D1029750

RICHARD WAGNER

TO

MATHILDE WESENDONCK

Mathilde Wesendonck

1860

From a Painting by C. Dorner.

Richard Wagner to Mathilde Wesendonck

TRANSLATED, PREFACED, ETC.
By William Ashton Ellis

SECOND EDITION

VIENNA HOUSE
New York

Originally published by Charles Scribner's Sons
New York, 1905

First Vienna House edition published 1972

International Standard Book Number:
0-8443-0010-1

Library of Congress Catalogue Card Number: 74-163794

Manufactured in the United States of America

CONTENTS

PAGE

INTRODUCTORY vii

ZURICH LETTERS I

VENICE DIARY 29

VENICE LETTERS 83

LUCERNE LETTERS 115

PARIS LETTERS 171

AFTERMATH 295

FROM HER TO HIM 333

VALEDICTORY 367

INDEX 376

Dein Verhältniss zu mir ist so heilig, sonderbar, dass ich erst recht bei dieser Gelegenheit fühlte : es kann nicht mit Worten ausgedrückt werden, Menschen können's nicht sehen.

GOETHE TO CHARLOTTE VON STEIN.

Ich gehe viel mit Richard Wagner um, welcher ein genialer und auch guter Mensch ist.

GOTTFRIED KELLER, Zurich, 1856.

❧

INTRODUCTORY

(To his sister, Clara Wolfram.)

"Geneva, 20th August 1858.

" My dear Kläre,

" I promised you something more detailed about the true causes of the serious step in which you now see me engaged. I will tell you what is needful, that you may also be able to refute any other gossip ; toward which, however, I am most indifferent myself.

" What for six years past has supported, comforted, and strengthened me withal to stay by Minna's side despite the enormous differences of our character and disposition, is the love of that young gentlewoman who at first and for long approached me shyly, diffidently, hesitant and timid, but thereafter more and more decidedly and surely. As there never could be talk between us of a union, our deep attachment took that wistful character which holds all base and vulgar thoughts aloof, and discerns its only source of gladness in the welfare of each other. Since the very commencement of our acquaintance she has felt the most unflagging and refined solicitude for me, and obtained from her husband in the most courageous fashion whatever might alleviate my life. For his part, in view of his wife's out-spokenness to him, it was only natural that he should fall into increasing jealousy ; but her grandeur has consisted in this,—that, always keeping her husband informed about her

heart, she gradually attuned him even to the fullest resignation toward her. With what sacrifices and combats this
could but be attended, may easily be judged : what made
its achievement possible to her, could only be the depth and
the sublimity of her attachment, remote from all self-seeking,
which gave her power to shew herself to her husband as
of such stature that, if she ended by threatening her own
death, he needs must abstain from her and prove his
unshakeable love even by upholding her in her solicitude
for me. In fine, it became a matter of retaining the mother
of his children, and for their sake—who severed our two
selves the most insuperably—he accepted his renunciant
position. Thus, whereas he was consumed with jealousy
himself, she was able so to interest him in me again, that—
as you are aware—he often-times assisted me ; and when it
became at last a question of procuring me a little house
with garden after my own wish, it was she who by
dint of the most unheard-of battles won him round to
buy for me the pretty premises beside his own. The most
wonderful part of it, however, is that I absolutely never had
a notion of these conflicts she was going through for me :
for love of her, her husband had continually to shew himself
friendly and unconstrained towards me ; not a black look
was to enlighten me, not a hair of my head to be touched;—
serene and cloudless should the sky envault me, soft and
yielding be my every tread. This the unparalleled result of
this purest, noblest woman's splendid love.

"And this love, which had still remained unuttered by
a word between us, was finally to cast aside its veil when
I penned the poem of my *Tristan* just a year ago, and
gave it to her. Then for the first time did she lose her
self-control, and confess to me that she must die !—Reflect,
dear sister, what this love must have meant to me, after a
life of toils and sufferings, of sacrifices and commotions, such

as mine!—Yet we recognised forthwith that any union between us could not be so much as thought of, and were accordingly resigned; renouncing every selfish wish, we suffered, endured, but—loved each other!—

"My wife seemed to understand with shrewd feminine instinct what here was proceeding: certainly she often shewed some jealousy, deriding and running down; yet she tolerated our companionship,—which on its side never violated morals, but simply aimed at consciousness that we were in each other's presence. Consequently I assumed Minna to be sensible enough to comprehend that there was strictly nothing here for her to fear, since an alliance was not to be dreamt of between us, and therefore that forbearance was her best and most advisable resource. Well, I have had to learn that I had probably deceived myself in that respect; chatter reached my ears, and finally she so far lost her senses as to intercept a letter from myself and—break it open. That letter, if she had been in anything like a position to understand it, might really have afforded her the completest reassurance she could wish, for our resignation formed *its* theme as well; but she went by nothing save the endearing expressions, and lost her head. She came up to me raving, and thus compelled me calmly to explain to her precisely how things stood, that she had brought misfortune on herself when she opened such a letter, and that if she did not know how to contain herself, we two must part. On the last point we were both agreed, I tranquilly, she passionately. Next day, however, I felt sorry for her; I went to her and said, 'Minna, you are very ill; get well first, and let us have another talk then.' We arranged the plan of a [medical] cure, and she seemed to quiet down again. As the day of departure for the place of cure drew near, she insisted upon speaking to the Wesendonck first: I firmly forbade her to. Everything depended on my making Minna gradually acquainted with the character of my relations to that lady, and thus convincing her that there was nothing at all to be feared for the continuance of our wedded life, wherefore she simply ought to behave wisely, sensibly and nobly, abjure all foolish thoughts of vengeance and avoid any manner of fuss; which she promised me at last. She could not hold her peace, however; she went across, behind my back, and—doubtless without realising it herself—affronted the gentle soul most grossly. After she had told her, ' Were I an ordinary woman, I should take this letter to your husband!' there was nothing else for the Wesendonck—who was conscious of having never kept a secret from her husband (which a woman like Minna, of course, can't comprehend!)—but to inform him at once of this scene and its cause.—Herewith, then, had the delicacy and purity of our relations been invaded in a coarse and vulgar way, and many a thing must alter. Not for a long time could I succeed in making it clear to my lady-friend that the very highness and unselfishness of such relations, as subsisted between us, made them forever impossible of explanation to a nature like my wife's; for I was silenced by her grave reproach that I had omitted this, whereas she had always had her husband for her confidant.

   " Whoever can estimate what I since have suffered (it was the middle of April then), will also appreciate how I feel in the end, now that I have to realise that the most persistent efforts to preserve the relations disturbed have absolutely borne no fruit. I saw to Minna's welfare at the health-resort with every care; to pacify her, at last I broke off all association with our neighbours pending her absence; careful only for her health, I tried every possible means of bringing her to reason and recognition of what beseemed her and her time of life: in vain! She abides

by the absurdest fancies, declares herself injured, and,
scarcely tranquillised a little, the old fury soon bursts forth
afresh. Since a month ago, when Minna returned—while
we were having company—it had to come to a decision at
last. The two women so close together, was impossible
any longer ; for neither could the Wesendonck forget, that,
in reward for her supreme self-sacrifice and tenderest regards
for me, she had been met on my side, through my wife,
with such coarse and insulting treatment ; moreover, people
had begun to speak about it. Enough : the most unheard-
of scenes and tortures never ceased for me, and out of
consideration as well for the one as the other, I finally
had to make up my mind to vacate the fair asylum that
had been prepared for me with such tender affection.

" Now I require rest myself, and the completest seclusion :
for the grief I have to weary down is great.—

" Minna is incapable of comprehending what an unhappy
wedlock ours has ever been ; she paints the past as something other than it was, and if I have found relief, distraction
and oblivion, in my art, she has brought herself to think
I never needed them. Enough: I have come to an issue
on that head ; no longer can I tolerate this everlasting
bickering and whimsical distrust, if I'm to have any heart
left to fulfil my life-task. Whoever has observed me closely,
must have been surprised from of old at my patience,
kindness, ay, my weakness ; and if I am now condemned
by shallow judges, I have grown insensible to all that
sort of thing. Never had Minna a finer opportunity of
shewing herself more worthy to be wife of mine, than
now, when it involved the preservation to me of the highest
and dearest : it lay within her hand to prove if she truly
loved me ; but she does not even understand what such
true love is, and her rage transports her over all !—

" Still, I exculpate her by her illness ; not but that even

this might perhaps have taken on another, milder character, had she herself been otherwise and milder. Further, the many adversities she has survived with me, and over which *I* have been lightly borne by my inner genius (which unfortunately I have never been able to communicate to her!), make me considerate towards her; I should like to give her as little pain as possible, since, after all, I'm truly sorry for her! Only, I feel unequal to enduring by her side henceforth; neither could I help her in herself by doing so: I should always be incomprehensible to her and an object of suspicion. Therefore—divided! But, in kindliness and affection: I would not have her shamed; merely, I could wish her to perceive in time, herself, that it is better for us not to see each other much again. For the present I afford her a prospect of my returning to her in Germany as soon as the amnesty arrives (which also was the reason why she was to take all our furniture and things with her); yet I mean to bind myself to nothing, and let everything depend upon my future feeling. So please adhere to it, yourself, that the present is merely to be a passing separation; whatever you can do to make her calm and reasonable, I beg you not to leave undone! For—as said—she really is unfortunate: she would have been happier with a lesser man; and so take pity on her, with myself! I shall thank you from my heart for it, dear sister!—

"I shall bide here in Geneva awhile till I can go on to Italy, where I think of passing the winter—presumably in Venice; already the solitude and the removal from all torturing company are reviving me a little. It was a sheer impossibility of late, to think of work; so soon as I find heart again to go on composing my Tristan, I shall regard myself as saved. Indeed 'tis *so* that I must try to help myself: I want nothing of the world except that it may leave me rest for works that some day shall belong to it; therefore let it also judge me charitably!—

"The substance of this letter, dear Kläre, you need not hesitate to use for explanations, wherever needful; in general, however, I naturally should not like much discussion of what has happened. Only the very fewest will really *understand* what is the case: for that one needs close knowledge of the persons here concerned.

"Now farewell, dear sister, and hearty thanks once more for your discreet enquiry, which I have answered, as you see, in confidence! Treat Minna leniently, but let her also gradually come to know how she stands with me!

"Your brother
"Richard W."

(*To Doctor Anton Pusinelli, Dresden.*)

"Venice, 1st November 1858.
"My dear faithful Friend,*
"I approach you to-day on a deeply intimate subject. —My wife will spend this winter in Dresden. In all probability she has already arrived; perhaps she has even called on you by now.—I remember the kind cheering opinion on her state of health you so touchingly sent me

---

* All these introductory letters, alike the two to the elder sister and those to the two intimate male friends, employ the second person singular where I have rendered "you" and "your." The present letter comes from a group of close on forty (out of an existing collection of eighty) addressed to Dr. Pusinelli, published in the *Bayreuther Blätter* Spring 1902, i.e. four months *before* Mathilde Wesendonck's sudden death, and therefore long prior to the publication of our main group. The letters to Clara Wolfram were first published in the Berlin *Tägliche Rundschau* within a month after that death, together with a few others to which I shall subsequently refer; whilst that to Sulzer made its first appearance in Herr A. Steiner's *Neujahrsblatt* of the Zurich Allg. Musik-Gesellschaft January 1903.—W. A. E.

last summer, after my description of her symptoms. Now I entrust to you the patient herself; be her physician, her adviser, helper—if you can, alleviator if you cannot. The profound conviction that a change of air and scene, also a temporary removal from my undoubtedly somewhat agitating presence, must serve to give the invalid at least a chance, combined with other things to make me fix upon a separation from her for a period. Dresden will certainly be homelike to her on the whole, and woo her finally to greater calm. She will occupy a little parterre flat in the Rottdorf house, where we first dwelt at Dresden, but will first alight at Tichatscheck's.—

"Recently she has been at her brother-in-law's, who is a doctor himself. As I wanted ease of mind on her condition, I addressed myself to him, and now enclose his answer, which I received yesterday. You see how little consolation there is in his report; I am deeply affected !*—

"She will be able to afford you but little clear information as to the genesis of her condition. An organic ailment (perhaps seated in the lymphatic system—for her mother died of dropsy in the chest) has probably been developing ever since and during our Dresden stay; but the constantly increasing havoc of her nerves dates chiefly from the many severe and troublous episodes in our later life. In 1853 the over-excitation of her nerves, with sleeplessness, was already very strong; a doctor treated her for gout, and employed

---

* The provincial brother-in-law must indeed have 'piled the agony' regardless of all consequences to the husband's own state of mind and health; for, on the one hand we find this report almost plunging Wagner to the bottom of the Grand Canal (pp. 69-71 *inf.*), on the other we find it much discounted by the expert metropolitan physician, since the very next letter to Pusinelli (Nov. 18) exclaims: "I breathe again, at knowing my wife to be under your treatment, in your guard. May Heaven bless you, if you can continue to give me relief such as you have already been able to indicate. You can scarcely believe what good you do me, with this care for the sufferer!"—W. A. E.

hot baths and douches, which drove her almost mad. Then she acquired a taste for laudanum, which had incautiously been ordered in small doses for her sleeplessness; as she could detect no result, she pushed the doses up to several scores of drops, as she confessed to me later. With her progressive irritability, moreover, frequent conflicts were not to be avoided between us; and for that reason—I admit it to you openly—our life together had latterly become unbearable.—But you will soon discover all about her physical condition for yourself. Be entirely candid with me, dear Anton, so that I may arrange myself in every way to back up your treatment as studiously as possible. My conduct and future relations to her will be governed by no other regard in the world, than the heartfelt wish to contribute to her healing, her soothing and sparing; whatsoever may serve towards that end, I shall make my most urgent concern. Should we succeed in preserving her life full long to come, in utmost painlessness and comfort, my heartiest wish will have been fulfilled; and I am prepared for any sacrifice, to attain that.—For the present I hear, to my relief, that she has somewhat quieted already—as was to be foreseen,—her appearance also is said to have improved. Let the poor woman, who moves my soul to deepest pity, be commended to your noble heart; be to her as much as ever you can, and count upon my fervid thanks!

" Of myself, and my extremely retired life, you will hear a little through my wife; I also will tell you something of it next time I write you; for which, as I instantly hope, you will very soon afford me and my gratitude occasion through friendly tidings of my wife! Goodbye, best Friend! Be saluted and blest by your

" RICHARD   WAGNER.

"Canale Grande, Palazzo Giustiniani,
"Campiello Squellini 3228."

(To Jakob Sulzer, former chief-magistrate of Zurich.)

"Venice, Dec. 3, 1858.

"My dear honoured Friend,

"Can you believe that I would run away from you like that, without so much as looking back? Whatever you may think of me, surely you at least have thus much good opinion of me, that I keep in inextinguishable fondness, and hold in an imperishable esteem, a figure that has left so deep and valuable a mark as yours upon my life? Of latter years our paths had lain much asunder. . . [etc., etc., see *Life of Richard Wagner* iv, 133.]

"Whatever may have come to your ears as to the cause of my seemingly so sudden departure from Zurich, I must leave on one side; yet [Alex.] Müller was initiated to some extent, I believe, and could have informed you; though it is to be doubted, in any case, whether he was intelligent enough to inform you correctly. It was impossible for me then to take a formal, ceremonial leave of Zurich; I had to put up with seeing my friends plunged into uncertainty about me for a time, whereas I myself must first gain time and quiet to turn back to them at last with needful explanations. You are the first to whom I now address myself in this sense too, and—in all likelihood you will also remain the only one; for, taken strictly, my only care can be for your opinion.

"Probably it had not escaped you from hints of mine before, that the state into which my wife had fallen, particularly through the worsening of her very painful heart-trouble, was becoming so unsettling to myself as well, that a radical change in our dwelling arrangements would have to be thought of at last. Ill-luck ordained that, owing to—what I can only call—a trivial misconception of certain of my personal associations that were really far remote from standing in any manner of relevancy to our conjugal relations, she believed herself actually wronged in these latter ; thereby, and particularly under the influence of her physical affliction—which in such cases, as we know, reacts so strongly on the mind,—she lost all her usual discretion and forgot herself to the length of words in our immediate neighbourhood ; which must necessarily lead to such unsettlement and disturbance of those neighbourly bearings themselves, that, in spite of my honestest endeavours to stave it off, the resolve was bound at last to ripen in myself—my very self—to give up our residence at Zurich. What I suffered through it all, between unreasonableness on the one hand and passionateness on the other, ought to absolve me of any share of blame for which I may have been answerable myself. When I formed my decision, and resolutely carried it out in the teeth of unusual obstacles, I had to give up much that had grown very dear to me ; among which I will merely name the sweet country-place I long had desired, with its equipment.—

"But enough ! it had to be ; and the result is already proving that, just as I did the most straightforward thing, I also did the best. Amongst the motives for the change was the necessity of effecting a temporary separation between my wife and me. In constant, close, immediate contact, without a jot of external distraction, it was not always possible for me to keep nothing but my regard for her ailing condition of body and mind in view, under every circumstance—with my own temper also inflammable : to my most penitent regret, conflicts arose again and again, and finally with daily aggravation ; conflicts in the vehemence whereof I could not stay without a part myself. Even for *her* health's sake I must have thought about an alteration ; so I now rejoice in the result. At Dresden, well tended, with pleasant old acquaintances and agreeable distraction by fit artistic entertainments, my wife already

b

feels much better ; which certainly is chiefly contributed-to by the fact that I can commune with her from a distance quite differently and more beneficially than was possible— with the best intentions—when close at hand. Now I can pick time and mood for my communication, also for correction of her passionate charges—still constantly recurring till a short time back—, and in this way I have already brought matters so far that she has begun to grow thoroughly calm. Particularly in view of her most ailing state of health, which makes her quite irresponsible, I am heartily concerned to ease her hard and painful life and make it as endurable as possible.

"About myself and my probable future I will tell you some other day ; moreover—and especially about my future —there is next to nothing to be said at present. I am working and striving to finish my Tristan, but unfortunately have been repeatedly hindered by illness. A malady that is keeping me tied to my chair for the second week, now, is also to blame for my break in this letter, which you will remark by its date [a second date is not given; cf. p. 76 *inf.*].

"You must have been wondering why Venice, which made such a disagreeable impression on yourself when passing through it, should have seemed to me the very place to meet my present needs. I sought a spot where I could live entirely unnoticed, completely retired, and work without the least disturbance. Uninteresting little places could never afford that. Here, on the contrary, I have everything I wish : a very quiet dwelling on the Grand Canal (of course with no noise of street traffic), where I pass the greater portion of my day ; then a promenade through the incomparable parts of Venice, ever new of effect, from S. Mark's square to the public garden, with an outlook across the lagunes to the sea ; an ever-lively populace, but altogether joreign to me, always remaining objective,—

this suffices and suits me exactly, in my present state of mind. A quite definite change in my situation must naturally take place next summer ; how and in what direction, however, I am unable as yet to say.

" Now I beg you to be satisfied with this morsel for to-day, also to give my best regards and heartiest greetings to your dear wife, the Herr son, and my friends Bohm and Hagenbuch—to Müller too—when you see them. Should you be paying a call on the Wesendoncks, don't forget to give them news of me and convey my kindest greetings. If you care to write my wife for once—which certainly would much delight her—address to 9 Marienstrasse, Dresden . . . [purely business matters.] Preserve a kind remembrance of me, just as I shall ever hold yourself in grateful friendship !

"Goodbye and let me hear from you soon.

"Your

"RICHARD WAGNER."

"(Canal Grande, Palazzo Giustiniani, Campiello Squilini, 3228.)"

" Lucerne, 7th April 59.

" Best thanks for your letter, dear Kläre, and don't be vexed if I write but little in reply. You would hardly believe the bulk my correspondence has gradually increased to, and how chary I often must be with words, not to be obliged to desist from work entirely . . . [3 sentences about a poor relation.]

" May I hope you understood me well enough, not to take offence at my begging you last autumn to avoid all agitating subjects with Minna ? She had been writing me in greater and greater heat and passion, so that I was bound to assume, there was too much talk about the sore point with her. Of course I might have told myself that it would be difficult, in fact impossible to avoid it, and there wasn't the smallest reproach in my plea to you; yet I felt I could not do enough, all round, to ensure a calming influence on her. A heart like hers, that will not come to rest at all, is a terrible affliction; I was deeply sorry for her, and as I had grown more and more keenly alive to the impossibility of reasoning with her reason, I recognised that there was only one choice left—between treating her with considerate cajolery, always evading, simply tranquillising, ignoring all her ebullitions, or—undisguisedly abandoning her to her misery. It stands to reason that I chose the first course; so far as anywise possible, in all my letters I have treated her according to this principle, now earnestly, now playfully, and the effect appears to be proving of gradual benefit to her. For money, ample money to live quite nicely on, I do not let her lack, and have just provided her again with enough to lead a life of really elegant comfort the summer through. Grant God that all this, combined with the summer cure at Schandau, may so materially improve her, as to make it possible for me to commit my home to her again this autumn without fear of fresh relapses to her old condition, which would deprive both me and her of any further hope!—

"As for myself, this solitariness is doing. me a power of good. True, I have often been unwell, but it has never oppressed my spirit: within me is the fairest, deepest calm. What confers it on me, and makes its preservation possible, is the noblest, most touching experience of all my life: here everything is high, upraised above the common plane; incredible sacrifice, but peace profound. I live henceforward to complete my works,—for that alone; and for that—towards that, I am helped.—Intimation enough!—

"I expect to write my third act here; my mood is

excellent.—Farewell, dear Kläre ; be thanked for your sisterly love, and ever count on my reciprocation.

" Your brother

"(Schweizerhof)   " RICHARD."

In the eyes of a select few readers of this book the above will be sufficient preface, and they may prefer to pass direct to the profoundly interesting collection of letters itself. The generality, however, will probably demand additional enlightenment as to the actors in this unique tragedy. Let me therefore begin with the one whose principal scene may be said to occur in its first act :—

MINNA WAGNER—to give her full baptismal name, Christiane Wilhelmine—was born at Oederan, a village between Freiberg and Chemnitz, about half-way from Dresden to Zwickau. Her father, Gotthelf Planer, is always described as a " mechanikus," or mechanician—a term that covers various kinds of workmanship of skilful fingers, rather than of sinewy arms or educated brain ; Praeger says " working spindle-maker,"—not inherently improbable. Of him and his wife (Johanne Christiane Meyer) we know nothing more, except that they had three daughters and a son, lived in Dresden most of their lives, and for many years (until their death ?) were supported entirely by Richard Wagner. The last we hear of them is on a visit to Zwickau in 1854 to meet Minna, apparently at the house of another married daughter. The first we hear, comes from that Oederan parish-register, where Minna's birth stands entered as having occurred on the 5th of September 1809,* i.e. nearly four years before that of her future husband.

It was at Magdeburg that Richard and Minna first met, he aged 21 and just embarked on his first conductorship, she 25 and engaged as actress at the same town-theatre. That she was "pretty as a picture" then, and remained so for some years to

----

* It is only within the past two years that the exact date has been definitely established (by Herr Tappert), since the actual place of birth was theretofore unknown ; in vol. i of the *Life of Richard Wagner* the year is erroneously given as "1814," owing to the *marriage* certificate having been misleadingly filled up—after a manner not unusual with our own census papers.

come, we hear on every hand; the quality of her professional talent, on the contrary, is difficult to ascertain, though Richard describes her in a letter of this period as "erste Liebhaberin," or leading lady. Within six months of their acquaintance, i.e. early in 1835, they had begun to rank as an affianced couple in the eyes of their associates; but it was not till the end of that year that he made her a formal offer of marriage, as we are told, in a letter vowing himself to the devil should she refuse him. Minna, who appears to have left Magdeburg at the time in search of a more enthusiastic audience, returns at once to complete her professional, and commence her conjugal engagement; and the pair get married in November 1836. That ceremony took place at Königsberg, where Richard was then waiting for the shoes of a conductor who betrayed no hurry to vacate them. Scarcely has he donned those shoes, when a Königsberg correspondent reports to Schumann's *Neue Zeitschrift* that "Herr Musikdirektor Wagner has already left us, it is said for family reasons;" those discreetly-veiled family reasons being, in fact—that his wife had left *him*, and little more than six months after their wedding.

It was a bad beginning, whatever the cause; but that cause has never been authenticated, since the master himself in later years was naturally loth to approach the subject. German marriage-laws inclining rather to the American, than the English code, we must not jump to the conclusion that Minna had done anything more serious than abandoning her husband, when we find him appealing to those laws for a divorce in June 1837; yet for his happiness during the next quarter of a century, and even for her own—to go by her remarks on her silver-wedding *—we can but regret that he withdrew his legal plea and welcomed back the penitent in the following autumn, so that the first anniversary of their wedding was spent together at Riga, after all, where he had meanwhile entered his third appointment as conductor. Not that Minna ever ran away again, or acted in any other fashion than that of a 'dutiful,' perhaps even an affectionate wife; but, as we have just heard her husband say, decidedly "she would

---

* "The 24th ult. was the day of our so-called silver-wedding, which I passed very dismally (solo). If I could cross these 25 years out of my life, perhaps I might be merry again" (to a feminine friend in Berlin, Dec. 15, 1861; see *Die Gegenwart* of Oct. 21, 1899).

have been happier with a lesser man." Whether the "lesser man" would have been happy, is quite another matter: for my own part I strongly doubt it, unless he had been an infinitely lesser, since the few letters that have been brandished by Minna's none too wise defenders positively set one's teeth on edge. I will reproduce one in an instant, as it is only fair that the poor sufferer should be given a hearing in person; we must first take a bird's-eye glance, however, at the course of the Wagners' married life down to the time of the great Zurich catastrophe.

From the first that life was her-relations-ridden, as his had always looked askance on what they deemed a mésalliance,—and rightly deemed ; for, albeit several of his brothers and sisters began their life on the stage, the whole Wagner family, with its antecedents for two-hundred years, distinctly belonged to the class of 'intellectuals.' Consequently Richard was virtually cut off from his own flesh and blood for long to come, and tied to a stock with scant sympathy for higher aspirations ; consequences far worse for his wife's mental development, than for his own. Even on her return to his hearth in 1837 Minna brought with her her sister Amalie, to fill a gap in the ranks of the Riga opera-troupe, and Amalie dwelt with the Wagner couple till they left that place some two years later (when she married a lieutenant of the Russian Guards, and we lose sight of her *).

In Paris—whither the Wagners next removed, and where they remained for two years and a half, 1839-42—there was no accommodation for a sister-in-law, as Richard found it more than difficult to procure sufficient maintenance for his wife and self. Is it no more than a coincidence, that *those* were the years to which he always looked back with tender memory, despite the hardships they had jointly endured? However that be, in this early Paris period Minna behaved as a loving wife should ; nor did she shrink from menial house-work to keep the home afoot. Yet her energies must have been confined to inside management, the washtub and kitchen ; for even 20 years later she confesses that she "can make no headway with French," whilst her husband himself has to conduct every detail of a removal for the same

---

* Similarly, our only knowledge of the brother is that Minna had generously assisted him before her marriage, and was plunged into the deepest grief by his death at the age of twenty-five, in Dresden, 1843.

specified cause. How was all the marketing and bargaining inseparable from a Paris ménage to be carried on, then, if not by his unaided self? Even a lady's-maid, when taken abroad, will generally have the wit to pick up enough of what she elegantly calls the 'lingo' to make herself intelligible for all useful purposes; wherefore we have here another reason for not ranking Minna's intellectual capacity as quite up to the average. Nevertheless in this Planer-less period the pretty little hand-toiling wife does seem to have been a comfort to her over-worked, half-starving husband.

With the acceptance of *Rienzi* for Dresden, its brilliant success there in October 1842, and Wagner's appointment as royal Kapellmeister a couple of months after, his wife was thrown once more among her old belongings, exposed to their banal influence; and certainly in the last year or two of the $6\frac{1}{2}$ they stayed there, if not long before, we find another relative enthroned in the house, namely Natalie, the youngest bearer of the Planer surname. Whether cause and effect may be linked here or no, the latter part of the Dresden period was embittered by perpetually recurrent domestic strife, goading Wagner on one occasion to the remark in presence of a young male friend, " Other people are lucky enough to have their enemies outside their house, but my bitterest foe I have at table" (*Life* ii, 373). This notwithstanding, he appears to have undertaken the entire support of Natalie, as well as of his wife and her parents, and immediately after his flight from Dresden (for a vague and trifling share in the insurrection of May 1849), behold him seeking to found a home for "my poor wife and her family"—so Planer-manacled is he!

For how *long* after Wagner's settlement in Zurich this extra mouth and tongue at table were imposed on him, I cannot definitely ascertain; manifestly the wife's relative was viewed so much in the light of a standing dish or dispensation, that one hardly catches a glimpse of her in his correspondence—in itself no flattering sign. By three direct but colourless references in his letters to Uhlig, however, we can trace her as clinging like a limpet to his bare walls from September '49 to November '51 at least, though she must have relaxed her hold by October of the following year (whether finally or not, I cannot say), since Wagner writes Uhlig November 1, '52, "Please see that my wife's family receives three tickets for the third circle, next Tannhäuser performance; yours must go to the amphitheatre"; and the nice distinction tells its tale. At any rate Minna must have soon after been robbed of her ally for good, if it was Natalie who married the doctor mentioned in the second of the letters printed above, and to whose new home at Zwickau Minna paid her visit in 1854.*

With his freeing from the Planer incubus Wagner had by no means been rescued from invasions of his domestic quiet. For Minna, entirely weaned from sympathy with her husband's inner self by now, not unnaturally felt lonely, and began going out to the Zurich theatre and an occasional ball or two; with the result that she picks up a little set of her own in the early part of 1852, and has to do some entertaining in return,—"tiresome visitors," her husband complains, "new acquaintances have forced themselves upon me," and "company that tortures me, and before which I withdraw to torture myself" (letters to Liszt and Uhlig). While the 'poor neglected wife' thus was gadding about in her mild philistine way, leaving her husband "sitting lone on the couch, staring at the lamp" (letter to Liszt Feb. '53), Providence brought him into the society of a lady with truer instinct for the needs of a genius' heart and mind, though, as we have seen in the first of the letters above, it was years before this pair of souls became consciously united. Nothing grosser than a union of souls did it ever come to,—that is plain on all the following pages; whereas Minna had long ceased to be a wife in anything but name, since she and her husband now met at little more than meal-times.

For the moment I will skip those intervening years, undoubtedly of physical pain for Minna, and call herself to the footlights in the interlude that succeeds the stormy ending of act i. After "raising halloo"—to quote that choice expression which is all her *Gegenwart* champion finds fit to cite from any of her early letters to the Berlin lady—she evidently went to stay awhile,

---

* Here again we are in the dark, as the unsystematic von Hornstein, who did not make Wagner's acquaintance till 1853 (*vid. inf.*), has this to say: "How small was his household! Himself, his wife and her unmarried sister—a simple, unassuming person—the parrot and a dog." But the whole question of Minna's relations awaits authoritative treatment.

first with *Richard's* sister Clara Wolfram at Chemnitz (*vid. sup. &*
p. 33 *inf.*), then with her own married sister at Zwickau, and
thence to Dresden—heralded by her husband's letters, not only
to his old medical adviser and benefactor Dr. Pusinelli, but also
to other of his own staunch friends who, he knew, would stand
by and assist her. From Dresden she writes the unnamed Berlin
lady as follows:—

"Dresden, the 29th December 1858.

"It is impossible for me to close this fatal year without
sending you first my heartiest greetings. Please, do write
me soon, whether things are going well with you.

"Unfortunately I cannot tell you that about myself; I
have been made wretched and ill by two abominations,*
and shall recover very slowly, perhaps never at all. My
poor heart still is thumping violently. I look so wretched
that my acquaintances do not recognise me.

---

* At first one might suppose the "zwei Abscheulichkeiten" to
be intended for Richard and Mathilde; but I do *not* hold Minna
capable of describing her husband thus to a correspondent who, it
appears, had once made a stay in his house. The first "abomination"
—especially, in view of that date "1853" in Richard's letter to
Pusinelli, i.e. the year of removal to the new flat—is far more likely
to be Emilie Heim, the singer mentioned in my footnote to p. 7 *inf.*,
wife of that "Papa Heim" whose name crops up from time to time
in the main collection of letters. It is one of the Zurich traditions,
that Minna was furiously jealous of Frau Heim before she transferred
that feeling to Frau Wesendonck; also that the earlier jealousy was
one of the causes of Wagner's wish to quit his Zeltweg flat (p. 13 *inf.*),
since its back windows looked straight on those of the Heims', and thus
the two women were constantly brought face to angry face. The
groundlessness of such jealousy is palpable, as Ignaz Heim himself
became Wagner's generous financer at the very time when Minna's
conduct had made it impossible for him to accept anything from Herr
Otto, and we shall find the master writing him from Venice (p. 72 *inf.*);
whilst Herr Steiner, an inhabitant of Zurich who himself has carefully
perused the documents, declares that in all the correspondence between
Heim and Wagner (unpublished), extending over twenty years, there
is "nowhere a shadow of ruffling" (*Neujahrsblatt* 1902).—Tr.

"I believe I wrote you that I had rented a small parterre here; I only wanted to have the necessary of our effects sent from Zurich, which, however, I luckily did not afterwards need, because good faithful Frau Tichatschek had so nicely fitted up my little lodging, consisting of two tiny rooms, with her own superfluity, that nothing lacked; she had even stocked the little kitchen and store-room; wood, coals, potatoes, eggs, flour, bread, butter etc., none are wanting. This act of friendship was extremely welcome to me in various respects, as my brother-in-law [of Zwickau] had not been able to advance me the needful money after all. I am living very sparingly, and yet left dry. My good man seems to run through very much himself at Venice, as always is the case when he lives alone, so that nothing remains over for me. New Year I was to have had money sent me by him; yesterday, however, he writes me that he will want it himself. A very nice thing, that; yet I submit, and shall not exactly die of hunger so long as I have a roof and a warm room. Richard is often ill in Italy; first he was threatened by a horrid nervous fever, which kept him twelve days in bed. Since nearly five weeks he has a large open wound on his leg, which has been discharging continually, so that he has felt acute pain with it. Walking is out of the question; he is carried into and out of bed, and naturally cannot think of work.

"That fateful Tristan, which I cannot bear for its origin, only seems able to be called into life with great interruptions and exertions. Let's see what happens between this and then. It seems to me as if with works like that there can be no luck. Perhaps I am mistaken; so we will see what the end brings, and whether this opera pleases people. I wish it from my heart! Yet for various reasons I cannot bring myself to attend a first performance.

"The [your?] communication of the little Guido's death

gave me quite a fright. May God hold every blow of Fate afar from this cold woman spoilt by happiness, but I believe that there is a Providence. I was always thinking, if only our Lord God would suddenly check such sauciness through the illness of a child—and now see! O it gives me a shudder!

"Of course I cannot keep a maid. I may not go to big parties, only to small family-gatherings; on the other hand, by my doctor's advice I am to attend the theatre often, where I have no need to speak, which tires me very much. It would not have been quite easy for me to carry out the theatre part if his Excellency Herr von Lüttichau, on whom I had to pay a call for politeness' sake, had not sent me a ticket next day for every performance, without my having had to waste a word on it. That was very obliging of him, and an exception but seldom made in anybody's favour. Altogether, people here are taking me up very cordially and kindly, and as I am bound to believe, purely for my own sake this time. Yet as said, I must keep quiet, not to agitate myself, which brings on my old sleeplessness again.

"My cure here will last a long time still, consequently I shall never see my husband again, or at least not for a very long while. I require peace and quietness. . . . [Please read footnote.*—Tr.] Sweet Christmastide is at the door. People are buying an immense deal, in spite of the shocking high prices here. Only I shall pass the festival quite silently and without any presents, as also the New Year.

"Richard writes to me much and heartily; I too, to

---

* The anonymous author of the strangely wry-brained article in *Die Gegenwart*, whence the above is derived, here obviously tacks on a fragment from a letter of a full week earlier; it is so illuminating, however, particularly when this inference is borne in mind, that I have translated it as it stands.—W. A. E.

him ; nevertheless I wish my being with him long deferred. I keep swallowing the thought, but down it will not stay.

" Apropos, in your next letter do tell me once more the name of that gentleman you met, and who said : What a pity the Wagner is going back to her husband ; she might have come to me, as I'm a widower, and so on. You know that I should neither go to him nor to anyone else,—I might have had that before if I liked ; yet it interests me to know who it was that said that. Do satisfy my curiosity." [Here ends the reproduction of this letter, or combination of two letters, without winding-up or signature.—Tr.]

Writing to Lotte and Caroline, Schiller once speaks of his profound interest on finding, through study of the old Greek tragedians, that " human beings are so alike in every age, the same passions, same collisions of passions, same language of passion ; with all this infinite variety, yet this resemblance, this oneness of the same human form " ; and Caroline answers him, " As life goes on, it has become to me a second nature to feel my soul at home with whatever things are beautiful and excellent, and to leave the common common, without deeming it bad, as may so easily happen to a heart that seeks for beauty."—After reading the effusion above, it is well to sip some such corrective, to remember that the voice of passion thrills to much the same chord whether high or low, and that " the common " is not necessarily " the bad." For commonness is stamped on all this document, and one now may better realise what Wagner meant when he told Pusinelli (Nov. 18, 58) that " the great intellectual divergence " between himself and his wife had been the source of their many painful differences. She has not even the sagacity to see that all the kindness showered upon her now in Dresden is by no means " purely for her own sake this time," but a very patent result of her husband's frequent messages to *his* good friends to do their best to make her happy. " My doctor " is the doctor we have just seen Richard begging to assist her in every way ; he prescribes her the theatre as an agreeable diversion of her thoughts, and between him and Wagner's other old friend, the great tenor Tichatschek, the "exception but seldom made in anybody's favour" is granted without her even having to ask for it. Tichatschek had been Wagner's own guest at the Asyl on the very eve of the disruption; Wagner writes him at the end of September (as also to old Chorus-master Fischer a fortnight later) announcing his wife's arrival, and the Tichatscheks kindly offer her provisional shelter. Presumably it is they, who secure her a flat in the house of-gentler memories, and behold!—when she arrives to take possession, it stands already furnished by a fairy hand. Her own relations, so long recipients of her husband's charity, cannot advance her the money they had promised to; yet she is so dense, or so vain at 49, as to imagine that his ancient Dresden friends are keeping the wolf from her door 'for the sake of her beautiful eyes,' as the French say! Moreover she must have completely drifted from their good atmosphere not long hereafter, and returned to what her husband ten years since had called "the dregs of Dresden vulgarity" (*Life* iii, 9); for, in justification of his wish to draw her to himself in Paris, he tells Pusinelli next October (1859): "Your reports about my wife do not take me unawares; from her letters and her own confessions it is manifest to me, how difficult a job it is with the poor soul. I also perceive, though, how much the success of your medical efforts is hindered by my wife's continuance in company that can but be injurious in its effect upon her. That my wife has found *yourself* as doctor, was a great good-fortune for her; the misfortune was, that this must be in *Dresden*. At any other place she would have been less exposed to all the influences I have hinted in brief." Poor Minna, incorrigible, I fear; but weak and silly, not morally "bad."

How about the wicked husband, though, who "wanted all the money for himself"?—In the first place, he was ill himself, in a foreign land without a single friend; no one there to provide *him* with coals and potatoes, or medical advice and physic gratis; no one to cheer *him* up with a free pass for entertainments. He was occupying a vast room in a palace, no doubt, but probably at very little more rent, as times then went in Italy, than she was charged for her small flat; and he had lately had to—pawn his watch. For, where was the money to come from? Minna herself had killed the goose with the golden eggs, and very little profit trickled from the theatres; since most of them had paid a miserably small lump sum down, some time before, for the performing-rights of all his marketable wares. In the second place, as I suspect to have been usual with her, Minna was only telling half the truth when she cited her husband's letter of "yesterday"; and as this really is an enlightening instance, I will furnish detailed proofs of my assertion:—

That "yesterday" gives her whole case away since 1903, when the records of the Hanover court-theatre, down to forty years ago, were published by Dr. Georg Fischer. On the 22nd of December 1858 Wagner writes a long business letter to the Director of this theatre, to the effect that, as they have already procured the score of *Rienzi* for performance, he expects the "fee of 50 Friedrichsd'or" to be paid at once, and begs that the treasurer be instructed "to address 20 Friedrichsd'or [£17] of the sum destined for me to my wife, Madame Minna Wagner, No. 9, Marienstrasse, Dresden; the rest, however, to myself at Venice"; whilst a fortnight later he is made acquainted by an official telegram with the money's despatch. Now, we happen to have a very close idea how long it then took letters to travel from Venice to the middle of Germany, since Wagner acknowledges on the 7th of January 1859 the "receipt to-day" of a letter Liszt had posted at Weimar on the 1st, and on the 22nd of February a letter Liszt had posted on the 17th; therefore five to six days was the length to Weimar, and it would be much the same with Dresden. Consequently the letter Minna received "yesterday," *i.e.* the 28th of December 1858, would be posted by her husband on the 22nd or 23rd—the day of, or day after, his letter to the Hanover director—and must indisputably have conveyed the intimation that he had ordered the said 20 Friedrichsd'or to be despatched to her direct. Even if she had small faith in its coming, she had no right to suppress the fact of its promise when complaining that some other amount—perhaps a contribution from his former benefactress, elderly Frau Ritter of Dresden—could not be set aside for her. And now we will turn to Wagner's letter of Jan. 19, 59, to Mathilde (pp. 101-2): "Karl Ritter returned on New Year's day, and now comes to see me at 8 every evening again. He has reported to me that he found my wife looking somewhat better. She seems to be doing tolerably, on the whole, and I take care that nothing lacks to her ease." So Karl—and he was always generous—had visited Minna on her husband's behalf only a few days before that letter of sour complaint !

Nor—to shake off this sordid business once for all—do we find the peevish wife " left dry " in the interval between January and next April, when we heard Wagner tell his sister that he had just sent Minna "enough to lead a life of really elegant comfort the summer through." For that interval we now have data in Dr. Wilhelm Altmann's most valuable synopsis, *Richard Wagner's Briefe nach Zeitfolge und Inhalt*, published only this year (1905). Here, among other things, Messrs. Breitkopf and Härtel supply particulars of never-printed letters from the master to their firm, extending over many years. Under date Jan. 31, '59, he asks them to send a Mannheim theatre-fee to his wife direct, on March 17th to make her an advance on others (her receipt whereof he afterwards acknowledges). That fully disposes of every innuendo that she was left to shift for herself, even when he was so hard put to it to find the wherewithal. Neither did he omit to send her whatever else conceivably might interest her : during the same period the Härtels' archives demonstrate that he ordered them to forward her in November '58 the vocal score of his revision of Gluck's *Iphigenia in Aulis*, and ten days later the poem of his *Tristan*,—his only publications that winter. He ministered to her in every possible way, and a woman who, despite all that, could send off such a letter to a friend (of both ?), must long before have grown most difficult to live with.

I have deferred the question of jealousy, as in the present instance that was pardonable to some extent, though with a different kind of wife there might never have been occasion for its cause. But if confirmation were needed for the dictum that the jealous person is the selfish person, this letter would furnish it down to the ground. Year after year had Richard treated Minna to every conceivable ' cure ' for her disease—far oftener and more sedulously than he had troubled to attend to his own ill-health—and coldbloodedly she can now recite her husband's bodily sufferings without a word of pity ! Surely he is right when he informs his sister that Minna " does not even under-

stand what true love is." A woman who had ever owned a spark
of love would at least have hinted sorrow that this painful wound
of his was left to alien hands to dress. Contrast her expressions
with his to Pusinelli, and say which member of this ill-matched
pair not only had the finer brain, but far the better heart.
Physically, indeed, there wasn't much to choose between the hearts;
as we shall see later on (p. 190), even nine years back he had
been warned against the danger to his, and it nearly carried him
off ten months from this (p. 183). But Minna had learnt to
make capital of hers, and it is the best capital in the world to
trade on if you want your own way. Listen to what dear old
Fischer hears this autumn (Oct. 58): "It's all very well for you,
to exhort me to come to rest at last. Lord, how I love rest,
in other people! Seriously though, my poor wife is a great
sufferer; she has a complaint of the heart, and one must have
experienced what that means! No rest to be thought of there,
either for the invalid or anyone around." The story of years
is condensed in that one phrase, yet we soon shall see that Wagner
manfully made up his mind—and clearly through the Wesendoncks'
persuasion—to shoulder his cross once again. After another
year of it, he falls seriously ill himself; and alike by Minna's
bulletin to her Berlin friend (p. 254*n*), and Mathilde's courageous
offer to come and tend him (p. 257), we may judge how utterly
unsympathetic a nurse Frau Minna made. Only by prodding it
into our memory that she really was an invalid herself, can we
divest our mind of the conclusion that "the common" in this
case came perilously nigh being "the bad."

Another excuse must also be remembered. Wagner has
already called her *unzurechnungsfähig*—"not accountable for her
actions"; four years after the Zurich catastrophe he writes sister
Clara again (June '62) "Arrived home, I found a letter from
Minna, which made me most terribly concerned about her; for
this letter really gave me the impression as if it had come from
a maniac. She must be terribly excited again." Of course the
heart alone would not do that, for its physical distress would
prevent any wielding of the pen till the attack was over and
reaction had set in : it *must* be the effect of a 'stimulant' of some
kind. And there we have every symptom of what nowadays
is morphinomania, but then was induced by the far more harmful

c

parent-drug, crude laudanum,—in which the effect of its solvent proof-spirit should not be forgotten.* Dr. Pusinelli was cautioned about it November '58, whilst Liszt had been told in the previous July, " My anxiety about my wife has been terrible ; for two whole months I actually had to be prepared every day for the news of her death. Her condition has become so much worse chiefly through the insensate use of opium—allegedly for sleeplessness ! " That *vermeintlich* (allegedly) tells us all ; the drug habit had become a virtual intoxication, with all its shocking consequences : consideration for truth is discarded, the wildest fancies spring unbidden to the victim's brain, any innate vulgarity grows rampant, a molehill is converted to a mountain. Thus must it have been for some time past at Zurich, and thus it certainly goes on in Paris. Early in 1861—when he seems no longer to have had a private sitting-room, poor man—Wagner writes Mathilde : " The odds are so against my profiting by any better-cultivated intercourse, that I willingly resign on every hand, and just accept whatever whim or hazard brings into the house " (p. 262 *inf.*). Immediately preceding this obvious allusion to Minna's mistrust comes a reference to Mme Ollivier, Liszt's elder daughter, ". . . I'm thinking, how it is that we so seldom see each other," and the reasons for the dots in that passage we are bound to respect ; but on the one hand we find the most odious insinuations anent the selfsame lady in Minna's letter of March 1860 to her Berlin friend (see *Die Gegenwart*), on the other, Liszt writes Princess Wittgenstein in May 1861, " Pour revenir à Wagner, je vous dirai qu' Ollivier a écrit une lettre fort sévère à Mme Wagner, qui, à ce qu'il paraît, a fait des cancans très déplaisants sur Blandine. Il est difficile que les relations se renouent après cela.† Pour ma part, je ne m'en mêlerai point, l'expérience m'ayant trop enseigné sur l'inutilité des replâtrages ! " At times the poor drug-victim must have behaved as a she-devil in the house, then ; outside it too.

---

* It may be needful to inform the layman that even drops of lavender-water, or eau-de-cologne on lumps of sugar, have been taken by the weaker sex with dire effect ; whilst in one of the worst cases I have seen of feminine addiction to stimulants, when every other was cut off, recourse was had to sal volatile.

† Together with his wife, Emile Ollivier, future premier of France, accompanies Wagner on a journey two months later,—after Minna's departure ; see p. 278 *infra*.

Not for a moment would I deny that Minna had amiable qualities, once displayed to her husband, now chiefly to her company; though when Challemel-Lacour terms her "la meilleure des femmes d'artiste" (quoted by Herr Tappert), either he must have had a lordly contempt for "artists," or those of his acquaintance must have been singularly unfortunate in wedlock—as Berlioz was indeed, his second time. Of notable acts to her credit, we do know of her attempt in 1854 to gain her husband's amnesty by personal intervention at the Saxon Court, and her visit to his friend Roeckel in prison; of her renewed efforts in 1859 and 1862, the latter whereof proved successful * ; also of an open letter, written at her husband's request Jan. 9, 1866, in which she gave the lie to "Munich and Vienna rumours" by declaring that "until now I have received a sustentation from my absent husband Richard Wagner, which secures me an existence free from care." That disavowal was published in the newspapers only just in time, for she died a fortnight later (Jan. 25)—alone in the night with an open window, as if she had been gasping for breath, after the excitement of a tea-party she had given at her rooms that afternoon. Poor soul, one cannot but feel deeply sorry for her; but it is an act of gross injustice to her husband's memory, to represent her as a martyr to anything but her own constitutional unfitness, and I am convinced that her loudest-mouthed champions would never have endured a whole week by her side in the last half of her life, to say nothing of her husband's score of years. His own epitaph upon her is still the best; writing to Clara a year after, he says: "Your [year-old] account of Minna's death has quite moved me to horror afresh; there was a calamity about the unhappy one, and nothing of it could be changed. In her fate lies something so disconsolate, that in my eyes it throws a shadow over all existence."

It is because that shadow looms so threatening in the back-

---

* August Roeckel's wife obtained *her* husband's release from his 13-year imprisonment at about the same time, not by any personal influence, but simply since the Saxon Ministry insisted on a personal apology, and were driven at last to accept it *by proxy*. The more important half of Wagner's amnesty, viz. permission to enter any part of Germany except his native land, was procured for him in 1860 by the Princess of Prussia, subsequently Kaiserin Augusta.

ground of the present group of letters, though her name occurs so seldom in them, that I have devoted to unhappy Minna a disproportionate share of this attempt at introduction, and shall even have to bring her in again. Without knowing something very definite of the poor earthen pot that cracked itself against the nobler vessels with which it swam awhile adown the stream, one cannot understand the nature of the dents it left on them. And nobler the other three were, far nobler, two of silver, one of gold.

Of OTTO WESENDONCK, the first of the two silver vessels, we know little more than is conveyed by these letters themselves and those others addressed by the vessel of gold to him. He was a Rhinelander, we are told, born March 16, 1815, therefore close on two years younger than his friend, and nearly fourteen older than his gentle wife—not a great discrepancy in age when the man is the senior. Partner in a large New York firm connected with the silk-trade, his knowledge of the world would naturally be extensive ; but, until thrown into Wagner's society, he does not appear to have devoted much thought to art, saving as applied to luxury. For good pictures to hang in his house, a fine house wherein to hang them, his taste was pronounced ; to judge by page 287 of the present book, however, he had not cultivated any great relish for reading, apart from the newspapers ; whereas his conversation seems to have betrayed a marked tendency to argument, on ' politics ' or other trifling matters (pp. 131, 135-6, 319). But it is as a knightly figure that he will ever abide in the memory of all who met him (he died November 1896), and surely truer knightliness than he displayed in a singularly difficult conjuncture can nowhere have been found, outside King Arthur's court. Undoubtedly 'twas *he* who was the greatest sufferer for several years,—by no means Minna,—years of perpetual heart-burning bravely borne. Not a line of his do we possess or are likely to, though Wagner once thanks him (1855) for a " long letter which I have accepted as the outpouring of the heart of a friend " ; but in the autumn of 1856, a year before the time of greatest trial, Wagner says to him, " If ever I am to play a rôle in the history of art, truly you should likewise occupy no scanty place therein,"—and those words stand true to-day.

The precise nature of those "conflicts" on Otto's private hearth, to which Wagner alludes in the first long paragraph of his narration to his sister, we shall never know; it would be unjust to all concerned, however, to imagine that they passed beyond the bounds of dignity; also we must make due allowance alike for the certainty that Wagner speaks of them at secondhand, and for his intense agitation at the moment of writing. Whatever form they took, and however long they had endured, their issue is sufficient warranty that Otto *knew* that his trust in his friend was not abused; and even though some coolness between the two men would be very natural after the repeated "scenes" which Minna's turbulence had caused, we find Otto writing Richard on a subject nearest to a father's heart, the death of a beloved child, barely two months after the Asyl was closed (see *Letters to Otto*, and p. 109 *inf.*). That in itself is ample refutation of the avid slanderers who not long since painted Wagner's voluntary forsaking of his haven as a humiliation inflicted by a wrathful husband. But the refutation is strengthened by the frequent interchange of visits in the following spring and summer; still more by Wagner's expression of October '59: "Children, that we are *three*, is my and your greatest triumph!" (p. 194). Here a triple renunciation, of a kind too sacred for the vulgar mind to grasp, was still in force; a renunciation which alone can explain those cryptic words on page 69, "Nay, he will not betray thee, — — —, not— he!"—the application whereof to Otto is so manifest when we remember that Wagner had but just received his tender tidings of bereavement.

One more point, before we pass to the other vessel of silver. Down to the time when Wagner knew at last the secret of Mathilde's heart, he may have guessed that her friendly interest in him was part-occasion of her husband's largesses, but the wildest imagination could never have dreamt that Otto's generosity was not dictated by his own free will *; for Jakob Sulzer also, no wife to influence him, had long ago combined with Wesendonck for the artist's assistance. From the moment that his eyes were opened, though,

---

* In a "Gedenkblatt," or "Souvenir" contributed to the *Allg. Musik-Zeitung* of Feb. 14, 1896 (nine months before her husband's death), Frau Wesendonck pointedly observes that "money-matters were never discussed" between herself and Wagner.

Wagner seeks help in every *other* quarter; and even a year thereafter, when the ideal trefoil spreads its leaves in peace, it needs
some pressure on Herr Otto's part, to induce his friend to accept
of his munificence again (p. 167*n*). One may wish that no
further acceptance had been necessary, but the eternal money-
trouble was the Achilles-heel in Wagner's lot, and for that his
laggard fellow-countrymen must be mainly held responsible; neither
has a golden vessel ever yet been known without its portion of
alloy.

MATHILDE, the chief vessel of silver, was born at Elberfeld the
23rd of December 1828, her parents Karl Luckemeyer and Johanna
his wife (née Stein). We hear of a brother and a younger sister,
but know nothing more about her family, except that her father
was a man of civic standing—a Kgl. Kommerzienrath, or member
of the royal Board of Commerce—and that they soon removed
to Düsseldorf, a very important commercial city on the lower
Rhine. Mathilde at first received her education there, thereafter
at Dunkirk; but as she tells us herself, she was a "blank page"
when she first met Wagner (1852). On the 19th of May 1848 she
married Otto, and their first son Paul was born at Düsseldorf
November 1849 (died four months old). They spent the following
year in "America," presumably New York, and by the middle of
1851 we find them settled in grand style in the Hôtel Baur au Lac
at Zurich, where Myrrha, whose name will often recur, was born
the 7th of that August. This hotel became their head-quarters
for another six years, and here were also born their sons Guido,
Sept. 13, 1855, and Karl on the 18th of April 1857;—they had
no further issue until June 16, 1862, their last child, Hans (died
1882). Probably when they first arrived at Zurich, a great silk
centre, they had no intention of making it a permanent home;
certainly they spent a good portion of each year away, and almost
a whole twelvemonth in Paris from early 1856 to early 1857 save
for a brief flight back and forth again. Not till 1855 did they
begin to build their stately villa in the rural suburb Enge, the
famous "Green Hill," which they occupied from August 22, 1857,
down to 1872; when they removed first to Dresden, and in 1882
to Berlin, with a country-seat "Traunblick" on the shores of the
Traunsee, Salzkammergut (1878 onward). It was at Traunblick

that Mathilde Wesendonck died, the 31st of August 1902, after
but eight hours' illness ; apparently, therefore, from a seizure of
the heart, as Minna and Richard Wagner before her.
A fair idea of Frau Wesendonck's mental capacity is scarcely
to be gathered either from her "Gedenkblatt" on Wagner in the
Allgemeine Musik-Zeitung,* written when age was creeping on, or
from the fourteen letters that terminate the present book ; for which
reason I have prefaced those letters by two little so-called children's-
tales from a collection lately re-issued, these bearing too close a
relation to the life-romance not to be doubly welcome in the
absence of any of the former of earlier date than June 1861.
The curious will find at the British Museum, as I am informed
by a friend, her five-act drama "Gudrun," Zurich 1868, a volume
of her "Gedichte, Volksweisen, Legenden und Sagen," Leipzig
1874, and her dramatic poem "Odysseus," Dresden 1878. Beyond
these, I can speak of a five-act tragedy "Edith oder die Schlacht
bei Hastings," Stuttgart 1872, a "Baldur-Mythos" after the younger
Edda, 1875, "Kalypso, ein Vorspiel" (without date), and a
four-act "Alkestis, nach dem Griechischen frei bearbeitet," 1898,—
for possession of all which I have to thank her heirs. Dr. Golther
(editor of the German originals of these letters) further mentions
"Natur-Mythen," Zurich 1865, and a drama "Friedrich der Grosse,"
Berlin 1871. Quite a respectable list, and of works of no mean
merit ; the main point for us, however, is that not one of them
was written before Frau Wesendonck's attachment to Wagner—
whose phraseology may be detected here and there—or published
till correspondence with him had practically ceased. These works
have little prospect of survival, but those which sprang from the
depth of her heart, the *Fünf Gedichte* (pp. 16-17 *inf.*) and the
poems sent to him with one of her later letters (pp. 351-54), are
bound to live as long as his own name.—
Her personality? No one admitted to the honour of Frau
Wesendonck's society during the last twenty years of her life—
and here I can speak from personal experience, however slight—
could for a moment believe her to have ever been the heroine

---

* Of Feb. 14, 1896, already referred to. As most of the facts in
that article have already been used in my vol. iv of the *Life*, I do not
think its reproduction needful here, more particularly as the chronology
is rather faulty at times.

of what the baser sort imply when they speak of a 'Tristan-and-Isolde romance.' This placid, sweet Madonna, the perfect emblem of a pearl, not opal, her eyes still dreaming of Nirvana,—no ! emphatically no ! *she* could not have once been swayed by carnal passion. And these letters, in bulk and in detail, most flatly contradict that implication : nay, more,—they prove the justice of my old contention, not mine alone, that the 2nd act of Wagner's drama excludes all possibility of *his* Tristan, *his* Isolde being victims to a coarse desire. In these letters all is pure and spiritual, a Dante and a Beatrice ; so *must* it have been in their intercourse. For my own impression of their recipient—whom I first met in that sad year at Bayreuth when the master was no more—it was that of the silver moon reflecting a sun that has set long since. Not a word ever fell from her lips on such a love as is revealed here ; but every accent of her voice, the gathering moisture in her eye, spelt worship, and from her it was, I earliest learnt a truth which added years have simply verified : that in Richard Wagner we have more than a great,—a profoundly good man.

RICHARD WAGNER :—

" The message from X greatly moved and affected me,* and in more than one respect. My art has ever fared quite well with women's hearts ; and that apparently arises from the fact that, amid all the prevailing vulgarity, it still is much more difficult for women to let their souls turn utterly to leather, than it has proved for our civilised men-folk with such ample success. Women indeed are the music of life ; they take up everything with opener mind and less reserve, to beautify it through their fellow-feeling " (To Uhlig, Dec. 1849).

" What set your letter in its ugliest light, was its coming as enclosure to a letter of E.'s, which I happened to read

---

* From other sources we learn that this " X " in the authorised edition of the *Letters to Uhlig* stands for Mme Laussot, the " Bordeaux lady " of page xlviii, a relative of Wagner's benefactors the Ritter family. The " E." in the next extract was a daughter of Frau Ritter's, and Wagner seems to have met none but the sons as yet.—Tr.

first of the two. Ask E. what I mean by that, and in
two words she'll make it plain to you ; for—believe me—
this girl is miles ahead of you,—and why ? By birth,
because she is a female. She was *born a human being,*—
you, and all men nowadays, are born *philistines ;* but painfully and slowly do we wretched creatures reach at last
to turning human. Only the ladies, those who have stayed
entirely what they are at birth, can teach us ; and were it
not for them, we men should go irreclaimably to ground
with our paper pellets. Do you suppose that the passage
in my letter, where—since you took it so for granted—I
answered that Paris was doing me a world of good, I was
perfectly delighted with it, and so on,—do you suppose
that E. would have taken that at its face value ? I can
hardly believe it, and presume she would have understood
the irony a little better than the Royal Chamber-musician
did " (To Uhlig, from *Bordeaux*, March 1850).

"Just one thing more,—it used to crop up in our old
debates :—never shall we be what we might and should be,
till—*Woman* is *woken.*—Ah, see what songs I'm singing
you, poor fellow ! Believe me, I am not blithe myself, that
I can merely sing" (To August Roeckel, political prisoner,
Aug. 1851).

" Exactly as Ahasuerus, the Hollander yearns for death
as end of all his sorrows ; but the Hollander may gain
this redemption—denied to the eternal Jew—through *a
woman* who shall sacrifice herself for love of him. Thus
it is the yearning for death that spurs him on to seek
this woman ; but this woman no longer is Odysseus'
housekeeping Penelope, wooed in days of old : no, she is
the archetype of womanhood, though non-extant as yet,
the longed for, dreamt of, infinitely womanly woman,—let
me out with it in one word : *the Woman of the Future* "
(Communication, autumn 1851).

These passages, and many, many like them, have lain open
to the world for years, alike in German and in English ; it is
amazing that their sense should have been grasped so seldom,
and the coarsest imputations cast on Wagner's moral character by
all sorts and conditions of writers, down to the last bumptious
tyro who fancies he can wield a pen. Somewhere, of course,
there must reside an explanation : it resides in this, that fifty
years ago the " Woman of the Future " was considered a fantastic
myth, at any rate in Germany; whereas she has become to-day
the Woman of the Present, whilst the Woman of the Past is so
extinct that her very history runs risk of being clean forgotten.
Unfortunately Wagner, whose whole mission it was to "make
revolution wherever I go," lived far in advance of his age—which
was mentally and morally incapable of understanding him in almost
anything—and still he has to pay the penalty. " Out of themselves
they blow them across to me, those clouds ; how much longer
must I scatter them, to shew them that I'm, after all, a good pure
man ? " (p. 106 *inf.*). Those clouds are still blown, and I cannot
too emphatically insist that, upon *all* reliable evidence, Wagner
was a clean-living, clean-thinking man ; in fact, it is the very
cleanness of his thoughts that has baffled so many a plumber,
—where he speaks of "the senses," for instance, "they" only
think of one.

Writing of the Paris 'sixties (when Minna scented vice in every
petticoat), Malwida von Meysenbug, a pure-minded spinster who
shared her friend Wagner's belief in the future of Woman, has
placed this on record : " In face of practical life he had that
awkwardness of genius which is so touching, since it coincides
with a profound naivety of ideas about the relations of ordinary
life which can be misunderstood alone by mediocrity and malice "
(*Memoiren einer Idealistin* III. 267). In his first edition of the
Communication he was naive enough, indeed, to include the
following passage concerning his *Liebesverbot* period, i.e. the year
or so before he fell in love with Minna : " *Woman* had begun
to dawn on my horizon. The shy reserve towards the female sex
inculcated on us all—that ground of all the vices of the modern
male generation, and no less of the stunting of the female—my
temperament had only been able to break it through by fits and
starts, in isolated utterances of a pert impetuosity : a hasty con-

science-stinging snatch had had to serve as most unsatisfying substitute for the instinctively desired bliss. That desire, which nowhere could still itself in life, found an ideal food in the reading of Heinse's Ardinghello, as also the works of Heine and other members of the 'Young-German' school of literature. The effect of these impressions shewed itself on my outward life in the only way in which Nature can utter herself under the pressure of the moral bigotry of our Society, namely as—what folk call, unfortunately to-be-tolerated—vice" (*Prose Works* I. 294 & 396). The next edition, issued twenty years later (1872), expunged for good the last clause and the *second* sentence; for which reason, when translating the work in 1892, I relegated them to an appendix; whence—oddly enough—they have not yet been unearthed by "mediocrity and malice." But is it not plain, on the face of them, that these are the words of a man disgusted with the wild oats which he, like myriads of others, had sown for a brief period of his early life? And does not their expunging connote that his traducers were a force to be reckoned with, people who even in 1872 would fail to comprehend his protest against that "shy reserve towards the female sex" which *still* prevailed in Germany and turned that sex into domestic animals or puppets? The Woman of the Future was only just beginning to be born, and rational liberty of comradeship was not yet tolerated.*—

To get back, or on—I almost forget which—to the time when Wagner first met the two Wesendoncks, namely February 1852:—

With a wholly unsympathetic wife by his side—a wife constitutionally disqualified to understand her husband's wish for more inspiring company,—Richard Wagner has arrived at a climacteric in his artist-life. His operas *Rienzi*, the *Holländer*, *Tannhäuser* and *Lohengrin* already are on the boards, though the last-named he has never heard himself; he has just rounded off his most important theoretic period, *Opera and Drama* and the *Communica-*

---

* To obviate any misconstruction of this deprecation of "Die uns Allen anerzogene schüchterne Zurückhaltung gegen das weibliche Geschlecht," I adduce von Hornstein (see p. xlv): "Once he happened to make a risqué joke in the presence of his wife and sister-in-law, and immediately blushed like a girl. That blush became him well." How many men past forty have retained the faculty of blushing?

tion to my Friends appearing together this selfsame winter; the full plan of *Der Ring des Nibelungen* has ripened in his brain, whilst its last two members lie versified on paper (subject to revision). Now he is simply waiting for the Spring, his favourite creative season, to attack the *Walküre* and *Rheingold* poems in earnest; but his health has ebbed to a wretched state—undoubtedly due to the eye-strain of so much literary work—and a fallow season is essential. To tide the interregnum over, he conducts subscription-concerts at Zurich (his place of refuge) with an inadequate orchestra and a tiny fee : at a rehearsal of his *Tannhäuser* overture, for one of these, he delights Mathilde Wesendonck, to whom and her husband he has been introduced at the house of a friend some few nights previously. His remarks to Uhlig (a young Dresden friend) in a letter of a day or two afterwards are eloquent of an instantaneous impression : "The feminine element remains the only one that can help me to illusions, off and on ; for I can form no more about the males"; and a month later, four days after the concert-performance itself : "Don't call me vain if I confess to you that the extraordinary effects, which I am spreading around me, restore me now and then to a pleasurable sense of existence ; ever and again it is the 'eternal womanly' that fills me with sweet illusions and warm thrills of joy-in-life. The glistening moisture of a woman's eye often saturates me with fresh hope again" (see *Life* iii, 272 *et seq.*).

I have just said that the mutual impression seems to have been instantaneous, but hasten to add that for a long time, a very long time, it was quite subconscious on both sides. In certain precipitate quarters—evidently acquainted with nothing but French *extracts* which lately appeared in a Paris review—capital has already been made of Wagner's Diary entry of August 21, 1858 : "Yesterday I wrote to my sister Kläre. . . . I indicated to her what thou hast been and art to me these six years since" (p. 33 *inf.*); but my readers have only to turn back to the said letter itself,—"at first, and for long, shy, diffident, hesitant and timid." A profound effect had been produced on Mathilde's mind by her first personal experience of that rarity on earth, a genius, and no doubt the effect was strengthened by a woman's quick grasp of the situation in Wagner's cheerless home : admiration and commiseration would thus go hand in hand, with the result that Otto was at once persuaded to exercise the duty of the rich and take upon himself, in some degree, the rôle of a kind Providence. That Otto did so from the very first, is proved by Wagner's earliest published letter to him, namely of July 1852, and still more strongly by a much later one, of February 1857: "You know how I told you 5 years ago of this greatest wish of mine,* and defined it as the longing for a cosy, quiet country-house with garden. It seemed a thing that ought to be attainable, and you offered me a hand thereto yourself." And so we shall find that, until a little later than the letter of 1857 just-cited, alike those to Otto and the tiny billets to his wife betray no feeling, certainly no consciously reciprocated feeling, other than that of a friendship which has ripened into camaraderie: brothers and sisters might address each other thus. Yet, in his passion for proselytising, Wagner soon undertook to form the beautiful young matron's untrained mind. There lay the unsuspected danger; with centuries of chains behind it, the feminine mind had not yet learnt to loose itself from the emotional heart; the "wakening of Woman" might prove to be a thought too soon.

From Frau Wesendonck's brief reminiscences, above referred to, there is really very little to be gleaned as regards this process; from her (later?) friend Frau Wille's absolutely nothing. The gossip gathered half a century thereafter from toothless survivors of their entourage, at second to fifth hand, is not worth the paper wasted on its printing. For this nebulous period we are therefore restricted to Wagner's private letters to contemporaries, and the testimony of the only one of his male associates whose recollections have as yet been made public, to wit, von Hornstein.†

---

* Namely, "untroubled rest to carry out my artistic drafts"; yet unless the above refers to a conversation, the "five" should be reduced to less than four if we may judge by that fragment of a second letter in the *Otto* collection dated "June 11, 1853," which seems to be an answer to Herr Otto's inquiry as to Wagner's needs.

† "Erinnerungen an Richard Wagner: Auszüge aus dem unge-druckten Nachlasse des Komponisten Robert Freiherrn von Hornstein," feuilleton of the *Neue freie Presse* Sept. 23-24, 1904. An editorial footnote tells us that Baron Hornstein was born 1833, and died 1890 (long before modern gossip on these relations had started), also that a collection of his songs has now reached its twelfth edition; whilst allusion is made to his "interesting reminiscences of Schopenhauer"

From these, combined, I will endeavour to 'reconstitute' the puzzling past:—

1852.—Jan. 30 : "With her natural strong need of love, a woman *must* love something" (to Liszt, just *before* this acquaintance). Then—

March 25 : "Yesterday I received a letter from Hamburg, from a lady of aristocratic birth [Malwida von Meysenbug, a total stranger] who thanks me for my essays, saying they have been her salvation; she declares herself a thorough revolutionary.—Thus it is ever the ladies that have their hearts in the right place in my regard, whereas I am almost compelled to give men up as lost already" (to Uhlig).—May 3 : "The *Holländer's* impression on my public was most unusual, deep and earnest. Naturally, the ladies were to the fore again" (to U.) ; 29th, "With all the *ladies* I have won a mighty feather in my cap" (to L.); and 31st, "Julie [née Ritter] is in the country with us here ; K[ummer, her husband] is at the baths.—Julie seems to have taken a great fancy to me ; at any rate she implicitly follows my word " (to U.).—July 15, "There are splendid women here in the Oberland, but only to the eye ; they're eaten up with raging vulgarity" (to U.).—Sept. 12 : "My personal affairs are shaping fairly pleasantly [*Tannh.* fees coming in], but alas ! I'm *much alone ;* I lack all satisfying company " (to Roeckel) ; 27th, "If I could only come to an agreeable rest: yesterday a young woman [perhaps a fortune-teller?] told me *what* would cure me ; she was very bold, and was right ! Good Lord, what a silly fool I am, to be such a squeamish beast ! But that's the way I'm built ! " (to U.).—Nov. 9, "I am living an inexpressibly good-for-nothing life ! Of actual enjoyment of life I know sheer nothing : for me the 'taste of life, of *love*' is simply a matter of the imagination, not of experience. . . . If I could visit *you* at Weimar, perhaps I might hope to recover, . . . perhaps a word of love might sound from here or there—but here ? ? Here I must perish in the very briefest space, and everything will come

---

published by the same journal in 1883. Making allowance for an obvious inaccuracy here and there, v. Hornstein's vindication of Wagner is the more valuable as it was written in 1884 and he confesses to having ceased to be on friendly terms about twenty years previously. Unfortunately the "Auszüge," or excerpts, give no dates, though these are easy to furnish on other internal evidence.

too late—too late. 'Tis so!" (to Liszt).—N.B., Theodor Uhlig,. Wagner's favourite disciple, died in Dresden this Christmas.—

1853 : the year the two families first became more intimate :—

May 30 (*re* the famous three Zurich concerts, consisting of extracts from the *Holländer, Tannhäuser* and *Lohengrin*) : " Indeed it was a festival for the little world around me ; the ladies were all in my favour " (to Liszt).—June 8 : " I might say I am living fairly pleasantly now [in the new flat] if—I were anybody else ! It is not only that I am bound to feel the dishonourableness of the world in general more acutely than many another does ; but even as regards my own personal life I'm bound to admit to myself more candidly each day that it is only in the last few years [*cf.* Jan. 1854] I've grown aware—too late !—that I strictly have not lived *at all* yet ! . . . My art is becoming more and more the lay of the blinded yearning nightingale, and this art would suddenly lose all its reason if I could but clasp the actuality of life. Ay, just where Life stops, there does Art begin ; from youth up we stumble into art sans knowing how, and only when we have forged through art to its very end, do we discover to our lamentation that 'tis just this life we lack. . . . O yes, there's one thing might console me :—not only am I wondered at, but also *loved ;* where criticism ceases, love steps in, and a number of hearts has it drawn near me. Yet *that* sort of love cannot but still remain far off me ; it enters my life most indirectly, and—the way this life of mine has shaped—it is only as into dimmest distance I can look into that realm of love. Could I become a proper egoist, things would be easier ; but as it is, it can't be helped, and—like yourself—only through resignation can I at least maintain myself in the truth of my nature " (to Roeckel in prison).— Dec. 29 : " When composing [*Rheingold*] I generally undertake too much, and drive my wife to justifiable wrath by keeping dinner waiting ; so that it is in the sweetest of humours I enter the second half of the day, with which I don't at all know what to do : solitary walks in the mist ; sundry evenings at Wesendonck's. It is there I still obtain my only stimulation ; the graceful lady stays loyal and attached to me, though there also remains much in this society that can but torture me " (to elderly Frau Ritter of Dresden).—One might place the commencement of the reading-lessons somewhere about here, with a good deal of pianoforte demonstration, as we know, including fragments from the growing *Rheingold.*

1854.—Jan. 25-26 (the famous homily to Roeckel) : "Whatever a man cannot love, stays beyond him, and he beyond it; here the philosopher may flatter himself he comprehends, but not the truthful human being. Well, in its fullest reality, love is only possible between the sexes : only as *man* and *woman* can we human beings love most really, whereas all other kinds of love are but derived from this . . . [and so on, for pages] . . . 'I' and the world, means nothing more than 'I' alone; to 'me' the world becomes a full reality but when it has become a 'thou'; and it becomes that only in the apparition of the loved individual. . . . Enough ! I venture to send you these confessions of faith without fear of rousing trouble for you, in your solitude, through a sharing of my views. Not only you, but I myself—as all of us—live at present in conditions and relations which point to none but surrogates or makeshifts ; for you, no less than for myself, truest, realest life can only be a thing of thought, of wish. I had become 36 years old ere I guessed the actual drift of my artistic impulse * ; so long

---

* Wagner became "36" on the 22nd of May 1849, so that—unless the "6" be a misprinted 9—the said epoch would fall within his first year of exile ; which confronts us with the never yet unriddled "Bordeaux episode" of March 1850. Ferdinand Praeger, who invariably embroiders what he does not invent, tells the story thus: "Feeling naught congenial to him in Paris, he left again for Zurich, via Bordeaux and Geneva [*such* a short cut]. At Bordeaux an episode occurred similar [?] to one which happened later at Zurich, about which the press of the day [?!] made a good deal of unnecessary commotion and ungenerous comment. I mention the incident to show the man as he was. The Opposition have not spared his failings, and over the Zurich incident were hypercritically censorious [it was not so much as known to any but a private circle before this wretched book of P.'s]. The Bordeaux story I am alluding to, is, that the wife of a friend, Mrs. H——, having followed Wagner to the south, called on him at his hotel, and throwing herself at his feet, passionately told of her affection. Wagner's action in the matter was to telegraph to the husband to come and take his wife home. On telling me the story, Wagner jocosely remarked that poor Beethoven, so full of love, never had his affection returned, and lived and died, so it is said, a hermit" (*Wagner as I knew him* pp. 196-7). And that was published by a respectable London and New York firm during the lifetime of both the ladies mentioned, a few months after its author's

had Art found credence with me as the end, and Life the means.
But the discovery, it is true, had come too late, and none but
tragical experiences could respond to my new instinct of life.
Moreover, a wider glance into the world shews Love itself impossible
now. . . . Not one of us will see the Promised Land ; we all shall
perish in the wilderness . . . in the happiest event we must become martyrs. . . Now I can do nothing else than go on existing
as artist : all the rest—since I can embrace Life, Love, no more
—either disgusts me, or interests me solely insofar as it bears upon
Art. 'Tis an agonising life, to be sure ; still, 'tis the only life
possible."—What does that reveal to us,* but a man distraught

own decease ! Seeing that Frau Wesendonck was openly named 100
pages after, in course of further insolences regarding "the Zurich
incident" ; seeing also that a German edition was promised for speedy
appearance (also a French, but the German publisher's withdrawal
knocked that on the head)—the reader will not be astonished at my
warning that lady at once about the slander. That there was *something*
in the "Bordeaux story," quite unconnected with herself, is proved by
her reply (see facsimile), but Praeger's version is so little to be credited
that he does not even believe it himself : the "English" edition says
"At Bordeaux an episode occurred" etc., implying that "the husband"
was telegraphed-for from *there ;* the German edition, professedly "translated" by himself, says in the usual Praeger fashion, "At Bordeaux
he visited a married couple . . . . and when he resumed his journey, she
followed him and found him at a hotel en route. . . . but Wagner
telegraphed to the husband to come and fetch his wife back." After
that, one cannot trust a single word of the details ; but the very possession
of the story, in any shape, points either to a still graver breach of
confidence than is self-admitted (namely to garbled divulgence of Wagner's
closely guarded Memoirs), or to something far more likely in this instance,
an unbosoming by the "solitary, heroic Minna"—with whom the tattler
made great friends during his fortnight at the Asyl in summer 1857
(of course he persistently dates it "1856"). The latter supposition,
coupled with P.'s soup-brewing tendencies, would account for the impossible suggestion (Engl. ed.) that the Bordeaux lady was Emilie Heim,
—who with her husband first came to Zurich in 1852. Whatever the
right or the wrong of the story may some day prove to be, there is
not the smallest probability of· *Richard* Wagner's having betrayed
it to so garrulous an acquaintance, and never in this world "jocosely,"—
see "tragical experiences" above.

* There is *no* directer personal allusion in the letter. Incidentally
it should be remarked that, apart from all despondence caused by
a Leipzig *Lohengrin* fiasco, the acuteness of the present psychologic

with love, driven almost to despair by its apparent hopelessness? Resignation has yet to come, though only just below the offing, as we shall descry in an instant; *consciousness* of being loved in return is many, many a league away.

April 9, '54: "Ah dearest, dearest, onlyest Franz! Give me a heart, a mind, a feminine soul, in which I might **wholly** merge myself, that would embrace the whole of me,—how little should I ask of this world!... But I'm wool-gathering again! Send me to the right-about, as I deserve;—nobody will ever make anything of me but a fantastic idiot!" (to Liszt).—June: "Seek me no copyist; Mad. Wesendonck has presented me with a gold pen—of indestructible writing-power [cf. page 152 *inf.*]—which is turning me into a caligraphic pedant again. These scores will be my most consummate masterpiece of penmanship: one can't escape one's destiny" (to L.); his saving gift of humour, so often coming to the rescue, has stood him in good stead once more. But that gift will not forever stay his tears, as is shewn by the following reminiscence of von Hornstein's, who first met him at the zenith of the Zurich festival in '53, and now runs over from Lausanne for a wild-goose concert chase at Sion (*Life* iv, 365-70) and its sequel at Karl Ritter's bridal home near Chillon: "Several times was Wagner overcome by yearning for the talented and beautiful Frau Wesendonck, for whom he had conceived a passionate regard; the refined lady accepted the artist's homage without compromising herself in the smallest degree. Once we surprised him, sitting in the garden, with tears in his eyes. Apart from such attacks of weakness, he was cheerful, amiable, full of intellectual talk." Later in July, Wagner invites Liszt to Zurich, "Come, if you can, in the second half of August; the Wesendoncks will be back by then, I think" (as Liszt was unable to come, he cannot have met them till autumn '56).

Then the *Walküre* music is taken seriously in hand, some of it under the eyes of von Hornstein, who has come to Zurich for a while and tells us, evidently of September: "In the presence of Ritter, Wesendoncks, Heim and myself, he sang and played the whole first act. Frau Heim, a capital singer, supported him;

---

crisis itself accounts for the strangely inconsequential 'explanation' of the Ring-poem contained in this, the favourite epistle of the modern axe-grinder: Wagner himself is hardly to be recognised here.

it was a rare première.—For himself, he did not sing at all badly ; with little voice he managed much ; just an ordinary sort of voice, but the higher notes rang better. His piano-playing was about the same ; without being a proficient, he could bring out every-thing.—That evening he was very happy."—On the sketch of the prelude to that first act of *Die Walküre* Wagner's pencil traced "*G*....... *s*.. *M*.......," deciphered later by Frau Wesendonck as "*Gesegnet sei Mathilde*"—"Blessed be Mathilde!" Even though the initials may date from this period, however, it is impossible for the sketch itself to have been made away till long thereafter ; at first he needed it until completion of the full score, and then he left it in London for Klindworth to make the pfte version (1855 onward, see no. 213 of *W.-L. Corr.*).

Meantime this same month of September 1854 brought his first acquaintance with the works of Schopenhauer, without which he might have been unable to endure the strain of so hopeless a passion ; for his thoughts had often been attuned to suicide of late. Schopenhauer taught him very soon a nobler way—of *resigned* renunciation ; and it is in that mood that his *Tristan* dawns on him before "this mournful year" goes out. Mid-December to Liszt : "As I never in my life have quaffed the actual delight of love, I mean some day to raise a monument to this most beauteous of all dreams, wherein that love shall glut itself right royally for once. In my head I've planned a *Tristan and Isolde*, the simplest but fullest-blooded musical conception ; with the black flag that floats at its end I then shall shroud myself —to die." Certainly *Tristan* is deferred for nearly three years, three years of ripening and refining, as the *Ring des Nibelungen* blocks the way; but, the *Walküre* composition-draft completed (Dec. 27), for a fortnight he suddenly takes up and finishes a subject just as symptomatic of his present state,—he revises his *Faust* overture of fifteen years ago, "the solitary Faust."

1855.—It would seem to have been Mathilde's expressed desire to hear this work, that prompted the *Faust* revision ; for she in-forms us that he had wished to dedicate its publication to her, but recoiled with horror at the thought of its gloomy motto (after Goethe) : "Impossible—he cried—to pin that fearful motto to your breast!" Whether those were his actual words or not, he simply presented her with "the score" (rough draft?), presumably without the motto, and wrote upon it, "R. W. Zürich 17 Jan. 1855 zum Andenken S. l. F.," i.e. "In remembrance of his dear Friend." *

The next piece of evidence we have in this year is a letter to Roeckel of February the 5th : "With my own life-experiences I had arrived at the exact point where it needed nothing but Schopenhauer's philosophy, to determine my whole course. Through ability to accept his very, very serious truths without reservation I most positively conformed to my innermost bent, and albeit he has set me on a somewhat different tack from before, yet this veering was the only one to answer to my deeply suffering sense of the world's essence. . . . With a truly reverential feeling, then, do I send you this work that has strengthened me to endurance, and given me power of renunciation, at a very decisive catastrophe of my inner life"; whilst the meaning of that "catastrophe"—i.e. crisis, and an *inner* one, mark you—is distinctly outlined in a previous passage of this letter : "At last I have finished composition of the *Walküre*—amid great inner sufferings whereof no one knows anything, and least of all my good wife" (she had visited the prisoner some three months back).—Then from London, to Roeckel again, next April or May : "Long had I found it hard to keep an optimistic footing, in face of the perpetual evidence of my own eyes, and friend Sch. simply helped by his enormous impetus to rid me of the last Judaic heresy, and, with great grief indeed, but the consolation of having cast off the last wilful illusion, to make myself as free as ever man can be. . . . In summer I shall return to my dear Switzerland, which I think of never quitting more. Retirement, beautiful Nature and—work : 'tis the only element for me to live in, and I shall not let myself be torn from it again." That is the reverse of the reflection of a declared, still more of an accepted lover.—In September, and on

---

* Dr. Golther—evidently going by Frau Wesendonck's *Gedenkblatt*, where she had cited the inscription as "Der lieben Frau"—interprets the initials as "Seiner lieben Frau"; but that *possessive* pronoun makes a vast difference, and I therefore believe that the "F" should be read as "Freundin," i.e. "Lady-friend." In Lotte's letters to Schiller we constantly find this abbreviation "l.f.", or "l. Fr.," standing for a male "dear friend."—The revised *Faust* overture was first performed Jan. 23, 1855, at Zurich.

the day of Guido's birth, it is followed by an invitation to Liszt to bring Princess Wittgenstein and her daughter to Zurich at Christmas : " One can pass *the winter* very spaciously and comfortably, for *very little*, at the *Hôtel Baur au lac* where you stayed before [1853]. . . . The Wesendoncks are living there, and you might set up quite a famous—half joint—household ; which would much divert me."

Richard and Minna had passed a few weeks at Seelisberg on the lake of Lucerne just previously ; von Hornstein went to stay there too, and this is what he tells us :—" He [they ?] occupied two small rooms, in which one could not have placed even an upright piano, even had there been one to procure. There was a grand in the public conversation-room ; but that was never empty, and Wagner never set his foot inside. . . . On our walk, as we came to a part dropping sheer to the lake, he begged me to let him go first, as he had what is called sympathetic dizziness and felt nervous for the man in front [cf. p. 167 *inf.*]. On our return it was exactly time to go to supper. Then for the first time I saw his wife, who gave me the impression of a very kind, good-natured woman ; we soon became great friends. She always had a high opinion of me * ; moreover, Ritter [?] and I always took her part,—which could not be said of everyone in Zurich. The three of us sat down to the general table-d'hôte : Frau Wagner, who sat opposite her husband and myself, stood [!] very well with all the company, and chatted briskly with her female neighbours ; Wagner held aloof from the whole company, which was taken very ill of him. They were mostly ladies from Zurich and Basle, few gentlemen ; a fairly home-baked gathering —Immediately after table, Wagner retired with us to his room ; his wife brewed him a grog, which he used to drink every evening then. He would often change his diet. . . We parted rather late that night, against his usual custom.—At Seelisberg he rose early, and worked till dinner at a desk-stand near the balcony, from which one looked down on the lake, with

---

* To judge by Hornstein's literary style, one can quite believe it ; to make any coherent sense of his six-word gasps, I have been compelled to reduce the rank of their full-stops, from time to time. Needless to say, his paragraphs are, equally jerky ; they are represented by the dashes introduced above.

the Mythensteine opposite.—I posted myself on this balcony to
study Schopenhauer, and in those few weeks at Seelisberg I got
the principles of Schopenhauer's philosophy by heart [would that it
had also been his style!]. As I took a daily walk of several hours
with Wagner, and passed the evenings with him, my penetration
into that philosophy was much assisted by the fact that Schopenhauer formed our chief topic of conversation.—Wagner had a
pencil-sketch of the 'Rheingold' in front of him [it was *Walküre* act ii],
and was fair-copying the score. For this he used a platinum pen
which a Russian lady had presented to him [poor Frau Wesendonck].
He wrote most distinctly, almost beautifully. When I asked if
the copying did not weary him, he replied : It was no mere
transcribing, but thus he went over the work again and altered
in detail.—At the dinner-table things passed exactly as the night
before ; the Swiss had a kind of awe of Wagner, and got out of
his way. Directly after table Wagner withdrew to his room, to
read and rest; Frau Wagner and I remained with the company,
and entertained ourselves quite well with the excellent philistines,
who were very nice to us and appreciated our affability ; Frau
Wagner, in particular, did all she could to furnish a corrective of
her husband. Later, I retired to my room in the side building,
which looked upon the Uri-Rothstock. Towards evening I fetched
Wagner for a walk.—Thus our life repeated itself with great
regularity ; it was fine weather almost all the time, so that this
day's plan was little altered.—I learned to love and admire
Wagner. At Seelisberg he did not turn one of his disagreeable
sides outward. He was full of wit, and often enchantingly adorable.
Even with his wife he had not the smallest rencontre, which frequently occurred at Zurich later."—Had Minna but *encouraged*
her husband to go his harmless way, as he let her go hers, no
"rencontre" need there ever have been,—clearly he was steering
away from the rocks toward which her non-company temper
lashed him back ; and of this "later" we have von Hornstein's
testimony again, though he specifies no definite period : "He
was charming when he went for walks with Ritter and myself
alone. Clever aperçus flew through the air ; he lavished upon us
his rich store of experiences. Many a golden saying leapt to ear,
original views of men, relations, art and politics, to light ; his
whole goodness of heart, of which he possessed a large dose,

mounted to the surface. His love of animals had something touching. When his pity was aroused, he found himself disarmed. He long had ceased to love his wife, and was consumed with passion for another; yet he would turn sulky, hasty, perverse, never coarse. With one little word he might have thrust a poniard in the woman [cf. p. xxii]: he never breathed it."—

1856.—In January of this year the Wesendoncks were still at Zurich (cf. a letter of Gottfried Keller's), but they must have left for Paris, or possibly the Riviera, quite early in the year ; nor did they return, save for a brief spell or two in autumn, till about commencement of the following Spring,—practically a twelvemonth's absence.

In the meantime Wagner has finished scoring *Die Walküre*, middle of March, and repeated attacks of illness have compelled him to take a long rest at a place of so-called 'cure.' In May he sketches that scenario for *Die Sieger* to be found in vol. VIII. of the Prose Works, with Ananda and Prakriti (alias Sawitri) as hero and heroine (pp. 54-56 *inf.*). This is highly significant, especially as it appears from his letter to Roeckel of August 23rd that the Buddhesque variant of Brynhild's farewell words in *Götterdämmerung* has been drafted soon thereafter, whilst "The chief thing I desire is health, to be able to execute all the sketches of which I am full. Unfortunately I'm fuller than I need ; for, beyond the Nibelungen pieces, I have still a Tristan und Isolde in my head (Love as fearful agony), and a latest subject of all, 'die Sieger' (supreme Redemption—a Buddhist legend), which so compass me about that only with great pertinacity can I drive them back in favour of the Nibelungen." Love as "*furchtbare Qual*,"—that is his own experience, like Tristan's in act iii, and he has just described it on another page of this letter as the "devastating" element in his *Ring*,—so at variance with the earlier termination ! Further : "Can you conceive a *moral action* otherwise than as an act of *renunciation* ? And what else is highest holiness, i.e. fullest redemption, than the conversion of this principle into the basis of our every deed ?— But even with these simple questions I'm faring too far afield, no doubt, and becoming more abstract than is good for me ; wherefore I will merely add something about my concrete personality.—I am nothing but Artist,—and that's my blessing and my curse ; otherwise I would fain become an anchorite, and have my life mapped out for me in the simplest of modes. As it is, fool that I am, I run about in search of rest, i.e. that complex rest to be supplied by an untroubled life of ease sufficient to enable me to—do nothing but work, be nothing but artist."

We shall find that paradox running as a thread of scarlet through this volume, the cause of all its hero's seeming inconsistencies. But the interesting point at present, is that *Otto's* sympathy had also been claimed a fortnight previously alike for the *Tristan* and *Die Sieger* projects, whilst we can plainly detect a week hence that Mathilde has taken such alarm at the Grand Duke's offer of a *Weimar* sanctuary as to induce her husband to forestall it (*Letters to Otto*). Wagner himself had wisely endeavoured to secure a rural house, whose whereabouts we must leave the Zurichers to trace, but which clearly was not near the Wesendoncks' then half-built villa (p. 10 *inf.*) : Mathilde, listening to the dictates of her heart, not her reason, holds out to the renunciant that fateful apple of the Asyl. Of that there can be no doubt, since Wagner's letter to Otto of September 10 bears all the marks of a response to a spontaneous offer : " To be sure of enjoying total quiet and retirement in the immediate neighbourhood of a family so kind and dear to me as yours, of always finding harbourage and sympathy for joy and sorrow in these most intimate relations, would be a happiness *no* other could replace ! " Nothing could be more positive proof, that on September the 4th Otto himself had written : If I can succeed in buying it, will you oblige me by accepting tenancy of the little property adjoining mine? And Wagner follows up our last quotation with a serious monition : " But can I cast this whole burden of my existence upon you, and after repeated experiences of the great difficulty of my position, ought I not to recognise that the load would grow too heavy for you ? " Here we can see that the temptation to accept relief is becoming too strong to be resisted, but it is manifest that Wagner believes himself strong enough to resist any other temptation which may flow from that acceptance. Another thing manifest, is that neither Richard nor Minna can as yet have had the least suspicion of Mathilde's secret love of him.

In that letter of Sept. 10 to Otto one passage, given us merely in oblique narration, refers to Wagner's "anxious waiting for

Wesendonck's return." Soon thereafter the friends must have met once more, followed by the little dispute between the two wives anent the merits of *Rienzi* (p. 12 *inf.*); a mere passing tiff, however, for it is the present owner of the future Asyl who frustrates the "harbourage" proposal, by declining to be bought out.—In mid-October Liszt with Princess Carolyne and her daughter arrive, for about six weeks at the Hôtel Baur, and it is clear from messages sent to and fro immediately hereafter that they make the Wesendoncks' acquaintance. More than that,—Wagner at last makes his bosom-friend a confidant and counsellor, for we read in a letter of November '57 : "Now take my hand, and take my kiss ; a kiss such as you gave me a year ago, when you accompanied me home one night—you remember, after I had told my doleful tale to both of you. However much may lose its impression on me,—what you were to me that night, the wondrous sympathy that lay in what you told me as we walked,—this heavenliness in your nature will follow with me, as my most splendid memory, to each future existence " (note *in jedes Dasein hin;* the English edition fogs it into "everywhere"!).—

To wind up his visit, Liszt makes a little concert expedition with Wagner alone, and the latter, on his return to Zurich, writes friend Otto (back in Paris with his wife by now) Nov. 30: "Last Thursday I returned to my domestic quiet (?)"—the note of interrogation being explicable by the letter's close—"The great kind-heartedness of the princess has attuned me to a greater gentleness and control of my so very irritable temper ; so that I am returning to my solitude as from a school, with the feeling of having learnt something. And how much should I not have to learn yet, to conform a little to the claims I make upon myself, and shew myself worthy to myself of what I hold for good and noble in this life of woe and weakness ? Never has it become clearer to me than now, what lenience the very best of us requires, and how, above all others, he must exercise the greatest goodness, not to become the greatest wretch !" If it was not a *good* man who wrote these lines, there never was one ; and as they seem to point to 'rencontres' with Minna whereof Otto himself had been witness, it is fairly plain that jealousy of Otto's wife cannot have been the exciting cause as yet.

1857.—February the 8th Liszt is informed of Otto's purchase of the little property on the grass-clad moraine ridge * that runs up to a commanding prospect, Kilchberg (p. 100) between the Sihl valley and the lake of Zurich, and of his offer of a tenancy thereof for life. Here it should be remarked that in the very next breath Wagner speaks of the necessity of "securing my livelihood in an *independent* fashion," namely by a sale to Härtels of the *Ring;* composition of the third member whereof, the *Siegfried,* he had commenced last September. His ambition for independence was not to be wholly fulfilled, since Härtels would not come to terms; but its sincerity is past all cavil, whilst nothing could be more beautiful than the expression of his thanks to Otto, ending with the words : " Could I depict to you the wonderful deep calm that fills my soul to-day !" (*Letters to O.*)—

April 18, as we have seen, Karl Wesendonck is born, and Hornstein shall be called into our witness-box for the last time : "At the christening of a child of Frau Wesendonck's I stood at Wagner's side ; we were in the background. He was very moody ; all at once he muttered to himself, 'It is like attending one's own execution.' That utterance did not suggest an intimate relation ; moreover we were all convinced that the connection never broke through certain bounds." Vulgarly as it is put, this corroborative evidence is vital, and it is confirmed by the entire absence in *all* contemporary correspondence of any belief in such "relations"—whatever the prurient know-alls of half a century later may fable to the contrary.—

At the end of April the Wagners move into the Asyl, on which Wesendonck's own architect has meanwhile been hard at work. May 8 Wagner writes Liszt : "I have a trying time behind me, but it now seems clearing to quite an agreeable state. Ten days ago we moved into the little country-seat you know of, beside the Wesendoncks' villa, which I owe to the truly great sympathy of this friendly family. I had to go through many a trouble first, though : the fitting of the little house, which certainly has turned out very neat and to my mind, required much time ; so that we were compelled to move out before there was any possibility of moving in. Then my wife fell ill, to boot, so that I had to

---

* Herr Steiner tells us that the ridge (not the little house) is locally called the "Gabler." After the Wesendoncks left the Green Hill, the next proprietors were goths enough to pull the "Asyl" down.

shoulder the whole removal out myself, and alone. We went to
the hotel for ten days, and finally moved-in in terrible weather and
cold ; so that really nothing but the thought of a definitive migration
could have kept my spirits up.   But it's all got over now, all set
and stowed for permanence just as we want it, everything in its
proper place.   My workroom is furnished with the pedantry and
elegant ease well known to you ; the writing-table stands at the
big window with the splendid view of lake and Alps ; quiet and
tranquillity surround me.   A pretty garden, already very well
cultivated, offers me room for little walks and sittings-down, and
to my wife the pleasantest of occupation and diversion from her
crotchets about me ; in particular, a good-sized kitchen-garden
absorbs her tenderest care.   Quite a nice soil for my retreat is won,
you see, and when I reflect how much I have been longing after
such a thing for long, and how hard it was even to get a prospect
of it, I feel compelled to look on this good Wesendonck as one
of my greatest benefactors.   Next July, too, the Wesendoncks hope
to be able to take possession themselves, and their neighbourship
promises me all that is friendly and pleasant.—So, something
achieved !—and I hope very soon to be able also to resume my
long-discontinued work."

Work is resumed a fortnight later ; for act i of the *Siegfried*
' composition-sketch ' bears as final date " 20. Januar 1857," act ii
the dates " 22. Mai 1857— 30. Juli 1857."   The real trouble,
however, is only about to commence, and that with the Wesendoncks'
own definite removal from their Zurich hotel to their new villa
(August 22).   Not one of Wagner's brief notes before that date
suggests the faintest shadow of a passion shewn,* and we may
dismiss F. Praeger's observation " During my stay I saw Minna's

---

* At first I felt inclined to place the letter concerning " die Liebe " and
"die Muse " (now numbered by me " 49 ") in May 1857 owing to a verbal
kinship with no. 28, where a " visit of the Muse " is also referred to; but
we find a similar reference even so late as the Venice diary of December
1858 : " Da klopfte Koboldchen ; es zeigte sich mir als holde Muse " (p. 80
inf.), whereas the Muse of letter 28 as yet bears no " endearing " epithet.
A still more convincing reason for assignment of letter " 49 " to its present
position, is the fact that *Minna* plainly quotes it to her Berlin friend
in July '59 : " Möchte diesmal seine Muse . . . in der Ferne,"—thus
practically identifying it with the letter she had intercepted in April 1858
(p. ix *sup.*).

jealousy of another," and his connection thereof with what he grossly misterms "a public scandal," as on a par with his usual unreliability. Certainly he was one of the series of guests who enjoyed Wagner's hospitality for periods ranging from three days to three weeks in this summer; but he had left before the neighbours settled in, and Frau Wesendonck herself informed me years ago that she had *no* recollection of ever meeting him. Whatever gossip the magpie picked up, must have filtered through a very dubious channel *afterwards :* "Minna had been in correspondence with me" —he tells us, of a later epoch indeed, but his chronology is always negligible—"Of her letters I publish nothing."

At the end of July the *Ring des Nibelungen* is laid aside for years, no business person wanting it, and *Tristan* taken up instead. Authority has it, that Parzival himself originally was meant to meet with Tristan in act iii, but the first was sundered from the second in the early Asyl days and made the subject of a separate scenario (cf. p. 94)—for further particulars of which we still must wait. What is documentarily established, is that Wagner wrote Frau Ritter as to *Tristan* July 4, "The poem is slumbering in me yet, and I shall summon it to life ere long"; also that "20. August 1857" is the date upon the *Tristan* prose-draft found among Frau Wesendonck's effects and soon to be presented to the world elsewhere.

A fortnight later, the Asyl guest-chamber is occupied by very memorable visitors; after a week in neighbouring apartments, Hans von Bülow brings his bride there—married in Berlin two days before that draft was signed. Sept. 4, Hans writes to Richard Pohl: "How I regret not having found you here still ; we might have passed magnificent days, as yesterday for instance. Wagner was in splendid vein, and what a glance at the score of 'young Siegfried' revealed me is colossal. What a giant of a man ! . . . Wagner has promised to read us a new poem, at which he is working this instant."—Then Wagner himself, to Frau Ritter again: "The visit of the young Bülow couple was my most delightful episode of this summer. They stayed in our cottage three weeks; seldom have I felt so agreeably stimulated, as by this intimate visit. Of a morning they had to keep quiet, as I was writing my Tristan then, a fresh act of which I read them out each week. The rest of the day we almost always made music, when Frau Wesendonck would come loyally across, and thus we had our most grateful little audience close at hand." Could anything be more dramatic, than this daily gathering under the *Tristan* poet's roof of the only three women who ever had or were to have a share in his human destiny?

The last act of *Tristan und Isolde*—do not forget that *third* act—is read to this "most grateful audience" the 18th of September 1857. Wagner's diary of a twelvemonth hence completes the history of that day (p. 42 *inf.*), and this is what Hans von Bülow tells a correspondent on the next: "I can imagine nothing that could confer on me so great a boon, such spiritual refreshment, as the being with this glorious, unique man, whom one must reverence as a god. In presence of this great, good man I thaw from all life's misère, and ascend." If in these *Tristan* days a happy bridegroom can use such terms about another man, is it at all astonishing that Mathilde also should have thawed at last, confessed her pure and gentle love? O yes, this testimony of von Bülow's is worth a hundred times von Hornstein's: did the wonderful epistles in our volume leave the faintest shadow of a doubt— which emphatically they *do not*—it would be dispelled at once by that immediate evidence of one who had seen the reflex of chaste radiance on his hero's face.

And now I beg you to take up that phrase, again, of two months hence to Liszt,—"will follow me *to each existence.*" Indeed it is the key to all the mystery: this love held no fulfilment in the present life, but a sacred promise for the next. We have seen how deeply Wagner had been steeped in Indian lore, how his *Sieger* was an ideal of the most unstained renunciation. In the Venice diary we shall see how he arrives "with greatest certainty, at proving in Love a possibility of attaining to exaltation above the instinct of the individual will" (p. 76). One other link alone is needed, a link supplied by his demonstrable familiarity with Goethe's letters to Mathilde's prototype, Frau Charlotte von Stein, where we find the idea of such renunciant love embodied in these lines:—

"Sag, was will das Schicksal uns bereiten?
Sag, wie band es uns so rein genau?
Ach, du warst in abgelebten Zeiten
Meine Schwester oder meine Frau"—

and even still more appositely in prose: "If I come upon this earth again, I will pray the gods to let me love but once; and were you not so averse to this world, I would beg you for companion of that life of mine."

" Happy Ananda ! Happy Sawitri ! "—Wagner cries (p. 56)—and what filled von Bülow's hero with such exaltation that the younger man felt ready to fall down and worship him, was the sense of a very real, but spiritual victory : " And no one then shall lose, when *we—are victors* " (p. 28).

Let me intrude no further, but reserve till the close whatever else may still be requisite to say.

W. A. E.—February 1905
(slightly amended July 1905).

ILLUSTRATIONS

Mathilde Wesendonck, after an oil-painting by C. Dörner . *Frontispiece*

Facsimile of a letter from Mathilde Wesendonck . . . *facing p.* 1

Photograph of the "Green Hill" and "Asyl" . . . ,, ,, 13

Facsimile of a theme for "Parzival" . . . . . ,, ,, 23

Facsimile of concert-close and programme, prelude to *Tristan und Isolde* . . . . ,, ,, 198

Photograph of Richard Wagner, Brussels 1860 . . . ,, ,, 233

Facsimile of Sachs' Cobbler-song, *Meistersinger* poem . . ,, ,, 291

Medallion-portrait of Mathilde Wesendonck . . . . ,, ,, 333

FACSIMILE OF A LETTER FROM
MATHILDE WESENDONCK

(See page xlix.)

Milan. März 26. 1892.

Dear Sir!

Your kind lettre of the 20th
reached me at Milan, where I stay
a couple of day's, on the way home to
Berlin, Jelten 21., after an absence of
almost a year, past in Austria and
in Italy. —

You will believe me that the content
of your writing, deeply afflicts me.
It is a base and hateful beginning,
that of Mr Ferdinand Prager's, in
writing and publishing a book, merely
to darken the Meister's Memory to
mankind, by making "Gossip" on the

Intimacy of his private Life,
a Life, full of Conflicts, affliction
and Suffering." —

What hath the Public to do
with it? Did he not bequeath to
him, his unequaled, unrivaled
everlasting Works? And is this holy
Testament not above all Doubt
and Calumny? Is it not sufficient
to secure him for ever, the grateful
and tender Respect, the awe and
the Consideration, due to his Greatness and his Genius? —

The "Episode" of Bordeaux,

has been related by the "Meister" himself, and is to be found in the Edition of : "hinterlassene Schriften." May we not be content with what He tell's us about it? Need we know more ? –

The truth is : that R. Wagner's affection and Gratefulness to the Wesendonck's remained the same throughout his life, and that the Wesendonck's on their side, never "ceased to belong to his most true and sincerest friend's unto to Death : –

What shall I say more ! Is it

worth while, to speak in so serious a matter, from my own personal self? —

The tie that bound him to Mathilde Wesendonck, whom he then called his "Muse", was of a so high, pure, noble and ideal nature that, alas, it will only be valued of those, that in their own noble chest find the same elevation and selflessness of Mind! —

Many, many thanks for your kind interference and communication. Yours truly

Mathilde Wesendonck

ZURICH

1852 *TO AUGUST* 1853

❉   ❉   ❉

1.

Herr and Madame Wesendonck are most kindly requested to join us on Sunday at dinner-time.

R.S.V.P.

FAMILIE WAGNER.

2.

Busy in the kitchen, my wife advises you to take the carriage, which you would probably have made use of even had the weather been fine ; further, that it will be extraordinarily warm in our abode.

All which is to signify that we have no intention to give you up yet.

3.

Many thanks for the kind invitation, which I unfortunately shall be unable to obey.

Fare you well !

4.

Esteemed Lady !

God will guard you henceforth from my rudenesses ; for you certainly perceive by now that it was no idle whim of mine when I often dreaded accepting your kind invitations lest my nasty temper might torture my good friends as much as it torments myself   If in the future, also, I become more abstinent in this regard—and ought I not to end by being so, after experiences like those of yesterday?—rest assured that it is simply to earn your pardon through presenting myself to you in a better light.

3

I hope to hear from your husband to-morrow at Basle
that at least your precious health has suffered no ulterior
harm through my unruly tongue.*   With this heartfelt wish
your kind indulgence is besought by

RICHARD WAGNER.

Zurich, March 17, 1853.

5.

[Easter 1853.]

Fairest good-day!

My poor wife has become quite ill ; consequently I accept
to-morrow's invitation for myself alone.

Presumably you are not at home to-day ; otherwise I
should have inquired toward evening.

At my house everything is dull and dismal, despite the
growing "gaiety" of the apartments.

I hope things are going right well with you, and that you
are keeping Easter-day [March 27] with joy.

Many kind regards to all!

Your

R. W.

6.

Friday morning.

The Herweghs have invited themselves for this evening.

If you think it would help you to recover from the
exertions of your last invitations, it would much delight us
if you consented to take part in our entertainment.

Kindest regards.

R. W.

7.

Here's syrup, for yesterday's ice.†

[May 29, 1853.]

---

* A clue to the above may be found in Letter 95.—Tr.

† Accompanying a few bars of a polka, whereon stands the date.
[Cf. *Life of R. Wagner*, iv. 132.—Tr.]

8.

Esteemed!

You gave me permission to inquire to-day whether you would be able to come to us again this evening. In case of a favourable answer, I would suggest your passing a couple of quiet hours with us till 10 o'clock : I would invite nobody else, not to spoil this sacred evening in any way.

Hoping for a kind consent,

Your

RICHARD WAGNER.

June 1, 1853.

9.

[*To Herr Otto.*]

Your disposals are excellent, best friend : I thank you for them from my heart.

To enter my fresh indebtedness in a manner worthy to arouse your confidence, I am paying an old debt to-day : *
please give your wife the accompanying sonata, my first composition since the completion of Lohengrin (six years back !).

You soon shall hear from me again : but first send us news how you're faring yourselves.

Your

RICHARD WAGNER.

Zurich, June 20, 1853.

10.

The best of good-mornings !

Getting on pretty well.—Sincerest thanks for all kind-

---

* As is to be gathered from a fragment dated June 11, published in the *Letters to O. Wesendonck*, Herr Otto had just advanced a sum of money. The "composition" is that afterwards issued as "Album Sonata" (see *Life*, iv. 131 and 448).—Tr.

ness!—I propose going proudly on foot to the rehearsal.
If it must be, however, I accept the carriage for ¼ to 2.
You would follow soon after.

I meant to send the accompanying yesterday!
Auf Wiedersehen!

11.

The best of good-mornings!

Just skim a little of this book [A. Schmid's biography of Gluck, 1852].
It is badly written, and one is compelled to skip all where
the author thinks anywise needful to trot out an opinion
of his own; yet the facts, particularly from Gluck's Paris
period, are highly interesting; moreover, this passionate,
yet entirely self-centred Gluck, with his calm vanity, large
savings, and embroidered court-dress, has something quite
amusing and refreshing about him in his old age.—

Only, make a big skip at the beginning.

12.

Homer was stealing out of my library.
Whither? I asked.
He replied: To congratulate Otto Wesendonck on his
birthday.
I answered: Do't for me, as well!

RICHARD W.

March 16, 1854.

13.

With the present weather-outlook and west winds, will
you be travelling?
Merely a question.*

Your

R. W.

---

* A joint excursion to Glarus, Stachelberg, and the Muotta-Thal had
been arranged. [Footnotes unsigned are the German editor's.—Tr.]

14.

Is it necessary to remark that my question of yesterday, touching a trip to-day, requires no answer?

R. W.

15.

As Herr and Madame Wesendonck seem to have abandoned that footing of intimacy whereon they would drop in on us of an evening uninvited, I suppose we must ceremoniously inquire whether they perhaps could deign to take us unawares to-day, or—in case certain Professors have been given this day for imparting their learning to the gentleman and lady—whether we might expect a similar surprise to-morrow?

16.

My Lady!

Frau Heim cannot sing before Tuesday,*—so for to-morrow (if show you must have) a simple piano-evening.

I shall see you soon!

Your
R. W.

17.

What should I do to cheer you up—poor invalid? I gave the programme [Philh.] with the translations to Eschenburg [professor of English at Zurich]: but how shall *that* profit

---

* At the Zurich Subscription Concert of Tuesday, January 23, 1855, when Frau Heim sang songs by Schubert, and Wagner conducted Mozart's *Zauberflöte* overture, Beethoven's C minor symphony, and his own revised *Faust* overture?—Tr.

you? Otto must at once procure you "Indian Legends edited by Adolf Holtzmann, Stuttgart." I brought them to London with me: their reading has been my only pleasure here. All are beautiful: but—*Sawitri* is divine, and if you wish to find out *my* religion, read *Usinar*. How shamed stands our whole Culture by these purest revelations of noblest humanity in the ancient East!—

At present I'm reading a canto of Dante every morning ere I set to work: I'm still stuck deep in Hell; its horrors accompany my prosecution of the second act of Walküre. Fricka has just gone off, and Wodan must now give vent to his terrible woe.

Beyond this second act I shall in no case get here; I can work but very slowly, and each day brings some fresh upset to contend with.—

My London experiences are determining me to withdraw from public music-making altogether, for some years to come: this concert-conducting must have an end. So don't let our Zurich gentry put themselves to any expense on my account! I now need total inner equilibrium, to complete my big work; for which, as a grotesque chimera, I fear this eternal outrageous contact with the inadequate and insufficient might easily put me out of sorts.

—To enliven yourself, just reckon up how many fugues ought to appear in my London oratorio, whether * * * * * should wear white or black kid-gloves, and if the Magdalene should carry a bouquet or fan. When you have settled these important points, we'll go into it farther.

To-day is my fourth concert: the A major symphony (which at any rate will not go anything like so well as at Zurich), and with it a number of lovely things I never dreamt of having to conduct again in my life. However, I'm fortified for it all by the certainty that this—will have been the last time.—

Best wishes to Otto, whom I heartily thank for his last kind letter : if it really amuses him, I'll write him once more. Is Marie [sister of Frau Wk] not coming to you soon ?—

To-morrow, after the concert, I shall write my wife : she won't have any mighty news to give you, though.

Kind love to Myrrha too [the Wesendoncks' little girl]! Farewell, and—keep your spirits up!

London, April 30, 1855.

18.

[July 8, 1855.]

I fear my good old faithful friend—my Peps—will pass away from me to-day. It is impossible for me to leave the poor thing's side in its last hours. You won't be cross with us, if we beg you to dine without ourselves to-day? In any case we shall not leave [for Seelisberg] till Wednesday : so that we can still make up for what we miss to-day.

You surely will not laugh if I am weeping?

Your

R. W.

Sunday morning.

19.

[September 1855 ?]

I am not well, and presumably shall have to keep my wife's birthday [Sept. 5] a prisoner to the house.

Cordial thanks for your kindness !

20.

Take notice :—

Wednesday : Othello

Ira Aldridge.*

Tickets should be booked in good time.

(The top of the morning!)

R. W.

---

* " The African Roscius " (1805-66).

21.

If the Familie Wesendonck will give Heinrich of the Hotel Baur that errand, they can obtain my wife from the theatre too ; otherwise they must put up with my single self.

By the way, I, too, know English.

R. W.

22.

Dear Friend,

My wife has just told me a happy thought of hers, which leads me to address you quite a big petition.

It is a matter of making one more effort to obtain a life-lease of the Bodmer property at Seefeld, near Zurich. Were it to succeed, I should be relieved of all cares about an estate of my own, and for a mere rent I should arrive at the same enjoyment I am seeking. This place is let at present as a summer residence to a family by the name of Trümpler ; so that the Bodmers would have to be persuaded to give these ancient tenants friendly notice and let me have the place for life, or perhaps for a term of ten years.

So far as we know, it is rather a habit than a requirement of the Trümplers, to occupy the Bodmer place, and if the Bodmers themselves were *glad* to let us have it, I have no doubt they would find no difficulty in inducing the Trümplers to stand back. Therefore it is merely a question of winning the Bodmers to my wish in earnest ; and my wife, whom I have commissioned to make overtures to Frau Bodmer, desires the help of a third person who should tell that lady all the ingratiating things which neither she nor I can say : and to act as that third person, honoured friend, my wife considers nobody more fitted than yourself. So the heartfelt prayer goes up to you, to write Frau Bodmer and try to win her to my part. For that—my wife thinks—it might be advisable if you laid stress on my great want and need of such a quiet country home as her estate affords; perhaps also—so thinks my wife—if you pricked the lady's pride a little, and pointed out to her the honour it might conceivably bring her, to have her premises supply me with a fostering haven for my future art-creations.—

What do you say to it? Will you undertake it?—

On my approaching return to Zurich I should very much like to see this affair, which exercises me so urgently now, brought so far forward that I might take a swift decision.*

Need I say how much it would please me to be able to bid good-day to you as well [as Otto] at Berne?

Many hearty greetings from

Your

RICHARD WAGNER.

Mornex, August 11, 1856.

23.

[September (?) 1856.]

Most faithful of all Protectresses
of the Arts!

My sister [Clara Wolfram] is obliged to keep her bed: if you are not a victim to the same necessity, I beg you to dispose of the vacant cover, or else to save it (something of a consideration in these hard times, with the silk-crop failure!). In the former event I would propose (without dictating) Boohm.—†

Your

R. W.

---

* It came to nothing, for Wagner writes Herr Otto three weeks later: "Here you have the B.'s letter back; please give your dear wife my best thanks again for her attempt at intervention.—Once more I feel much and deeply humbled," etc.—Tr.

† Wilhelm Baumgartner. Frau Wesendonck adds a note concerning "a beautiful poem" delivered by Gottfried Keller at the Schweiz. Musikfest, 1867, in memory of B.'s then recent death. She further explains that she had warmly defended *Rheingold* and *Walküre* against Minna's admonition to return to the style of *Rienzi*.

The house is about my ears, through your speaking disrespectfully of Rienzi yesterday !—

24.

[Autumn 1856?]

Would it entertain you, perhaps, to see what my Weimar Councillor has brewed about my poem ?

Various hints which I had given him are strewn with marvellous fidelity amid his own gallimathias ; which makes the thing fairly amusing.*

Much satisfaction is wished you by

Your much dissatisfied

R. W.

25.

O happy swallow, wouldst be mating,
Thyself thou build'st thy brood a nest ;
In quest of quiet for creating,
I cannot build my house of rest !
The peaceful home of stone and pine—
What swallow'll build that nest of mine ?

26.

All in order.   Will you be coming over for the last act of the Walküre ?

I—hope so.—

[*May* 8, 1857, *evidently referring to a matter of some two months previously, Wagner tells Liszt of a private rendering*

---

* Liszt, August 1, 1856 : "Franz Müller will visit you at Mornex the middle of this month, and bring you his work on the Nibelungen." Wagner finished his Mornex 'cure' Aug. 17, met Otto at Berne on the 18th, and returned to Zurich next day ; where he not only found his sister Clara, but also that his "Weimar Regierungsrath and red-hot enthusiast had arrived, bringing novelties foretold by Liszt." Clearly, then, our no. 24 refers to an ensuing MS. revision, for Müller's *Ring*-book was not published until six years later.—Tr.

The Green Hill, Enge, near Zurich.

of " the big last scene from 'Die Walküre'" with Frau Pollert as Brünnhilde, himself as Wotan, and Th. Kirchner as accompanist: " We did it three times in my rooms," i.e. the Zeltweg flat, from which he moved out the middle of April; *see p.* lviii sup.—*Tr.*]

27.

Herewith the music-journal * and a letter of Princess Wittgenstein's, which please return to me when read.

   I am to give you my wife's best wishes.

         R. W.

28.

           May 21, 57.

I have naught to say to the father of my country : if he were to presume to call upon me in my swallow's-nest, I should shew him the door.   His colours are white and green; this for Baur.†—

The Muse is beginning to visit me : does it betoken the certainty of your visit? The first thing I found was a melody which I didn't at all know what to do with, till of a sudden the words from the last scene of Siegfried came into my head. A good omen. Yesterday I also lit on the commencement of act 2—as Fafner's Rest; which has an element of humour in it.   But you shall hear all about it, if the swallow comes to inspect her edifice to-morrow [his birthday].

        RICH. WAGNER.

---

 * Probably the *Neue Zeitschrift* of April 10, 1857, containing Wagner's article *On Franz Liszt's Symphonic Poems*, which originally formed a letter to Pss Wn's daughter (February 15, 1857).   The last clause would seem to refer to the birth of little Karl, April 18.—Tr.

 † Expecting King John of Saxony at his Hôtel du Lac, Baur had inquired as to the correct colour for decorations.

29.

[Early July 1857.]

It seems to me as though we had forgotten to send you a proper invitation for Sunday evening [12th]: permit us to remedy the omission herewith! As you are aware, it is a feast in honour of Sulzer. I am also to inform you that tea will be served at 7 o'clock.

We hope to see you appear quite punctually with Herr Kutter,* whom we likewise beg you most cordially to invite on our behalf.

For your personal gratification I may also tell you that of late I have been unable to work again at night ; Calderon, however, is committed to rest.—Devrient sends you his kindest regards. For the rest, the world is still standing, Fafner alive, and everything as it was.

30.

[Mid-August 1857 ?]

There you make acquaintance with a very amiable person [Robert Franz?].   Good-morning !

[*The poem of " Tristan und Isolde " was completed and its last act given to Frau Wesendonck on the* 18*th of September* 1857 ; *a memorable day—cf. p.* 42 *inf.   In all likelihood the next letter refers to a recital thereof, such as we know the Herweghs etc. to have been present at.—Tr.*]

31.

To the

highly-esteemed Familie
Wesendonck
(Myrrha, Guido, Karl etc.)

I don't want to leave it to Fortune whether you turn

---

* Of the firm of Kutter & Luckemeyer, New York. [Luckemeyer, it will be remembered, was Frau Mathilde's maiden name.—Tr.]

up this evening, but to ensure that good fortune by begging
it of you. I am expecting Semper and Herwegh. So—
early, please!

R. W. LAZARUS.

32.

October 1, 1857.*

[*To Otto Wesendonck.*]

Thus, dear friend, you also receive your first
[nominal?] rent from me. In time I hope to get the
length of offering you the actual equivalent : perhaps it's
not so far off now; then you shall say—

> " Hei, unser Held Tristan,
>   wie der Zins zahlen kann!!"—

And so for to-day, as for ever, my heartiest thanks again
for all the goodness and kindness you have shewn me!

Your
RICHARD WAGNER.

33.

[October 1857.]

> " Die Morold schlug, die Wunde,
>   sie heilt' ich, dass er gesunde,"

and so on

has come off capitally to-day—I must play it to you by
and by!

---

* Also the date of commencement of the 'composition-draft' of
act i., *Tristan.*—Tr.

34.

[December 1857.]

The great outburst duet between Tristan and Isolde has turned out beautiful beyond all measure.—

In the first flush of joy thereat.

35.

[Dec. 1857.]

[*The following is a memorandum by Frau Wesendonck herself, found in company of the said two additional closes to* "Schmerzen," *the last whereof is the same as that now in use. The difference between the 1st and 2nd versions of* "Träume" *consists in addition of the sixteen introductory bars, the first version having commenced with our bar 17.—Tr.*]

On the 30th *of November* 1857 *Richard Wagner wrote the music to the song :*

" In der Kindheit frühen Tagen " [= " Der Engel "].

December 4, 1857, *the first sketch for :*

" Sag', welch' wunderbare Träume ? "

December 5, 1857, *the second version of* " Träume."

December 17, 1857, " Schmerzen "; *with a second, somewhat lengthened close. This was soon followed by a third close, beneath which stood the words :*

" It must become finer and finer !

" After a beautiful, refreshing night, my first waking thought was this amended postlude : we'll see whether it pleases Frau Calderon, if I let it sound up to her to-day."—*

---

* " Träume " was also scored for a small orchestra, and, conducting eighteen picked Zurich bandsmen, Wagner performed it beneath Frau Wesendonck's window, as a birthday greeting, Dec. 23, '57 : possibly he played or sang "Schmerzen" on the same occasion.—Tr.

February 22, 1858, " Sausendes, brausendes Rad der Zeit " [= " Stehe still "].

May 1, 1858, " Im Treibhause."—

All five songs subsequently came out at Schott's Sons, Mainz [1862], *by the master's own instructions.—Before their publication,* " Träume " *and* " im Treibhause " *were named by himself* " Studien zu Tristan und Isolde."

36.

[December 1857 ?]

Here is another winter-flower for the Christmas-tree, full of sweet honey, without the smallest bane.

37.

Hochbeglückt,
Schmerzentrückt,
frei und rein
ewig Dein—
was sie sich klagten
und versagten,
Tristan und Isolde,
in keuscher Töne Golde,
ihr Weinen und ihr Küssen
leg' ich zu Deinen Füssen,
dass sie den Engel loben,
der mich so hoch erhoben!

R. W.

Am Sylvester, 1857.*

38.

I have not had the best of sleep, and was just hesitating

* New Year's Eve, 1857, together with the composition-draft of the first act of *Tristan*, completed that day. Bare prose must serve for a rendering: " Thrice happy, out of reach of pain, free and purely ever thine—Tristan and Isolde, what they bewailed and forwent, their tears and kisses, in music's chaste gold I lay at thy feet, that they may praise the angel who has lifted me so high!"—Tr.

whether I should come to-day, in spite of Vischer and ice.
Now, however, I think of looking in for half an hour.

I have much on my heart—yet everything, again, is but
the one thing without which poorest I should have no footing
more upon this earth.   That one thing!

A thousand greetings.

38a.

Thanks!   Slept   well—go   it   must!—And   the   one
thing!—*

Sincerest greeting!

[*From Jan.* 16 *to Feb.* 2, 1858, *Wagner was in Paris,
whence he sent at least one letter that has not been preserved
(see p.* 68 *inf.).   Perhaps the following note refers to a small
commission executed there.—Tr.*]

39.

Here is the lamp-shade.   May it shed a rose-beam on the
snow!

I have had quite a passable night.   And how was
Wahlheim † off for sleep?

Best greetings!

40.

[February 1858.]

I   already   have   Soden   too,‡—unbound,   and   soon   at
disposal.

---

* Ranging this and the preceding note here, I take the "go it must"
to refer to the 'orchestral sketches' of *Tristan* i,—commenced Nov. 5,
1857, completed January 13, 1858,—since the Härtels were to commence
engraving the work at once, and Wagner in fact began sending them his
fair-copy of the score in February.—Tr.

† "Home of Choice"; perhaps from Goethe's *Werther*, Dr. Golther
suggests.—Tr.

‡ Count J. von Soden's translation of Lope de Vega's dramas.

I knew the whole catalogue before, through Schulthess.*
Perhaps the volume with Kaiser Otto at Florence would
also be worth reading.

Beyond these, Richard's translations seem to me not
uninteresting, as far as the matter goes.†

We might also think of Cervantes' tales—I possessed
them once myself.

For the rest, I can still help out awhile with my own
provision; I'm—reading little.

Best thanks for Iphigenie [his own revision of Gluck's?].

Herewith a present from Strassburg; ‡ no *pâté de foie
gras*, though, our God be praised!

Shall we see each other this afternoon, perhaps?

41.

After a wonderful night, blest with almost ten hours of
Goethian sleep,§ I wish you serenely happy Good-day, send
(*schicke*) you Schack, ‖ and promise to read aloud quite
beautifully this evening, if Herr Otto has nothing against it.

---

* Zurich bookseller.

† C. Richard, Lope de Vega's *Romantic Poems*, 1824-8.

‡ A Strassburg playbill, dated January 15, 1858:—

Aujourd'hui, *Le Fou par Amour*, par MM. Bourgeois et A. Denncry.
Le spectacle commencera
par Ouverture de *Tannhäuser*, Musique de R. Wagner.

[*En route* for Paris, Wagner had stumbled on this performance and
become the recipient of an impromptu ovation.—Tr]

§ In Goethe's letters to Charlotte von Stein allusions to sleep abound:
once he writes, "I have only two gods, Thyself and Sleep;" still more
to the point, on two different occasions he says, "I slept 10 hours last
night." This in corroboration of my remark, p. lxi, on Wagner's manifest familiarity with those letters.—Tr.

‖ Count A. F. von Schack's *Geschichte der dramatischen Literatur in
Spanien.* [Wagner subsequently became next-door neighbour at Munich
to Schack and his famous picture-gallery; in the 'eighties he was still
recommending this "History of Spanish Dramatic Literature" to his
friends.—Tr.]

42.

So that one may not fall into the plight again, of having to tell good stories badly, I deposit in the Wesendonck house the accompanying exemplar [Grimms' *Deutsche Sagen*, 1816, No. 72] ; for black on white is a glorious thing.

You see, you won't be rid of me in a hurry ! I'm burrowing so into your house, that, even if you burned it down, a very well-known voice would cry to you from out the salvage :

" 'Twas time that we got out ! "

43.

I'm sending to the bookbinder, and should like to get [Lope de Vega's] " Star [of Seville] " etc. bound at the same time. Do you still require it first?

44.

Telegram.

Lucerne, 8.55 [A.M.]
Zurich, 31 March 58 ; 9.10.

To Herr Otto Wesendonck, Zurich.

The trusty Kapellmeister unfortunately cannot conduct the concert to-day. Saint Gotthart has taken toll, and given him in exchange a violently orthodox catarrh. The concert shall still be conducted, though, if the bandsmen only keep in good tune.*

Your

RICHARD WAGNER.

---

* Wesendonck must have been as much puzzled as ourselves by the "·soll aber doch noch dirigirt werden, die Musiker mögen nur immer noch gut einstimmen." The printed programme of this famous Villa concert (detached movements from Beethoven's symphonies) bears the date March 31, 1858, and no contemporary speaks of its postponement; wherefore it is probable that, when telegraphing, Wagner meant to get Heim to take his place, but on reaching Zurich (2.30 p.m.—cf. p. 122) he felt better, and

45.

Madame Mathilde Wesendonck.

[Easter Sunday, April 4, 1858.]

Best thanks for the splendid flowers! The old plant, well looked after, is as magnificent as ever; so I still shall keep it.—A good thing I finished the act yesterday and sent it off.* I should have been unable to work to-day; the catarrh has increased, and I am not free from a touch of fever. Otherwise things go well—and brightly; how go they in the neighbour-land?—

46.

Madame Wesendonck.

Best thanks!—I am still a little feverish and very limp, but think of tasting a mouthful of the lovely air to-day.

Kindest wishes!   R. W.

47.

To the entire Familie
Wesendonck.

Children, am I not to get a glimpse of you to-day? I'm feeling better than yesterday.

R. W.

48.

[April 1858.]

I'm doing tolerably. How does the zealous lady-pupil of de Sanctis? †

---

conducted that evening himself—thereby "increasing his catarrh" (see no. 45). As he held a rehearsal on the 27th, he cannot have been absent *more* than three days; so that the allusion to "der heilige Gotthart" sounds like some private joke—a pun on "catarrh"?—Tr.

* The German edition conjectures May 1857 as the date of this letter, connecting it with *Siegfried* i; but later research shews that no *Siegfried* music was ever "sent off" to Härtel's, whereas the final pages of act i of *Tristan* were, full score, on the 3rd of April 1858.—Tr.

† Francesco de Sanctis (1818-83), an Italian scholar, then professor at the Zurich Polytechnic.

Thanks for the Cervantes meanwhile.   It will tune me gradually for work again.   The second act is beckoning me.*

Shall we see one another to-day ?

49.

[April 1858?]

And my dear Muse still stays afar ?   In silence I awaited her visit; with pleadings I would not disquiet her.   For the Muse, like Love, beatifies but freely; woe to the fool, woe to the loveless, who fain would constrain what will not yield itself of its free will.   They cannot be constrained; is it not so?   Not so?   How could Love be Muse withal, did it let itself be forced?

And my dear Muse stays far from me?—

50.

[Mid-April 1858 ?]

That letter—how mournful it has made me !   The demon moves from out one heart into the other.   How subjugate it ?   O we poor creatures !   We are not our own.   Demon, change to god !

That letter has made me mournful.   Yesterday I wrote to our friend.†   She will be sure to come in, before long.

50a.

[*The following unused sketch for "Parzival" was found by Dr. Golther in the same envelope as letter 50, which would*

---

* My arrangement of this little group of notes—which seem to have followed each other pretty closely, and during their writer's temporary confinement to the house by illness,—of course is purely tentative; but I now should guess the next of them, viz. no. 49, to have been the very one "intercepted" by Minna (see pages ix and lix), thus accounting for composition of act ii *Tristan* not being actually commenced till May 4.—Tr.

† Frau Wille ?   *Cf.* p. 51, *inf.* also p. x *sup.*—Tr.

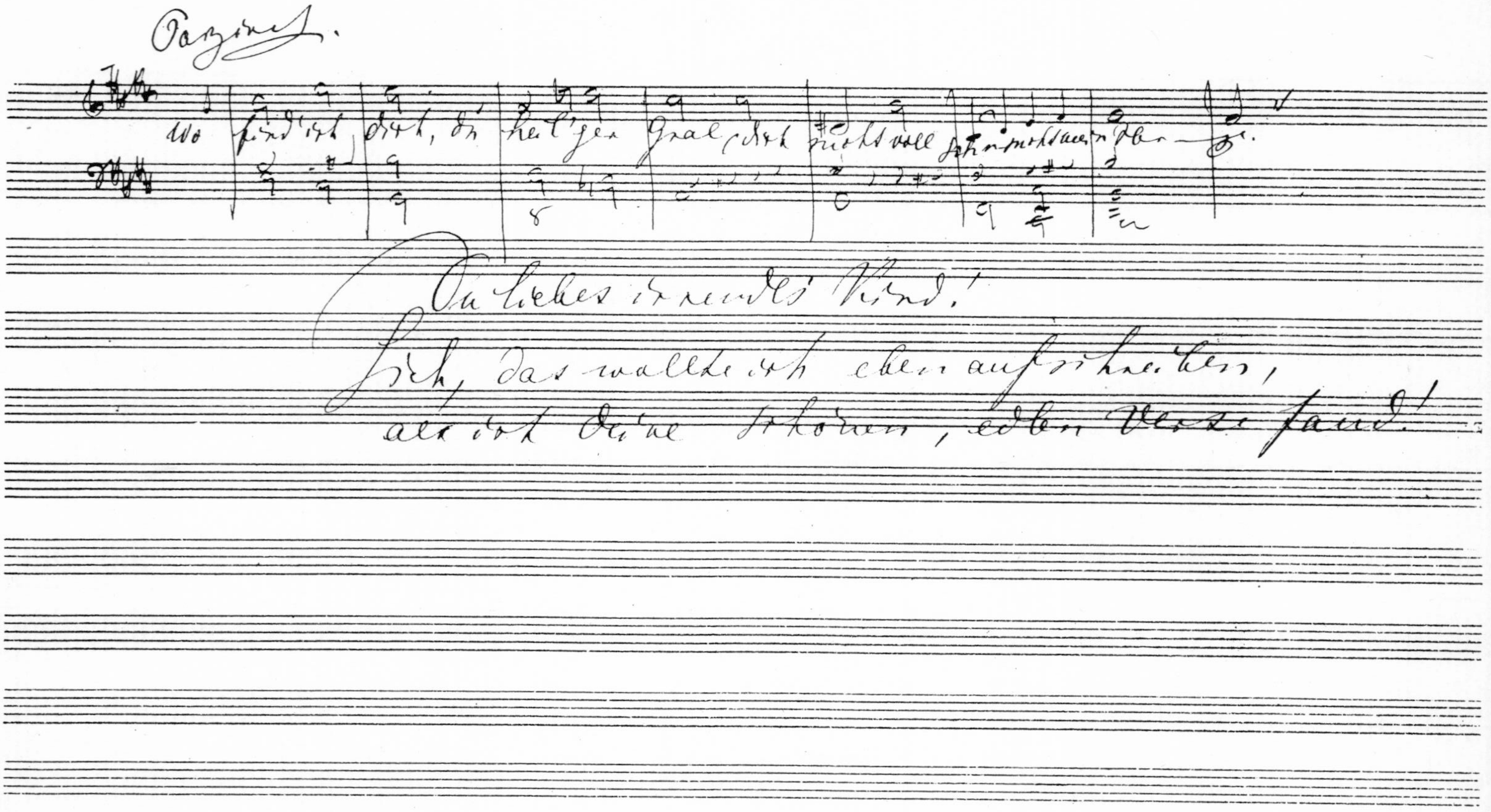

thus appear to have been answered ere long by the poem "Im Treibhaus," set to music May 1.—Tr.]

PARZIVAL.

Wo find' ich dich, du heil' - ger Gral, Dich
Where find I thee, thou ho - ly Grail? With

sucht voll Sehn - sucht mein Her - ze.
yearn - ing heart have I sought thee.

Dear errant child!
See, I was just about to write this down, when I found
thy lovely, noble verses.

51.

[April or May 1858?]

I have just been reading [Calderon's] holy "Ferdinand" and found it very beautiful and touching. Perhaps it was my frame of mind. Were death foretold me surely for this year, I should embrace it as the most fortunate and consecrate of all my life. Only the uncertainty, how long remains for us to live, makes us frail and prone to sin ; that certainty, however, would hallow me completely.—How were it to be gained, that certainty so ardently I yearn for ?—

52.

[May 22, 1858?]

Ah, the lovely pillow! Too dainty, though!
Tired and heavy as often is my head, I should never

dare to lay it on it, not even in sickness ;—at most, in death !
Then I may couch my head for once as easily as if I
had a right to ! Then you shall spread the pillow under
me.—There you have my testament !

R. W.

53.

[Late May or early June 1858.]
Madame Mathilde Wesendonck.

Here is my little musical home-goblin [Tausig];
may he find a kind welcome !

54.

[July 2 (?) 1858.]

What a wondrous birth of our child of sorrows !* Had
we to live, then, after all ? From whom could it be asked,
that he should forsake his children ?—

God stand by us, poor creatures !

Or are we too rich ?

Must we help ourselves unaided ?—

55.

[July 6 (?) 1858.]†
Tuesday morning.

Surely thou didst not expect me to leave thy marvellously beautiful letter unanswered ? Or was I to forgo
the privilege of replying to the noblest word ? And how
could I reply to thee, but in a manner worthy of thee ?—

The stupendous conflicts we have passed, how could
they end but with the victory over every wish and longing ?

In the most fervent moments of approximation, did we
not know that this was our goal ?—

---

* With the sketches for act ii *Tristan*, completed July 1. [Full score
begun July 5.]

† The original is missing. [Here for the first time " Du " appears instead of " Sie," apart from the verses of No. 37 and the lines under the
" Parzival " theme.—Tr.]

Assuredly ! Only because its difficulty was so untold,
was it only to be reached after the hardest of combats ; but
have we not fought out all our battles now ? What others
could there still remain ahead ?—Of a truth, I feel it deep
within : they are at end !—

When a month gone by I told thy husband my resolve
to break off personal commune with you [" *Euch*"—plural] I
had—given thee up, albeit I was not yet altogether whole in
that. For I merely felt that nothing save a total severance,
or—a total union, could secure our love against the terrible
collisions to which we had seen it exposed in these latter
times. Thus the sense of the necessity of our parting was
haunted by the possibility—present to the mind, if not to
the will—of union. In that still lay a racking suspense
which neither of us could bear. I approached thee, and clear
as day it stood before us, that that other possibility involved
a crime which could not be so much as thought of.

But hereby the necessity of our renunciation of itself
acquired another character : the strain resolved into a gentle
reconcilement. The last taint of egoism vanished from my
heart ; and now my decision to revisit you (*Euch*) was the
triumph of purest humanity over the last stirring of selfish
desire. I wished naught any longer but to reconcile,
assuage, console—cheer up ; and thus procure myself withal
the only happiness that still can come to me.—

So deeply and terribly as in these last few months, have
I never been affected in my life. All earlier impressions
were void of meaning 'gainst these last. Shocks such as
I endured in that catastrophe were bound to plough deep
furrows in me ; and if aught could add to the great seriousness of my reflections, it was my wife's condition. For two
whole months I was threatened each day with the possible
news of her sudden death ; for the doctor had felt obliged
to warn me of that possibility. Everything round me

breathed the scent of death ; all my prospects and retrospects became images of death, and life—as such—lost its last lure for me.   Admonished to the utmost sparing of the un-happy soul, nevertheless I had to make up my mind to raze our last hearth and home, so lately founded, and at last to tell her so, to her deepest dismay.—

With what feelings dost thou think in this sweet summertide I viewed this charming Asyl,* the sole and perfect counterpart of my whilom aims and wishes, when I wandered through the tiny garden of a morning, watched the flowers springing into bloom, and listened to the white-throat that had built her nest within the rosebush ?   And what this tearing loose from my last anchor meant for me, that tell thyself, who know'st my inmost thought as none !

If I have fled from the world once before, dost dream I could return into it now ?   Now, when each nerve of me has grown so sensitive and tender with the lengthier weaning from all contact with it ?   Even my recent interview with the Grand Duke of Weimar [mid-June] shewed me plainer than ever that I can thrive in nothing but most absolute independence, so that I earnestly had to decline every possible kind of obligation to be entered, even towards this really not unamiable prince.   I cannot—cannot face towards the world again ;   to settle down in a big city, is inconceiv-able to me.   And if not that—how could I think again of founding a new refuge, a new hearth, after having to break up this, scarce tasted, which friendship and the noblest love had founded for me in this charming paradise?   No, no !—To go forth hence, for me is tantamount to—going under !

With wounds like these in my heart, I can try to found me no new home again !—

---

* " Refuge," or " Haven of Rest "—the name he had given his little house.—Tr.

My child, there's only one salvation for me I can think of; and that can only arise from the innermost depth of the heart, not from any sort of outer dispensation. Its name is Rest! A truce to yearning! Allaying of every desire! Worthy, noble overcoming! Life for others, for others—in relief to ourselves!—

Thou know'st the whole solemn resolve of my soul now; it relates to all my views of life, to my whole future, to all that stands anigh me,—and so to thee, too, who art dearest to me! Upon the ruins of this world of longing, let me—bless thee!—

See, never in my life, in any manner of relation, have I ever been importunate, but always of an almost exaggerated sensibility; so for the first time will I seem to be importunate, and implore thee to be profoundly tranquil as regards me. I shall not often visit you (*Euch*), for in future you must only see me when I'm sure of shewing you a calm and cheerful countenance.—Of old, maybe, I have sought thy house in suffering and longing: thither, whence I wanted solace, have I brought unrest and suffering. That shall be no more. Wherefore if thou dost not see me for a length of time, then—pray for me in silence!—For, then be sure that I am suffering! But when I come, be sure I'm bringing to your house a gracious gift of my being, a boon such as lent perhaps to me alone to shed, who have endured so much and willingly.—

Probably, nay, certainly, the time is at hand—I conjecture the beginning of next winter—when I shall depart from Zurich altogether for a spell; my amnesty, expected soon [in vain!], will reopen to me Germany, whither I shall periodically return for the only thing I could not make good to myself here. Then I often shall not see you for long. But then to return again to the Refuge so endeared to me, to recover from worry and unavoidable vexation, to breathe pure air, and gain new zest for the old work for which Nature has chosen me,—this, if you grant it me, will ever be the point of mellow light that buoys me up there, the sweet relief that becks me here.

And—wouldst thou then have shewn my life no highest benefaction ?   Should I not owe to thee the only thing that yet can seem worth thanks to me upon this earth ?   And ought not I to seek to requite what thou has won for me with suffering and sacrifices so indicible ?—

My child, these last months have perceptibly blanched the hair on my temples ; there is a voice in me that cries with yearning after rest,—that rest which long, long years ago I made my Flying Dutchman yearn for. It was the yearning after "home,"—not after the seductive joys of love : only a grandly faithful woman could gain for him that homeland. Let us vow ourselves to this fair death, which stills and buries all our hankerings and cravings ! Let us fade away, with peacefully transfigured gaze, and the holy smile of beautiful self-victory !—And—no one then shall *lose*, when we——*are victors !*

Farewell, my dear hallowed angel !

56.

[August 1858 ?]

It must be so !*

57.

[August, 17, 1858.]

Farewell !   Farewell, dear love !

I'm leaving tranquilly.   Where'er I be, I shall be wholly thine now.   Try to keep the Asyl for me auf Wiedersehen ! Auf Wiedersehen !   Dear soul of my soul, farewell—auf Wiedersehen !—

---

* English in the original. This clearly refers to his irrevocable decision to break up his home at once.—Tr.

DIARY

AUGUST 1858—*JANUARY* 1859

VENICE

(With one entry, April 1859, *Lucerne)*

❦ ❦ ❦

DIARY

Since my flight from the Asyl
17. August 1858

❧

GENEVA.

August 21.

The last night in the Asyl I went to bed at
11 o'clock: I was to start at 5 next morning. Before I
closed my eyes, it flashed through my soul how I had
always sent myself to sleep here by the thought that on
this very spot I once should die: thus should I lie when
thou approachedst me for the last, last time, clasp'dst my
head in thine arms, in open view of all, and with one final
kiss receiv'dst my spirit! That death was my fondest
conception, and it had framed itself entirely to the locality
of my sleeping-room: the door toward the staircase was
closed, thou enter'dst through the curtains of the study;
thus didst thou wind thine arm around me; thus, gazing
up to thee, I passed away.—And now? Even that possibility
of dying had been snatched from me! Cold, as if hunted,
I was quitting this house, in which I had been shut with
a dæmon I no longer could ban save by flight.—Where—
where shall I die, then?— —Thus I fell asleep.—

Out of troubled dreams I was wakened by a wondrous
rustling: as I woke I plainly felt a kiss upon my brow:—
a shrill sigh succeeded. 'Twas all so lifelike, that up I
sprang, and peered around me. All still. I struck a light:

31

it was just before 1, at end of the ghosts' watch. Had
a spirit stood guard by me in that drear hour? Wert
thou awake or sleeping, near that time?—How fared it
with thee?—Never an eye could I close thereafter. For
long I vainly tossed in bed, till at last I rose, completely
dressed myself, shut the last trunk to, and, now pacing up
and down, now stretched full length on the divan, uneasily
waited for daylight. This time it appeared later than I
had been accustomed-to on sleepless nights in the summer
past ; shame-flushed the sun crept up behind the mountain.
—Then I gazed across once more and long.—O Heaven,
not a tear came to me, but it seemed as if every hair on
my temples were turning grey!—I had taken leave ; now
everything was cold and set within me.—I went downstairs.
There my wife was waiting for me ; she offered me tea,
'Twas an awful, lamentable hour.—She accompanied me.
We paced down the garden. It was a magnificent morning :
I never turned my head.—At the last farewell my wife
broke out in tears and lamentations ; for the first time
my eyes stayed dry. Once again I exhorted her to gentleness and nobleness and quest of Christian comfort ; once
more the old revengeful vehemence flared up in her. She
is incorrigible,—I could not help telling myself,—yet I
cannot venge myself on the unhappy woman ; herself she
must work out her own sentence.—So I was in terrible, sad
and deadly earnest ; but—weep I could not.—So I set forth.
And lo!—I won't deny it : it was well with me, I breathed
free.—I was faring into solitude : there I am at home ;
in that solitude where I may love thee with every breath
I draw!— —

Here I haven't spoken to a soul as yet, save servants.
Even Karl Ritter I have written not to call upon me. It
does me so much good, not to have to speak.—Thy diary *

* See pages 50 and 56, *infra.*—Tr.

I read ere going to my first sleep since my departure.
Thy diary! Those fair deep imprints of thy being!—I
slept well.

Next day I moved into a lodging,* which I have hired
by the week. Here I am quiet and undisturbed, collect
my thoughts, and wait till the heat is past, to let me go
to Italy. I keep the house the whole day long.—

Yesterday I wrote to my sister Kläre,† whose acquaintance thou madest two years ago: she wanted brotherly
explanation from me, as my wife had written and announced
herself. I indicated to her what thou hast been and art
to me these six years since; what a heaven thou hadst
prepared for me, and with what strifes and sacrifices thou
hadst stood by me; and how that wonder-work of thy high,
noble love had then so rudely and so clumsily been mauled.
I know she'll understand me—she has the heart of an
enthusiast in a somewhat unkempt shell—and I was bound to
shed a little light on that side; but how my soul and bosom
heaved as I ventured to delineate thy lofty, noble purity
with tender touch!—Of a surety, we shall forget and forgive
all, all, and nothing but elation will remain; the consciousness that here a miracle has happened, the like whereof
Dame Nature weaves but once in centuries, perhaps never
so nobly before. Away with grief! We are the happiest;
with whom would we exchange?—

August 23. 5 in the morning.

In a dream I saw thee on the terrace, dressed as
a man, with a travelling-cap upon thy head. Thou peer'dst
toward the direction in which I had departed; but I drew
near from the contrary: thus thy gaze was ever turned from

---

* Third floor of the "Maison James Fazy," subsequently Hôtel de
Russie, corner of the Quai du Léman and Rue du Montblanc.—Tr.

† The letter reproduced in the preface to the present volume.

me, and I sought in vain to signal my approach, until I
softly cried : Mathilde ! then louder and still louder, till my
bedroom echoed with the sound, and my own cries awakened
me.—Then, when I had relapsed a little into slumber, I
dreamed I was reading letters of thine, wherein thou confess'dst to me a youthful love-affair ; thou hadst renounced
thy lover, yet kept'st singing his praises, so that I appeared
in the light of a mere would-be consoler,—which somewhat
galled me. I would not let that dream proceed, and arose to
write these lines.—The whole day I had had vehement
longing, and a grievous impatience of life had mastered me
once more.—

> August 24.
> Yesterday I felt utterly wretched : Why go on
living ; why live ? Is it cowardice—or courage ? Why that
immeasurable happiness, to be so boundlessly unhappy ?
— —The night brought sound sleep.—To-day has gone
better.—I have had a beautiful portfolio made here, expressly
to lock away thy keepsakes and letters : it will hold a great
quantity, and what once gets in, will not be given out again
to naughty children. Therefore take good care what thou
send'st me in future : not a jot thereof wilt thou have back
—until after my death ; unless thou wouldst fain commit it
to the grave with me.—To-morrow I go direct to Venice.
I am dying to get there, where I think of settling calmly
down, tho' the journey in itself is most distasteful to me.—It
is a week to-day since I saw thy terrace for the last time !—

> Venice, the 3rd of September.
> Yesterday I wrote thee and our lady friend,* so
long had I been withheld by the journey and my accommodation here. Now the diary shall be kept right methodically.—

---

* Frau Wille : the letters are not preserved.

My route lay over the Simplon; the mountains, particularly the long valley of Wallis [Valais], weighed me down. One lovely hour I spent on the garden-terrace of the Isola bella; a wondrous sunny morning; I knew this spot,* and dismissed the gardener at once, to be alone there. A beautiful sense of calm and uplifting came over me—so beautiful, that it could not last. Yet what raised me up, what was with and in myself, that lasted : the happiness of being loved by thee!

At Milan merely a night's halt; on August 29 arrived in Venice after noon. On the way down the Grand Canal to the Piazetta, melancholy impressions and graveness of mood ; grandeur, beauty and decay, in close array : yet comfort in the reflection that here no modernity flourished, and in consequence no bustling triviality. S. Mark's Square of magical effect. A wholly distant, outlived world, it admirably fits the wish for solitude : nothing to strike one as directly real life ; everything objective, like a work of art. I *will* remain here,—and accordingly I shall.—Next day, after long debate, apartments taken on the Grand Canal in a mighty palace where I am quite alone for the present ; wide, lofty spaces, wherein I can wander at will. Since the question of Abode is so important to me, as the housing for my labour-mechanism, I'm devoting all possible care to arranging it after my wish. I wrote for the Erard at once ; it ought to sound wonderful in my vast, high palace-salon. The peculiarly intense stillness of the Canal suits me splendidly. Not till 5 in the afternoon do I leave my abode, to dine ; then promenade towards the public garden ; brief halt in the square of S. Mark, which gives a thoroughly theatrical suggestion through its absolute uniqueness and its sea of utter strangers void of all concern to me, merely distracting

---

* See letter to Otto of July '52.—Tr.

one's fancy. Toward 9 return home in a gondola; find the lamp lit, and read a little till bedtime.—

Thus will my life flow outwardly on, and thus would I have it. Unfortunately, my stay here is already known; but I have given orders, once for all, to admit nobody.— This solitude, possible wellnigh here alone to me—and so agreeably possible—caresses myself and my hopes.—Eh! I hope, for thy sake to get well! To save thee to me, means to save me to my art. With it—to live for thy consolement; that is my mission, that fits with my nature, my fate, my will,—my love. Thus am I thine; thus, too, shalt thou get well through me! Here will the Tristan be completed—a defiance to all the raging of the world. And with that, an I may, shall I return to see thee, comfort thee, to make thee happy; there looms my fairest, my most sacred wish. So be it! Sir Tristan, Lady Isolde! help me, help my angel! Here shall your wounds cease bleeding, here shall they heal and close. From here shall the world once learn the sublime and noble stress of highest love, the plaints of agonising joy. And august as a god, serene and hale, shalt thou then behold me back, thy lowly friend!

.   .   .   .   .   .

September 5.

This night I have been sleepless, long my vigil; my sweet child does not tell me how it fares with her?— Marvellously beautiful, the Canal by night; bright stars, last quarter of the moon. A gondola glides by; from the distance the chant of gondoliers calling to each other. This last is extraordinarily beautiful, sublime: Tasso's stanzas are recited to it no more, they say, but the melodies are in any case of hoary eld, as old as Venice; certainly older than Tasso's stanzas, which must simply have been fitted to them after. Thus the everlasting has preserved itself in the melody, whereas the stanzas were but taken there-into as a passing phenomenon, at last to be engulfed.* These profoundly melancholy ditties, sung with full ringing voice, borne across the water from afar, and dying into still remoter distance, have sublimely moved me. Glorious!—

September 6.

Yesterday I saw Ristori as Maria Stuart. I had seen her first a few days since as Medea, in which she pleased me much, nay—made a fairly deep impression on me. Uncommon virtuosity, and in the play of emotions a certainty of gesture never known to me before in such perfection; but what I missed from the first—and as for that, is necessarily foreign to Medea—I plainly recognised now as the chief defect in her art, since it is imperatively demanded of Maria Stuart. Here ideality, enthusiasm, deep, rapturous warmth, are needed. It was humiliating, how painfully the artist fell short here; and with no little pride I felt the height and the significance of German art, when I remembered how enkindlingly, ay, transportingly I had seen this very task fulfilled by many a German actress;† whereas the Ristori, with her abrupt leaps from sophisticated prose to almost animally plastic passion, shewed that she had not even remotely guessed the nature of her task, to say nothing of being born to it. It was truly deplorable and exasperating. This strain of ideality in German art, however, is that which makes my music possible, and by means thereof my poetry. How distant, on the other hand, are these French-Italian evolutions from all I can ever conceive; and yet the ideal element casts

---

* Cf. *Prose Works*, vol. v. 73-4 (the *Beethoven* essay).

† Minna herself had played the part at Riga in 1839 as "guest," and therefore presumably before her marriage also.—Tr.

an unconscious spell over Italians and French themselves, when it comes upon them from without, so that I cannot let it merely rank as a sort of specifically German onesided-ness of character. I myself have experienced this in the effect on individuals of my performances.—In what, then, consists the difference between the ideality I mean and that realistic comedy of passion? Glance through the scene in the third act of Maria Stuart, in the garden where she welcomes freedom, and imagine that Ristori left out the greater part here, nay, almost all that did not lead up to a point of hatred against Elisabeth, and thus afford an opening for development of her rapid changes of impassioned byplay.—Yet, that will not make it quite clear to thee, but thou'lt know what I mean in an instant, if I remind thee of our love. . . . . . .

September 7.

To-day I had a note from Frau Wille; it was the first tidings I had had of thee. Thy mind is made up, she says, calmly and resolutely to go through with the renuncia-tion : parents, children—duties.—

Oh but how foreign it sounded to me, in my solemn cheerfulness!—

Thinking of thee, never have parents, children, duties, come into my mind : I simply knew that thou lov'dst me, and that everything sublime must be unhappy in the world. From this height it startles me to see a written catalogue of *what* makes us unhappy. Then of a sudden I see thee in thy gorgeous house, see all *that*, hear all *those* to whom we must ever remain unintelligible; those who, strangers, yet are—near us, all anxiety to keep the Near afar from us; and anger takes me at the thought: *To these*, who know naught of thee, comprehend naught of thee, but want everything from thee, thou'rt to sacrifice all !—I cannot, will not see or hear it, if I'm to finish worthily my earthly work! Only from the inmost depth can I gain the strength; but— everything from without, that would usurp my resolutions, stirs bitterness up in me.—

Thou hopest to see me for a few hours in Rome this winter? I fear—I cannot see thee! To see thee,—and then depart from thee for the delectation of another,—can I do that now already? Surely not!—

And no letters, wouldst thou?—

I have written thee,* and sincerely hope not to be rejected with *that* letter;—ay, I am sure of thine answer!—

Away with these foolish thoughts!—I hope.—

Sept. 8.
> " O blinde Augen!
> Blöde Herzen!" [*Tristan* i.—Tr.]

Sept. 10.
Yesterday I was downright ill, with fever. In the evening, too, I received another letter from Frau Wille:— enclosed was my note to thee—sent back unopened!—

Nay, *that* should not have been!—Not that!—

To-day I have nothing for the diary as yet; no thoughts,—merely feelings. Those must first come to clearness.—

That thou art recruiting thy health, and feeling strong, is my consolation. I have yet another, that almost looks like a revenge:—Some day thou'lt read this rejected letter also—and realise what an appalling injustice has been done me with its rejection!—But much the same has occurred to me quite often before.—

---

* See entry under date September 3.—Tr.

Sept. 11.

Ha!—a direct address from thee! Three words—nothing more!

Yet mere go-betweens, were they the most intelligent and sympathetic, can make up for nothing. How hard it is for two to understand each other fully, how necessary, even for that communion, that they should be in a happily like mood, such as nothing but the fullest feeling of the loved one's actual presence can really bring to pass; but a third person stands ever apart. Who could efface himself and his particular standpoint so entirely, as *only* to be a channel for two others? That Frau Wille, purely for her own part, cannot prevail on herself to convey to thee letters from me, I can but deem intelligible: of course there can be no regard paid to their contents there, no consideration how quieting, therefore how needful such communications are;—enough, they're letters, and she feels, perhaps must feel, compunction in delivering them. As for that, whatever can the "lady friend" advise in general, save what her attitude toward all concerned makes possible to her, and possible in the best and noblest sense?—But—she also acted according to thy wish! What!—a case of conscience *between* us two?

Enough for to-day!—Peace! Peace!—

September 13.

I felt so sad, that I meant to confide nothing even to the diary: then thy letter came to-day—the letter to Frau Wille.—That thou lov'st me, I knew full well, and thou art good as ever, profound and wise; so I had to smile, almost to rejoice at my late vexation, since thou prepar'st me here so excellent a satisfaction. I understand thee—even where I think thee a shade in the wrong,—for everything is a wrong to me, that savours of defence against im-

portunacy. By that terrible departure from Zurich I should
have thought I had given final proof that I can—withdraw ;
consequently I have a right to resent any doubt of my
resignative nicety as an unmerited and deep affront.—Yet
to what purpose *that* now?—My beautiful exaltation has
been cast down ; it needs an effort, to mount again : forgive me if I still am tottering !—I'll be cheerful again—
so far as I can ; to Frau Wille, too, I'll write ere long ;
but even with letters to her I'll be moderate. God ! every
single thing is so hard, and yet the highest can only be
attained through moderation.—Yes ! 'tis well, and all will
turn out well. Our love stands high above all obstacles, and
every hindrance makes us richer, more spiritual, nobler, and
ever more intent upon the substance and essence of our love,
ever more indifferent toward the inessential. Yes, good,
pure darling ! we shall triumph,—we are already in the
midst of victory.—

September 16.
        Behold me well and cheerful. Thy letter rejoices
me yet. How apt, how sweet and beautiful, is everything
that springs from thee !—Our personal fate seems to me
almost a matter of indifference now, everything within is
so pure, so altogether fitted to our nature alike and necessity.
With that harmonious feeling I wish to return to my work,
and am waiting for the piano. The Tristan will cost much
still ; but once it is quite ended, meseems a vastly important
period of my life will have then been rounded off, and I
shall look with new senses, calmly, clearly and with deep consciousness into the world, and through the world up to thee.
For that it also is, I now feel so much drawn to work.—
        Meanwhile I have all manner of dreadful and tedious
correspondence, that takes away my time ; yet ever thou
quicken'st me in midst thereof, and Venice gloriously assists

thee to cheer me up. For the first time I breathe this pure, delicious, ever even air ; the magic of the place enfolds me in a tender melancholy charm, which never ceases to exert its beneficial power. Of an evening, when I take a gondola trip to the Lido, it vibrates round me like one of those mellow long-drawn fiddle-notes I love so, and to which I once compared thee. Judge thence how I feel, in the moonbeams there on the sea !—

September 18.

A year gone by to-day I finished the poem of Tristan and brought thee its last act, thou led'st me to the chair before the sofa, placedst thy arm around me and saidst : " I no more have a wish ! "—

On this day, at this hour, was I born anew.—To then was my before-life : from then began my after-life : in that wondrous instant alone did I live. Thou know'st how I spent it ? In no tumult of intoxication ; but solemnly, profoundly penetrated by a soothing warmth, free as if looking on eternity.—I had been painfully, but more and more definitely detaching myself from the world ; all had turned to negation in me, to warding off. Painful was even my artistry ; for it was a longing, an unstilled longing, to find for that negation, that warding off—the positive, affirmative, self-wedding-to-me. That instant gave it me, with so infallible a certitude that a hallowed standstill came o'er me. A gracious woman, shy and diffident, had taken heart to cast herself into a sea of griefs and sorrows, to shape for me that precious instant when she said : I love thee !—Thus didst thou vow thyself to death, to give me life ; thus did I receive thy life, thenceforward from the world to part with thee, to suffer with thee, die with thee.—At once the spell of longing was dissolved !—And this one thing thou knowest too, that ne'er since have I been at variance with myself. Perplexity and pang might come to us ; even thyself might'st be swept by an eddy of passion :—but I—thou know'st!—remained ever the same ; never, by never so awful a moment, could my love to thee be reft of its fragrance, were it but of one minutest film. All bitterness had vanished from me ; I might mistake, feel pained or tortured, but ever it stayed clear as day to me that thy love was my highest possession, and without it my existence must be a contradiction of itself.—

Thanks to thee, thou gracious, loving angel !—

September 23.

The drinking-vessel [see p. 88] and cup have arrived ; once again the first friendly token from without. What am I saying ? " von Aussen " ? How can anything come from without to me, that comes from thee ? And yet,—it comes from out the distance ; from that distance where my nearest now is. A thousand thanks, thou dear inventive soul ! Thus mute, how plainly can we tell each other what is so inexpressible !—

September 26.

I can't even get to my diary now, such an odious mass of business letters I have to attend to. How· foolish I am, though ! This constant vulgar care for life,—and at bottom so deep a disgust with it ; a life I always have to dress up artificially, not to see it constantly before me in its natural offensiveness ! If people only knew what lies between me and a final possibility of rest for work !—Yet I'll hold on, since I must ; I do not belong to myself, and my griefs and troubles are the means to an end that scoffs at all these sufferings. Tut, tut !—no shirking !—

September 29.

The waning moon now rises late : at its full it furnished me fine comfort through agreeable sensations which I
needed.   After sunset I regularly took a gondola to meet
it, toward the Lido, for the battle twixt day and night was
always an entrancing vision in this limpid sky : to the
right, amid the dusk-rose æther, gleamed kindly bright the
evening star ; the moon in full splendour cast its flashing
net towards me in the sea.   Then when I turned my back
upon it for the journey home, my gaze—athwart toward
where thou dwellest, and whence thou look'dst towards the
moon—would meet the comet, stern and brilliant with its
tail of waxing light, close above my affinity the Wagoner.
For me it had no terrors, just as nothing can inspire me
any more with fear, because I absolutely have no hope,
no future more ; rather, I could but smile quite earnestly
at people's awe of such a visitant, and chose it with a certain
insolent pride for my star.   I could see nothing in it but
the unaccustomed, dazzling, marvellous.   Am I such a comet
myself ?   Have I brought misfortune ?—Was it *my* fault ?—
I could not lose it from my ken again.   Silent and at peace
I reached the gaily-lighted, ever-lively Piazzetta.   Then
down we go the melancholy grave Canal : to left and right
stand lordly palaces : without a sound : only the gentle
gliding of the gondola, the plashing of the oar, broad
shadows from the moon.   At my dumb palace steps I
disembark : wide halls and spaces, now inhabited by me
alone.   The lamp is burning ; I pick up a book, read little,
ponder much.   All's still.—Music there, on the canal !
An illuminated gondola with singers and musicians : more
and still more boats with listeners follow in its wake : the
flotilla spans the breadth of the canal, gliding all but moveless
past.   Fine voices, passable instruments, render songs.   All
is ear.—Then, scarcely perceptibly it curves round the bend,

and vanishes still more imperceptibly. For long I still can hear the tones, ennobled and transfigured by the midnight stillness, tones that as art could hardly captivate me, but had here become part of nature. At last all ceases : the last tone as if dissolves into the moonlight, which softly goes on shining as a visual remainder of the sound-world.—

Now the moon has waned.—

I have not been well these last few days : I have had to give up my evening cruise. Nothing remains but my loneliness, and my futureless existence!—

On the table before me lies a little picture. It is the portrait of my father,* which I no longer could shew thee when it arrived ; a noble, gentle, sufferingly pensive face that infinitely moves me. It has become very dear to me.—Whoever enters, would probably suspect at first the picture of a lady-love. Nay! Of her I have no picture, but her soul I carry in my heart; there let him peep who can!—Good-night!—

September 30.

To-day I have gone through much. I heard of my beloved's care for me, and quite a beautiful letter lay by.† I have answered as well as I could, sadly and gladly, just as I felt!—

.   .   .   .

Once more I have experienced a thorough horror of youthful marriages;‡ except with persons of absolutely no

---

* Surely this must be meant for "stepfather"; see the letter of Jan. 5, 1870 to Otto, also the portrait of Geyer on page 34 of Mr. H. S. Chamberlain's *Richard Wagner*.—Tr.

† See letter of same date to Frau Wille, printed below.

‡ Comparing this sentence with the said letter to Frau Wille, I take the preceding dots to represent some allusion to Karl Ritter, whose marriage, contracted four years previously, had by no means proved a happy one.—Tr.

importance, I have not yet encountered one the radical
mistake whereof has not shewn forth in time. What misery
then! Soul, character, parts—all must warp, unless exceptional, and then of course most sorrowful new relations
supervene. Thus all around me is quite doleful; what has
any manner of significance, helpless and suffering: and
only the insignificant can thoroughly enjoy existence. Yet
what recks Nature of it all? She goes her blind way, intent
on nothing but the race: i.e. to live anew and anew, commence ever again; spread, spread—utmost spread; the individual, on whom she loads all burdens of existence, is
naught to her but a grain of sand in this spread of the
species; a grain she can replace at any moment, if she only
gives an extra twist to the race, a thousand- and a million-
fold! Oh, I can't stand hearing anyone appeal to Nature:
with finer minds 'tis finely meant, but for that very reason
something else is meant thereby; for Nature is heartless
and devoid of feeling, and every egoist, ay, every monster,
can appeal to her example with more cause and warranty
than the man of feeling.—What, then, is such a marriage,
which we contract for life in giddy youth at the first stir
of the sexual impulse? And how seldom are parents made
prudent by their own experience; when they themselves at
last have steered out of misery and into ease, they forget
all about it, and heedlessly allow their children to plunge
along the selfsame track!—Yet it is just like everything
in Nature: for the individual she holds misery, death and
despair, in readiness, and leaves him to lift himself above
them by his highest effort of resignation:—she cannot
prevent that succeeding, but looks on in amazement, and
says perhaps: "Is that what I really willed?"—

I'm not quite well yet, but have great hopes of to-night
if it brings me calm sleep. Thou wilt not grudge me
that?—Good-night!—

October 1.

The other day, in the street, my eye chanced to light on a poulterer's stall; unconsciously I was looking at the heaped-up wares, all neatly and appetisingly dressed, when, as a man at one side was busy plucking a fowl, another thrust his hand into a cage, dragged out a live hen, and tore off its head. The bird's horrible shriek, its pitiful clucking while being overcome, sent a shudder through my soul.—Often as I had experienced the impression before, I haven't got rid of it since.—It is ghastly, the bottomless abyss of inhumanest misery on which our existence, for the most part bent on pleasure, is really poised! This has always been so manifest to me, and with increasing sensibility has become so stamped upon my mind, that I recognise the rightful cause of all my sorrows as strictly residing in my inability to give up life and strife as yet for good. The consequences thereof are bound to shew in everything; and my often unaccountably changeful behaviour, my not infrequent acrimony toward my dearest, is to be explained by this conflict alone. Where I observe decided ease, or marked tendency to procure it, I turn aside with a certain inward horror. So soon as an existence appears to me painless, and carefully planned for avoidance of pain, I am capable of dogging it with implacable bitterness, because I account it so far removed from the right solution of man's task. Thus, with no feeling of envy, I have felt an instinctive dislike of the rich: I admit that, despite their possessions, even they are not to be called happy; but they have a very pronounced aspiration to be so, and that so alienates me from them. With studied aim they hold at arm's-length whatever might bewray to their dormant fellow-feeling that misery whereon all their wished-for ease is based; and that alone divides me from them by a whole world. I have searched my heart and found that I am drawn with sympathetic urgency towards that other side, and nothing seriously touches me save in so far as it awakes my fellow-feeling—that is : fellow-suffering. This compassion I recognise as the strongest feature in my moral being, and presumably it also is the wellspring of my art.

What characterises compassion, however, is that its accesses are not determined by the suffering object's individual qualities, but just simply by the witnessed suffering itself. With love 'tis otherwise : in it we ascend to communion of joy [" Mit-Freude "], and we can share an individual's joy only when his or her particular qualities are in the highest degree agreeable and homogeneous to us. Among ordinary personalities this is far more lightly possible, because purely sexual regards are almost exclusively at work here ; but the nobler the nature, the more difficult this integration to communion of joy, and should it succeed, behold the highest height !—On the contrary, compassion can bestow itself on the commonest and meanest creature, a creature which apart from its suffering has absolutely nothing sympathetic to us, ay, is positively antipathetic to us in what it is able to enjoy. The cause hereof in any case is infinitely deep, and if we espy it, we see ourselves thereby raised above all stricter barriers of personality ; for in this exercise of our compassion we encounter Suffering itself, irrespective of personality.

To deaden oneself to the promptings of pity, one generally argues that lower natures have been proved, you know, to feel pain itself far more slightly than is the case with higher organisms ; that pain increases in reality in direct ratio to the degree of heightened sensibility which enables one to pity : therefore that compassion bestowed on lower natures is a squandering, exaggerating, ay, a cockering of our emotions.— But this opinion reposes on the fundamental error from which all realistic readings of the world proceed ; and it is precisely here that idealism shews itself in its true moral import, since

it lays that bare to us as egoistic hebetude. Here it is not a
question of what the other suffers, but of what *I* suffer when
I know it to be suffering. Indeed we know all that exists
outside us only in so far as we figure it to ourselves, and as
I figure it, so it is to me : if I ennoble it, it is noble because
I am ; if I feel its pain to be profound, so it is, because
I feel profoundly when figuring its pain,—and whoever,
on the contrary, may figure it as small, merely shews
thereby that he is small himself. Thus my compassion
makes the other's suffering a verity, and the smaller the being
with which I am able to suffer, the more extensive and encompassing is the field of my emotion in general.—Herein
resides that attribute of mine which to others may appear a
weakness, and I grant that one-sided dealing is much impeded
thereby, though I am certain that when I do deal, I deal
conformably to my nature, and at any rate never inflict pain
on anyone intentionally. For all my future dealings, however, I shall be guided by this consideration alone : to occasion
others as little pain as possible. In that way I shall find
myself entirely at one with myself, and only so can I also
hope to give others joy ; for there is no true, sterling joy,
save of agreement in compassion. That, however, I cannot
compel : it must be brought me by my friend's own nature
of itself, and therefore—have I only once been fronted with
it whole and full !—

But another thing has also grown clear to me : why
I can feel even more compassion for lower natures, than for
higher. The higher nature is what it is for very reason that
its own suffering uplifts it to the height of resignation, or
that it has the germs of that uplifting in it, and tends them ;
it stands directly near to me, is my equal, and with it I
attain to communion of joy. Wherefore I feel less compassion for men, at bottom, than for beasts. To these I
see the capability of elevation above pain, of resignatio⸣

4

and its deep, divine tranquillity entirely denied ; so that when they fall on suffering—for instance when they're tortured—I see with torturing despair myself just simply absolute suffering, void of redemption, without any higher purpose, and with death alone for liberation ; a liberation which goes to prove that it would have been better had they never arrived at existence at all. Wherefore if there be any purpose at all in this suffering, it can only be the wakening of pity in Man ; who thereby takes the animal's failed existence up into himself, and becomes redeemer of the world inasmuch as he recognises the error of existence in general. (This meaning will become clear to thee some day from the third act of Parzival, Good Friday morning.) Now, to see this capacity for world-redemption through pity innate in a man, but undeveloped, and rotting through studious neglect, makes just that man repellent to me, and weakens my compassion for him to the point of complete insensibility towards his want. In his want he has the very road to redemption which is closed to the beast ; if he does not recognise it, but absolutely wills to keep it blocked to him, I on the contrary feel urged to throw that door wide open to him, and can go the length of cruelty, to bring the want of suffering to his consciousness. Nothing leaves me colder than the philistine's howl over a disturbance of his ease : here any compassion would be complicity ; just as it is a property of my whole nature to rouse people out of vulgarity, I am driven also here to naught but goading, to give them to feel of the great sorrow of life !—

Now with thee, child, I also have no compassion more. Thy journal which at last thou gav'st me,* thy latest letters, shew me thee so high, so true, so clarified and glorified by sorrow, so mistress of thyself and the world, that I now can feel but communion-of-joy, but reverence, worship. Thou

* See pages 32 and 56.—Tr.

beholdest thy pain no longer, but the pain of all the world ;
thou canst not so much as figure it to thyself in any other
form than of the suffering of the world at large ; in the
noblest sense, thou hast become a poet.—

But terrible compassion I had for thee then, when thou
thrust'st me from thee ; when, no longer a victim to pain
but to passion, thou deem'dst thyself betrayed, believ'dst the
noblest in thee misconstrued ; then wast thou to me as
an angel abandoned by God. And just as that thy state
soon freed me from my own bewilderment, it made me inventive to convey thee balm and healing ; I found the
lady friend * to bring thee solace and uplifting, relief and
reconciliation. See, it was pity did that ! Of a truth, I could
forget myself for that sake, will to renounce for aye the bliss
of seeing thee, of being near thee, if but I knew thee calmed,
enlightened, given back to thine own self. So contemn not
my pity where thou seest me exert it, since I have nothing
left to bestow on thyself save communion of joy ! Oh, that
is the sublimest ; it can only appear where sympathy is at
its full. From the commoner nature to which I gave pity
I must swiftly turn away so soon as it demands of me
community of joy ; that was the cause of the last embroil-
ment with my wife. The unhappy woman had understood
in her way my resolve not to set foot in your house any more,
and read it as a rupture with thee ; so she thought that ease
and intimacy were bound to be established between us on
her return. How fearfully I had to undeceive her ! But—
quiet ! quiet ! Another world will rise for us ; be thou blest
therein, thrice welcomed to eternal unity of joy !—

October 3.

What a hard life I have of it, to be sure ! When I
think of the vast expenditure of care, worry and pain I need,

---

* See letter 50, page 22.—Tr.

merely to procure myself a little leisure from time to time, I'm inclined to be ashamed of going on imposing myself in this way on existence, since the world, speaking strictly, will really have nothing to do with me.   Thus for ever and ever to be fighting for provision of the needful, often obliged for whole long periods to think of absolutely nothing but how to set about obtaining outward quiet and the requisites of existence for a little time ahead ; and for that to have so entirely to depart from my own way of feeling, to appear to those through whom I want myself maintained so altogether different from what I am,—it truly is revolting.   And added to it all, to be framed the very way to recognise it as none other.   All these cares come so naturally to a man who views life as an end in itself, who finds in concern for provision of the needful the best of sauces for his imaginary enjoyment of the finally procured.   For which reason, also, no one else can quite understand why this is so absolutely repugnant to a man like me, seeing that it is the lot and condition of all men ; that for once in a way a man should just not view life as an end in itself, but as an unavoidable means to a higher end—who will comprehend that right earnestly and clearly ?—There must be something peculiar about me, that I should have put up with all this so long already, and more-over should still go on doing so.—The hideous part of it is the growing more and more aware that really not one human creature—certainly, no male—is quite sincerely and seriously interested in me ; with Schopenhauer, I begin to doubt the possibility of any genuine friendship, to rank as utter fable what is dubbed so.   People have no idea how little such a friend is actually able to place himself in the other's position, to say nothing of his mode of thought.   But that, too, is quite explainable : by the nature of things, this superlative friendship can be nothing but an ideal ; whereas Nature, that hoary old sinner and egoist, with the best of will—if she could possibly have it—can do no else than deem herself the whole exclusive world in every individual, and merely acknowledge the other individual so far as it flatters this illusion of Self.—'Tis so, and yet, one holds on! God, what a worth it must have, the thing for whose sake one holds on, with such a knowledge!—

October 5.

A while ago the Countess A. announced a "little figure" that would soon arrive for me; I didn't understand her, and meantime finished reading Köppen's History of the Religion of Buddha. An unedifying book: instead of sterling features from the oldest legends, which I expected, for the most part a mere account of development in girth, which naturally turns out more and more repellent, the purer and sublimer is the core. After being so thoroughly disgusted by a detailed description of the ritual at last established, with its relics and preposterous simulacra of the Buddha, the "little figure" arrives, and proves to be a Chinese specimen of one of these sacred effigies. My abhorrence was great, and I could not conceal it from the lady, who fancied she had hit the very thing.

One has much trouble in this distortion-loving world to hold one's own against suchlike impressions, and keep unwarped the pure-beheld ideal, everybody is so fond of representing the noblest, if he cannot reach up to it, as akin to himself, i.e. a parody. Nevertheless, in spite of the Chinese caricature, I have succeeded in keeping pure to myself the son of Çakya, the Buddha.

Yet I did find in that history one new, or hitherto unheeded feature that was very welcome to me, and probably will lead to an important point. It is this:—Çakya-Muni at first was quite against the admission of women into the community of the elect; he repeatedly expresses

the view that women are far too subjected by Nature to
the sexual function, and consequently to caprice, wayward-
ness, and attachment to personal existence, ever to attain
that concentration and breadth of contemplation whereby the
unit cuts itself loose from the Natural drift, to arrive at
redemption.   Now, it was his favourite pupil, Ananda—the
same to whom I had already assigned his rôle in my
" Sieger "*—, who finally induced the master to depart from
his severity and allow women also to be received into the
flock.—In that I have an uncommonly weighty gain ; without the least forcing, my plot acquires a great and powerful
expansion.   The difficulty here, was to adapt this entirely-
liberated mortal upraised above all passion, the Buddha
himself, for dramatic, and particularly for musical treatment.
It is solved at once by his attaining himself one final step
in evolution through acceptance of a new cognition ; which
is here conveyed to him—as all cognition—through no
abstract combination of ideas, but through intuitive
emotional-experience, namely by way of a shock to his
inner man, and therefore displays him in one final advance
to consummate perfection.   Ananda, standing nearer to life
as yet, and directly affected by the young Tschandala maiden's
impetuous love, becomes the medium of this last perfecting.
—Ananda, deeply stirred, can reciprocate that love in none
save his, the highest sense, as desire to draw the loved one
up to him, to let her also share the last salvation.   Herein
the master crosses him, not harshly, but deploring an error,
an impossibility ; finally, however, as Ananda in profoundest sorrow believes he must give up hope, Çakya—
attracted by his compassion, and as it were by a last
fresh problem solution whereof has still detained him in
existence—feels moved to examine the girl.   In her deepest

---

* See *Richard Wagner's Prose Works*, VIII. 385-6 ; the date of the
sketch is " Zurich, May 16, 1856."—Tr.

distress, of herself she comes to implore the master to wed her to Ananda. He recites the conditions, renunciation of the world, discardal of all the bonds of Nature. At the final decree she is frank enough to lose all command of herself; whereon there ensues (perhaps thou recall'st it?) the opulent scene with the Brahmins who cast in his teeth, as proof of the perverseness of his teaching, his intercourse with such a girl. While denouncing every kind of human pride, his growing interest in the maiden, whose prior existences he reveals to herself and his opponents, reaches such a pitch, that, when she—recognising in her own sufferings the vast concatenation of the sufferings of the world—declares herself ready to take any vow, he admits her among the saints as if for his apotheosis, thus regarding his world-career for the redeeming of all beings as finished, since he has been able—directly—to accord redemption to Woman also.—

Happy Sawitri! thou now durst follow thy beloved everywhere, be ever near him, with him. Happy Ananda! she is nigh thee now, won never to be lost!—

My child, surely the glorious Buddha was right when he sternly prohibited art. Who can feel more distinctly than I, that it is this abominable art which forever gives me back to the torment of life and all the contradictions of existence? Were this strange gift not within me, this strong predominance of plastic phantasy, clear insight might make me obey my heart's dictate, and—turn into a saint; and as saint I durst bid thee, Come, quit all that holds thee, tear down the bonds of nature: at that price do I point thee out the open road to healing!—Then were we free: Ananda and Sawitri!—But so it is not now, for see! even this, this knowledge, this plain insight—, it makes me ever and again but poet, artist. At the instant I attain to it, it stands before me as an image, with the most lifelike, soul-filled visuality, but—an image that enraptures me. Perforce I must regard it ever closer, ever more intimately, to see into it still more definitely and deeply, sketch it, execute it, breathe life into it as my own creation. For that I need mood, elation, leisure, a comfortable sense of having overcome the common, sordid needs of life ; and all this I have to wrest from just this crabbed, refractory, at all points hostile life, at which I can only get in its own, its sole intelligible way. Thus, with self-reproach at heart, I must incessantly be seeking to beat down misunderstanding (which I feed myself), worry, want, vexation,— merely to say what I see but cannot be ! Not to go under, I look up to thee ; and the more I cry, Help, be near me !— the farther dost thou vanish, and a voice makes answer to me : " In this world, where thou burden'st thyself with this want, to realise thine images,—in this world she belongs not to thee ; for that which mocks thee, racks thee, everlastingly misunderstands thee, it compasses even her about ; to it she belongs, and it has a claim on her. Why does she, too, delight in thine art ? Thine art belongeth to the world, and she—belongeth likewise to the world."—

Oh, if ye foolish men of learning but understood the great love-brimming Buddha, ye would marvel at the depth of insight which shewed him the exercise of art as the most certain of all pathways from salvation ! Believe me, I know what I am saying !

Happy Ananda ! Happy Sawitri !

October 6.

The piano has just arrived, been unpacked, and set up. While it was being tuned, I read thy Spring diary through again. There, too, the Erard figures.—I have been very much moved since its arrival, for the history of this instrument is full of meaning. Thou know'st how long

I had wished for it in vain. Then last January, when I went to Paris—thou know'st for why?—strange, how it struck me to sue so actively for just such a piano! Not one of my projects did I take in earnest; all was indifferent to me; nothing did I pursue with an atom of zeal. Yet it was different with my visit to Frau Erard; in presence of that altogether dull, insignificant person I became rightdown inspired, and transported her—as I heard thereafter—to regular enthusiasm: with the turn of a wrist I won the instrument, as if in fun. Odd instinct of nature, how it comes out in every individual, according to his character, as simply that of preservation of his life!—The import of that acquisition was soon to grow yet clearer to me. On the 2nd of May, just ere thou too wast to start for "change of scene," and I must be left so wholly forlorn,— the long-expected came to hand. While it was being set in my room the weather outside was bad, raw and cold; I had abandoned every hope of seeing thee that day upon the terrace. The piano was not quite fitted, when—of a sudden—thou stepp'st from the billiard-room on to the front balcony, sitt'st down on a chair, and look'st over here. Then all was ready, I opened the window, and struck the first chords; but thou hadst no idea, as yet, that this was the Erard.—For a month I saw thee no more, and in that interval it became clearer and surer to me that we must henceforth stay apart! Then I should really and truly have done with my life, but this wondrous soft, sweet melancholy instrument wooed me right back to music once more. So I called it the swan that had come to bear poor Lohengrin home again!—Thus did I begin the composition of the second act of Tristan. Life wove its web around me like a dream of existence.—Thou returnedst; we did not speak with one another, but my swan sang across to thee.—

And now I've fared right forth from thee, the Alps
lie piled up heaven-high between us, it becomes ever clearer
to me how all must turn, how everything will be, and
that I now shall live a life no more.—Ah! if the Erard
but came, it must help,—have I often thought—for, when
all's said—things *must* be! I had long to wait, but here
it is at last, that cunning tool with its lovely timbre, which
I won in those weeks when I knew that I should lose thy
presence. How symbolically plain my genie here speaks
to me,—my dæmon! How unconsciously I erst happed
on the piano, yet my sly vital spark knew what it wanted!
—The piano!—Ay, a wing,*—were it the wing of the angel
of death!—

> October 9.
>   I have begun—what with?
Of our songs I had only the pencilled jottings, often
entirely unworked up, and so faint that I was afraid of
clean forgetting them some day. So I first set to work
playing them over to myself again, and calling every detail
back to memory; then I wrote them carefully out. Now
thou need'st not send me thine again; I have them all
myself.—

So, that was my first task, my pinions are preened.—
Better than these songs have I never done, and very little
in my works will bear setting beside them.

> "und löst dein Räthsel—
>   heil'ge Natur"—†

I had a strong mind to re-christen the "heil'ge Natur"—
the thought is right, but not the expression: Nature is no-

---

* "Flügel," the ordinary German name for a "grand" pianoforte
also, on account of its shape.—Tr.

† The last words of "Stehe Still!"—Tr.

where holy, saving where she revokes and denies herself
—but for thy sake I have let it stand. . . . .

. . . . *

October 12.

My friend Schopenhauer somewhere says : " It is
much easier to expose the faults and errors in a great mind's
work, than to give a complete and lucid exposition of its
value. For the faults are single things and finite, which
therefore can be fully surveyed ; but this, on the contrary,
is the stamp impressed by Genius on its works, that their
excellence is unfathomable and inexhaustible."—

I apply this saying with sincerest conviction to thy last
letter. What to me seemed erroneous therein was so easy
for me to review, and therefore at first I could deliver myself
on that alone : but the deep, divine and beautiful thereof is
so infinite and inexhaustible, that I can only enjoy it, not
speak about it even to thyself. What profound consolation,
the only one possible, it affords me to know thee so high
and sublime, I can attest to thee through nothing save the
whole further and concluding tendence of my life. How its
outward course will shape, I certainly cannot foretell, for
that belongs to Fate ; but the inner core, from which to
shape the dispensations of my outward fate, is settling in me
to a firm, clear consciousness, whose purport I will outline
here as well as I am able.—

My course of life till the time when I found thee, and
thou at last becamest mine, lies plain before me. The
nature of the world, in its contrast with my own, had been
making itself more and more painfully and cheerlessly clear
to me, and more and more consciously and definitely had

---

* Six pages, pp. 23-28, are missing from the manuscript [—a hiatus
probably to be explained by the nature of the reference to Mathilde's
" last letter " in the next entry.—Tr.].

I been withdrawing from my relations therewith, yet without being able as artist and indigent man entirely to snap all bonds that chained me to it. I shunned men, since their contact pained me, and sought with strenuous design for isolation and retirement ; yet the more ardently did I cherish the yearning to find in *one* heart, in one specific individual, the sheltering, redeeming haven to harbour me entire and whole. By the world's nature this could only be a loving woman : even without having found her, that was bound to be clear to my clairvoyant poet's-eye ; and the sheer impossibility of finding what I longed for in the friendship of a man, could but be proved me by the noblest attempts thereat. Yet, never did I dream that I should find what I sought so absolute, so realising every wish, so satisfying every longing, as I found it in thee. Once more :—that thou couldst hurl thyself on every conceivable sorrow of the world, to say to me "I love thee ! "—redeemed me, and won for me that solemn pause * whence my life has gained another meaning. But that state divine indeed was only to be won at cost of all the griefs and pains of love : we have drunk them to their dregs !—And now, after suffering every sorrow, being spared no grief, now must the quick of that higher life shew clear which we have won through all the suffering of those birth-throes. In thee it lives so pure and sure already, that I need only shew thee to thy joy, thy fellow-joy, what shape it now takes in myself.

The world is overcome ; in our love, our sufferings, it has overcome itself. No longer is it a foe that I flee, but an object void of substance, indifferent to my will, towards which I bear myself now without dread, without pain, and therefore with no actual revulsion. I feel this ever more distinctly, in that I no longer recognise the bent to absolute retirement as theoretically strong in me. That

---

* " Stillestand "— see the words of their song " Stehe Still."—Tr.

bent itself had heretofore the sense of longing, seeking and desiring : but that—oh yes, I feel it!—is now completely stilled ; the last issues between us have brought me the clear consciousness that I have simply nothing more to seek, no more to yearn for. After the fulness wherewith thou hast given thyself to me, I cannot call it resignation, still less despair. That reckless mood confronted me before with exit [by death?] from all my seeking and yearning : from its necessity, beatified by thee, I am redeemed. My feeling is one of a sacred satiety ; the bent is slain, because it is completely satisfied.—Informed with this consciousness, I look afresh upon the world, which consequently dawns upon me in an altogether new light ; for I have nothing more to seek in it, no more to discover a spot wherein I might be sheltered from it. To me it has become quite an objective spectacle like Nature, in which I see day come and go, seeds of life sprout and decay, without feeling my inner self dependent from that coming and going, that sprouting and decay ; I bear myself towards it almost solely as seizing and re-presenting artist, as a man who feels and fellow-feels, yet without willing, seeking or striving, himself. Even in purely external regards I recognise this new relation, inasmuch as that craving, so well known to thee, for a lonely and sequestered dwelling-place has practically left me ; tho' I admit that the sad fruit of experience has had its share in that. For what could best have met my fondest wishes, in that sense, yet left me in the end unsatisfied ; since it was precisely there I had to learn from our severance, and the necessity of that severance, that the longed asylum neither can nor ever shall be furnished me.

And where in the world now, should I will to found myself a fresh asylum ? When I left the fatal last one, I became entirely insensible to such a wish.—On the contrary,

I feel so strengthened and soothed in my inmost depth now, so sheltered and protected from all the world by the everlasting, inviolable and indestructible haven I've won in thy heart, that from its refuge, which accompanies me throughout the world, I can look with calmly pitying smile upon this world; to which I may now belong without a shudder, just because I belong thereto no more—no more as suffering, but merely as fellow-suffering subject. Wherefore I now yield myself completely wish-less to the figuration of my outward fate, submissive to it just as it may hap. I strive for nothing : what presents itself, and is not against my deep enlightenment, I shall tranquilly take, without hope, but also without despair, and go on proffering to the world, as well as the world permits, the best I can, untroubled for reward, ay, even for understanding.—Following this tranquil trend (the fruit of endless battles with the world, and finally of my redemption through thy love!), presumably I shall some day pitch my tent where ample artistic means are to be had without my needing first to fash myself for their procuring (to me the game no longer is serious enough for that!), so that I may give myself a periodic hearing of my works according as the spirit moves me. Naturally, any kind of " position " or " appointment " could not even remotely enter my plans. Neither, for that matter, have I the slightest preference for this or that particular spot; for—nowhere shall I seek again for something definite or individual, to say nothing of intimate : from that craving, in truth, I am freed! On the contrary, I shall simply grasp whatever allows me the most general, maybe even the most superficial, bearings towards my surroundings; and that is like to come the easier, the larger is the place. I haven't the remotest idea of withdrawing into any sort of intimacy, e.g. to Weimar; in fact, such a thought is distinctly repugnant to me. For I can only act up to my deeply settled attitude towards the world by taking men quite in the general, without any sort or kind of closer individual relationship; an endeavour like that at Zurich, where I tried to draw each single creature to me, can never attract me again.—

There thou hast the main features of my frame of mind. What will come of it outwardly—as said—I cannot predetermine, as it also is indifferent to my deepest soul. Of anything permanent for my future I do not think at all : while striving after permanence I grew so used to change, that I the more willingly yield the latter play now, the less I have a—wish.

How our personal intercourse, thine and mine, will shape itself—the only question left to agitate me—I suppose we must also leave, my love, to Fate.

Here lies, in truth, the one sore point, the thorn of suff'ring and of bitterness toward others, who make the heavenly boon of nearness impossible for us, without securing for themselves the smallest gain thereby ! Here we are not free, but hang from those to whom we sacrifice ourselves and to whom we turn back, with the one great sacrifice at heart, to exert on them our next compassion. Thou wilt bring up thy children :—accept my full blessing thereon ! Shouldst thou have joy of them and their flourishing, I shall ever look towards thee with naught but deep contentment.—*
Haply also we shall meet again, yet meseems but as in dream at first—like two departed spirits that meet on the scene of their sufferings, once more to feast on the look, the

* See the letter of some few days later to Otto :—" My last words to your wife were my blessing on the rearing of your children."—*Letters to Otto Wesendonck*, p. 43.—Tr.

pressure of the hand, that raised them from this world to win them Heaven. If perchance—by cause of my profound appeasement—a green old age be granted me, perhaps 'tis yet reserved me to return for good to thy proximity, some day when every pang of jealousy is overcome. The " Asyl " then might yet become a truth at last. Maybe I then should even need some tending : I am sure it would not be denied me. Perhaps—one morn thou yet wouldst step through the green workroom to my bedside, and with one parting kiss receive my spirit in thine arms.—And thus my diary would close as it began.—Yes, my child, so let this diary be closed herewith ! It offers thee my suffering, my lifting up, my struggles, my looks into the world, and over all—my ever-lasting love to thee ! Entreat it kindly, and forgive me if on any page it opens up a wound.—

I shall now return to " Tristan," to let the deep art of sounding silence there speak for me to thee. As for present things, the great isolation and retirement in which I live refreshes me : in it I'm collecting my sorely shattered vital forces. Already since a little while I enjoy the boon, almost never known by me to this extent, of deep and quiet sleep at night : would I could give it to everyone ! This I shall enjoy till my amazing work has thriven to completion ; not until then will I look around for once, to see what face the world presents to me. The Grand Duke of Baden has [?] effected thus much, that I may return awhile to Germany for the personal production of a new work ; perhaps I shall make use of it for the Tristan. Till then I stay alone with that in my dream-world turned to life here.

If aught occurs to me worth telling, I shall jot it down, store it up, and thou shalt receive it as soon as thou wishest. We shall give each other tidings of ourselves as frequently as possible ? They can do naught but delight us now, for all is crystal-pure between us, and no misunderstanding, no mistake, can cumber us again. So fare thee well, my heaven, my redemptrix, my pure, angelic love, farewell! Be blessed from the devoutest depth of my soul!

[*Here ends the first diary, despatched forthwith.*]

VENICE 1858.
   October 18.
         A year ago to-day we had a beautiful day at the Willes'. It was the season of wonders, we were celebrating the 18th of September [completion of the *Tristan* poem]. As we returned from our walk and were mounting the hill thy husband offered Frau Wille his arm, so I also might offer thee mine. We spoke of Calderon : how well he served! Indoors I went straight to the new grand piano : myself, I did not understand how I could play so finely.—It was a glorious, a glutting day—hast thou kept it to-day? Oh, that fair time had to bloom for us once! It passed— but the flower fades not ; that breathes its everlasting perfume in our souls.—

A letter from Liszt arrived also to-day, and gave me great joy ; so that—with fine weather here too—I'm in quite a calmly-cheerful mood. I had written him lastly on various tender points : I had to, as he really is so dear to me, and I therefore felt candour a duty ; and behold, he answers me with unwavering gentleness. From this beautiful experience I learn that I have not to repent my recognition of the impossibility of a perfect friendship such as floats before us as ideal ; since it has by no means made me insusceptible, but on the contrary, all the more grateful and sensible to what presents itself as some approach to that ideal. Between Liszt's intelligential character and my own there is so great and essential a difference, that the

5

difficulty—I must believe, in fact, impossibility—of making myself understood of him, often tortures me and drives me into bitter irony: but here love steps so beautifully in, with its very own allowances and satisfactions, that I'm half inclined to think warm friendship possible twixt man and man only when their modes of view are different. For it really is this friendly feeling alone, that can bring about agreement in the male sex: probably they never will fully concur in their views, or at most when they are insignificant persons and their views relate to common everyday things; if they touch on something higher and uncommon, it could wellnigh only be a case of the equations of practical logic, such as may occur in the sphere of science: the true glow of friendship, however, first enters at the very point where differences are equalised thereby and shewn to have no importance, as it were by a higher intervener. This agreeable feeling I have repeatedly received through Liszt before; yet I will not deny, that—on calm reflection—I think it well we should never be long and close together, since I should then have to fear too strong a salience of our dissimilarity: at a distance we gain very much to each other.—

But we—: far and near, we are united—mated—one!—

October 24.

How much I hang from thee, Beloved, I again have felt most keenly at this serious time. My mood of deep and beautiful tranquillity I had really won through thee alone: I knew thee so serene and lofty, that I could but be it too. And then this mourning, this woeful suffering, to know thee smitten with the loss of thy little boy:* how everything

---

* Guido, born Sept. 13, 1855, died Oct. 13, 1858. [See the beautiful epistle of condolence in the *Letters to Otto Wesendonck*, cf. note to page 63 *sup.*—Tr.]

of a sudden was changed! All pride, all calm, dissolved so swiftly into fear and trembling; deep trouble, weeping and lamenting; the built-up world all tottering, my gaze on it blurred by tears. Truly, an outer Power has come once more to knock at the gate of our hearts and prove if all is right within. It has been a time of seriousness; thou wilt recognise that only with an effort, wellnigh not at all, could I think of my work in days like these?—Yet from that I don't infer that there is something amiss with me; rather is it growing clear to me that even this work is merely *one* utterance of my being, which has other, surer channels of expression at command. I am able to suffer and mourn with thee: could I do aught finer, when thou art suffering and mourning?

Now let me hear from thee soon, that I may behold thee with utmost distinctness in this trial of so grave a meaning! What thou tell'st to me, as everything that comes from thee, will teach me and enrich me with a noble gain. Speak to me out of that feeling which habituates itself to embrace the whole world, wherein thy child with its existence—its tender death—was held as well; be sure of being kindly and devoutly understood of me in everything!—Thou poor dear child!—

October 31, evening.

Dost not know, then, my child, that I depend from thee alone—from thee alone—that the earnest cheerfulness which closed the diary sent to thee was a mere mirror of thy beauteous mood as told to me? O, hold me not so great that I could be what and how I am entirely of and through myself! How deeply I feel that now, when unspeakable grief and woe have cloven me to the midriff!—I have received thy packet, read thy diary, thine answer,—dost really not yet know, then, how I live on thee alone? Didst not believe

it, when I had it told thee but lately again ?* To be like
thee, worthy of thee, is the holdfast of my life! So do not
chide me if I once more tell thee, I am altogether as thyself,
feel as thou, entirely share thy every mood, thy faintest grief,
not merely because it is thine, but because it so clearly and
surely is also my own!—Hast forgotten how we wrote each
other when I was in Paris,† and that joint lament burst
simultaneously from our hearts, after we had told each other
our resolves as if inspired? So it still is, so will it remain,
for ever and ever!—Everything is *Wahn*, everything self-
delusion! We are not made, to square the world to us. O
thou dear angel of pellucid truth, be blest for thy heavenly
love! O, I knew all; what fearsome days did I live through,
what waxing apprehension! The world was at a stop, to
me, and I could breathe but when I felt thy breath.—O my
sweet, sweet girl, I cannot comfort thee to-day, poor doleful,
broken-down man that I am! Neither can I give thee balm,
and—" have I indeed no healing for thee?" How should
I have power to give thee healing? My tears are flowing in
full salt streams—: might *they* have power to heal thee?—
I know, they are the tears of love, of such love as never was
before: in them flows all the lamentation of the world, and
yet the only rapture I would fain experience now, to-day,
they give to me; they give me a deep, deep inward certitude,
an inexpugnable, inalienable right, for they are the tears of
my eternal love to thee. Might such tears heal thee?—O
heavens! more than once I have been on the point of starting,
to come into thy precincts: have I refrained out of care
for *myself?* Nay! oh, nay; but of care—for thy children!
Wherefore—once again—and ever: courage!—'tis needed for
a while yet. Methinks—methinks—I might—ere long present

---

* See the letter of Sept. 30 to Frau Wille, p. 86.—Tr.

† Last January; the letters are not preserved.

myself more fairly to thee, more acceptably, worthier of thee : and how gladly would I !—but what boots Would ?—

No ! no ! sweet child, I know all ! I understand all :— I see clear, clear as day— — —! I'm going mad !—Let me break off now ! Not to seek rest, but to deliver myself over to drown in the rapture of my grief !—O my precious ! —Nay ! Nay ! He'll not betray thee.— — — — Not— he !—

November 1.

To-day is All Souls' day !—

I woke out of brief, but deep sleep, after long and fearful sufferings such as I never had suffered before. I stood upon the balcony, and peered into the Canal flowing black below; a tempest was raging, my leap, my fall, would have been noticed by no one. I were free of torments, once I sprang, and I clenched my fist to mount the hand-rail.—Could I—with my sight on thee,—upon thy children ?—

Now All Souls' day has broken !—

All Souls ! peace be with you !—

Now I know it still is granted me to die within thine arms ! Yes, I know it !— — I shall see thee soon again : certainly by the Spring ; perchance the middle of this winter.—

See, my child, the last sting has left my soul ! . . . . . I can bear anything now. We soon shall meet again !—

Place no reliance on my art ! I have discovered all about it now : 'tis no solace, no compensation to me ; it is simply the accompanist of my deep harmony with thee, the fosterer of my wish to perish in thine arms. When the Erard arrived, it could lure me only since thy deep unfaltering love shone out more fixt and brightly on me after the storm than ever : *with* thee I can do all things—*without*

thee nothing, nothing! Don't let thyself be cheated even
by the expression of calm serenity that concluded my last
diary; it was nothing but the reflex of thine own fair,
noble elevation. Everything falls asunder with me, so soon
as I espy the slightest want of harmony between us; believe
me, only one!—thou hold'st me in thy hands, and with thee
alone can I—achieve.—

So, after this terrible night I pray thee :—Have trust in
me, unconditional, boundless trust! And that but means
again : Believe that *with thee* I can do all things, *without*
thee nothing !—

So thou knowest who disposes of myself, my acts and
sufferings ; 'tis thou, e'en when I'm seized with foolish
qualms about thee. And thus, too, am I sure of thee ; thou
wilt not forsake me, not turn a deaf ear on me, but
guide me loyally through want and misery. Thou canst
not else : this night I have won a fresh claim on thee—thou
canst not know me given back to life, to grudge me any
act of grace. So help me, then! and I will help thee
loyally too.—

Help me also to bear the frightful load that weighs on my
heart!—A load it is ; but on my heart it weighs.—Yesterday
I received from a reliable physician the exact report on
my wife's illness [see p. xiv] : she seems past saving. She is
threatened with development of dropsy in the chest :
increasing, perhaps protracted, but ever more agonising
pain, with death for sole prospect of rescue. The only
thing to ease and make it bearable, is utmost quiet,
avoidance of all moral agitation.—Help me to tend the
unfortunate ! True, I shall only be able to do it from a
distance, since I myself must deem remoteness from her
the aptest of means. When I'm near her, I become incapable of it : my presence, moreover, is bound to upset
her ; only at a distance can I calm her, as I then can

choose my time and mood so as ever to be mindful of
my task towards her. But neither can I do that, unless—
thou help'st me. I must not know *thy* heart bleeding; I
must not feel *myself* in the misery of being able to offer
thee no physic for thy wounds! That breaks me in a
thousand pieces, and leads me thither whence I returned
last night to thee once more! Thou understandest me,
my angel, dost thou not? Thou know'st that I am thine,
and thou alone disposest of my actions, steps, my thoughts
and resolutions? Do not scruple to acknowledge it—for
so it *is!* No Swan can help me, if thou help'st me not:
nothing has sense or meaning, save through thee! O believe
it, believe it!—So, if I bid thee, Help me, help me to this
or that, I merely mean: Believe that through thee alone
can I do aught, and naught without thee! That is the
whole secret.—I have become more deeply cognisant thereof
than ever. Since the death of thy little son, it has stood
sadly with my work; then I saw right clearly that it was no
comfort to me, but merely the expression of the lone man
who felt himself made one with thee and had not to distress
himself about thee. Ah, that's why it long has gone hard
with it: in truth, 'tis but a game to me; my true earnest
abides not therewith, as it never was really quite in it, but
over and away from it, in what I yearned for, and now in
what alone still makes me capable of life and art-work!
O believe! believe me that thou alone art my earnest!
—Last night, when I drew my hand back from the rail
of the balcony, it was not my art that withheld me!
In that terrible instant there shewed itself to me with wellnigh visual distinctness my life's true axis, round which
my resolution whirled from death to new existence: it was
Thou!—Thou!—Like a smile the thought stole over me:
Were it not sweeter to die in her arms?— . . . . . .
. . . .

Be not vexed with me, my child: "Die Thräne quillt, die Erde hat mich wieder!"*—All Souls' day! The day of resurrection!—

I'm writing Heim to-day, to retain me the free pass for the Erard, after all; I think of making use of it, some day, to take the instrument back into Switzerland duty-free. The swan has lost much of its meaning since last night; it is hardly worth my promising thee delight therefrom in future!—

Our lot is hard, very hard, my beloved child; yet in exchange, we're rich enough to be able to pay each debt of life and still keep for ourselves the most infinite gain. But thou'lt not be dumb towards me, wilt thou?—and— if I cannot "heal" thee, at least thou'lt not despise my " balm "?—

We shall see each other soon. — — — — — —

Farewell!

All Souls' day!

Farewell!—

And wish me well!—

November 24.   Venice.

Karl [Ritter] has left me for a while, to congratulate his sick mother on her birthday; he will come back shortly. At our parting he much affected me, the queer creature could hardly tear himself away. I really think, whoever has been much with me in these last months, must have derived a good impression; certainly I have never been so clear in everything, as now, or felt so little bitterness, wellnigh none at all. Who knows so surely that he has nothing left to seek, and henceforth but to give, is really also re- conciled to all the world; for his quarrel with it had

---

* " Tears flow, the earth regains me "—Goethe's *Faust.*—Tr.

consisted simply in his seeking something, where nothing could be given him. And how does one attain this wonder-gift of Giving? To be sure, but through one's own desiring nothing more oneself: he who is conscious that the only happiness to touch the bottom of his heart lies quite beyond the power of the world to give him, at last feels, too, how justified it is in refusing what it cannot give. But what do we signify by the World? In our sense, all those human beings who are practically able to give to themselves what their happiness asks: honour, fame, property, smooth wedlock, diverting society, Possession in every shape; and who does not attain it, scolds the world for his pains. But how ill were it of us, to scold the world, since we truly ask naught of all that it can give and take at its good pleasure! So I pityingly turn my gaze back to mankind, and rejoice in the gifts which allow me the power of comforting where Illusion lays up sorrow for itself. Who stands so high, however, so wondrously upraised above the world, should also under no condition ask aught of it, or aught accept of it, but what upraises and endows the giver's self through that acceptance. If, on the contrary, we craved of it an actual sacrifice, felt by it as such—something it grudged to give,—that ought to shew us at once that we had descended from our plateau, and were in act of somewhat derogating from our dignity. This, too, was the meaning of the Buddhist mendicancy; the monk, who had renounced all possessions, quietly took his station in the streets and before men's houses, to bless those who should tender him alms by acceptance thereof. What would the pious renunciant have thought of himself, if he had had to wring a gift from an unwilling giver, perchance to stay his hunger; his, to whom hunger was a devotional exercise? I was glad to find my mind already clear about this doctrine of giving and receiving, when I had to answer the

letter of a friend on the Lake of Zurich not long since.*
How despicable, eh! how criminal would that have been
which in that evil sense I should have had to extort from
the spirit of the world itself, a spirit which would believe
itself making a concession to me at the very time I fancied
it raised up to me by my high opinion of it. How proud
I was then, but not bitter; the Buddhist beggar had
stationed himself before the wrong house, and hunger
became a devotion: where I dreamed of rendering happy,
one thought of being called to sacrifice oneself to me.
Needed it more, than to recognise that error? And had I to
renounce my last breath of life, what lives within me stays
pure and divine if no sacrifice of the World's attaches to it.
This is the knowledge—this the will—that magnifies us
so, that gives us the stupendous power of feeling pain itself
no more, and—making hunger a devotion.

— I had a winter-journey in view. That is abandoned,
but I see the world still clearer now; with each devotion
my spirit strengthens to a power of working miracles. I
must have much control over people now: that I judged
by Karl, when he said goodbye for a little while.—I am not
always quite well, still my mood for the most part stays
bright and unruffled, nor can I help smiling when Koboldchen flits †: I heard its rattle yesterday again.—

December 1.

Here have I been, poor wretch, confined to my
room once more for a week, and this time even to my chair,

---

* There can be little doubt that the said " friend " was François
Wille, if one compares these few sentences with the letter of Sept.
30 to Frau Eliza—*vid. inf.* p. 87. Their meaning, of course, is impossible to define precisely, but it looks as though Dr. Wille had bluntly
declined a proffered visit; see also p. 144.—Tr.

† See Grimms' fairy-tale, referred to in letter 42.—Tr.

from which I dare not rise, and out of which I have to be carried to bed of nights. Yet it is nothing more than an outward affliction, which I even regard as altogether determinant of my health ; so that my condition even fills me with hope of being able to keep to my work quite undisturbed in future, whereas its interruption was the main thing that made my previous illnesses so insufferable to me.— At such times my intellect is always wide awake, plans and sketches actively engage my fancy ; this time it was philosophic problems that engrossed me. Of late I have slowly been reading friend Schopenhauer's chief work straight through again, and this time it has extraordinarily incited me to expansion and even—on some points—amendment of his system. The subject is uncommonly weighty, and perhaps it had to be reserved for my peculiar nature, precisely at this quite peculiar epoch in my life, to arrive at insights which could open to no other man. For it is a matter of demonstrating a path of salvation recognised by none of the philosophers, particularly not by Sch.,— the pathway to complete pacification of the Will through love, and that no abstract love of mankind, but the love which actually blossoms from the soil of sexual love, i.e. from the affection between man and woman. It is conclusive, that I am able to use for this (as philosopher,—not as poet, since as such I have my own) the terminology which Sch. himself supplies me. The exposition leads very deep and far, for it embraces a preciser explanation of the state in which we become able to apprehend Ideas, as also of that of Genius (*Genialität*), which I no longer conceive as a state of disengagement of the intellect from the will, but rather as an enhancement of the intellect of the individual to a cognitive organ of the race itself (*Erkenntnissorgan der Gattung*), thus of the Will as Thing-in-itself ; whence alone, moreover, is to be explained that strange enthusiastic joyfulness and rapture in the supreme moments of geni-al cognition which Sch. seems hardly to know, as he can find it [i.e. that mode of cognition] only in repose and in the silencing of the individual passions. Quite analogously to this conception, I then arrive with greatest certainty at proving in Love a possibility of attaining to that exaltation above the instinct of the individual will where, after complete subjection of this latter, the racial will comes to full consciousness of itself; which upon this height is necessarily tantamount to complete pacification. All this will be made clear even to the inexperienced, if my statement succeeds; whilst the result cannot but be very significant, and entirely and satisfactorily fill the gaps in Schopenhauer's system. We will see if I'm in the mood for it some day.—*

December 8.

To-day I have been into the open air again for the first time. I'm not completely well yet, nevertheless this last illness—in which I really was quite helpless, as I could not stir a foot—has enlightened me about myself quite satisfactorily, through the experiences reaped from it. Karl has been away nearly 3 weeks [p. 72], so that I had almost

---

* The idea, so far as it touches Love, seems never to have been worked out farther than the following fragment of an uncompleted letter, never sent to Schopenhauer, which made its posthumous appearance in the *Bayreuther Blätter* 1886, and now is definitively dated by the above:—

" *Metaphysics of Sexual Love.*—' Each year presents us with one or another case of concerted suicide of a loving, but outwardly impeded pair. To myself it nevertheless remains inexplicable, how two persons assured of mutual love, and anticipating the utmost bliss from its fruition, should not rather adopt the extremest steps to extricate themselves from all relations and suffer any ignomiry, than give up with their lives a happiness beyond which they can conceive of no greater' [*Welt als Wille u. V.* ii. § 44].

" It flatters me to suppose that you really have not yet discovered any explanation of this, as it tempts me to connect with such a point

nobody to talk with except my doctor and the servants;
oddly also, I never felt the least desire for company, but
quite the reverse. When a Russian prince here *—whom
I could not quite shake off, and who combines a right
good-heartedness with much intelligence, particularly in
respect of music—came to call on me one day, I was heartily
glad at bottom when he left; I always feel it a useless,
altogether profitless exertion, to—entertain myself with
anybody. On the other hand, I'm always glad to see the
servants; here the still naive man appeals to me, with all
his faults and merits. And they have tended me right well,
in fact with some self-sacrifice, for which I am very grateful:
Kurwenal, for once, stands nearer me than Melot. Moreover,
communications from without kept silent almost all the
time, the postman hardly ever shewed his face. When
I reached the Piazza to-day in the gondola, the whole place
was swarming with life and colour; but I have chosen an
hour for dining when I'm sure of being quite alone in
the restaurant, so I slipped unnoticed through the motley
throng once more, back to my gondola, and fared down the
silent canal to my earnest palace. The lamp is burning,

---

to submit to you a view whereby I think I can see in the beginnings of
sexual love itself one path of salvation, to self-knowledge and self-denial
of the Will, and that not merely of the Individual will.

"You alone supply me with the terminology whereby my view may
be imparted philosophically; and, in attempting to make my meaning
clear, I rely on nothing but what I have learnt through yourself. Please
attribute it to my inexpertness, perhaps also to my inaptitude for
dialectics, if it is only by a circuitous route—and in particular, by first
reciting the highest and most perfect instance of that resolution of the
Will which I refer to—that I arrive at an explanation of the case adduced
by you; which, again, I can only regard as an imperfect and lower grade
of that other."

Combining the two passages, we could wish for no completer refutation of the "Tristan and Isolde" slanderers old and new.—Tr.

* Prince Dolgorucki; see letter 58a, also of Nov. 21 to Liszt.—Tr.

everything is so still and grave around me; and within the sure, unequivocal feeling that this is the world for me, from which my longing can reach forth no more without grief and self-deception. So I feel happy in it; the servants often catch me in the blithest humour, and then I'm fond of joking with them.—

With reading, too, I stay most limited; little tempts me. In the long run I always hark back to my Schopenhauer, who has led me to the most remarkable trains of thought, as lately indicated, in amendment of some of his imperfections. The theme becomes more interesting to me every day, for it is a question here of explications such as I alone can give, since there never was another man who was poet and musician at once in my sense, and therefore to whom an insight into inner processes has become possible such as could be expected of no other.*—

I meant also to read Humboldt's Letters to a Lady friend, but could only get the booklet of Elisa Mayer, about him and with extracts from him. I laid this little tract down much dissatisfied : unmistakably the best of it was what *my* lady-friend already had extracted from it for me. Whoever knows Humboldt well, will certainly make acquaintance with a very able scientific student and inquirer. As man, too, he must have been most pleasing and attractive ; I cannot quarrel with Schiller for having frequented his society ; such a man would have been very valuable to myself. Productive minds need closer contact with such decidedly receptive natures, were it only because one often wants to give of oneself unchecked ; whereas one easily consoles oneself for discovering, on a final valuation, that

---

* To this period must accordingly be assigned at least that jotting found among the Posthumous papers, "The great joy," etc., *Prose Works* VIII. p. 391; whilst the larger subject gets developed at length in the *Beethoven* essay (1870).—Tr.

the assumption of one's having been quite grasped was really nothing, after all, but our own good faith. As a fact, Humboldt didn't comprehend much of the essence of things; there he remains decidedly shallow and ordinary, and this parson-like cant about Providence and the kind God is a little surprising in the intimate friend of Schiller, the pupil of Kant. I very soon saw that this man, too, was one of those of whom Jesus said: it is easier for a camel to go through a needle's eye, than for them to enter the kingdom of Heaven! The perpetually-recurrent ensurance of his easy circumstances is positively droll: to two inherited fortunes he weds two others, and further receives from the State the present of a fifth; robust and well brought up, he marries young a wife he can love with full sincerity until his death: add to all which a lively mind, an era of Schiller and Goethe, and I should say one couldn't be more luckily equipped by " Providence "; neither for his becoming a statesman and diplomat, one hopes, had he Providence to blame.—The more touching and affecting, however, is the love of this man, and his gentle exit from the world. Above all, *I* thank him for one deep and final anodyne, through a tiny immaterial saying which my lady-friend, however, repeated to me with so wondrous beautiful an accent of innocence that those few lines have made a great impression on me, pointing out the only path to hope: it was the passage about "confidence" and "confidences."—

Since yesterday I have been occupied with the Tristan again. I'm in the second act still, but—what music it's becoming! I could work my whole life long at this music alone. O, it grows deep and fair, and the sublimest marvels fit so supply to the sense; I have never made a thing like this! But I also am melting away in this music; I'll hear of no more, when it's finished. In it will I live for aye, and with me—

December 22.

A lovely morning, dear child !

For three days had I been plodding at the passage
" Wen du umfangen, wem du gelacht" and " In deinen
Armen, dir geweiht," etc.—I had been long interrupted, and
could not find the corner in my memory for its working
out ; it made me seriously uneasy. I could get no farther,—
when Koboldchen tapped, it shewed its face to me as
gracious Muse, and in an instant the passage was clear ; I sat
down to the piano, and wrote it off as rapidly as if I had
known it by heart for ever so long. A severe critic will
find a touch of reminiscence in it : the " Träume " flit close by ;
but thou'lt forgive me that—my sweetheart !—Nay, ne'er
repent thy love of me : 'tis heavenly !—

1859.

January 1.

Nay ! ne'er repent them, those caresses wherewith
thou deck'dst my threadbare life : I had not known them,
those flowers of bliss, bloomed from the purest soil of noblest
love ! What I had dreamt as poet, was destined once to
turn out for myself so wondrous true, on the common clay
of my earthly existence was destined once to fall that
gentle quick'ning and refreshing dew : I never had hoped
it, and yet it is to me as if I still had known it. Now
am I raised to nobility, I have received the highest badge
of knighthood ; at thy heart, in thine eye, by thy lips—
have I been raised out of the world, every inch of me now
is free and noble. As with holy awe at my lordship, I'm
thrilled through and through with the sense of having been
loved by thee with such abundance, so exquisitely tenderly,
and yet so altogether chastely !—Ah, I still breathe it, the
magic fragrance of those blooms thou pluck'dst me from thy

heart! They were not buds of life: so smell the wonder-blooms of heavenly death, of life eternal; so decked they of yore the hero's corse, ere it was burnt to godlike ashes. Into that grave of flames and perfumes leapt his loved one, to mingle her beloved's ashes with her own—and they were one! One element, not two loving mortals: one divine ur-substance of eternity!—Nay, ne'er repent those flames; their fire was radiant, pure and white! No lurid glow, no fumes, no acrid vapour soiled it aye, the clear chaste flame that shone for no one yet so pure and so transfiguring as for us, and therefore also none can know of.—Thy caresses—they are the crown of my life, the sweet roses that blossomed from the wreath of thorns wherewith alone my head was clad. Now am I proud and happy! Not a wish, not a longing! Delight, supreme consciousness, strength and aptitude for everything, for every storm of life!—Nay! nay, repent them not! Repent them ne'er!—

January 8.
> O Tag! Du aller guter Geister Gott
> Sei mir gegrüsst!
> Gegrüsst nach langer Nacht!—
> Bringst Du von ihr mir Kunde?—*

|April 4.

Lucerne.
The dream of Wiedersehen is dreamt; so—have we met again. Was it not in reality naught but a dream? These hours I have passed in thy house, in what do they

---

* "O Day, thou god of all good spirits! I greet thee, greet thee after weary Night!—Bringest me word of her?"—Tr.

differ from that other dream I erewhile dreamed so fondly
of my coming back? Almost it stands before me more
distinct, than the triste reality to which my memory will lend
itself so little. To me, it is as if I actually had not seen
thee plainly at all ; thick mists lay between us, through
which scarce pierced the sound of voices. Also it is to me
as if thou actually didst not see myself; as if, in my stead, a
ghost had come into thy house. Didst recognise me?—O
heavens! I recognise it: this is the road to sanctity! Life,
reality, ever more dreamlike, the senses numbed; the eye—
wide open—sees no more,—the willing ear forgoes all echo
of the Present ; where we are, we see each other not; only
where we are not, rests each's gaze on each. Thus is the
Present non-extant, and all our Future null.—Is my work
really worth my preserving myself for?—But thou, thy
children ?—Let us live !—

And when I read on thine own face the traces of so great
a suffering, when I pressed to my lips thy shrunk hand—a
deep throb shot through me, and called me to a finer duty.
Our love's miraculous power has helped till now ; it
strengthened me to win the possibility of a return ; it taught
me this dreamlike oblivion of all the Present, enabling me to
approach thy presence undeterred thereby ; it quenched all
my chagrin and bitterness, so that I could kiss the very
threshold which permitted me to pass to thee: so let me
trust it ! It will also teach me to see thee plainly once again,
e'en through the veil—which we have donned as penitents—
to shew myself as well to thee all bright and clear !—

Thou heavenly saint, have trust in me !

I shall be able !—

VENICE LETTERS

SEPT. 1858 *TO MARCH* 1859

❧ ❧ ❧

58.

To Frau Eliza Wille.*

Believe me, dear honoured Lady, I must keep tight hold on myself, to hold out at all! Almost every hour I have cause to remind myself: Sit tight! otherwise all flies asunder!—The one thing now left me is isolation, complete seclusion. It is my only comfort, only rescue; and yet it's so unnatural, especially for me, who am so fond of unrestrained communication. However—unnatural is just the word for everything about me. I have no experience what family, relatives—children are: my wedlock has been nothing but a trial of my patience and pity.—By me no friend is thinkable, to whom I could fully unbosom myself without repenting it; every day I become more aware how misunderstood I always am, wholesale and retail; and an inner voice, the voice of my truest nature, assures me it were better if I relentlessly freed, not only myself, but also my friends, from all illusion in that regard.—

For, the whole world is nothing if not practical; but with me the ideal gains such reality that it makes out my true life, and I can bear no jot thereof to be disturbed. Thus, arrived at my forty-sixth year, I'm forced to see that

---

* " An die Freundin Frau Eliza Wille." As the original of this letter is missing, presumably the superscription is an addition of Frau Mathilde's. The Willes lived on the opposite side of the Lake of Zurich, but had become intimate with the Wesendoncks, probably through Wagner himself. See also the letters to Frau Wille published together with the *Letters to Otto Wesendonck.*—Tr.

solitude must be my only solace and I must stand altogether alone. 'Tis so and I cannot deceive myself, 'tis this
insight that keeps me from collapse, and were I once to act
against it, I know I should be utterly lost: then bitter
ire would deluge everything. So my motto is simply, Hold
out—hold thy tongue!*—

When fancy gets full play at last, then things will go;
and mental work indemnifies, so long as it proceeds untroubled. But mind, in the long run, always feeds upon
heart: and how waste that region stands with me!—

All foreign and cold around! No lulling, not a look,
no soothing sound. I have sworn not even to procure
myself a little dog: it shall never be that I've a pet about
me.—After all, she has her children!—

Nay, but that is no reproach, merely a moan; and I
think she likes to take me as I am, moaning and all. True,
I have my art! Yet even that affords me no delight, and
I can but shudder if I look away from my work to the
world it will have to belong to; a world that only in the
most repulsive mangling can make it its own!—

Yes, I ought not to think on it, as on so much else:
I know that. Wherefore I also don't mean to, but keep
on calling to myself: Sit tight! it must be! Go it must—and
go it shall!—

Indeed she helps me charmingly! What a heavenly
letter was that you sent me to-day from her! The dear
sweet soul—let her be comforted; her friend is faithful to
her, lives on her alone—and therefore holds out!—

Ay! it must go, and—go it shall;—I imagine that
Venice will help, and believe the selection was excellent.
I really meant to write Wille a word or two about my
life here; but that also you must take on your shoulders.

---

* See next page, also the Diary entry of Nov. 24, p. 74.—Tr.

He has already vouchsafed me an unheard-of sacrifice, a letter in which he simply gave me to understand the sacrifice it cost him. Tho' that was and sounded very waggish, I won't put him to the pains again; * best for us to have another chat, about Venice this time, on the sofa in his red study with the fine antiques. Give him my very best anticipations!—

I am not leading an actual life as yet here; there can be no question of that till I'm at work once more : and I still am waiting for the piano! So rest content with a description of the terrain on which I have had to fix to live. Did you not write me, you knew this part? My palace lies about midway between the Piazzetta and the Rialto, close to the knee the Canal here makes, which is formed the sharpest by the Foscari palace (barracks now) at my side; right opposite is the Palazzo Grassi, which Herr Sina at present is having restored. My landlord is an Austrian, who received me enthusiastically for my famous name, and shews himself extraordinarily obliging to me in every way. (He also is the cause of my arrival's getting into the newspapers at once.) You have read how people regarded my being here as a political move, to worm my cautious track through Austria into Germany. Even friend Liszt was of that opinion, warned me, but also exhorted me to count on no successes of my operas in Italy, on which I surely must have had an eye: it really was not my terrain, and he was surprised at my refusal to see it. The answer to that I found most hard!—

I was supposed to be on my way to Vienna, too, as you probably know, but scarcely believed?—

I'm still the solitary guest (lodger) in my palace, and occupy spaces that scared me at first. However, I could

---

* See pages 74 and top of 86.—Tr.

find little cheaper, absolutely nothing more convenient;
so I moved into my big drawing-room, which is exactly
twice as big as the Wesendoncks', with a passable ceiling-
picture, splendid mosaic floor, and what is bound to be
glorious resonance for the Erard. I took some pains forthwith to overcome the stiff unhomeliness of the upholstery;
the folding-doors between a huge bedroom and a little
adjoining cabinet had to be removed at once, and portières
took their place, though of no such beautiful material as
my last in the Asyl; cotton must serve for the nonce to
establish the stage-decoration. The colour had to be red
this time, as the rest of the furniture was that already;
only the bedroom is green. An immense hall gives space
for my morning promenade; on one side it has a balcony
over the canal, on the other it looks into the courtyard
with a little well-paved garden. So here I pass my day till
about 5 in the afternoon. Of a morning I make my own
tea: I have two cups, one of which I bought here and
Ritter gets to drink from, if I bring him back in the evening;
out of the other, which is very large and handsome, I drink
myself. I also have a proper [? soda-]water-apparatus,
which I didn't buy here: it is white with gold stars, which
I have not counted yet, but presumably are more than
seven.*

About 5 the gondolier is called, for I'm so situated that
whoever wants to get at me must cross the water (which also
affords me a pleasant shut-offness). Through the narrow
alleys right and left, yet "sempre dritto" (as you know!) to
the restaurant in S. Mark's Square, where I find Ritter as a
rule. Thence "sempre dritto" in the gondola to the Lido
or the Giardino publico, where I usually take my little
promenade; then back by gondola to the Piazzetta for

---

* See p. 44 about the "Wagoner," alias Ursa Major. For the cup and
"Wassertrinkgeschirr" (which might also mean a filter), see p. 43.—Tr.

another saunter, my glass of ice in the Café de la Rotunde,
and then to the traghetto, which returns me through the
sombre night of the Canal to my palace, where a lighted lamp
awaits me about 8!—

The singular contrast of the still and melancholy grandeur
of my abode and its site with the constant mirth and glitter
of the Square and its belongings, the pleasing sense of
personal indifference towards this throng, the perpetual din
of wrangling gondoliers, and finally the quiet transit in the
twilight or as night falls—hardly ever fails to make a grateful,
and at last an agreeably calming impression upon me. And
at this I have stopped, for the present; as yet I have felt no
craving for inspection of the art-treasures; I reserve that for
the winter: I'm glad enough, for now, to be able to taste
this placid rise and setting of my day with equable content.—
My mouth I open to no one but Ritter, who is so taciturn as
never to disturb me; he likewise is alone, his wife having
stayed behind. We part on the traghetto every evening, and
very seldom does he set his foot in my abode.—It would
have been impossible for me to choose a spot better suited to
my present needs. Utterly alone in an insignificant, uninteresting little place, a gregarious hankering after company
would have been bound in the end to make me seize some
opportunity of social intercourse; and an acquaintanceship
sprung from that sort of need, and finally consolidated, is just
the thing to torture one at last. On the contrary, I could
nowhere lead a more retired life than here; for the interesting,
theatrically absorbing spectacle that here renews for me its
vivid contrast day by day prevents the faintest wish arising
to play a definite individual rôle therein, since I feel I
should then lose all the charm which the spectacle offers me
as a purely objective beholder. Thus my life in Venice
until now is a perfectly faithful image of my whole bearings
toward the world at large; at least as, in accord with my

knowledge and resignative need, they must and shall be. How I have to regret it, every time I step beyond them!—

When they've played pieces from Tannhäuser and Lohengrin in S. Mark's Square—where we have a military band on Sunday evenings—it really seemed to me, for all my anger at the dragging tempo, as if I had nothing whatever to do with it. For that matter, I'm already known everywhere; in particular, the Austrian officers often astonish me with signs thereof in delicate attentions. It has got about, however, that I wish to remain in most thorough seclusion, and after a few callers have been persistently refused admittance people are leaving me in peace. With the police I'm on excellent terms: certainly my pass was demanded again, after a while, so that I began to think of measures commencing; but it was soon sent me back with due ceremony, and the assurance that there was absolutely no objection to my continued stay in Venice. Thus Austria decidedly vouchsafes me refuge, which really is something worth acknowledgment.—

What gives my life from within out so peculiar, almost dreamlike a character, is its utter lack of future; the sentiment of Humboldt and his lady friend is altogether mine. When I go on the water of an evening, survey the mirror-bright expanse of sea, which, stretching motionless to the horizon, there joins the sky with absolutely no distinction to be noted, the evening red of the heavens completely wed to its reflection in the water—I have before me a faithful likeness of my present: what is present, past or future, is as little to be distinguished as there the sea and sky. Yet streaks then shew, flat isles that give the picture drawing here and there, and far away a ship's mast points on the horizon; the star of evening shines, the fixed stars twinkle, above in the sky and below in the sea:— which is past, which future? I see but stars and pure rose-tinted clarity, and in between them glides my bark, all noiseless with light plashing of the oar,—maybe that is the present.—

Greet the dear angel many-thousand times, and tell her not to scorn the gentle tears that drip for me! And if you partake of all as well, in power of your noble friendship, indeed, indeed we're happy !—

Farewell !

Your

R. W.

[*To Frau Wesendonck henceforward.*]

58a.

[Mid-December 1858.*]

Our letters have crossed: yours came just after I had posted mine !—

I have been quite alone for some time past; Karl Ritter left me to congratulate his sick mother on her birthday [cf. p. 72]. When he went, I was just recovering from an

---

* In the German edition this letter is printed as an integral part of that numbered "61," there filling the position indicated by the line I have left blank on p. 107. Its contents, however—more particularly in their similarity to the Diary entries of Nov. 24, Dec. 1. and 8, 1858—assign it beyond all doubt to somewhere between the 12th and 15th of December '58 ; a point of considerable interest in view of the concluding information as to the printing of the *Tristan und Isolde* poem. Nor is it difficult to guess how the confusion arose, if we bear in mind that of letter 61 "the original is missing": clearly, in copying-out at some distant epoch, Frau Wesendonck has in this instance misarranged a sheet of Wagner's manuscript. The only point uncertain is that of the location of the brief sentence " Our letters have crossed " etc : placing it *here*, I am influenced by the consideration that it is far more appropriate to a letter's beginning, than to its middle or end. If that conjecture of mine is correct, we have an indication of the former existence of at least one other letter of Wagner's concurrent with his Venice Diary. Finally, I have to observe that the " Du," which still appears in the intimate Diary, is replaced in this and all subsequent letters by the more ceremonious " Sie."—Tr.

illness that had interrupted my work—then scarce commenced ;
I promised him, if he returned, to have another large slice
of the Tristan ready, but I had to reconcile myself once
more to keeping my room, and this time—in consequence
of an outer lesion on my leg—a captive even to my chair, on
which I had to get myself carried to bed.   That lasted more
or less till now ; only the last few days have I been out
in the gondola again.   I tell you this, to link to this chapter
of misfortunes the tidings that I did not lose my patience
for a moment, although I had to give up work again, but
kept my mind free and cheerful through it all.   I didn't
see a creature all the time except my doctor, Louisa—my
Donna di servente, who nursed and bandaged me very well—
and Pietro, who had much stoking to do, fetched me food,
and with aid of a gondolier, morning and night, bore me
out of and into bed again upon my chair : a manœuvre
I called the " traghetto " and always gave orders for with
the habitual Venice " Poppéh."   Louisa and Pietro were
surprised and delighted to find me in such constant good
spirits ; what particularly pleased them, was my explanation
why I was such a bad hand at talking with them, namely,
because they had the Venetian dialect, whereas I knew
nothing but pure Tuscan.—

A good-natured, well-informed and intelligent man, a
Prince Dolgorucki, called on me one day ; I was pleased
when he came, still more so when he went away, I feel
so happy not to be amused and distracted.   I didn't do
much reading, however—even in such predicaments I read,
tho' little—yet I sent for W. v. Humboldt's letters, which
didn't particularly please me.   In fact I found it difficult
to read much of them, as I already knew their best part
through an extract : four lines of that were dearer to me
than all the diffuse, confused remainder.   I wonder if you
will guess the four lines ?—

I am more interested in Schiller. With him I'm uncommonly fond of consorting now : Goethe has had a hard
job to hold his own beside this intensely sympathetic nature.
How everything here is pure ardour for knowledge ! One
fancies, this man never existed at all, but was simply always
on the watch for intellectual light and warmth. Apparently
his ailing health didn't stand at all in his way : at his
maturity, though, he also appears to have been altogether
free from overpowering moral sorrows ; in that quarter
all seems to have gone fairly well with him. And then
there was so much still for him to know—at a time when
Kant had left such weighty points unsettled—so much
that it was difficult to acquire, especially for a poet who
also tries to be quite clear in his thinking (*im Begriffe*).
One thing lacks to all these men, though—Music ; albeit
they felt a need thereof, a presage. This often comes
out quite distinctly, for instance in that most happy sub-
stitution of the antithesis of " plastic " and " musical " poetry
for that of " epic " and " lyric." With Music, however, a
puissance has been won compared wherewith the poets
of that wondrous seeking, strenuous age of evolution were
but as outline-draughtsmen in their works ; and that is just
why they belong so intimately to me, they're my incarnate
heritage. Happy were they, tho'—happier without music :
the intellectual concept (*Begriff*) gives no pain, but in
music Begriff becomes Feeling ; that consumes and burns,
until it bursts into bright flame and the wonderful new
light can laugh aloud !—

Then I did a lot of philosophy, and arrived at some
big results, supplementing and correcting my friend
Schopenhauer : I prefer to ruminate a thing like that in
my head, however, to writing it down. On the other hand,
poetic schemes are looming again very lifelike before me.
The Parzival has occupied me much : in particular a singular

creation, a strangely world-dæmonic woman (the Grail's messenger), is dawning upon me with ever greater life and fascination—if I bring this poem off some day,* I should have to do something very original with that. Only, I have no idea how much longer I ought to live, to carry out all my various plans. Were I really in love with life, I might fancy quite a long existence guaranteed me by this multitude of projects; yet it does not necessarily follow—Humboldt tells us that Kant still proposed to work out quite a mass of ideas, from which, however, and very naturally at his great age, death stopped him.—

Even against the completion of Tristan I remark quite a fatalistic opposition, this time. Not that that can induce me to scamp it: on the contrary, I'm composing away as if I meant to work at nothing else my whole life long, and in return it will be finer than anything I've ever done; the smallest phrase has the import to me of a whole act, with such attention am I carrying it out. And as I happen to be speaking of the Tristan, I must tell you of my delight at having just received a first copy of the newly-printed poem, in the nick of time to send it you as birthday present.†—

---

* " Wenn ich diese Dichtung noch einmal zu Stande bringe, müsste ich damit etwas sehr Originelles liefern." Since the *noch einmal* is repeated in the next sentence, "wenn ich all' meine Pläne noch einmal ausführen soll," in respect of "plans" which certainly had not been "carried out" before, it cannot here be held to signify that Wagner had actually written a Parzival "poem" already. On the other hand, in his preface to the German edition of these letters, Dr. Golther informs us that "the three acts of Parzival were provisionally sketched in brief at the end of April 1857,"—for which, in the absence of more exact specification, and as Wagner was *then* in the thick of a household removal (p. lix.), I take the liberty of reading " April 1858 " (cf. pp. 22-23).—Tr.

† " Angebinde," i.e. for Dec. 23. Presumably there was more than this in the original letter, of which the above appears to be but a stray fragment, as it does not come to a full close, and one would naturally expect some sort of signature.—Tr.

59.

Venice, Jan. 19, 59.

Thanks for the lovely fable, Lady-friend [see p. 98]. 'Twere easy to explain how everything that comes from you always reaches me with symbolical significance. Precisely to the hour, the moment, came your greeting yesterday, as if a necessity conjured by magic ; I was seated at the piano ; the old gold pen was spinning its last web over the second act of Tristan, its touch just lingering on the fleeting joys of my pair of lovers' first re-meeting. When I yield to the sedative of a last enjoyment of my own creation, as happens with its instrumenting, I often get plunged in an infinitude of unbidden thoughts withal, which display to me the utterly peculiar nature of the poet, of the artist, forever unintelligible by the world. Then I plainly recognise herein the wonder of it, its total opposition to the usual view of life : whereas that view turns ever on the pivot of experience, poetic intuition, preceding all experience, embraces altogether of its ownest potency what first lends all experience a sense and meaning. If you were a regular adept at philosophy, I would call to your mind that here we meet in strongest measure the phenomenon whereby all manner of cognition first grows possible, to wit, by this : the whole scaffolding of Space, Time and Causality, wherein the world presents itself to us, pre-exists in our brain as its most distinctive function ; consequently these conditioning attributes of every thing, namely its dimension, duration and effectuation, are already contained in our head before our cognition of the things themselves, which we otherwise could not cognise at all.—

Now, that which is upraised above Space, Time and Causality, and does not need these helps for its cognition ; that which is loosed from these conditions of finitude, and whereof Schiller so finely says that it alone is *true* (wahr) because it never *was* (war) ; this which is totally incomprehensible by the common view of the world only the poet cognises with that full prefigurement residing in himself, and governing all his fashionings, that he is able to represent it with infallible certainty,—this Something that is surer and more definite than any other object of cognition, albeit it bears on itself not one attribute of the world which we know by experience.—

The supreme marvel must be, tho', if that foreknown essential Something should enter at last the poet's own experience.   His Idea then will take great part in this experience's shaping : the purer and higher that, the more unworldlike and incomparable this ; it will purge his will, his æsthetic interest will become a moral one, and to the highest poetic idea will link itself the highest moral consciousness.   Then will it be his task to prove it in the moral world ; the same foreknowledge will guide him, that, as cognition of the æsthetic idea, had moved him to present that idea in his artwork and qualified him for the experience.—

The common world, still standing under the influence of experiences forced upon it from without, and grasping nothing that is not driven home to its sense of touch, so to say, can never comprehend this position of the poet toward his experiential world.   It will never be able to account for the striking positiveness of his fashionings, otherwise than that they must at some time have come as directly to his own experience as all that it has made a note of in its memory.

That phenomenon I have observed the most surprisingly in my own case.   With my poetic conceptions I have been so far ahead of my experiences, that I may consider my moral development as almost exclusively induced and brought about by those conceptions ; Flying Dutchman,

Tannhäuser, Lohengrin, Nibelungs, Wodan—all existed earlier in my head than my experience. But the marvellous relation in which I stand to the Tristan now, you will easily perceive yourself: I say it openly, since it is an observation due to the initiated mind, though not to the world, that never has an idea so definitely passed into experience. How far the two predestined one another, is so subtle, so wondrous a regard, that the common mode of perception will be able to conceive it only in the sorriest distortion. And now, when Sawitri—Parzival—are filling my mind with previsions and striving to mould themselves next to the poetic idea—now to be bending o'er the work of artistic completion of my Tristan with all the calm of plastic meditation,—now! who will divine the wonder that must fill me, and so waft me away from the world that to me it seems all but wholly overcome already? You divine it, You know it! Ay, and haply you alone!—

For if another guessed it, knew it, then no one would chafe at us more; and every triste experience, invading his heart from without, he must needs offer up with a noble's sense of exaltation as a sacrifice due to, and in sympathy with, the higher ends of the World-spirit, which moulds from out itself experiences wherein to suffer, and through those sufferings to lift itself still higher. But—who will comprehend it?—would there be such nameless sorrow in the world, if our cognition were so much alike as the eudæmonistic will is like in all of us? In this alone resides men's misery: if we all cognised the Idea of the world and of Existence alike and accordantly, that misery would be impossible. But whence this hurly-burly of religions, dogmas, opinions and eternally warring views? Because all wish the same, without cognising it. So let the clearer-sighted save himself; and above all—let him dispute no more! Let him mutely suffer of the madness that grins around him, thrusts at him in every shape, in every reference, demanding, where it is blind, coveting where it misjudges. Here nothing helps but—silence and endurance !—

All this will strike you as another fairy-tale ; yet perchance, as another, it holds the key to yours *: the grey sparrow extols its Creator, and as good as it understands Him, so good sounds its song !—

You see, I'm so happy as to be able to work again. And verily that is a happiness, whereas a really serious illness is no such great misfortune, since it also liberates the mind and sets the moral force in action. The worst of states is that in which we are not absolutely ill, yet hampered and unsettled ; where profound discomfort takes us in our contact with the outer world, wishes and requirements try to raise their voice, the instinct of activity finds no right fulcrum, all is barred, all clogged, nothing permitted, naught will fit. Where this void and cheerlessness arise—this longing, yearning, wanting—it is given to no mortal to maintain himself continually at height of his true nature ; for his whole existence is strictly based on one perpetual struggle with the more subsidiary conditions of its very possibility, and his higher nature can express itself through nothing but the final victory in this fight ; ay, it is nothing else except that victory, the force which compasses it, and thus at bottom one perpetual negation—namely, a denial of the sway of those subsidiary conditions. And this comes out so strikingly in the purely physical groundwork of our body itself, where all, even the chemical (*vegetalen*) components of the whole are forever pressing on to dissolution, severance ; conspicuously succeeding, too, at last in bodily death, when the vital force is finally exhausted by the constant fight. Thus we have to be ever, ever fighting, merely to be what

---

* " The stranger bird " [see p. 339 *inf*.—Tr.].

we are ; and the more subsidiary and lowly are the elements of our existence from which we have to wrest submission, the less worthy of our highest essence can we shew ourselves when at war for the time being with them alone. Thus I have to do battle every day, and almost all day, with the purely corporeal base of my existence. I'm not exactly an invalid, but quite uncommonly susceptible ; so that I feel a smart in all those regions which in people of lesser sensibility never enter consciousness at all. Naturally I suppose that this malaise of mine would vanish in great part if my extremely acute sensibility were deflected and agreeably absorbed by an element in life's surroundings such as perhaps might be my due, but is entirely denied me ; I lack the kindly, coaxing entourage to draw my sensitiveness (*Empfindlichkeit*) towards itself and gently curb it into sentiment (*Empfindsamkeit*). Lady-friend—be it said with quite a placid smile—what a wretched life I lead ! Indeed I dare not read the account of Humboldt's life, if I'm to reconcile myself to mine !—

Well, that you know ! Neither do I say it to get myself pitied ; merely—I repeat it to you just because you know it !—No longer can I feel any sort of wellbeing save when I've swung myself up to my topmost height, but that height itself is hard to scale, and the harder as it *is* a height ; judge, then, how relatively brief must be my wellbeing, how lasting the reaction. But you have judged all that before, and know it ; then why do I speak of it ? It can only be *because* you know it ;—I need any number of good wishes, and tell it you since I know how your wishes are with me !—

So I'll just go on complaining.—My abode is big and beautiful, but horribly cold. Hitherto I've frozen—now I know it—in Italy alone ; not in the Villa Wesendonck, least of all in the Asyl. Never in my life have I made such friends with the stove, as in lovely Venice. The weather is mostly bright and set fair, thank goodness!—but it's cold here, too, though perhaps colder where you are and in Germany. The gondola merely serves as a hack conveyance now, for pleasure-trips no longer ; for one freezes badly in it,—which comes of the incessant north-wind, which is just what gives such brilliant weather here. What I am getting to miss the sorest, are my rambles over hill and dale : nothing remains for me but the fashionable promenade from the Piazzetta along the Riva to the public gardens, half an hour's walk, with a fearful crush of people always. Venice is a wonder : but that's all it is.—

I often long for my dear Sihl valley, for the Kilchberg slopes where I met you also proudly driving. So soon as it turns warmer, and I can make a little pause in my work (my solitary help now !), I think of an outing, first to Verona and the neighbourhood, where the Alps come quite close. It makes a strangely triste impression on me, when, in very clear weather, I can watch from the public gardens the far procession of the Tyrol chain. Then I'm often seized with a yearning of youth that draws me to the mountain-top whereon the tale once built the shining palace with its beautiful princess inside ; 'tis the rock on which Siegfried found Brünnhilde sleeping : the long, flat level, that surrounds me here, looks like nothing so much as resignation.—

My relations with the moral world are not inspiring, everything is leathern, tough and dull, precisely as it must be. How my personal lot will shape, God only knows ! A suggestion has been made me from Dresden, to go there with a safe-conduct, surrender my person to the law, and let action be commenced against me ; in consideration whereof, even in the event of conviction, the King's pardon would be a certainty. That would be all very fine for a man who might attain all he needed for life's happiness by such a submitting to the most odious chicaneries etc. of a trial; but, good God! what should *I* gain by it? In return for highly problematic refreshment by a possible few performances of my works, the quite certain annoyance, worry and over-exertion, which are now the more inevitable as my ten-year retirement has made me susceptible in the highest degree to any contact with this atrocious art-boggle I still should have to use as means. With that Dresden suggestion I therefore have not fallen in [see next letter]. To tell the truth, I'm altogether in the air with my works, none of my new cnes could I possibly allow to be produced without my personal assistance.

The Grand Duke of Baden seems to be the most faithful and energetic of my princes. He sends me word that I'm to reckon for certain on producing the Tristan at Carlsruhe under my personal supervision ; they wish to have it the 6th of September, the Grand Duke's birthday. I should have nothing against it, and the persevering sympathy of this amiable young prince inclines my heart towards him ; so we will see if he carries it through, and whether I—am ready. I still have a great, a serious task before me, and altho' I hope to keep to it now without disturbance, in no case shall I be able to finish it before June.—Then, if no change occurs, I think of withdrawing from Venice and visiting the mountains of my Switzerland again ; when I may even inquire at your house one day, my friend, whether you still remember me, and if my call is welcome.—

Karl Ritter returned on New Year's day, and now comes to see me at 8 every evening again. He has reported to me that he found my wife looking somewhat better. She seems to be doing tolerably, on the whole, and I take care that nothing lacks to her ease. At anyrate the awful beating of her heart appears to have quieted down, though she continues to suffer from sleeplessness, and, now that she has grown a little calmer, complains of increasing oppression in the chest with prolonged paroxysms of coughing—which unfortunately cannot hold out good prospects to me of her mending. The doctor, a tried friend of mine [Pusinelli], makes the prognosis of her illness depend on a lengthy cure in the country next summer; after such fearful derangement, and particularly in view of the obstinate sleeplessness and consequent malnutrition, we must therefore wait for Nature's decision about this poor tormented soul which finds itself so much a stranger in the world now. You haven't a moment's doubt, dear friend, that my attitude toward the unhappy one is nothing but forbearance and heartily kind consideration ?—

Thus I have care upon care—wherever I look the world makes life hard for me, dear child! Can it then be otherwise, than that I give you worry too? Yet you worry yourself for simply nothing but my cares, and ah! indeed you always help me so kind-heartedly. And where you cannot help me, I help myself with you: do you know how? I heave a great deep sigh until I smile : then to a good book, or—my work. Then all vanishes in an instant, for you are with me then, and I'm with you.—

If you'll send me a book from time to time, that you have read, I shall accept it with profoundest thanks. True, I read very little ; but then I read well, and you shall hear about it every time. To yourself I likewise recommend a book: read "Schiller's Life and Works—by Palleske" (only one volume has appeared as yet). Such a piece of reading, the intimate history of a great poet's life and evolution, surely is the most sympathetic thing in the world ; it has uncommonly appealed to myself. Now and again one must obliterate Palleske, though, and keep to the direct communications of Schiller's male and female friends. It will fascinate you greatly ; ay, in some parts you'll be quite— amazed. In his youth, when connected with the theatre at Mannheim, Schiller stood on a brink whence he was withdrawn by a glorious apparition, which he was lucky to have enter his life thus early,—you must tell me much about that ! And—if I may—I'll write you oftener in return now. Then you shall learn all you would like to know of curious exiled me : all—I hide nothing from you, as you may judge by to-day !—

I'll write Myrrha too, for once, of course : what eyes she'll make ! Only prepare her for my hand in advance. And if Wesendonck wants to hear from me some day, I'll write to him as well : already I have told him that. For to-day, give him my kindest regards !—

Thus I part from you with the palm ! There where my wreath of thorns rests, my roses shed unwithering scent ; the laurel tempts me not,—wherefore, if I am to decorate myself before the world, I choose the palm !

Peace ! Peace be with us !—

A thousand thousand greetings !

Your

R. W.

60.

Venice, February 22, 59.*

According to the law of the most-gloriously-perfect Buddha, the accused shall confess his offence aloud before the congregation, and thereby alone is he absolved : you know how I have involuntarily become a Buddhist.† To the Buddhist beggar maxim, also, I have unconsciously ever

---

* The original is missing.

† " Sie wissen, wie ich unwillkürlich zum Buddhisten geworden bin." Though the " unwillkürlich " *might* be translated " instinctively," I take this to be a more concrete allusion, either to some passage omitted by

adhered.   And that's a very lofty maxim : the monk comes
into the towns and streets of men, shews himself naked and
reft of possessions, and thus his appearance confers on
believers the precious opportunity of practising the noblest,
the most meritorious work of gifts and alms.   Consequently his acceptance is the most visible grace he can
bestow, and in that grace resides the blessing, the exaltation, he sheds upon the givers.   He needed not the gifts,
since of his own free will he had given up all for very sake
of reviving men's souls through his receipt of alms.—

I mean to be privy to my fate, down to its minutest
ramification ; not to divert it from its course, but merely to
face it without a vestige of illusion.   For my future, however,
I have no need : the noblest need of my life—you know
that !—I have to restrain ; how, then, could I flatter myself
with any kind of ordering of my fate ?   Only for others do
I wish : if those wishes are unrealisable, I must learn to
renounce them as well.   For, after all, the blessing of each one
of us must flow from his inner self : medicaments are snares.

Does that sound sad and serious ?—And yet I say it
for your comfort.   You needed that relief, I know, because
you need reassurance about me ; so we will vie with one
another in this sweet exercise, relief for relief !—

I renounce Germany with cold and placid heart ; I also
know that I must.   I have determined nothing for my future,
however—except—to complete the Tristan !—

As a beginning, immediately on receipt of my memorial
the Archduke Max had the measures for my expulsion
quashed [see footnote], so I'll see if I can bring the draft

Frau Wesendonck when transcribing, or to the petition for *amnesty* rejected about this date (see *Die Musik* I. 20-21), as the Archduke Max
is mentioned there in the same terms as later in this letter—which unfortunately is so disconnected as to suggest more than one involuntary
transposition—Tr.

of the third act also off here. Then I should instrument it in Switzerland, presumably not far from you, at Lucerne, which I rather liked last summer. Next winter I shall probably pass in Paris,—so I imagine at least, albeit without a spark of wish, but rather with great reluctance.—

I thank Wesendonck much for his offer, but don't let my correspondence with America etc. worry you and him too much. It is my lot, to have to help myself in this way, and the help's unproductiveness makes me suffer less than the road thereto ; from which, however, none can spare me. To be sure, posterity will some day wonder that I, of all men, should have been compelled to turn my works to wares : for, only as posterity (*Nachwelt*) does the world ever come to a little understanding, and then forgets with childish self-complacence that it also is a contemporary (*Mitwelt*) itself ; in which latter capacity it stays as dense and feelingless as ever. But that's the way it wags, and we can't alter it. Eh, and that is what you tell me of people in general, neither is there much chance of alteration in myself : I retain my little weaknesses, am fond of nice rooms, love carpets and pretty furniture, like to dress for my indoor work in silk and velvet, and—have to pay for it in correspondence !—

No matter, if but my Tristan turns out well : and that it will, as never anything yet !—Is Koboldchen laid, and Lady-friend relieved ?—

Don't forget Vienna ; perhaps it will give you a little delight—I would gladly go there myself some day : for the present you must take my place. Again and again I hear very good news of the representation of Lohengrin there, and from all I gather, it is the best of any of the performances of my operas. I'm waiting for definite notice from there, how long the season still lasts and you will be able to hear the Lohengrin ; as soon as I know, I will send you word !—

And now kindest greetings and thanks to Wesendonck.—
Koboldchen has been on its best behaviour, and I greet
Lady-friend from the bottom of my heart! Adieu!

R. W.

61.

Venice, March 2, 59.*

Best thanks to the fair Fairy-tale-teller, she tells so
beautifully, and yet is a long way off having such experienced
wrinkles as the Grimms! I'm in good humour owing to the
second act's success. Of evenings of late I've had Ritter,
and Winterberger into the bargain,† to play me the chief
portions bit by bit, and so it seems I've done a pretty thing:
all my earlier works, poor creatures, are thrown into the
shade by this single act! Thus I'm storming away at myself,
and ever reducing my children to one.—

Ah, dear Heaven! Thou knowest what I *will!* 'tis pure,
clear and transparent as Thyself when Thou spread'st Thy
fairest crystal o'er me! From my truest inner man not a
cloudlet rises more, that could cloak from any human soul
the aspect of my clarity! Out of themselves they blow them
across to me, those clouds; how much longer must I scatter
them, to shew them that I'm, after all, a good pure man?
Nor is it for my own sake, I scatter the clouds—fain would
I remain what I am; but they hide themselves away from
me behind those clouds, and I cannot rejoice them!—

Lady-friend, my case is hard, oh—very hard! But in
return, my guardian angel also becks to me. It comforts me,
and gives me rest when I need it most. Therefore will I
thank it, and tell myself: "Thus was it bound to be, that—
so it might be!"—Only he knows the palm, who has worn

---

* The original is missing [see footnote to next page.—Tr.]

† Alexander Winterberger, pianist and organist, a pupil of Liszt's.
[See also Wagner's letter of Feb. 22, 59, to Liszt.—Tr.]

the wreath of thorns : and it rests so soft, so swaying in the hand, and bows above the head like the airiest angel's-wing that cools and supremely revives us with its fanning !—*

As I still am very poorly, without exactly being ill, the other day I set my heart upon a land excursion. I wanted to go to Vicenza, but a train was leaving in the other direction, and so I arrived at Treviso. After a miserable night, as the sun was shining I started on a good long walk of about three German miles [14 English]. Out through the gate I made straight for the Alps, which proudly drew their splendent chain against me ; my thoughts were many. Tired out, I returned to the city of lagunes that evening, and asked myself my chief impression of this trip to the main land ; I was so melancholy at finding nothing in my memory but the dust and poor tortured horses, which I lit on again. I looked mournfully down on my silent Canal : " Dust and poor wretched, tortured horses—eh, those thou hast not here ?—but they exist in the world." Then I put out my lamp, prayed my angel for its blessing—and my light went out too,—dust and torment blew away.—

Next day work was resumed.—

And then I had letters to write—but I have told you that before. Tomorrow I intend to work again, but this letter had got to be written first. With it I glide across, away into the night, where the light goes out, where dust

---

* Here, following Frau Wesendonck's transcript, the German edition prints those passages which I have transplanted as a separate letter to pages 91-94 for reasons there stated. The whole remainder of this letter, however, is so at variance with the "good humour" proclaimed in its opening paragraph that it *must* be a compilation of various extracts, now undeterminable of date.—Tr.

and torment vanish.—Have thanks, child, for this convoy! could anybody grudge it me?—

And a thousand greetings, a thousand good, kind greetings!

R.W.

62.

Venice, March 10, 59.

My dear Myrrha,*

That was quite a wonderfully pretty, really a copy-book letter, you wrote me! If anyone will not believe it, let him look at it for himself. My child, I cannot write so prettily; I am far too old for that now! So, if there is anything you cannot understand in my answer, please ask Mamma, who has given you such beautifully success-ful writing lessons, to help you now in reading too. Of course there is much you are able to read, even without Mamma,—I do not doubt that for an instant; but a letter from me will be much harder, if only because I never yet have taught a Myrrha writing. So I have got used to writing all my own way, you see, which perhaps you will find a little indistinct. But Mamma must kindly help.—

Well, I thank you ever so much, my dear Myrrha, and it was very nice of you not to have doubted that I wept with you all for dear Guido. When you make him a present of flowers again, give him my love as well. It pleased me much, to hear from you that Karl is growing up so pretty. If he has not the same face as dear Guido, that need not stop you from taking him for exactly Guido, all the same. Believe me, he is every tiny bit Guido over again; only—he just has another face. As he has another

---

* The Wesendoncks' daughter, born August 7, 1851, at Zurich; married Freiherr von Bissing [a nephew of Frau Wille's], and died at Munich July 20, 1888.

face, perhaps he will also look at things in the world some
day a little otherwise than Guido would have looked at
them. But that is all the difference, and really does not
so much matter as most folk think, although it does cause
some confusion now and then—which mostly comes from
all men looking at each other with different faces, and therefore believing they all are something different, too, and each
of them the really only right one. However, that passes
off, and when it comes to the main affair, to crying
or laughing, why, one face is as good as another; and
when we die some day, as may happen in the end too,
we shall all be right glad if we each have such a face
as Papa wrote me that dear Guido had. So stand
true to your looking upon Karl for Guido ; merely, he
wanted to bring his little features earlier to that beautiful
repose which most men can only make theirs after very
much crying and laughing and other wry faces. Still, each
one gets it there in time, the more so if he is very good
and kind. Now Karl wants first to laugh and cry a deal,
and has taken up that task for Guido; that's why his face
still looks different. I wish him from my heart that he
may laugh his fill with it ; for crying comes soon enough,
quite of itself, and to be able to do a good laugh helps over
many a stile, take my word for it !—

Now, think all this out for yourself, my dear Myrrha ; and
as you invite me so sweetly to visit you, I really will come
one day soon, to talk more about these things with you.—
And give Papa and Mamma my best regards. To Mamma,
who is always so good as to write what goes on in your
house, give the letter enclosed, and beg her very prettily
to be cheerful and calm ; in return for which you can promise
her to be quite diligent at reading too, so that you may
soon read my untidy characters without assistance. Then
we two will keep a regular correspondence !—

And now goodbye, dear Myrrha. Accept my thanks once more, and give Karl, too, best love from your

Friend and Uncle
RICHARD WAGNER.

62a.

Venice, March 10, 59.*

To Mamma.

Yesterday I got finished with my second act at last, the big (musical) problem so dubious to all, and know it solved in a manner like nothing before ; it is the acme of my art till now. I still have a week to employ on the manuscript, then to attend to my awful correspondence ; whereupon I think of honouring Verona and Milan with a few days, and crossing my old Gotthardt viâ Como and Lugano. Rejoice me ere that with one more account of yourself !—

Best thanks, too, for the punctual execution of my "business ; " † God knows what will come of all these follies ! If only *I* know what I will, I am fairly phlegmatic as to what the world wills with me, so we'll wait and see ; meantime I turn dizzy at the thought of having to spend any sort of pains on my existence ! For my art I feel less and less need of the world ; so long as health permits I could keep working on, even tho' I never heard a scrap thereof performed.—

Yesterday Winterberger, who is going to Rome, took leave of me ; whereat he wept and sobbed convulsively. Karl, too, when he left me last November, was incredibly moved. They really are all very fond of me, and I must have something—I almost fancy venerable, in their eyes. Karl I leave behind me ; he is miserable about it, quite dreads my departure.—

---

* The original is missing.
† The American offer ? see pp. 105 and 128.—Tr.

With the fairy-tale I've already made it up, though I sometimes am dense, as you have often learnt before. You weave so deftly out of Nature, that all one needs is to have leant over your terrace with wits alert, to perceive whence you mould that fairy-world whose every strand of life so beautifully conflows.—Fare you well. Kindest regards to Wesendonck, and thanks for his practical forethought !—Fare you well !—

Your
R. W.

63.

Milan, March 25, 59.

So I have taken leave in your name, Lady-friend, of my dreamy Venice. Like a new world the hum of streets surrounds me, a world of dust and dryness, and Venice already seems a fairy dream.—

Some day you'll hear a dream I brought to chiming there ! A few nights ere my departure, though, in reality I had another wondrous pretty dream ; so sweet that I must tell it you, albeit it was much too beautiful to bear the telling. All I can describe of it, was somewhat as follows :— A scene I witnessed in your garden (which looked, however, a trifle otherwise). Two doves passed over the mountains ; I had despatched them to announce to you my coming, and there were two of them : why two, I cannot tell, but pair-wise they flew, close together. When you espied them, of a sudden you soared aloft in the air to meet them : in your hand you were swaying a mighty bushy laurel-wreath ; with that you caught the pair of doves, and drew it fluttering toward you, playfully waving the wreath and its prisoners to and fro. Then suddenly, somewhat as the sun bursts forth after a storm, so blinding a radiance fell upon you that it woke me up.—Now, you may say what you like, I really dreamed that, only infinitely more beautiful and exquisite than it can be described : my poor brain could never have invented such a thing of set purpose !—

Else, I am tired, and, presumably from the onrush of Spring, had of late been very agitated, with thumping heart and boiling blood. When I took your violet in my hand, to wish myself something, the poor thing trembled so between my hot fingers that the wish came to me quick : Quiet blood ! Quiet heart ! And now I confide in the violet, for it has heard my wish.—I was in the Brera to-day, and gave S. Anthony your greeting ; it is a glorious picture. Not far from it I saw the S. Stephen of Crespi, the splendid martyr between two churls who stone him—realism and idealism directly side by side : of profound significance ! I cannot understand how these subjects, in such wonderful execution, have not always been recognised by everyone as the sublimest pinnacle of art ; whereas many, and Goethe himself, have regarded them as oppugnant to painting. It is certainly the supreme glory of the newer art, that, what philosophy can only conceive in the negative—as world-renunciation—this has been able to give us in such positive, appealing truth, and so beautiful withal, that I hold as poverty-stricken every image of the joy of life and every Venus, against these sacred transports of the martyr-death such as van Dyck, Crespi, Raphael, and so on, portray them. I can find nothing higher, more deeply satisfying, more beautifully ennobling.—

I have also been into, and on to the roof of, the marble cathedral ; but really that is imposing to tediousness !—

And now, tho' I shall get no more letters at Venice, the weather is favouring me, the snow of the Gotthard about to revive me, and I soon shall no longer be far from you. I'm uncommonly glad at the thought of Lucerne, and promise myself great refreshment from weekly rides on the Rigi, Pilatus, Seelisberg etc. I mean to beat up glorious quarters there, and some day you must come over to see me with all the Wesen-hood of Wesen-home—friend Swan [pfte] is already en route.—

If you give a great big party soon, in memory of our house-concert, bear myself in mind a little too.—

Bless Antonio and Stefano, and all the saints. Hearty greetings to Wesendonck and my little girl-correspondent. I cannot rightly bid farewell, as I'm coming so near you that almost nothing but " Ave ! " seems fit.

To-morrow ahead to the Alps! Adieu, Lady-friend !

Your
R.W.

" Luzern, Poste Restante."

❧

LUCERNE

APRIL TO AUGUST

1859

64.

Lucerne, April 7, 59.

Things old and new for my dear Saint Mathilde!—
No letter can I manage—to-day. But by and by.—

The piano has come; it crossed the Gothard safely,
and without getting in the least out of tune.

The weather is heavenly! This solitude is very beneficial to me. I have rediscovered some favourite walks.
The finches are warbling more blithely than I have heard
them for long; they touch me much, these ever-hopeful
voices of Nature.—

Adieu! More news soon. I hope to be at the Tristan
tomorrow!

R. W.

65.

Lucerne, April 10, 59.

So the child is teaching the master!—This one thing,
that was only to be won by experience, was new to me too
through its startling veracity, and triumphantly leavened
each pang at the last:—only because there is no such thing
as severance, for us, could we go through this re-meeting!
I, too, was almost amazed at the feeling of absence of all
surprise; it was as if we had parted but an hour since.—

That is a miraculous soil, from which some glorious
thing must flourish yet. Ay, I foretell it:—we yet may
yield much happiness!—This noble, heavenly feeling will
ever prompt my Lady-friend more actively, strengthening her, and giving her that inflexible serenity which

preserves to us eternal youth.—Let her repose! I also am reposing, as a man just recovered from death!—

The third act is begun [yesterday]. It shews me distinctly that I shall invent no new thing any more: that one supreme blossom-tide awoke within me such a multitude of buds, that I now have merely to stretch back my hand, to rear the flower with easy tilth.—It also is to me as if this seemingly most sorrow-burdened act will not so sorely harass me as one might think. The second act still taxed me severely; Life's utmost fire flamed up in it with such unspeakable fervour, that it burned and consumed me almost personally. The more it quenched toward the close of the act, and the soft radiance of death's transfiguration emerged from the glow, the calmer I myself became. That portion I will play you, when you come.—Now all I hope for, is a good ending!—

But I can hardly wait much longer for your visit. Imagine it! a Kobold brought me yesterday a whole tea-service, and with the best of will I cannot inaugurate it all by myself. Perhaps you're not aware that I brought away with me a very fine big cup which another Koboldchen had sent to me at Venice, and out of which I always drink? So what am I to do with all these lovely new, delicate cups? O do come soon, to install them; I promise you, you shall be pleased with my quarters already.—But—seriously, was not the gift too rich? I almost thought so. What say you?—Wasn't it too much?—You'll be astonished at all the tokens of you you'll find with me!—

Now, write me when Wesendonck is coming back; then I'll present myself one afternoon again,—if I didn't weary both of you too much the last time.—

My love to Myrrha—also to Karl, who gave me an uncommonly prepossessing surprise. I called him Siegfried at his birth, and thus became his uninvited sponsor in my brain. And truly that christening has brought him luck : see what a splendid urchin he is growing !—

Are you not glad ?—

Adieu ! All's well and beautiful ! To the noble heart the world is fashioned from within ; only to the common dolt does it arise from without.

Life is ours !—

A thousand greetings !

Your

R. W.

66.

Child ! This Tristan is becoming something *terrible*.

This last act !!! — — — — — — —

I fear the opera will be forbidden—unless the whole is turned into a parody by bad production—: nothing but indifferent performances can save me ! Completely *good* ones are bound to send folk crazy,—I can see nothing else for it. To this length has it had to come with me ! Heigho !—

I was just in full blast !

Adieu !

R. W.

67.

Child ! Child ! Tears have just been streaming from me while composing— : Kurwenal :

" Auf eig'ner Weid' und Wonne
im Schein der alten Sonne,
darin von Tod und Wunden—
du selig sollst gesunden."—

That will be very harrowing—especially as it makes no impression at all upon Tristan, but passes o'er him like a hollow sound.

There's immense tragedy in it ! Overwhelming !

68.

April 15.

Child, the weather is abominable. For two days work has been suspended ; the brain stubbornly refuses its service. —What's to be done?—I snatched at the Tasso to-day, and read it through right off. Indeed it is a unique poem, and I know absolutely nothing to compare with it. How could Goethe have ever written it!—Who is in the right here? who in the wrong? Each sees as he sees, and cannot see otherwise ; what seems to the one a gnat, to the other is a giant. In the end, however, our heart is captured by the one who suffers most, and a voice tells us also that he looks the deepest. Just because he sees in each case *every* case, does the smallest seem to him so huge, and his sorrow shews us what is really in a case if one but probes it to its deepest bottom. The mere fact of this process being so terribly swift with the poet, since his eye takes in everything at a glance, makes him unintelligible to the others.—

But the mistress of Sorrow is manifestly the Princess. For him who looks deep enough there virtually is but one antithesis here, that between Tasso and the Princess : Tasso and Antonio are lesser contrasts, and their conflict interests the thinker less, since it admits of adjustment. Antonio will never understand Tasso, and only occasionally—by way of relaxation—will the latter hold the former worth the pains of understanding. Everything at stake between these two men is altogether inessential, simply a means of bringing Sorrow into play for Tasso so soon as ever he vehemently desires a thing. If we look beyond the piece, however, nothing remains to us but the Princess and Tasso : how will these two antitheses get balanced? As it here is a question of suffering, the lady has the advantage ; will Tasso learn of her? With his vehemence, I should rather fear madness for him. That the poet has foretokened marvellously.—

This set me also thinking, tho', that it was rash of me to publish the Tristan thus early. Between a poem altogether built for music and a purely poetic stage-play the difference in plan and execution must be so fundamental, that, if the former is viewed with the same eye as the latter, its true import must stay almost entirely lost,—that is, until completed by its music. Recall what I wrote in the letter on Liszt [*Prose Works III.*], apropos of Berlioz' Romeo and Juliet scene, about the binding difference here. It is precisely those many little touches whereby the poet must bring his ideal object quite close to the common experience of life that the musician leaves out, laying hand instead on the infinite detail of music, thereby to present the ideally distant object convincingly to men's emotional experience. But that makes an immense alteration in the form of the poetic work itself. Without the mass of small, nay, trifling details from the common wont of life, from politics, society, eh, the home and its needs, which Goethe employs in his Tasso, he would be unable to clothe his idea in pure-poetic guise at all. Here is the point, moreover, where everyone is with him, where each may fasten on a notion, an experience, and at last feels so at home that he can be imperceptibly led to what the poet really wills. Naturally, it always ends with each man's being left exactly where his feet will carry him no farther; still, each has an understanding of it after his kind. And the same thing happens when the music is furnished to my work : then melodic phrases enter into play and inter-play, engross and incite; one holds to this theme, another to that : they hear and guess, and provided they're able, they also grasp the object, the idea, at last. But without the music, that handle still lacks; unless we're to suppose a reader so gifted as to feel out the convincing trend from the uncommonly simplified plot itself.

Now you may imagine how I feel when bad weather and a heavy head pull me up in my music! If I knew that Wesendonck were back and had no objection, I would come to you tomorrow, if the weather continues so bad. Just fancy : I am still without my box of music and ruled paper! The military escort have detained it in Italy [see pp. 128, 136]. If I cannot work again tomorrow, I would far rather be up and about ; even the railroad would give me a chance then. So we'll arrange it so : if Wesendonck isn't back yet, you will telegraph to me at once ; if I receive no telegram in the forenoon, and the weather remains equally bad, I will telegraph *him*, begging him at the same time to send the coupé to the station at 9 P.M. (if that is not asking too much). Then we'll see how we can kill the bad weather together on Sunday.—Will that suit you ?

Kindest regards.

R. W.

If you were able to send me a telegram time enough, I should prefer to leave here in the morning (arriving at Zurich 2.30), I'm so afraid of my bad-weather idleness !

But the telegram would have to be here by 9 A.M.

69.

Good Friday. [April 22, 1859.]
Ere going to bed.

I have just finished reading the Egmont. Really, the last act is very fine. Otherwise I was put out, this time, by the prose in the piece : after the Tasso, a thing like

that strikes one as nothing but an undeveloped sketch,—
many animated features, yet no true life-filled whole.   It
does not reach the level of a work of art, and in this
respect I also think the Tasso is unique.   However, I have
been much moved by it again, but principally by the
last act.—Has the child nothing nice for the master to
read ?   Something soft, poetical—relaxing.   How glad I
should be of an unknown masterpiece of poetry.   Can I
really know them all already ?   Have you by any chance
a translation of Tasso—Jerusalem Delivered ?—

    To-day has been another day of downpour : I never
went out at all.   Still, my work has gone fairly.   I require
time for it, however.   Do you know this ?—

[See note to next example.—Tr.]

    Scarcely yet ?—

    I'm looking indescribably forward to your [plural] visit !
Everything is arranged already, and shall go as by clock-
work.   Making music will do me thorough good for once,
and I still owe you a glimpse of the Erard.   Things are
turning nicely green already.   If only the weather is fine—

eh ? I also promise Wesendonck to put plenty of closes into my playing ; every 8 bars a small gratification.

My best blessing on your house !

Many good wishes !—To our meeting soon !

R. W.

70.

Easter Tuesday [April 26, 1859].

Here's a reliable morning at last ! We must see how the day keeps it up ; what with your note, and the fine weather, it has made a very good beginning. I thank you ! On the whole I'm somewhat fretful and inert. I have really been too long about this work, and feel too keenly that my productive-force is simply feeding on the buds and blossoms which a brief-lived season, like a fertilising thunder-storm, awoke in me. At actual creation I can rightly arrive no more with it ; but the longer it lasts, the more happily attuned must I constantly feel, if the inner store is to come to full wakening ; and such attunements are compellable by no reflection,—like so much else, as far as that goes, in face of the world. True, I do some work each day, but brief and little, just as are the intervals of light ; I often would rather do none, if the horror of a day left thus entirely bare did not goad me on.

An odd case is that of a man like me. One doesn't lead a natural life at all ; yet, to make it semi-natural, it would have to be much more artificial ; somewhat as my artwork itself, which also finds no parallel in Nature and Experience, yet receives its new, its higher life precisely through the most consummate application of Art.

But imagine it : I have been unable to persuade myself to look through my 2nd act again ever since I've been here ; so that it already lies behind me like a shadowy dream. I feel no craving for it : the element in which alone I still could live, I lack entirely. If I'm to prosper, my art and its reactions on me would have to enfold me to the point of intoxication, of complete forgetfulness of self. But before me, of all men, lies nothing but life; life, in which I play so unnatural, so doleful a rôle. That really is not as it should be; and to stay true to my will, wellnigh a species of wilfulness will have to help me in the end. Nothing goes naturally and of itself, with me, not even my artistic creation. To me it is as if I took no genuine pleasure even in the Tristan any more: at the least it ought to have been finished last year. Well, the gods vetoed that! And now my sole feeling about it, is that it has got to be finished somehow, as otherwise just everything would suddenly come to an end. It's a case of main force.—

That sounds pitiful, does it not?—Perhaps the bad weather must bear much of the blame. Perhaps also a share of that attribute we found so unalloyedly developed in Tasso. Still, it always is a last relief to me to be quite candid, and especially to make up my mind to hide nothing from myself; then I take that sad insight also into account, and if after that I still intend a thing, I see that it probably must be. And that, in turn, gives me renewal of courage; just as it already revives in me now that I've told you this, since I know that I'm even more candid toward you than toward myself.—But—perhaps I ought to leave a thing like that untold you. It might distress you; and why should you be distressed? Were it not splendid for me, to know you unconcerned in any case?—But, by dint of illusions? Then all indeed were null and void again: how could your unconcern profit me then?— —There's no help for it; one must be able to avow all to oneself, the whole misery of the world and existence, fully and entirely to gain the power to taste the only thing that lifts above it.—

That is my whole philosophy, in face of those also

who labour to make life endurable by declining to admit its badness, or wilfully shutting their eyes to it. What they then feign to enjoy, still stays just nothing save the self-sufficiency of their illusion : but the otherwise-minded well knows what he has to rejoice at, namely the over-coming of grief; which alone yields strength, and pride, and—happiness.— — —

Best thanks for the brother's letter ; I'm returning it with hearty greetings to Uncle Wesendonck [see p. 128]. May he give marching-orders for Lucerne as soon as possible ! Then we'll have a famous dispute about the war ; which one can do to one's heart's content, since it absolutely doesn't con-cern one at all, and there one can make absolutely nothing depend on one ; but where it is otherwise—where decision and crisis depend on our innermost will, then that will itself should speak for us, in deed, in mode of dealing. So we'll stick to that !

You scarcely need have troubled Herr " von Heiligen " (German translation of "de Sanctis") : "Gries"*—that's how " Tasso " is called in German.—Am I not quite shameless ?

And now I come on you for something more ; only, for Heaven's sake don't breathe a word of it to Wesendonck. — I carry my blankets and bedding about with me—pampered mortal that I am ! The silk coverings look so terribly dirty, however, that I'm ashamed of the chambermaid seeing them. Could you spend a spare moment on trying if you can find the material in Zurich ; they were green, but could be red at a pinch, as the leaf turns in autumn. But I should require a good quantity. If you found something, you should give the order quite secretly (not Heim-ly ! †) to forward the whole piece to me here ; then I would take what I want of it, and settle the account without your further intervention.

---

* Translator of Tasso's poems.
† For the pun (*heimlich*) see p. 72.—Tr.

For the rest, you'll find everything spruce here. The big marquee ["Marquise"—apparently an awning] is ready ; only the sun for it to protect from is missing. Stay, though : we have some to-day, so perhaps things will go somewhat better. About that one may rightly say— : Heaven grant it !

And now my felicitation to the " Others " and " Röckly's " *
—and for an absolute close something new and silky †

from   Your   R. W.

71.

Mid-day Saturday [Apr. 30, 59].

The timorous sun gives me no heart for the Rigi ; wan

---

* "Und nun noch meinen Glückwunsch zu den 'Andren' und 'Röckly's.' " Dr. Golther tells me that "Röckly" is Swiss patois for "Röcklein," i.e. a little coat ; but I rather suspect it to be meant for "Köchly," the name of a Zurich professor (cf. p. 344).—Tr.

† It is rather curious that this excerpt should be given as " something new," just four days after the passage which in *Tristan* it directly *precedes*. It will be recognised, with a faint difference, as the accompaniment to the hero's words, "Wen ich gehasst, den hasstest du ; wen ich geminnt, den minntest du" (vocal score p. 204), thus proving that nearly a third of the music of act iii had already been sketched within a fortnight, for all the composer's self-reproaches of "inertness."—Tr.

vapours cloud the sky, and I now shall save myself the witches' expedition for the 1st of May.

I'm very sorry for Wesendonck's telegraphic headache ; as it fares so ill with him, it's only fair that the Rigi should vanish into smoke, this time, for me as well.   I hold firm to his acceptance for next week, however, and beg to be given a word of notice the day before.

Best thanks for the Tasso ; it shall compensate me for the Rigi.—I also owe thanks for the American letters, and beg you for the present to convey to Herr Luckemaier my heartiest recognition of his efforts.   For that matter, I feel somewhat Londonish again about it ; I have determined nothing, and at bottom could almost have wished Herr Ullmann's counter-offer had relieved me of all doubt. I really am to get a sight of this man, however, and therefore will not split my head till then.*

The war's a nuisance to me ; I still lack that box from Venice ; strangely enough, I have been unable to obtain any news of Ritter either.   In hypochondriacal fits I often think I ought to have gone to Paris sooner, to avoid getting the war between me and my future quarters.   On the whole it is interesting that, upon an outbreak between Germany and France, I should be seeking refuge in the enemy's

---

* As long ago as Dec. 24, 58, Wagner had replied to a Dr. Hartenfels of Frankfort, theatrical agent, concerning a vague invitation to go to New York and conduct his operas under " Herr Direktor Ullmann "; and on the 1st of February, 59, to Klindworth, " I'm keeping it open, but have a good mind to recommend *you*—as my substitute." May 26, immediately after a reference to the Austro-Italian-French war, he writes Otto, " My projected American alliance is therefore becoming of more and more weight to me ; " but, probably owing to the " counter-offer " proving too meagre, the scheme fell through.—Bernhard Ullmann was partner for a few years with Strakosch in the management of an Italian operatic company which toured the States, in 1859 including Adelina Patti as a member for the first time.   " Herr Luckemaier," of course, is " the brother " of Frau Mathilde mentioned p. 126 ; cf. p. 110.—Tr.

capital; I'm much afraid of losing all my patriotism and being secretly delighted if the Germans received another sound thrashing. Bonapartism is an acute, a passing ailment for the world,—but German-Austrian reactionism a chronic, an abiding one. Yet more: of late I've felt a longing to give some newspaper an "unpolitical view" of Italy, which is criticised by our politicians with a stupidity verging on impudence,—as soon as the weather improved a bit, though, those notions took flight. If only I were well into my work again! But that "well into," I fear, will never return: 'tis a memory of youth!

Apropos, if you leave me in the lurch much longer, I shall get Kirchner to come to me.*

Your sending me the Schiller [to Lotte] letters was a very happy thought of yours. Converse with that sort of people is what I like best, even better than politics. Their tiniest billets I read with interest; they are just what make one enter the dear creatures' life. And that's the very thing one seeks; one wants to be quite intimate with such people.—

I have absolutely nothing new to tell you; from nowhere have I had a letter all the week.—

Farewell! The month of May will help, and refresh yourself too!

Your
R. W.

72.

[Monday, May 9, 1859.]

Child, child! The Zwieback [a kind of rusk] has done the trick: with one tug it landed me over an awkward passage where I had been sticking for a week, unable to move any farther. Yesterday's attempt at work was execrable. My temper was awful, and I gave vent to it in a long letter to Liszt, in which I informed him that it was all up with

---

* Pianist, etc.; see p. 13 and *Life* iv, 135.—Tr.

my composing, and Carlsruhe must think of something else. Neither has the sun helped, and I've had to confess to myself that its shining on Friday morning was a mere gallantry of mine; it was the candle I set to light you home. To-day I stared with utter cheerlessness into the grey vault of the sky, and simply sought a target for some bitter word. As 8 days since I could get no farther with the actual composition (at the transition, in fact, from "vor Sehnsucht nicht zu sterben" to the sick man's voyage), I had then let it be, and taken up instead the working-out of the commencement, which I played to you. To-day, however, I could get no farther with that either, because it seemed to me as if I had done it all much better once before, but no longer could remember exactly how.—

As soon as the Zwieback arrived, I knew what the matter was: my rusks were much too sour here, so that nothing decent could occur to me; but the sweet familiar Zwieback, dipped in milk, at once put all into its groove again. So I cast the working-out aside, and went on with the composing, at the story of "der fernen Aerztin." And now I'm perfectly happy: the transition has succeeded beyond belief, with a quite wonderful concord of two themes. God, what the proper rusk can do!—Zwieback! Zwieback! thou'rt the only medicine for lamed composers,—but it must be the right sort!—Now I have a fine provision of it; when you notice that it's running short, please think of a fresh supply: I observe it is a potent drug!—

Friday evening I had to laugh a lot again with Schiller; he has that absolutely unique humour, which I don't find in this lovableness with Goethe. The laurel-wreath* (his landlady, I believe), the chambers in whose heart are infinitely cheaper than in her house—though there would be

---

* Schiller had conferred this title on his motherly Jena friend, the wife of Professor Griesbach.

more likelihood of damage there—is capital. I thank you
very much for these letters ; I should like to read simply
nothing but such intimacies.

Yesterday was detestable ; I could think of nothing all
day long, but the political nonsense. God, how heaven-high
one is lifted above these " most momentous questions of the
now-time," as soon as one's in one's right senses ! Whoever
can occupy himself incessantly with politics, proves incon-
trovertibly that even He doesn't know what to do with
himself : so the outer world must come in, and the broader
that stretches, the sublimer he deems the stew.—

I wrote Frau Ritter again the day before yesterday, and
I believe—for all forbearance—very plainly, helpfully and to
the point. Let's hope !—

Just fancy : the letter about the bass-clarinet [*Lohengrin ?*] I only read yesterday.—

Literally nothing has happened. While you were being
entrained again "vers les Wille's " I amused myself from
the balcony with my Lucerne pit, which makes a regular
fanaticism of the advantage it enjoys over you—namely, of
being able to admire my new dressing-gown daily. It really
must be very beautiful !—

Now let me soon hear, not merely taste, from you. Give
my kindest regards to the Excited, and thank him again in
my name for the visit, also for the champagne to which he
treated me ! Zwieback it was not, however—Good Lord !
Zwieback !!—

A happy week with some sun is wished you by one
who has to put up with Sunday without sun.—Adieu !

73.
                              Lucerne, May 21, 59.
I really must let you into a most comical discovery
which I have only just made. It suddenly appears to me

as if all the trouble with my work reposed on hypochondria. Everything I have dashed off looks so shockingly bad to me, that I lose all zest, and refuse to go farther.   To-day I forced myself to work clean out a passage from the sketch which had so displeased me of late that I believed I must wholly recast it.   Nothing better had occurred to me, however, and I was so wretched about it that I thought of giving up, and so on. Finally—in my despair—I fair-copied the passage out to-day, leaving it precisely as in the sketch, save for correction of a few small trifles here and there ; I try it over to myself, and—behold you, I find it so good, that I was unable to improve it for that very reason.—Isn't that laughable ?—And yet it's ill, for the very happening of this hypochondria is proof enough that something isn't as it should be.   I simply cannot prevail on myself to take a thing I have rapidly sketched and render it to myself with warmth and expression.   God knows, I'm so entirely the reverse of frugal reserve, that in communication I gladly go beyond all bounds.   Yet I also know that I've often had to rue my precipitance in imparting my sketches to out-siders with whom I had no sympathy, and whence I con-sequently never drew the proper warmth for my own lively grasp of my subject ; wherefore I have frequently sworn to do it no more.   Now that is avenging itself, and I no longer arrive at making friends with my inspirations at all.   How-ever, I'll take a lesson from to-day's experience, and see that I'm not so mistrustful of my drafts another time.   That way I shall end by becoming quite flighty, and carrying out the first thing that crops up in my head !—

Enough : for to-day I would rather say no more to you.   I'll write you a sensible letter by and by, when I can get hold of other paper than this coquettish pink which the elegant Schweizerhof has purveyed to me.—Even if the weather were quite propitious, I couldn't go up the Rigi tomorrow, as I have had to resort to a medical conference, in result whereof I am Rigi-unfit for some days.

Kindest regards. Keep my birthday for me ; I make you a present of it. Consequently—*I* congratulate !

R. W.

After work !

74.

Lucerne, May 23, 59.

Your war-song, Lady-friend, was quite admirable, and by all means a good inspiration. There's something in it like the storm-spell of my Donner in Rheingold, which pleased Liszt so much. By the music for it, though, there hangs a curious tale, which you'll hardly credit when I tell it you. On my last journey home to Lucerne the rhythm of the railway-carriage made music for me again, and brought me to Beethoven's music for Egmont. I ran that through my memory once more, closely scanned the "Leidvoll und freudvoll," and found that this was not a success. The Soldier-song stood the test all the better, and I had to find it so thoroughly original and excellent that I sang it through twice over, in my head. I hadn't an inkling of purpose about it, but simply tumbled on this song out of comparison with the other. So you may judge my surprise when I found your song awaiting me at home, built on precisely that melody in favour of which I had just rejected the "freudvoll und leidvoll"—whose text, by the way, I had also amended while criticising the music ; viz., the false rhyme

> "himmelhoch jauchzend,
>   zum Tode *betrübt :*
>   glücklich allein
>   ist die Seele die *liebt*"

I altered into

"glücklich allein
ist wer Redlichkeit *übt*,"

[" happy alone is who honestly deals "—Goethe having written, " happy
alone is the spirit that loves."—Tr.]

which obviously sounds better.

So that matter of the Soldier's song and its music has
succeeded completely. Heavens, though! Supposing you
were to run away from us one day, and join the military!
Already I can see you serving in the Engineers ("*Genie*").

And how goes everything else? Was Myrrha able to
decipher my yesterday's despatch? I wrote it very neatly.
But Myki's handwriting is growing lovelier every day; if
she goes on at this rate, she'll arrive in due course at the
hand of her mother, beyond which, of course, 'twere useless
to aspire.

Besides yourself, Liszt also congratulated me, telegraphi-
cally; for which I promptly thanked him by telegraph, in
my turn. Apart from that, one of my hopes has been
dashed: you know how I hoped that Karl Ritter would not
permit himself to leave me without a greeting on that day,
which would also have given me tidings of his whereabouts;
nothing having arrived, however, I am much concerned, as
he evidently doesn't want to compromise me in the eyes
of his family. I was luckier with Frau Ritter (the mother),
from whom I likewise found a letter on my last return
home, which shewed me that I had to some extent succeeded
in enlightening, and consequently even in reassuring her.
Remarkable—she replied to certain hints of mine: "good
Karl often acts too imprudently; when he suddenly resolved
on one of the most momentous steps in life, all my pleadings
to give himself a little time, and not bind himself by an
engagement so quickly, were in vain." O Fatum! [cf. p. 45.]

Who is right, and who wrong, in this world? It is a
jumble of likes and dislikes, attraction and repulsion: if a

man wants peace of life, at last he plants a boundary-post,—
here shall things stop, and not change any further! And
the post stands exactly where the craving meant to stop:—
but it did not stop, and then?—

"Who then is happy?" [Goethe's *Tasso*]—

After all, that's the best quietive;—and one can always
answer it with:

"wer Redlichkeit übt"—

or, if you like:

"die Trommel gerührt,
das Pfeifchen gespielt."*

Do you think me crazy??

Just a wee bit out of my senses I probably shall go in
time. Such a random life as mine has assuredly never been
led. Everything that might resemble a plan in me, falls
to pieces the instant I look at it fixedly; nothing holds
water. I positively don't know where to deposit myself
four weeks hence, and as not a single plan is good, I am
yielding myself with true fanaticism to hazard, drink Kissinger water since yesterday, force myself to nothing, in particular not to my work, look out on how it threatens rain
each day again, don't answer Härtels, who worry me for
"manuscript" (!), let children give me cushions, and grown-
ups Zwieback, and reflect "who leaves the issue in the hands
of God!" So it jogs along quite passably at last, and I
simply leave it to a miracle; who knows? maybe one will
occur!—Indeed, it isn't worth the pains of fretting; the
best things come to one "unbidden, unbesought—the
readiest," as sleep to Egmont.—

See, I could go on chattering with you by the hour, if
Wesendonck didn't start a discussion on one point or other,

---

* "The drums are rolling, fifes shrill clear"—the opening lines of the
aforesaid Soldier-song in *Egmont*.—Tr.

and thus give more precision to the chatter [such as]:—It's warm in the world, these days; Heavens, what lovely weather! Stay, though : one may go about lightly clad,—which ought really not to be, you know, for it's better when the weather's cold and one can go warmly clad against it. Over that a nice little dispute could be raised at once!

—Still no news of my box from Venice! But that also is becoming indifferent to me, even whether the Siegfried gets lost. What more can I do for it, save at utmost to harass myself unsuccessfully? On the other hand, I have made another altogether new invention for the Parzival, notwithstanding that I haven't read your book yet.* Neither am I reading anything else whatsoever, except the Allgemeine of an evening, which I mean to throw aside soon, however, and that for good cause. I'm not particularly keen on anything, but will take a turn at the Plato ; a dip into it did me much good. One ought never to associate with aught but the noblest ; everything else is debasement, a thousand-fold dilution of the primal fount. (Well, is that at least a rational maxim?)

Perhaps Tausig will come to me presently : he's to be had, and would like it.

To-day I've worked a little, which passed off once more as the day before yesterday. What will you say to me, you bellicose person?—me so peaceable that I don't even wage war with myself any more!

But one thing is good and enduring :—
thousand thanks for your wishes. Write me soon again, how I appear to you ; it will shew me what to think of myself! Kindest greetings—and hearty thanks.

Your

R. W.

---

* San Marte's " Parzival, Rittergedicht von Wolfram von Eschenbach,' 1836, second edition 1858 ; see next letter.

75.

Lucerne, May 29, 59.

So May is drawing to a close, and I am not to get up the Rigi? Everything was ordered yesterday, when the Lord of the Sky put in his veto once more. Luckily it had gone fairly well with the work: which helps.

Meanwhile we have buried the good soldier also [her poem]! I rather think he must have stood with Garibaldi, who is reputed not to spare his men ; for which reason I'm right glad de Sanctis did not join him. I'm rejoiced at your being in such high spirits. I am in neither good nor bad ; the vile weather is teaching me submission. After all, one has only got oneself to live on : fair weather in the heavens and upon earth may help one to live on oneself better and easier ; but there too in the long run, as in every circumstance, one must bear the costs oneself. Nothing enters into us that isn't already inside us by sympathy, and when one has consumed one's whole self there's an end of it, let one stick as much plaister as one likes upon it from outside.—So—patience, as long as aught's left to consume !—

Let that pass for a little philosophy. Regarding poetry, my change in Goethe's " freudvoll und leidvoll " has falsely alarmed you : you should simply have laughed at it,—nothing more ! Among all vaunted things, unfortunately this " honesty " has been turned to something risible for me ; and that springs perhaps from
      " Ueb' immer Treu' und Redlichkeit,"
which was the first little piece I learnt on the piano ; then came " God save the King," and then the " Maiden's wreath." Heine also once poked some neat fun at it, describing the Hamburg Exchange, "where our fathers dealt as honestly as possible with one another." It will ever be the same, where one converts an accidence, a symptom, into the actual substance of a line of conduct. The genuine man,

concerned for nothing save the genuine, cannot help being honest: and what were honesty without genuineness?

And—Karl Ritter did write me, after all, only his letter got delayed in the post. That has made me very glad. He has drifted to Rome, met Winterberger in front of S. Peter's, fallen in love with the flat dome of the Pantheon, and writes me excruciatingly naïvely about his interesting affairs. He is and remains a most original fellow. It was by no means for fear of compromising me in the eyes of his people, that he had not written me earlier, but simply because he fancied I was in receipt of far too many letters already, and didn't want to bore me. I have paid him well out for that!—

May 30.

After work I generally lie down awhile, to shut my eyes for a quarter of an hour. Yesterday I wouldn't give way, but tried to write to you instead. It avenged itself, however: a regular faintness came over me; I was obliged to stop.—Now you see how things stand with me.— To-day I'm sitting down before work, for a moment, and also have the pleasure of being able to reply to a kind couple of lines this lovely morning brought me from you. For—lovely it is to-day!—: whether it will last, remains doubtful. At present the early morning is the important weather-point for me, and the afternoon may look after itself at a pinch. Only think: I've been on my legs at 6 o'clock each morning since my birthday, drinking my Kissinger and promenading withal till about 8. Luckily the mornings have at least been bearable till now. Dear child, I could wish you also the refreshment of these morning promenades: I find myself quite perceptibly better since taking them; the slight fatigue of the unaccustomed early walk soon wears away, after a little rest, and has all

the more freeing and lightening an effect. Of course you
know that yourself, from your various bath-cures. One
is liable to forget it though, and yet should maintain this
regime all the summer, as it is a true nerve-strengthener
and blood-restorer. In summer one really can't pass the
real day out-of-doors : the mornings are the actual fortifiers,
whereas the evenings merely calm. Throughout the day-
time one had better take a good siesta ; at evening, too,
not go to bed too late. But the whole thing fits hand in
glove. For my part, I mean to stick to it the summer
through, wherever I may be, perhaps even rise still earlier,
later on ; so vividly has the effect of these early morning-
walks impressed itself upon me this time. Do follow my
example ! Wesendonck will certainly have nothing against
it ; on the contrary, he'll praise you. What you lose on
such a morning, the whole day, even including the evening,
can never make good to you: 'tis the fair rosebud of the
day, the quick of summer's joy, and as we're always so
wishing for sun and for summer, one ought also to know
the real cream of them.—

For my work, too, I'm exceedingly fond of the sun ;
but the kept-off sun, the sun one seeks to shade to pleasant
coolness. It then has the effect of fame and honours, which
one despises, yet which kindle a comfortable feeling of our
leaving them outside for very wealth. In the opposite event
we're reminded of our poverty ; for whoso has to seek for
light and warmth, is badly off.

I'm busy working out the first half of my act now. It
always costs me a deal of time to get through the suffering
passages ; there, even in a good vein, I can finish very
little at a sitting: but the brisk, swift, fiery parts get
reeled off infinitely quicker. Thus with the technical completion, too, I'm living it " leidvoll und freudvoll " all through,
and hang entirely from my subject's thread. And this

last act is a veritable ague—profoundest, most unheard-of
suffering and pining, and immediately thereon the most
turbulent exultation.   God knows, no one yet has taken
the thing in such earnest, and Semper is right.   Which
itself has set me once again against the Parzival.   For it
has struck me again, only quite recently, that this is bound
to be another very nasty job.   Considered strictly, *Anfortas*
is the centre and principal subject.   There you have a pretty
tale at once.   Imagine, I ask you, what is up!   To
myself of a sudden it has grown too appallingly clear :
it is my Tristan of the third act with an inconceivable
increase.   The spear-wound—haply yet another—in his
heart, the poor man knows but one longing in his fearful
anguish, that for death ; to win to that uttermost cordial,
again and again he craves the aspect of the Grail, if that
at least might close his wound, since every other aid is
impotent, nothing—nothing serves !—Yet again and again
does the Grail but renew him this one thing, that he *cannot*
die ; its sight but multiplies his torments, adding undying-
ness to them.   Now, the Grail, after *my* reading, is the
cup of the Last Supper, wherein Joseph of Arimathea
gathered the blood of the Saviour on the cross.   Now see
what a terrible import is gained by Anfortas' relation to
this wonder-cup ; *he*, stricken with the selfsame wound,
dealt him by the spear of a rival in a passionate love-
adventure,—for his only sustenance must yearn for the
boon of that blood which erst flowed from the Saviour's
like spear-wound, when, world-renouncing, world-redeeming,
He pined world-suffering on the cross! Blood for blood,
wound for wound—but from here to there what a gulf
between this blood, this wound! All transport, worship,
ecstasy, at the wondrous presence of the chalice which
reddens into soft entrancing radiance, new life is poured
through all his veins—and death can not draw nigh him !

He lives, re-lives, and more fiercely than ever the fatal
wound ravens him, *his* wound! Devotion itself becomes
a torture! Where is an end to it, where redemption?
Suff'ring of mankind through all eternity!—In the frenzy
of despair might he turn entirely from the Grail, shut fast
his eyes thereto? Fain would he, for a possibility of death,
but—he has been appointed Guardian of the Grail himself.
And no blind outer power appointed him,—no! but since
he was so worthy, since none had wist the marvel of the
Grail so deeply and so inwardly as he; as even now his
whole soul ever turns again towards that sight which
withers him in adoration, blends heavenly unction with
eternal ban!—

And I'm to execute a thing like that, to boot? make
music for it too?—Declined with thanks! Let him do it
who likes; *I'll* keep it fairly off my neck!—

Someone may do it, who will manage just à la Wolfram;
that won't much matter, and after all may sound like something, perhaps even something quite pretty; but *I* take
such things far too seriously. Look, if you please, on the
other hand, how easy even Meister Wolfram made it for
himself! Never mind his understanding simply nothing of
the inner content; he strings incident to incident, adventure to adventure, turns the Grail-motive into rare and
curious happenings and pictures, fumbles around, and leaves
the earnest seeker with the question what he really meant.
To which his answer would have to be: Hm, I really don't
know that myself, any more than the priest his Christianity,
which he also mumbles at the altar without a notion what
it is.—And that's the truth. Wolfram is an utterly unripe
appearance, the blame for which must largely be laid on
his barbaric, altogether mongrel era, hovering between
primitive Christendom and the newer State. Nothing in
that age could be carried right through; poetic depth

immediately is merged in insubstantial fantastries. I am
almost coming to agree with Frederick the Great, who,
upon the Wolfram being handed him, told the publisher
he mustn't bother him with such rubbish !—Seriously, one
must have so lived into the heart of a subject like this
through its legend's sterling features, as I now have don(
with this Gralssage, and then taken a bird's-eye glance at
the way in which Wolfram represents the same thing to
himself—which I also have done in skimming through your
book [cf. p. 136]—to be repelled at once by the poet's in-
capacity (with Gottfried v. Strassburg's Tristan it already
had gone much the same with me).   Take merely one point:
among all the meanings given by the legends to the Grail,
this superficial "penetrator" selects the one that has the
very least to say.   Certainly the identification of this marvel
with a precious stone occurs in the earliest sources one
can trace, namely in the *Arabic* of the Spanish Moors; for
one observes, alas ! that all our Christian legends have a
foreign, pagan origin.   In this case our onlooking Christians
were amazed to learn that the Moors in the Caaba at
Mecca (dating from the præ-Mohammedan religion) paid
reverence to a wondrous stone (sun-stone—or meteoric
stone—indubitably fallen from the sky).   The Christians,
however, soon framed the legends of its miraculous power
their own way, and brought it into rapport with the Christian
mythos; a proceeding simplified by the persistence of an
ancient legend in the south of France, that Joseph of
Arimathea once fled there with the sacred bowl of the
Last Supper—which harmonises perfectly with the enthusiasm of the early Christian age for relics.   Sense and meaning
thus entered at once, and with true rapture do I marvel at
this splendid trait of Christian myth-development which
devised the most pregnant symbol ever yet invented as
physical garb for the spiritual core of a religion ! Whom

does it not thrill with the most affecting and sublimest feelings, to hear that that goblet whence the Saviour pledged his last farewell to his disciples—and wherein the Redeemer's deathless blood itself was gathered and preserved—is still extant, and the elect, the pure, may gaze at and adore its very self? How incomparable! And then the doublec meaning of one vessel, as chalice also at the holy eucharist— unquestionably the Christian cult's most lovely sacrament! Thence, too, the legend that the Grail (Sang Réal—hence San(ct) Gral) alone sustained its pious knighthood, and gave them food and drink at meal-times.—And all this so senselessly passed over by our poet, who merely took his subject from the sorry French Ritter-romances of his age and chattered gaily after, like a starling! Conclude from that to all the rest! Fine are none but single descriptions, the strong point of all the medieval poets : there visuality reigns finely-felt, but their *whole* remains ever invertebrate. Then think of all I should have to set about with Parzival himself! For with *him*, too, Wolfram knows not what to do : his despair of God is absurd and unmotived, still more unsatisfying his conversion ; that matter of the "question" is *too* entirely flat and meaningless. Here, accordingly, I should have to invent just everything. Added to that is one more difficulty with Parzival. As the longed-for saviour of Anfortas, he is wholly indispensable : but if Anfortas is to be set in the true light due him, he acquires such intensely tragic interest that it becomes wellnigh more than hard to let a second main-interest crop up beside him ; yet Parzival must be accorded that main-interest, unless he is merely to come on at the end as a damping deus ex machina. Consequently Parzival's evolution, his sublimest purification, albeit predestined by his whole pensive, profoundly compassionate nature, has to be placed in the foreground once more. And for that

I can choose no spacious outline, such as Wolfram had at disposal: I must so compress the whole into *three* main situations of drastic intent, that the deep and branching contents yet may stand forth sharp and clear; for, to operate and represent *thus*, when all's said, is *my* art. And—I'm still to undertake a task like that? Heaven preserve me! To-day I bid farewell to this insensate project; let Geibel write, and Liszt compose it!—When my old friend Brünnhilde leaps into the pyre, I'll make my plunge beside her and hope for a blessed end! You have my word on it. Amen!

Eh! haven't I nicely de-grailed myself? Take it as a lecture, for which you have not needed to go to the Zurich Rathhaus! You will get no more to-day, despite the last fine Zwieback!—I'll see if I can do a little music now! Farewell, keep Whitsuntide in view, and—promenade right early in the garden. A thousand greetings.

Your

R. W.

76.

Lucerne, June 3, 59.

Freundin, I feel as if I shouldn't find the frame of mind to please yourself and myself in the Willes' house next Sunday. Therefore I enclose for Frau Wille a few lines of apology— dated direct from Kissingen [!]. Sometimes I suffer so much from my friends' cowardice [cf. p. 74], that it becomes better to help oneself without friends—at least for a while, till the power of illusion sprouts out of one's heart again and the whole world contains naught but dear friends. That also will return : until then, please convey my best compliments.—

And kindest thanks for the still kinder letter. More about that by word of mouth.—

Hearty greeting to your house!

R. W.

77.

Child! Child, dearest child,

Here comes a terrible tale! The master has made something good once again!

I have just been playing through the finished worked-out first half of my act, and had to tell myself what dear God once told himself when he found that All was good! I have nobody to praise me, any more than dear God had then—circa 6000 years back—and so, among other things, I told myself: Richard, you're a d—l of a fellow!—

Eh, I can understand now, why the lumber gave me such attacks of hypochondria! One has to keep reaching out God knows where, you see, to fetch the smallest pebble for one's building; and for all its grief and misery, it has to sound fine in the end, and insinuate itself in such a fashion that one gets a trouble round the heart without ever marking what poor stuff it is! It all goes off capitally: I have found no lengths and no monotonies; quite the opposite, passionate life up to arrogance, to laughter of jest!—No: such a thing I haven't made before; you'll marvel, for once, when you hear it.—

Now for quiet, peace and some smiling of fate, soon to complete the second half as well! Then I must be as new-born!—Help me, yourself! else no one helps me. Outside there all of them are dolts, all, all!—

Adieu for to-day!

It really was my Rigi day again to-day, so of course it's sweetly raining!

What says Wesendonck to Garibaldi?

A thousand blessings on you!

Lucerne R. W.

June 5, 59.

78.

Lucerne, June 17, 59.

A couple of hasty lines before meat, and after work! Best thanks for the restored bijou. I have just despatched the first manuscript of the 3rd act to Leipzig [Härtels].

An old tale :—it's raining!

A new one :—for 3 days past I *ride !*

Ride ! !—It's continued every morning. My doctorkin insisted on it. I hope for much good from it. Don't tell Wesendonck, or he'll lock up all his horses next time I come to Zurich!

Absolutely nothing befallen—barring much rain !—To-morrow, if the sun shines, I'll try and set about composing again. The visit of you two did me good. It was very kind of you. I am calm and fairly cheerful. Be it yourself! Soon more :—for to-day a mere trifle of a thousand greetings.

R. W.

79.

Lucerne, June 21, 59.

Good spirits are evidently not to be kept on end by the best of will! How goes it with yours ?

The day before yesterday I resumed composition with relish, yesterday it halted, and to-day I cannot even make a start: this godforsaken weather checks all spirits, rain-clouds and rain weigh like lead! I was really hoping the Prussian mobilisation would send us some wind from the north, but it still adheres to south and west ; it's enough to make one desperate. And to endure it for 3 months at a place where fine weather is the conditio sine qua non of any chance of holding out! What annoys me most, is when the rain prevents my morning ride now. I have developed a regular mania for riding: there I have so direct an association with my steed, which becomes quite a part of me during the motion, demands my whole attention and engrossment, and thus provides a wholly pleasurable company, with the quite distinctive feature of its all being *one* continuous contact.

I could write you much more about riding. I must guard against allowing a passion for the horse to rise, because I might again be learning something that I must forgo. Many a thing and oft have I renounced already, and the wanderings of the immortal Jew should be doubled by no steed.

Nothing has occurred. My discreet friends preserve a reverential silence. Even the music-journal [*Neue Zeitschrift*] serves up the celebrated Future-feast in snippets.* Now I almost wish to have no visitors from over there this summer; before the finishing of Tristan, such a noisy incursion could scarcely do aught but disturb me. Indeed they all mean something so totally other than I ; one must admit that to oneself, without any bitterness. It is only with a positive shudder, that I can think back to the goings-on of autumn 1856 ;† and when I remember what torments the visits of last summer caused me, when I simply counted the hours at last to people's departure, I cannot rightly conceive how I'm to look forward to those visits now with any feeling save dismay. And yet they can have been inspired by nothing but affection for me. A queer state of affairs ! What a crank I must be growing ! Perhaps it will be different with me when the Tristan's finished. At present it holds me : then I shall hold it.—

---

* First Leipzig " Tonkünstler-Versammlung," June 1 to 4, 1859, under Liszt's auspices. The prelude to *Tristan* was played June 1, but the *N. Z.* of the 17th cuts its report before reaching that item, and leaves it till the 24th ! Cf. pp. 198 and 203.—Tr.

† The six-week visit of Liszt and Princess Carolyne Sayn-Wittgenstein to Zurich.—Tr.

Many fine Zwiebacks came yesterday : they're increasing my chattels prodigiously ; whatever's to be done with all the boxes ? We shall have to think out some use for them.

The other day I was amused by a supplement to the Intelligenzblatt [a Zurich newspaper] ; I guessed Herwegh as the author, and asked him in a couple of lines [17th]. He confessed with delight. Such zeal's a good joke to me. The article was rather high-faluting here and there, but really written with much wit—with more than I had suspected in Herwegh—and that is enough in itself to call for hopeful recognition. The subject [the war—see p. 128] is so gruesome that wit and irony, in truth, alone can make the aspect of the world endurable to one ; they constitute at once a frank admission of the world's atrocity, whilst our feebleness in its despite is not concealed, but equally admitted. Whoso can treat it with a serious face, and hope and will, himself is still stuck deep in the illusion. Well, that indeed's the case with H. as yet ; but it hides itself behind the zeal of his denunciation of the mistakenness of others' efforts : and just in that game he turns witty. With Shakespeare, whom he cites in passing, I had to have a good long laugh again ; which brought me back to my favourite theme, of company with the *great* being ever the best, in the long run, to help us across the world. That curiously witty smile of Shakespeare's ! That godlike contempt for the world ! It really is the summit to which man can soar from this misery : the Genius can mount no higher,—only the Saint ! The latter, however, has need of wit no more.

Myself, I first feel quite restored from pain, when this smile steals once more through my spirit ; a smile that under circumstances, and if an undeception as to special big illusions aids it, may grow into a hearty laugh. With politics I catch myself taking things too seriously at times : the faintest hope of good-sense and good-will among men is a snare; it lures us still to by-ways whence one cannot come quick enough back, since that road also but ends in one's doing men injustice. One should repeat to oneself again and again, that good-sense and good-will are never the factors of history, and only so much of them dwells in the nature of men as to prevent the race from going altogether under; whereas they may help the individual out from life, indeed, but not within it. How many hopes are being smashed again now! How plainly also will the issue of this present war shew the magnanimous that he has not to seek his redemption where every battlefield can teach him *who* is ruler of the world. Yet, who will understand it? Comes a new generation, and the old game begins afresh! Thus at the aspect even of a battlefield a smile may take one, over the eternal mock we make of ourselves. However—that leads far, so we'll drop it to-day—! One mustn't take even that in too much earnest, but close our eye!—A thousand greetings.—

R. W.

80.

Lucerne, June 23, 59.

Many thanks, Lady-friend,

I'm in the vein, and have made up my mind—if God does not forsake me altogether—not to come and see you before I can hand you over the red portfolio completely full. That is my wish; whether it can be fulfilled, I don't know. For I am aware enough how easily one may be put out of tune with such fastidious plans, and believe I owe my present good working-mood merely to the most desperate dudgeon that directly preceded it. What I wrote you about Herwegh, on that occasion, must have been very confused: I had a suspicion of it when I sent the letter off, and have since read H.'s article once more through;

which has shewn me that in my letter I must really have meant someone other than H. Let's drop that, and return to Shakespeare's "wagging of beards" [*Coriol.* ii. 1]. This and the "not so much brain as ear-wax" [*Troil. & Cres.* v. 1] are the kind of quips I find so drastic in Sh. ; and only a man to whom the hollowness of the world is so omnipresent could coin them so originally.

Yet we'll drop that too, for even there our own subjective frame of mind may be too strong a co-efficient. The main thing I wanted to tell you, is that I flatter myself I shall be able to end the composition of my act as if by storm now ; the whole vivid thing was revealed to me yesterday as in a lightning-flash. I'm sure you will be pleased at this cause of my staying at home, and wish me good luck on my courageous disobedience to your invitation. There is also a morsel of gourmandry in it : for I feel as if I must be unutterably well of a sudden, once the Tristan is finished : so, perceiving that I can arrive at a feeling of wellbeing no other way, I mean to ensure it by this sleight of hand. Everything eggs me on. My abode is growing more and more impossible. Pianos are closing in around me, strangers on strangers, shoulder-shruggings of mine host : already I've bid sum upon sum to guarantee myself the needful non-disturbance, and still my anxious spirit sees itself once more a wandering Latona ; who nowhere found a spot to bear Apollo on, till Zeus bade the island of Delos arise from the sea for her. (In parenthesis : fables have this advantage, that one always comes to something in their end ; in real life the island stays snugly tucked under the sea,—or at Mariafeld [the Willes' place]—in short, somewhere away !) Yes, my child, folk make things hard for me, and I've no easy time ; in return, there's but *one* being I can so much as allow to praise my Tristan to me, and that one—doesn't need to. Therefore no one shall even say me

"Bravo!" And—you are right: it really is a worthier life, in this exile of mine, than over there [at Leipzig?]; merely you are wrong about the 7–8 years, since it already has entered the 11th. I didn't mean to brag of that, however, but simply to cite Härtels as another cogent reason for my work. Their pouts would have left me indifferent, but their instant joy over the first manuscript instalment of the 3rd act has moved me so—it had come to their ears that I meant to break off for a long while again [cf. pp. 129-30]—so!—so that if you see me come to you, it will only be with the red portfolio, or—in despair. Choose you!—I hope for the red portfolio—: but I still require a little patience; it won't go fast. *If* it but *goes!*

This morning bon Dieu made a personal tour of the streets. It was Corpus Christi day; the whole town processed before the empty houses, led by the priests, who had gone the length of donning golden nightgowns. However, the file of Capuchin monks had a most moving effect: in the midst of that unspeakably repulsive tinsel-comedy of religion, all at once this earnest-melancholy file. By good luck, I did not see them too close; yet I had come across a pair of plain but reverend physiognomies under the capuchin here before; and the crucifix always enthrals me. Last evening, so soon as the sly-boots knew by the wind that to-day we should have fine weather, all the children in the churches had to pray for it; so this wonderful cloudless morn itself was nothing but a comedy. I drank my fill of it, all the same, and knew well that the weather had strictly been made for myself: I also know who made it. Many thanks!—

Are you cross at my not coming? Rather ought you not to see Lucerne for once yourself at last in lovely weather? To come hither, is forbidden to nobody!—

Many kind greetings to Cousin Wesendonck, Auntkin

and Unclekin! Keep me in all of your hearts, and I'll be
right industrious.—Adio!

Your

R. W.

Do, please, look in at the art-shop opposite the Post:
they had a stock of those big gold pens years ago; perhaps
there's still one left.

81.

Lucerne, July 1, 59.

And how goes it with Freundin?—My mood has been a
little oppressed by the weather these last few days: still, it
keeps aloft on the whole. The work is thriving, and I've
a very odd feeling about it. Once I mentioned to you
those Hindu women who leap into the odorous sea of
flames [see p. 81, and cf. Isolde's last words]. Surprising, how odours
recall the past so vividly. On my walk the other day a
sudden gush of rose-scent burst upon me: sideways stood
a little garden, where the roses were just in full bloom. That
recalled my last enjoying of the Asyl garden: never, as then,
have I so concerned myself with roses. Every morning I
plucked one, and set it in a glass beside my work: I knew
I was taking farewell of the garden. With that feeling this
odour has wholly inwoven: summer-heat, summer-sun, scent
of roses, and—parting. Thus I then sketched the music
for my second act.

What surrounded me then with such presence, such all
but intoxicant presence, now lives anew as if in dream,—
summer, sun, rose-scent, and—parting. Yet the heartache,
the anguish is gone: all is transfigured. That is the mood
in which I hope to bring my third act to a close now.
Nothing can sorely afflict me, nothing cast me down: my
existence is so utterly un-chained by Space and Time. I
know that I shall live as long as I have work to do: so I

don't worry my head about life, but go on working. When
that comes to end, I shall know myself safe indeed; so
I really am cheerful.—

Would that you also were !

May I count on a line soon?

82.

Lucerne, July 9, 59.

It was truly kind of you, dear Child, to send me your
news for once, and I'll see what I can find to tell you in
reply. The return of the cousin [Otto] by now will certainly
have also brought you many a piece of news, and gladly
would I profit a little myself of his reports on my birthplace
and youthful home [Leipzig]. No doubt he went to Dresden
too ? Lohengrin he would miss there : it is not to come
out, as I hear, till the second half of this month.

Meanwhile I have gone through much. First and fore-
most :—a week ago to-day I moved, i.e. they had me moved,
and transported me to No. 7 on the 2nd floor of the
" Ur-Hotel," in the " Independence "—Indépendance. I feel
somewhat degraded, pretty much as Count Giulay after
Magenta ; to my agreeable big salon in the " Dependence "
even my thoughts dare fly no more. The unkindest cut
of all, though, was my having to renounce my Margravine
[the " marquee," see p. 127]: the republican monster of a landlord
forbade my further intercourse with her. So it's all up
with my beautiful morning hour at the open window : a
closed shutter bars me from the sun, and at a pinch I can
imagine myself sitting in gaol. There you see that I'm
not so spoilt and pampered yet, as some folk would like
to cry out. I take it in good part, however, as my fellow-
prisoners, Tristan and Isolde, are soon to feel quite free ;
and so I now renounce *together* with them, *together* with
them to get free. Mostly every other day I am at least

happy in my work: in between I usually have a less good day, as the good day always makes me overweening, and then I overtax myself.—This time I don't feel that old dread lest I should die before the last note: on the contrary, I'm so certain of finishing, that the day before yesterday I even made a folk-song of it on my ride:

> "Im Schweizerhof zu Luzern,
> von Heim und Haus weit und fern—
> da starben Tristan und Isolde,
> so traurig er, und sie so holde:
> sie starben frei, sie starben gern,
> im Schweizerhof zu Luzern—
> gehalten von Herrn
> Oberst Seegessern"—

Sung to a folk-tune, I assure you it goes quite well: in the evening I sang it to Vreneli.* I'd make it a present to mine host if he hadn't forbidden me the Margravine.— But Vreneli is my guardian angel; she leaves no crafty stone unturned, to keep unquiet neighbours off me; children are not allowed in all the étage. Joseph, also, has padded the door to the adjoining chamber with a mattress, and hung one of my curtains over it; which gives my room quite a stately theatrical air. As soon as I've finished my work, though, the heaviest ground of my claims on Abode will have vanished. In Paris I shall hide my diminished head in a chambre garni, and calmly let Fate pass over me; only when I have my travails in view, do I trouble for a superfine cradle. Moreover, I am growing more and more conscious of my position in life, and the greatest retrench- ment now becomes a duty. Perhaps I shall sell my lovely indoor-clothes as well then: you can let me know, if you

---

* Verena Weitmann, who entered Wagner's service hereafter at Munich and Tribschen. [The naive flavour of the lines would be destroyed by a needless attempt to translate them.—Tr.]

want to have any of them for your future cabinet of curiosities.—Such are the reductive thoughts, you see, that come to me in my present house of degradation!—Never mind: it's nearly all over with Tristan, and Isolde, I fancy, will also have given up the ghost this month. Then I shall throw the pair of them and myself into Härtel's arms.

Otherwise I know absolutely nothing of the world! Not a creature bothers about me, and that's really beginning to put me in good humour. God, how incredibly much one can do without! Only your company, my child, I forgo most unwillingly: once and for all, I know nobody to whom I unbosom myself so gladly. With men it can't even be attempted: at bottom, their only concern—for all their friendship—is never to come out of their shell, to stick to their private opinion, and let themselves be touched as little as possible. It strictly is so: the male lives on himself. But when I think how many good things you have enticed from me already, I can only rejoice at your having never had the least intention to, yet drawing out the best that was in me. How it delighted me, that I introduced S. Bach to you the other day! Never had he given such delight to myself, and never had I felt so nigh him. But a thing like that doesn't occur to me when alone. When I have music-ed with Liszt, it has been something quite different; it was music-ing, and technique and Art with a capital played a big rôle: there's always some hitch between men. But, dull as I perhaps appeared to you the last time at Lucerne, yet our being together has borne me good fruit—as you now may gather from my imperturbable mood for work. Is that no proof that I am grateful to you? and that as a genuine friend? Don't be surprised, if you don't get rid of me so soon yet! True, the fine weather is helping too. Even if one has to stay shut indoors the whole day, one knows that it's bright and fair outside, and the evening pertains to enjoyment. If it is hot, still the very breeze that sets the sky so clear, is sweet and comforting. Upon me it has quite a directly perceptible influence : a little agitating, but agreeable. Moreover, it's so beautiful to have the body's needs grow less and less ; I'm living on next to nothing but air now, and merely my heart bleeds at having to pay my landlord just as much for "board" as if I had to stock an English stomach.—

For all that, my relish for the gay preponderates. Just think : while working out the herdsman's merry welcome of Isolde's ship the other day, there suddenly occurs to me a still more jubilant melodic strain, almost heroically jubilant, and yet quite popular in cut. I was on the point of turning the whole thing inside out, when I at last discovered that this melody does not belong to Tristan's herdsman, but is Siegfried's to the life. I at once looked up the closing verses of Siegfried with Brünnhilde, and saw that my melody belongs to the words :

"Sie ist mir ewig,
    ist mir immer,
        Erb' und Eigen,
            Ein' und All'"—etc.

That will have an incredibly dauntless and jubilant air.— If at a whiff I was back in my Siegfried, ought I not still to believe in my life, then, in my—holding out ?—

Your having found such pleasure in Köppen's book [cf. p. 53] shews me how well you know how to read : *I* was provoked by so much in the book because I could not stop myself from reflecting how difficult it must make a clear knowledge of Buddha's doctrine to others ; so I'm glad you were not thrown off the scent. Yes, child, that is a view of the world compared wherewith all other dogmas must surely look parochial and petty ! The philosopher with his broadest thought, the explorer of Nature with

his most extensive deductions, the artist with his most
transcendent fantasies, the man with the widest heart for
all that breathes and suffers,—all find in this wondrous,
this quite incomparable world-myth a home the least confined, and in it their whole full selves again.—

Tell me, now that you have been dwelling there, how
our lordly European New-world looks to you? Do you
not find in it either the cruelest running to seed, or—the
very crudest rudiments of an evolution which blossomed
with that noble ur-folk long ago?—Railroads,—civic moralisa-
tion! O! O!——

The repellent effects of our historic Present I can mostly
ward off me in no other way than by a quickening drink
at that sacred wellspring of the Ganges: one draught there-
out, and the whole thing shrivels to the traffic of an ant-
hill. Within there, deep within there, is the world: not
there outside, where only madness reigns!—Well done,
then, even Köppen has not harmed you!—

And so we are soon to have peace, after all. Surely
the Cousin at Leipzig brought the armistice about? Perhaps
this peace may prove somewhat rotten—but: "who, then,
is happy?"—one must remind oneself of that again. In
any case Härtels will have helped much towards it, so as
to be able to pay me twice the fee [*Ring?*] upon prospects
improving. I really meant to charge the Cousin with some
such commission for Leipzig; now he seems to have guessed
it. Compliment him on that.—

And next time we three are together, I still have a
number of tales from my youth to relate to you; but they
won't work loose until we are together. Till then, have
all of you good cheer; praise the Most-gloriously-perfect
[p. 103], and keep a corner in your hearts for—my
Insignificance.

83.

[Mid-July 1859.]

Worse than in my work now, it can never have gone at Solferino ; now that those folk are putting a stop to the bloodshed, I'm pushing it on. I'm making a terrible clearance ; to-day I've struck Melot and Kurwenal dead, too. If you wish for a sight of the battle-field, you'd best come before everyone's buried.

A thousand greetings.

Your

R. W.

84.

Lucerne, July 24, evening.

I've read the beautiful fairy-tale out to the Erard : * it assured me by a doubly fine tone that it had understood it well !—

The same day you received my sketches [*Tristan*] ; so it was a case of exchange-of-matter ! I am obsessed by my work now, and regard it as a moral victory over myself if I can pause and abandon one page for the day. How ever shall I feel when I've ended ? I have still some 35 pages of the full score to do : in 12 days I expect to get through with them ; how ever shall I feel then ? I fancy, somewhat fagged at first ; even to-day my head's quite dizzy. And ah, how I depend on the weather ! If the air is light and free, you can do anything with me, the same as when one's fond of me ; contrariwise, if the atmosphere weighs on me, I can stoutly rebel, at utmost, but the beautiful comes hard.

I lack elbow-room. God, how the world is closing ever

---

* Presumably that called " The Swan " ; see pp. 57 and 334.—Tr.

tighter on me! How much easier might everything be made for me.

No matter, we'll console ourselves ; and after all, I know no one with whom I'd exchange.

—My salutations to Cleobis and Biton ; those were the names, if I mistake not, of your two good mother's-sons in Argos ? They're old acquaintances of mine. What a pity the Greeks were such a long way behind us ! There's absolutely nothing Abstract in their religion : 'tis nothing but a matchlessly luxuriant world of myths, and all of them so plastic and pregnant that one can never forget their shapes again : and whoso fathoms them aright, finds the deepest world-view sunk therein. But, they just made no dogmatic system of them ; they poesied and portrayed. Entire artists, profound and genial ! Glorious folk !—

Ah, how it revolts me when I look thence to our Europe ! And Paris ?—It will be a clear case of taking good care—to isolate oneself and keep alone !—

About the finished Tristan [July 16] another day.

It would be fine if we still could combine a Pilatus ascent ; farther than that I suppose I shan't get, with my " recreation-trips." I'll write you two best children of man exactly when I think to put the last stroke of my pen to the partitur. If it's possible then, do come : *alone* I won't go up Pilatus. And then we'll also plan our farewell dinner at the Villa (Franca) Wesendonck. I expect to have finished—as said—the end of the first week in August.

And now, good God protect you, and all your house, and the dépendance [Asyl] into the bargain ! Best thanks for all kindness and love, and especially for the fir-tale [?].

Hearty greetings to the cousin, niece and nephew !

Your

R. W.

85.

Lucerne, [Thursday,] Aug. 4, 59.

Before work a hurried pair of words to the dear students of the Herr Professor :

I must and will finish by Saturday, out of sheer curiosity to know how I feel then. Only, do not be cross if you find me somewhat slack : that really can't be altered. But I count on your rewarding me by arriving betimes Saturday evening ; I've somebody here [Felix Draeseke] whom I play nothing to, but keep consoling with that prospect. The Pilatus shall depend on the weather then, and I fancy it will be good, so that we can undertake the ascent Sunday afternoon. For the rest, let things abide by my suggestion, which you have so kindly adopted. Baumgartner won't slip through our fingers ; he is visiting me here now, and will be back in Zurich next week.—For my billeting I shall thank the excellent Cousin with clarion tongue. Meantime I have to worry around with the French envoy, who refuses to viser my passport once more. My vexation at this shamefully defenceless plight towards the world, which people leave me in so heedlessly, is only equalled by another, that I still can vex myself at such a thing.—

In other ways, too, I have been somewhat agitated of late, and therefore prevailed on myself—not to write to you awhile, so as to leave you nicely undisturbed ! I may tell you thus much, however, that I shall depart from Switzerland with great, almost solemn emotion now. Yet, as Fate wills ! I have lived through enough, to have left life behind me ; I will neither ordain nor prepare for aught in it again : nothing has sense any longer.—

But—three days more, and—Tristan und Isolde will be ready. What would one more ?—

A thousand thanks to the tiny weeny lady-student for

her charming notions; may it do her good hereafter, to
remember her girlhood's gardening!—

Fare you well, and give Wesendonck my very kindest
regards. If you don't mean to turn your backs upon me of
a sudden, I shall hope to see you Saturday.

Your

R. W.

86.

Lucerne, [Monday,] Aug. 8, 59.

Silly man that I am, I forgot one petition.* Tell me,
best child, would you have the great kindness to procure
me a pretty present for Vreneli right speedily? I believe
it will afford her more delight than a gift of money. Perhaps
a gown—wool and silk? I don't limit you in price: she
shall have a good present, cost what it may.—

But you would have to see to it at once, so that I might
receive it as early as Wednesday. If it's a nuisance to you,
as I shouldn't be surprised, merely tell me so.—

And the Willes, by *all* means invite them for Friday:
that is, if it will please them to come. I should like to see
Semper too; but Herwegh would shoot himself then.
Wille . . . will make me a deal of commotion among my
acquaintances; but what does that concern you two?—Merely
try and reserve me a room above the envoy: your influence
will certainly settle that difficulty [about the pass?—see p. 160]. It
is quite in keeping with the amiable character of the pair
of you, to offer me a sojourn in your house this time again;
it is for me to be discreet, however, and keep from your
necks the burden and embarrassment that might arise from
a prolonged stay.

---

* Evidently the Wesendoncks had been over to Lucerne on the 6th,
as invited, to celebrate the completion of the *Tristan und Isolde* full score—
with a little champagne, one might infer from the end of this letter.—Tr.

Since the day before yesterday, I am very displeased with myself; I have much to be ashamed of, and think of chicaning myself a little for it.

One memory will abide with me, however, and that will ever shew itself as heartiest and tenderest thanks !

A thousand greetings.

R. W.

87.

Lucerne, Aug. 11, 59.

Freundin,

Only in reliance on an indulgence possible almost to no one but yourself, did I pluck up courage to cause you the incredible upset, announcement whereof I committed to-day to the telegraph. Listen, please ! A departure from your house direct for Paris is not feasible to me ; much as I dread it, I also have no reason to assume as yet that every obstacle will be removed so quickly. Under various impressions—why deny it ?—I'm out of humour ; the chief cause of which, in any case, is bodily indisposition. Should I, then, let the parting hours be spoilt for me ? a parting whereto nothing urges me for days to come ? I really was afraid of it. And so I came by the resolve to refresh myself with mountain-air first, for the next few days ; I mean to go aloft, and think of arriving at Rigi-Kaltbad tomorrow (Friday) evening, when I shall see if I can tolerate a few days there. You shall hear from me thence. Then if I fix on a definite date of departure, I will let you know ; and although I cannot venture to insist on the former project being carried out, yet I hope to bring you a somewhat better-mannered parting guest into the house then, than you would have had to entertain tomorrow.

You are too good to me, and I repay it with the constant disturbance I cause you. I almost ought to have spared you the trouble about the Rütli [farewell gathering ?] from the outset ; but my own trouble, about leaving you with a good impression at parting, has also to be considered : I sacrifice yours to mine.

If you remain friends with me, please send me the Palleske [*Schiller*, cf. p. 102] too : sent as companion to me by you, he ought to be a firstrate guide aloft.

A thousand hearty greetings.

Tell me if you forgive me !

R. W.

88.

Lucerne, Aug. 16, 59.

So ! after the tension of work I have reached a point of recreation, at a glance to scrutinise the world that is to help me farther. It has a strange enough look to me, and appears to forbid me clean everything ; so that I ask myself seriously, what I still am to do in it ?—

Freundin, I *must* be brief hereon ; and you yourself lately made it my bounden duty to be a little careful in my utterances.* Will you take it as a sign of inner peace and harmony, if I tell you that I'm now resolved to yield myself quite passive to my destiny, lay my hands in my lap, and simply wait sans bestirring myself till people fash their heads about me ?—Enough ; I'm back in the Schweizerhof, as my last sanctuary, and mean to sit here till—they throw me out. My own free-will has nothing to do with it : there simply is nothing else left for me.

I enjoy good repute here, and think of committing myself to its agreeable shelter.—When congratulating Myrrha the

---

* See the dots after François Wille's name in the letter of August 8. Presumably this allusion explains the sudden cancelling of the " farewell dinner," on Wagner's side. No rupture, however, was caused thereby, for we find him thanking Otto in his first letter from Paris (Sept. 17) for " the four bright days on your hospitable hill " ; see *Letters to Otto Wesendonck.* —Tr.

day before yesterday, I telegraphed also to Liszt, telling him that I should wait for him *here*. Instead of his answer, I received a letter yesterday from Princess Marie [Wittgenstein], in which she announced her betrothal to a young Prince Hohenlohe, and—in her grief at having to quit the Altenburg so soon—begged me to accord her Liszt's unbroken presence till October (her wedding). So I'm now even robbed of the pleasant excuse of waiting for my friend here.—Ed. Devrient tells me, in his last letter, that he has something else to do than make a rendezvous with me.—

A peep into the Kaltbad on the Rigi convinced me that a stay there was not to be dreamt of; bad weather made the Rigi revival complete. In endurable humour, though semi-despair—since I found as good as no room *here* at all—the day before yesterday I made up my mind to go up Pilatus instead, at least to be able to give you exact information about this excursion in future. It is very beautiful, very handy, and Pilatus himself merits great propaganda. Returned here yesterday, I found letters that reduced me to a condition of abandoning every step towards self-help, and retiring for an unlimited period into a little chamber of the Schweizerhof. My piano remains nicely packed in the shed; but they have unpacked the divan for me, and also the child's cushion. So I'll follow your advice for once, and wait to see what will turn up.—Will that content you?—It ought to delight you, to hear that I'm letting the halm lie around me so coolly; my temper is quite excellent amid it all.

Tell me what the diplomats are doing. Accept a thousand thanks for your last indulgence and the Zwieback of to-day.

Many kind wishes from Your

R. W.

89.

Whatever can have put it into your head, Child, to
see, or wish to see in me a "wise man"? Am I not the
maddest subject one can possibly conceive? Meted with
the measure of a wise man, I must appear downright
criminal; and just because I know so much and many a
thing, and in particular, that Wisdom is so excellent and
wishable. But that, in return, gives me Humour, which
helps me over abysses the wisest doesn't even espy. And
then, you see, I'm a poet, and—what is far worse—a
musician. Now think of my music, with its tenuous,
mysteriously-fluent juices, that soak through the subtilest
pores of sensation to the very marrow of life ; there to over-
whelm all that bears itself the least like prudence or timorous
self-preservation ; to flood away all savour of the feint
of Personality, and leave but a sublime wistful sigh of
avowal of syncope :—then say, how *could* I ever be a wise
man, if I'm entirely at home in nothing but such raving
madness?

But I will tell you something. To the temple at Delphi
trooped princes and peoples from the uttermost ends of the
world, to get their fortunes told them. The priests were
the Wise who doled them out those revelations ; but the
priests themselves had first to gain them from the Pythia,
when she broke into a paroxysmal ecstasy on her tripod of
inspiration and wondrously groaned forth the god's own
oracles, which the wise priests merely had to transpose into
the world's vernacular.—I fancy, whoso once has sat upon
that tripod, can become a priest no more: he has stood in
the immediate presence of the god.—

Furthermore: reflect that Dante met his seldom-and-
soft-speaking wise men, not in Paradise, but at a shady
halfway place twixt Heaven and Hell. On the cross itself

tho', the Redeemer cried to the poor thief: This day shalt
thou be with me in Paradise.—

You see, you can't get over me: I'm of an arrant cunning,
and terrible reserves of mythology are stowed in my head.
If you will grant me that, I'll also grant you, that you—are
right; and still more: that it costs me no effort whatever
to grant that you're right, for whenever I catch myself in
that which you bring so concernedly home to me, I myself
am so cross and displeased with myself, that the only thing
I wince at then, is the having others rub my self-reproaches
into me as if they doubted my already feeling them. And
yet, you dear child, 'tis my final and fairest refreshment,
when I learn that all these inner processes of mine are so
delicately sensed by another.—Won't you be content with
me? Are you?—

Only remember how rarely you so much as see me
now, and how hard it is at those infrequent epochs to
be exactly what one might be. Indeed it is difficult now,
for— — — — — — —

So autumn has come down on us quickly; after a raw
and ruined Spring a short-lived blast of summer, and now—.
How the days draw in already! It all is truly like a dream.
A few days back the air was even nipping: every good
angel seemed flown. A little after-warmth has put in an
appearance, though: I enjoy it as a convalescent, yet as
one who must still take some care of himself. I'm boundlessly
idle, which perhaps may come—as I told my young friend
[F. Draeseke] the other day—from the great maturity at
which my talent has arrived.* I have received proofs for
correction [*Tristan* score], and stare at them aimlessly.
Possibly it is the catarrhal fever to which I last succumbed,
that has left me in this state: my nerves will not recover

---

* The little joke is not condensable in English, "*faul*" meaning both
" idle " and " rotten," therefore the next stage after *ripeness* of a fruit.—Tr.

quite, as yet ; perhaps it's the fault of the wind. Vreneli tells me that 4 persons in the hotel are already down with nervous fever. Well, I suppose I am safe against that.—

As for the rest, I've arranged my little room quite skilfully, so that you would be surprised at it, if you were to look in. I've even made it possible to find a place for the piano : so it's on its legs once more.—

Moreover, I already feel a shade more upright and respectable again : they sent me yesterday my passport visé.—Further, it's settled that I have no direct vertigo, but merely a sympathetic. That I found out again on Pilatus, where I looked quite calmly down into the deepest chasm at my feet, but was suddenly seized with a frenzy of terror when I looked at my guide, who had gone, like myself, to the brink of the precipice ; thus I really am not so concerned for myself, as for one who depends on me. On the other hand, I never can think without positive faintness of how my negligence was once to blame for the death of that dear little parrot, so touchingly attached to me, which I lost at Zurich before making your acquaintance.*—

Children ! Children ! I think the dear God will have mercy upon me one day.—Beg Wesendonck, also, not to be cross with me,† and think kindly yourself of

Your

R. W.

---

* See letter of February 1851 to Uhlig, also *Life* iii, 145–6.—Tr.

† Apparently for refusing the offer of a loan, as the German editor of the *Letters to Otto Wesendonck* mentions (without otherwise specifying) a letter of even date to that effect ; possibly the refusal was contained in an enclosure to *this* letter itself, and may explain the aposiopesis on p. 166. On the 28th Wagner changes his mind, however, in consequence of the failure of his negotiations with the Härtels for sale of the *Ring*, and writes to Otto that he is prepared " to do a little *business* with him "; a proposal willingly accepted by Herr Wesendonck, though with purely friendly intent.—Tr.

90.

Lucerne, Aug. 27, 59.

Herewith I send you Don Felix [Draeseke], who has kept me faithful company till now.   He's bringing you the Schiller, much of which (as you may easily imagine) has deeply affected me.   Your note of to-day was very satirical (*spöttisch*) to be sure, but still it rejoiced me, as testifying to your high spirits.   I feel in quite passable health these few days ; the landlord at Brunnen declared he had never seen me looking so well, as now.   A pleasantly confident mood has inspired me with projects,* about which I perhaps shall soon give [you] to decide whether they're monstrous or perfectly natural.   We shall see.—Don Felix pronounces the third act of the Tristan still finer than the second.   I entreat you to give him a good dressing for that.   Am I to tolerate that sort of thing ?

I have heard nothing new from the " world," and am still in the thick of the " wood."   There flit all kinds of Nibelungs and sleeping Valkyries.   I have promised Don Felix some Wotan this morning, as a last farewell ; he shall report to you how it turns out.†

---

* Clearly those referred to in the last note and concerning a purchase of the *Ring* by Otto.—Tr.

† It is just possible that this may imply the commencement of the ' composition-draft' of act iii *Siegfried*, the exact date whereof has not as yet been ascertained.   In favour of that supposition might be adduced the allusion to "sleeping Valkyries," the inference that Frau Wesendonck had not hitherto heard how *this* music "turned out," and the references to act iii toward the end of the letter of Sept. 24 (p. 177) and in that of Oct. 25 to Otto.   Against, we have " Wotan " where we should have expected " the Wanderer," the " Nibelungs " who do appear in act ii (scoring of which may alternatively have been commenced), and the contrast of "world" with "wood" so frequent in the first two acts.   No doubt it is a great temptation, to make that superb invocation of Erda directly succeed the last touch to the *Tristan* score, i.e. after an interval of barely three weeks ; but, all things considered, we must resist it until we have more definite data to go upon.—Tr.

To your cow you must soon add a lamb, and if possible, a pretty goat as well. That absolutely must be.—Yesterday I feared Vreneli was sickening for the nervous fever, and wanted to take energetic steps against it ; but she's better to-day. I think I shan't catch it myself, although it is now epidemic here.—Greet your Elves-hill and all that live thereon, and remember me !

Your

R. W.

PARIS LETTERS

SEPTEMBER 1859 *TO JANUARY* 1862

(Including four from Vienna)

❉ ❉ ❉

91.

"Ich sauge nur die Süssigkeit,
Das Gift, das lass' ich drin." †

A careless child thus bantered me some years ago : she has tasted since the bane of Care. But the little bee thrust in her sting, to boot; 'twas the spur to the best and noblest. She left it buried in my soul ; and was the bane so bad?—

Lady-friend, it is the latest years of my life that really have matured me to a man ; I feel at perfect harmony with myself, and whenever the True is at stake my will stands firm and fast. As for material life, I cheerfully allow myself to be guided by my instinct : something higher is meant with me, than the mere value of my personality. This knowledge is so rooted in me, that with a smile I scarcely ask myself at times an I will a thing or no ; that care is taken by the curious genie whom I serve for this remainder of my life, and who intends me to finish what only I can bring about.

Deep calm, then, is within me : the surging of the surface waves has nothing to do with my channel. I am—what I can be !—thanks, Freundin, to you.—

---

* Somewhere about a week after letter 90 Wagner had gone to the Wesendoncks for those "four bright days" adduced in my note to p. 163, and then set forth at once for Paris; where he has arrived by Sept. 12, and whence he writes to Otto Sept. 17—see *Letters to O. Wk.*—Tr.

† "I sip alone the honey, leave the bane behind."—Tr.

Now what will you say, when you hear I'm hard at work already?—

The young man who has made a translation of the Tannhäuser [Challemel?] gave it me to look through. After a fleeting glance I let it fall, and told myself: Impossible! Therewith a heavy load was shaken off, namely the thought of a French Tannhäuser, and I breathed anew. Yet that was only my person: the other, my dæmon—my genius?—said to me: "Thou seest how incapable this Frenchman is— or any one else, for that matter—of translating thy poem ; consequently thou'lt simply prevent thy work being given in France at all. But how when thou art dead, and thy works at last commence to live? How, when one has not to ask thy consent, but produces thy Tannhäuser in just such another translation as lies before thee and has been wreaked already on the noblest German poems (Faust for instance) with just as little understanding?" Ah, child! such a possible immortality in prospectu is a dæmon of peculiar sort, and lands us in the selfsame cares that fasten a mother and father to the welfare of their children far beyond their own term of life. I alone can contribute to a perfectly good translation of my works : therefore a duty lies in it I cannot forfend. So I seat myself with my young poet every morning, go over verse by verse, word after word, syllable by syllable ; seek with him, often by the hour, for the best turn of speech, the right word ; sing it to him, and make him thus clairvoyant to a world that hitherto was wholly shut to him. Well, his zeal rejoices me, his rising enthusiasm, his frank confession of his previous blindness,— and—we shall see! At least I know I'm providing for the future of my child as well as I am able!—

Otherwise I haven't gone much about as yet. My life stays the same, at Lucerne or in Paris. The outer rind can alter nothing in me : and just that pleases me.—

Sept. 24.

My Frenchman came [i.e. where the letter broke off]; in defiance
of a little feverishness, I worked somewhat too ardently with
him, and—he left me very tired : to-day I awoke to the
light with a strong catarrhal fever. Your and Wesendonck's
letter has delighted me; give him my hearty thanks! That
folk should be seeking me now that I've gone, is quite in
order : the world only seeks one when it suits it; as soon
as I have gone completely, folk will probably seek me the
most. Father Heim must have made quite an excellent
Posa [*Don Carlos*]; the kind-heartedness of such adherents
is always a joy, even though one can't suppress a smile at
indissoluble misunderstandings. I have seen nothing at all
of Bülow's letter on Tristan.* A Countess Charnacé, daughter
of Madame A., had received word from her mother, and
invited me to tea : I have been unable to go as yet ; now
the young lady is highly commended to me from Berlin
[by Bülow]. A more important point at present is that
of my abode ; for it was to " abide " somewhere again, that I
came to Paris. For the nonce I'm merely in a logis garni :
I still am seeking an unfurnished house. But, together with
the abode, I have yet another weighty " settlement " to think
of. Lady-friend, I have searched my heart, and determined
to carry out my resolution with the highest moral force that
I have gained ; yet I need a few easements towards it.
I am looking forward with delight to the uncommonly
clever, good and loving little dog [Fips] you once sent into
my home from your sickbed ; it will go for walks with me
once more, and when I come home after tiresome business
it will run like a friend to accost me. But please now

---

* Hans von Bülow had privately written to Brendel a most glowing
eulogy of the *Tristan* music; Brendel indiscreetly published the letter in
the *Neue Zeitschrift*, and a Dr. Zeller maliciously pounced upon it for his
Blätter für Musik—all in September.—Tr.

procure me another good house-sprite, select me a servant; you know what need I thus express. Your present porter's kind face pleased me much : what has become of his predecessor, who was such a favourite in the house? Without hurting your own interests too much, could you not effect an arrangement in my favour there? I want to make my household as congenial to me as possible : I would rather not fix anything about the female part of it, however; otherwise I should already have opened the Parisian colony to Vreneli. I insist upon my wife's picking out and bringing with her a girl of education, partly to attend to her, partly to keep her company. Beyond that, I have a cook to engage, for whom Madame Herold [widow of the composer] is going to look out. Accordingly the man-servant would have as his duties the tidying of the rooms (which the garçon always does in Paris), cleaning of silver etc., waiting at table, running on errands, and further, my valeting, especially at the bath ; on journeys he would accompany me, and look after my luggage. These attentions I greatly lack : looking after such things myself I always bustle far too much, get uselessly excited, catch cold, and so on. And above all : I so need a pleasant, sympathetic human soul about me, were it only as my servant.—

Now then : lend a kind ear to this plea. The man could enter *any moment.*—So it's a case of providing a Zwieback once more, and a big one this time !—

As for my outward lot, I am sure it will shape quite endurably. Upon that side I'm still on the ascending plane now ; and latterly it seems as if the ascent would even be fairly rapid,—at least, according to a conversation yesterday with the director of the Théâtre lyrique (a really pleasant, decent sort of man), it lies in my own hands how soon I will make even a Paris fortune. I shan't mind, though, if everything will only serve to keep me in good trim this

winter, so that I may visit my dear Switzerland next Spring ;
for there alone can Siegfried wake Brünnhilde,—in Paris
it would scarcely do, you know.—From Carlsruhe I'm
expecting a very circumstantial answer very soon, on many
points : I insist upon everything being taken very strictly
there. I may thereby place those gentry in embarrassment
enough ; but it can't be helped,—the fruit of Tristan is
no easy one to pluck.

How good it would be of you, children, if you
sent me a photograph of the Green Hill : that was indeed
a capital idea ! I still regret not having sent you my
Venetian palace.

I have much more [to tell you] concerning what we lately
spoke about ; but I'll save it for another time. To Frau Wille
I really will write soon : we could not see each other this
time ; but I'll offer her amends.—Now let me exorcise my
fever for good and all by rest and reading (Plutarch). I
shall hear from you soon again, perhaps even through
Fridolin.* Kindest wishes to cousin and children, deepest
obligation to Karl, and faithfulest love to Lady-friend !—

Richard Wagner.

92.

Paris, Oct. 10, 59.

In expectation of speedy good news of Karl's condition,†
I'll chatter all I can, dear Child, for your distraction.

To-day I've had a most astonishing adventure. I inquire
at a custom-office after my goods that have come from
Lucerne : the packages were on the books, but not my
name. I produce my letter of advice, and tell my name ;
then one of the officials rises : " Je connais bien Mr. Richard

---

* The man-servant above referred to, " der treue Knecht " [" faithful
hind "].

† Oct. 5 : " You make me anxious too, with your news of Karl's
illness"—*Letters to Otto Wesendonck.*—Tr.

Wagner, puisque j'ai son médaillon suspendu sur mon piano
et je suis son plus ardent admirateur." " Quoi ? " " Ne
soyez pas surpris de rencontrer à la douane de Paris un homme
capable de goûter les incomparables beautés de vos partitions,
que j'ai étudiées toutes " etc.*

It was all like a dream. An enthusiast at the Douane,
just as I was expecting such great difficulties with the
receipt of my furniture ! The good fellow leapt, and ran,
and helped me : he himself had to inspect. He has a wife
who plays the piano very well ; for himself, he has literary
aspirations, and meanwhile earns a living by his present
berth. He told me of a fairly wide circle which has formed
itself exclusively through spread of an acquaintance with
my works. As he doesn't understand German, I replied
that I could not conceive his taking pleasure in music
that depended so entirely on the poetry and expression of
the verse. He : Just because it tallied so precisely with the
diction, was he so easily able to argue out the poetry from
the sound, so that through the music the foreign tongue became
completely understandable. What next ? I shall have to
begin to believe in miracles !—And that at the douane ! I
begged my new friend, who much affected me (you may
imagine how happy I made him), to come and call.—

Do you know, my operas no longer really seem to me
such a paradoxical impossibility in Paris ? Bülow gave me
an introduction to an author-doctor of this place, a Dr.
Gasperini, who—with one of his friends, likewise a thorough
Frenchman—is in exactly the same case as my visitator at

---

* " I know Mr. Richard Wagner well, since his medallion hangs above
my piano, and I am his most ardent admirer." " Eh ? " " Do not be
surprised at meeting in the Paris Custom-house a man capable of
appreciating the incomparable beauties of your scores, all of which I
have studied " etc.—The young customs-officer was Edmond Roche,
subsequently joint translator of *Tannhäuser*, who died of consumption
very soon after that work's performance at the Paris Grand Opéra.—Tr.

the douane. These people play Tannhäuser and Lohengrin
to me, without my having a word to say to it; their not
knowing German doesn't gêne them in the least.—And then
the director of the Théâtre lyrique [Carvalho] announced
himself, to hear my Tannhäuser first-hand. They all assembled, and so I had to victimise myself once more, first
with a minute French explanation of the text (what that
cost me!), then with singing and playing. That made light
dawn on them at last, however, and the impression seemed
quite extraordinary. To me it all is so unheard-of with
these Frenchmen!

On the contrary, I receive none but dismal, sullen news
from Germany. Friend Devrient makes it his chief concern
to maintain his "institute" in smoothest equilibrium, and
keep all unhabitual, transient things aloof from it. A totally
voiceless high soprano, for whom Isolde's music lies too low
throughout, and who consequently can't even screw her mind
up to it yet, is the only one offered me for my heroine,
since she is said to be a good performer otherwise.* And
not one spark of warmth in anything : the only *pro* in all
the enterprise, that I'm to be there myself; but even on
that no definite reply as yet to all my recent queries, as the
Grand Duke still is not get-at-able. So I feel strongly
inclined to break off short : it really is not a genuine article,
and I ought to be able to wait till the genuine trots to my
hand; it's so odious to me, to have to hunt it!—

Yes, children, had you Zurich people, out of thanks for
all the honest sweat I shed there, but gone the length of
building me a middling decent theatre, I should have had
what I want for all time, and need go courting nobody again.
Singers and orchestra, whenever required for the first pro-

---

* According to Dr. Altmann, this was a Frau Hewitz—*not* Malvina
Garrigues, wife of Ludwig Schnorr von Carolsfeld, who ultimately
'created' the rôle of Isolde at Munich.—Tr.

duction of a new work, I should always be able to procure
as I wanted them ; foreign conductors and singers would
have been bidden to these performances, to take a pattern
by the rendering,—and that once called into being, I should
have felt I had cared for all the rest, and might thenceforth
lead a quiet life, without troubling for the further fate of my
works. How fair, how fine, how quite befitting me, would
that have been ! I should have needed then no prince, no
amnesty, no good or evil word : free stood I there, bereft of
all cares for my progeny. And nothing more than a decent,
by no means luxurious stage-building : people ought to be
thoroughly ashamed of themselves ! Don't you think so,
too ? !

Dear Heaven, one's mite of freedom still is all, to make
one's life endurable ! No otherwise can I hold out at all,
and every concession would gnaw at my heart as a deadly
worm. Genuine—or nothing !—Thus too, despite my Parisian
enthusiasts, I continue to live in great and total stillness :
I'm alone indoors almost the whole day long, and positively
every evening. This month I have yet to undergo my
moving-in : there again I've slung much on my neck, and
strictly in quest of nothing but peace for my work. My little
house will be quite pretty, though ; L. is here, and I'll shew
it him tomorrow, so that he may describe it to you.* The
close air and altered mode of life do not agree with me as
yet; I expect I shall have to take to riding again. Once
more I've a terrible number of letters to write ; my best
remain in my head, however : those to you. There I should
find plenty to say, yet nothing but the same old song you've
heard so often, and nothing of which will alter. With

---

* The German edition has "Liszt," but that is quite impossible ;
see Wagner's letters to him of Oct. 20 and Nov. 23 ("You couldn't come
to Paris "). Most probably the "L." stands for Luckemeyer, Frau
Wesendonck's brother.—Tr.

Plutarch's great men I feel pretty much as Schiller (not quite rightly, though) with Winkelried ; about these one might rather say, Thank God I don't belong to them. Ugly, small, violent natures, insatiable—because they have absolutely nothing inside them, and therefore must be ever gulping something from without : a fig for these Great men ! I swear by Schopenhauer's dictum : Not the world-conqueror, but the world-overcomer, is worthy admiration. Please God to keep these "powerful" natures, these Napoleons etc., off my neck !—And what is Eddamüller doing ? * Have you poor Heinrich ? Are you cross with me ? Or do you still retain a scrap of fondness for me ? Do tell me that ! And greet me the cousin,—and fare you well ! A thousand greetings from

Your

R. W.

From the 15th inst. I shall be living at 16 Rue Newton, Champs Elysées.

93.

Paris, Oct. 21, 59.

I found your letter, Lady-friend, at my new dwelling, when I moved in yesterday to sleep my first night there ; the beautiful æsthetic calm in your communications has done me a power of good, although it wellnigh shamed me.

Now let me be silent awhile : 'tis the only consecration open to me now ; I know how much my silence may be worth. Confide in it !—

I am not to have you at the Tristan ! How shall that be possible ?—Let me hear that you're tranquil and well on the fortunate isle [Sicily].—

---

* A characteristic nickname for Prof. E. M. L. Ettmüller, translator of the Eddas ; see *Life* iii, 271-2 and 323. The "poor Heinrich" must be Hartmann von Aue's *Der arme Heinrich* (circa 1200).—Tr.

When I write to you next, it shall be better. For the rest, I'm alone, see no one, and have to do—alas!!—with none but workmen. I am—housing myself once more!— Hearty greetings to Wesendonck. Thanks and fidelity!

Your

R. W.

94.

Paris, Oct. 23, 59.

My precious Child!

The master has seen Death once again since that All-Souls night last year : this time as friend and benefactor.

A while ago I went to pay a call on Berlioz. I found him just returning home in a lamentable condition ; he had just been getting himself electrified, as a last expedient for his ailing nerves. He depicted his torments to me, which, beginning the moment he wakes, increase in mastery every hour. I recognised my sufferings, to the life, and the sources whence they feed to excess ; among which I reckon in particular those incredible nervous exertions, entirely foreign to all other men, while conducting or otherwise eagerly rendering. I knew I should be a still greater sufferer than Berlioz himself, were it not that I expose myself so seldom to those exertions now; for I feel that, even as it is, they act more and more destructively upon me. In Berlioz' case, unfortunately, the stomach already is seriously affected ; and—trivial as it may sound—Schopenhauer is perfectly right in naming among the chief physiological requirements for Genius a good digestion. Through my extraordinary moderation I have mostly kept that requisite in serviceable order ; still, I foresaw in Berlioz' sufferings those probably predestined for myself, and said goodbye to the poor fellow in a frame of general awe.

I had to give my Frenchmen the other half of Tannhäuser ;

the strain was great, a moral bitterness preponderating [*vid. inf.*] ; next day a small error of diet (1 glass of red wine with my bouillon at lunch), and soon afterwards a regular catastrophe, which laid me by the heels in a trice. As I lay full length in utter prostration, seized at the body's very citadel [see p. 190], of a sudden I felt heavenly well. Gone was all chagrin, each trouble, every care, all will and must : profoundest accord of my innermost self with my physical condition ; silence of all life's passions ; repose, entire dropping of the tight-clutched reins of life.—

Two hours did I taste this happiness. Then life returned : the nerves twitched again ; pain, distress, desire, will, came back ; dearth, discomfort—future, confronted me once more. And so I gradually awoke completely, even to troubling about my new—housing.—

Yes! I am housing once more—without faith, without love, without hope, on the bottomless basis of dreamlike indifference !—

So be it then ! One belongs not to oneself ; and whoso thinks it, merely weens it.—

I am not quite well again yet (what people call well!)— yet I'll add one latest piece of information. The dramatic idyll at Carlsruhe has come to full stop and an ending ; Devrient himself has relieved me of the pain of having to refuse his songstress ; herself she has declared herself unequal to Isolde. I suppose it's all for the best : in any case, the whole Tristan adventure is postponed for a fairly long time, and the door stands again wide open for other good chances to throng through. Dream the time sweetly away in your Sicily : you'll miss nothing by it. How I wish you open weather, warmth, invigoration, recovery, from the deepest bottom of my heart ! Your plan is excellent, and cousin Wesendonck to be praised and extolled for it !—

The Green Hill has arrived :—why to me now this peaceful emblem of repose and innocence ? !—

Adieu for to-day.   You shall soon hear more.

A thousand greetings to the Lady-friend !

R. W.

95.

Paris, Oct. 29, 59.

Of one attribute that I have acquired in my art I am now becoming more and more distinctly conscious, since it influences me in life as well.   It is inborn in my nature to swing from one extreme of temper to another : the uttermost rebounds, moreover, can hardly help but touch ; in fact, life's safeguard often lies therein.   At bottom, too, true art has no other subject than the display of these extremes of mood in their ultimate relations to each other : that which alone is worth aiming at here, the weighty crisis (*die wichtige Entscheidung*), can really be won from nothing but these uttermost antitheses.   For art, however, from a material use of these extremes there may easily arise a vicious mannerism, which may degenerate into snatching at outward effect.   In this snare have I seen caught, in particular, the modern French school, with Victor Hugo at its head. . . . .*

Now, I recognise that the peculiar tissue of my music (naturally in exactest agreement with the poetic structure)— what my friends now consider so new and significant †—owes its texture in especial to that intensely touchy feeling which prompts me to mediate and knit together all the nodes of transition between extremes of mood.   My subtlest and deepest art I now might call the art of Transmutation, for my whole artistic woof consists of such transitions : I have

---

* Judging by the next sentence, I take the omission to be that of a reference to a certain someone else's music.—Tr.

† By this time he must have read that letter of Bülow's mentioned p. 175.—Tr.

taken a dislike to the abrupt and harsh; often it is unavoidable and needful, but even then it should not enter without the *Stimmung* being so definitely prepared for a sudden change, as of itself to summon it. My greatest masterpiece in this art of subtlest and most gradual transition is assuredly the big scene in the second act of Tristan und Isolde. The commencement of this scene offers the most overbrimming life in its most passionate emotions,—its close the devoutest, most consecrate desire of death. Those are the piers: now see, child, how I've spanned them, how it all leads over from the one abutment to the other! And that's the whole secret of my musical form, as to which I make bold to assert that it has never been so much as dreamt before in such clear and extended coherence and such encompassing of every detail. If you knew how that leading sense inspired me here with musical contrivances—for rhythm, harmonic and melodic development—such as I never could light on before, you would grow aware how, even in the most specific branch of art, there can be no true invention if it does not spring from such main principles.—So much for Art! But with me this art is very close-allied to Life. I suppose a strong conflict of extremes of mood will always remain part of my character: it is painful to me, however, to have to measure their effects on others: to be understood is so indispensably important. Well, as Art has to bring to understanding those extreme grand emotions of Life which remain unknown to the generality of mankind (except in rare epochs of war or revolution), so this understanding is only to be compassed through the most definite and cogent motivation of transitions; and my whole artistic work consists in nothing but evoking the needful, willing mood of receptivity through such a motivation.* Nothing has been more horrifying to

---

* "Wie nun in der Kunst die äussersten, grossen Lebensstimmungen zum Verständniss gebracht werden sollen, die eigentlich dem allgemeinen

me, in this regard, than when skips are made in the performance of my operas ; for instance in the Tannhäuser, where I
first went to work with a growing sense of this beautiful,
convincing need of Transmutation, and carried out a most
pregnantly-motived transition (even musically considered)
from the outburst of horror after Tannhäuser's appalling
confession, to the reverence wherewith the intercession of
Elisabeth is heard at last ; a transition I always was proud
of, and that never failed of its convincing effect.   You may
easily imagine how I felt, when I learnt that folk saw
'lengths' in this (as at Berlin) and positively struck out one
of the most essential portions of my artwork !—

Thus does it fare in my art.   And how in life ?   Have
you not often been witness how people found my language
domineering, wearisome, interminable, when, led by an
identical instinct, I meant nothing else than to lead over
from excitement, or after an unusual expression, to a rational
conciliation ?—

Do you remember the last evening with Semper ?   I
had suddenly forsaken my calmness, and wounded my opponent by a vigorous thrust : hardly had the words escaped
me, than I inwardly cooled down at once, and felt nothing
but the necessity—precisely to myself—of making amends,
and restoring the conversation to a seemly groove.   At like
time, however, I had a definite feeling that this could never

---

Menschenleben (ausser in seltenen Kriegs- und Revolutionsepochen)
unbekannt bleiben, so ist diess Verständniss eben nur durch die
bestimmteste und zwingendste Motivirung der Uebergänge zu erreichen,
und mein ganzes Kunstwerk besteht eben darin, durch diese Motivirung
die nöthige, willige Gefühlsstimmung hervorzubringen."—Even by a slight
paraphrase it is impossible to do justice to this pregnant sentence, as,
among other things, we have no single English equivalent for *Stimmung*—
the meaning of which may range from " key," or " pitch," to " frame of
mind."—Tr.

be done by sudden muting, but only through a gradual and conscious leading-over. I remember that even while still loudly championing my own opinion, I was already handling it with a certain artistic deliberateness, which, if people would only have let me go on, quite surely would have led to a conclusion alike intellectually and morally conciliating, and ended with agreement and appeasement in one. I grant you that this is demanding too much; for when actual temper once is roused, then each man wants to gain his point, and would far rather pass for insulted, than be brought to agreement. So upon this, as on many another occasion, I simply incurred the charge and rebuke of loving to hear myself speak. You yourself, I believe, were misled for a moment that evening, and feared that my continuing at first in a loud tone of voice proceeded from sustained excitement; and yet I also remember having answered you quite tranquilly, "Only let me lead back again; it really can't be done so quick!"—

You will believe me, that such experiences have something very painful to me?—Indeed I am companionable, and it is no surly egoism that drives me more and more away from all society. It isn't wounded vanity, if I'm sensitive to charges of perpetual talking, but the doleful feeling—What canst thou ever be to people, what can they be to thee, if in your mutual intercourse it is no question of attaining understanding, but just simply of retaining one's unaltered opinion? On subjects foreign to me, concerning which I have neither experience nor a settled feeling, I certainly never dilate any otherwise than with a view to gaining information: but when I feel that I have something rational and coherent to say about a subject with which I am quite familiar, then to have to let the thread of my argument be snapped for mere sake of giving another the semblance of right to an opposite opinion—that really makes it futile to speak a single word in company at all. I now decline all so-called company, and—really feel better for it.

But there I go, talking too much again perhaps, and bringing too much into conjunction that might as well be left apart? Will you understand me, if my feeling toward yourself impels me this time also to " transition "—to leading-over ; if I try to adjust the rough ends of my moods, and do not like to cease abruptly, just to blurt out that I'm calm and cheerful? Could that possibly seem natural to you? No : to-day as well, pursue the path I fain would lead your sympathy along, to arrive at a reassured feeling about me ! Nothing can be more painful to my heart, than to rouse a grievous sympathy ; if such a cause has slipped my lips, accord me the fair liberty of tranquillising gradually and gently. Everything, with me, is so ,linked together : that has its disadvantages, as it enables common and (under circumstances) remediable grievances to exert a frequently excessive influence on me ; yet it also has this advantage, that I derive from that same inter-connection the means of reassurance ; for, just as everything streams towards my ultimate life-task, my art, so from it flows back the fount that dews my arid paths of life. Through the heartfelt wish to soothe and reassure your sense of sympathy, to-day I've been able to make myself conscious of that highest artistic attribute which I find more fruitfully developed in each of my new works, and thus to speak to you as if from the very sanctuary of my art without the least constraint, the smallest self-deception, veraciously and sans pretence.—

Thus, too, my whole situation is gradually clearing toward a definite outlet, an outlet which faces a side of the world whence friendship and noble will may operate composingly upon me.—Everything will be arrangeable, and once I'm quite at rest again, once full recourse to my art, my creating,

is again made possible to me, all will soon lose its disturbing
influence on my mind : then shall I look tranquilly outwards,
and when I'm troubling least in that direction, perhaps
there'll soonest come from there as well a thing I have
to welcome.*—So—patience !—

From my [box of] books I've picked out our dear Schiller.
Yesterday I read the Jungfrau [*Maid of Orleans*], and felt
so musically attuned that I could capitally have filled with
tones Johanna's silence, in particular, when she is publicly
accused : her offence,—the miraculous.   To-day a speech
of Posa's about innocence and virtue (at close of the second
act [*Don Carlos*]) absolutely set me in amazement at the
incredible beauty of its poetic diction.   How I regret my
inability to comply with an invitation that reached me lately
from the committee of the Schiller-festival at Berlin (to write
a chant for it).   Bemoan me, but also rejoice when I tell
you that I've brought off this letter to-day amid countless
interruptions by workmen, under the hammering and rapping
of upholsterers, the instrument-maker, the wood-chopper,
and so on.   Ere long I might have had leisure, perhaps,
to bring a Schiller chant about : but the term is too short,
and the Muse has no niche in my houselet as yet.—

---

* Without a key, this whole paragraph is enigmatic, and more
especially its commencement:—"So klärt sich mir denn auch meine
ganze Lage allmählich nach einem bestimmten Ausgange hin ab, der
ja einer Seite der Welt zugekehrt ist, von wo Freundschaft und edler
Wille beruhigend auf mich wirken können.   Es wird sich Alles einrichten
lassen " etc.   Perhaps such a key may be found in the letter of Oct. 25
to Otto : " The Dresden Intendant sends me word that he hopes to
persuade the King of Saxony to summon me to Dresden for a first
representation of the ' Tristan,' but that could not take place before July
next year.   At least I should have singers with good voices there."
Moreover, Glasenapp informs us that on Nov. 4 Wagner wrote his old
friend the Dresden tenor Tichatschek, who had conveyed the intimation,
begging him to try to get the production arranged for an earlier date ;
whilst Minna, on her side, had lately been doing her utmost in Dresden
to procure her husband's amnesty (*Das Leben R. Wagner's* II. ii, 227-8).

Farewell; be kind to me, and trust me! All will have to be endured a while longer. A thousand greetings and hearty wishes!

R. W.

96.

Paris, Nov. 11, 59.

My precious Child,

You give me great delight! Yesterday I meant at last— I had been so obstructed!—to write yourself with the letter to Wesendonck,* to tell you how much your last letter rejoiced me: interrupted once again, this morning came round and brought me, too, the Schiller dithyramb. Never had I understood that so well, as to-day: you are always teaching me to see new beauties. How gladly I judge from it all, that you have recovered your health!—

I also am slowly recovering, and that—I can tell it you now—from a serious illness. Ten years ago—in Paris too— I suffered from acute rheumatics; the doctor particularly cautioned me to do all I could to drive them outward, lest the attacks should find their way to my heart. And so, in fact, just now each ailment of my body coalesced, and threatened one last exit through my heart. This time I really believed I was done for. However, it has all got to be thrust to the outside once more; by some kind of fitly distracting activity I shall try to foil the swarming toward my heart. You will stand by me, both of you; won't you, good souls?—

My first good tidings reached me from myself. The proofs of the third act of Tristan turned suddenly up. How a glance into this last completed work revived, filled strengthened, and inspired me—you will be able to feel

---

* A letter not preserved, at least not included with the *Letters to Otto.*— Somewhere about this date (the day before?) Minna must have returned to her husband.—Tr.

with me.   This joy, I should say, a father can scarcely
experience at sight of his child!   Through a river of
tears—why mask the weakness?—it cried to me: No!
Thou shalt not end yet; thou still must achieve!   A man
who has only just made *such* a thing, is full to overflowing
still!—

So be it then!—

To return: Your letter, also, rejoiced me so much; and
nothing in it more so, than when I see the child, now grown
so mightily sagacious, yet straying every now and then into
a small mistake about me.   Then I say to myself: She
will have the additional pleasure of getting quite clear upon
this point as well; for instance, that, when I dispute about
Politics, I have my eye on something other than the seeming
theme, etc.   But how glad I am, to be in the wrong when
I argue with you: I always learn some new thing by it.—

For the next, a very melancholy work of love has fallen
to me.   I suddenly learn that my dear fatherly friend Fischer
of Dresden is sick unto death (you will remember how
often I've spoken to you of his singular attachment and
fidelity); a complaint of the—heart at last had brought the
greybeard to death's door.   As my wife goes in to visit him,
under the most terrible seizures he presses out the piteous
moan: "O Richard! Richard has forgotten me, and cast
me off!"   I had expected him this summer at Lucerne, and
not written him since; so I wrote to him at once.   Then
I receive the tidings of his death; he had been too weak
to have my letter read him.

So a few days since I penned a Homage to the dear
departed:* as soon as I get back a print of it, I will send
it on to you.—That also was a piece of work!—

---

* First published in the Dresden *Constitutionelle Zeitung* Nov. 25,
then reprinted in the *Neue Zeitschrift* of Dec. 2, 1859, and finally in
vol. v of Wagner's *Ges. Schriften*—see *Prose Works* III.—Tr.

And I still am not rid of the workmen : these Parisians seem to think one's house their own. Only now, is *my* little étage in order at last : * were you to walk in, you would almost think I hadn't left the Asyl ; the same furniture, the old desk, the same green hangings, engravings, everything—just as you knew it. Merely the rooms are still smaller, and I have had to divide : my little salon holds the Erard, the green sofa and two fauteuils that used to stand in the tea-room ; on the walls the Kaulbach, Cornelius and the two Murillos [former presents from Otto]. Next to it a little cabinet with bookcase, work-table, and the well-known causeuse (of Lucerne memory). I have had my bedroom papered in plain pale violet, with a few green bands to frame it in ; the Madonna della Sedia forms its decoration : quite a tiny cabinet adjoining it is fitted as a bathroom. So this will have been my final planting of a household foot. You know I can abide by what I very seriously determine : so— : never, never will I " set up house " again ! God only knows *what* will put an end to this last settlement : but *I* know that an end will come to myself, before I die ; and I know that I shall trim myself no nest again then, but await entirely devoid of goods that spot where somebody shall seal my eyes at last.—

Once more I was seized, after all, by a ridiculous eager-ness to get my things arranged as speedily as possible, that I might find rest again. At such times I overdo it, not out of pleasure in the thing itself, but simply to arrive more quickly at a state where this and that requirement, satisfied to the last inch perhaps, shall no longer act disturbingly upon me. It must be so : for I cannot otherwise explain this ridiculous zeal wherewith I set about a thing like that,

---

* In Paris the Asyl arrangement was reversed ; Wagner occupied the ground-, his wife the first floor.—Tr.

since I know on the other hand how little I cleave to it all, and how recklessly I can throw it all behind me. Yes, laugh at me, do ; I'll stand it again.—

A few days back I was invited to a musical soirée, where sonatas, trios etc. from Beethoven's last period were played. Alike reading and rendering put me very much out, and they won't get hold of me so soon again, yet I had a few experiences. I took a seat next Berlioz, who presently introduced the composer Gounod to me—an amiable-looking, upright-endeavouring, but it seems not very highly-gifted artist—who was sitting on his other side. Hardly had it become known who I was, than people thronged round Berlioz from all sides, to be introduced by him to me ; remarkable to say, a bevy of enthusiasts who have studied my scores without knowing German : at times that makes me quite bewildered. I'm dreading a number of callers, in consequence, and must be a little on my guard ; the young Charnacé lady I have disgracefully neglected hitherto ; I don't quite see my way yet—as regards Paris. However, on the whole I've a mind to undertake something, purely to conduct—my "rheumatics" outward.

I am reading Liszt's Music of the Gipsies.* Rather too turgid and phrasy : still, the forcible portrayal of the Gipsy nature (unmistakably the Tschandalas of India) took me vividly back to Prakriti (alias Sawitri). About that another time.

And now, for to-day—a thousand thanks ! Ah, what does that not include ! I'll soon gossip again with the child.—

R. W.

---

* First French edition (orig.) *Les Bohémiens*, published in Paris 1859. Evidently on this, as on similar occasions before, Wagner was unaware that the work was largely the product of Princess Carolyne Sayn-Wittgenstein.—Tr.

97.

Paris, Nov. 29, 59.*

What great joy you again have given me, Lady-friend!
Believe me, if I had to recognise myself in none but the
mirror held up to me by the world and *all* my friends therein, I soon should have to turn away with dread of any
looking back. Nor can I be quite open and true with any
one of them: there always remain spots and blind places,
which I know not how to fill up. But if You answer me
for once, how splendid I then appear! Everything, including
myself, then seems to me noble: I know that I'm safe.
Children, that we are *three*, is really something wonderfully
grand! It is incomparable, my and your greatest triumph!
We stand inconceivably high above mankind, inconceivably
high! The noblest had to come true for once: and the
true is so incomprehensible because so wholly for itself.
Let us revel in this high good-fortune: it has no uses,
and is here for naught—it can but be enjoyed, and but
by those who are it.—

Now be you finely welcomed to French soil:† herewith
the poet of the Nibelungen steps forth to meet you, and
stretches out his hand. I felicitate you joyfully on your roving
to Italy; you go to meet a benefit that I am not to taste,
and which I therefore wish you doubly. Enjoy the balmy
heaven, the poetic land, the living past, for me as well,
and be you thereby twice made glad! How inexpressibly
gladly would I be with you both!—

Nothing remains for me now, but to make one final
energetic effort to rid myself of an eternal cumbrance of my

---

* The first two paragraphs, which by then had appeared in the
Allgemeine Musikzeitung 1898, I have already published with the
Letters to Otto.—Tr.

† Evidently taking the Marseilles route to Rome; see letter of Dec.
12 to Otto.—Tr.

life for good and all. Ruined and devastated as my relations
to life are, yet I have come to see that much therein may
shape itself endurably and acceptably if only I can get
myself the needful outer means to dispose at all times of
my mode of life, my projects, doings and leavings-undone,
according to my need and judgment, without being forever
arrested by that single point which nowadays has power
over freedom, and whose settlement removes all scruples
as to what we do or leave undone. I now have learnt
more forcibly than ever—tho' strictly it was always so—
that I can bear each failure, every undeception, each closing
of all prospect, all, all, with great, contemptuous indifference ;
but those said troubles make me furiously impatient. Disdain everything, let nothing turn me from the inner fount,
renounce all recognition, all success, even the possibility of
producing my own works myself—all this I can ; but with
gnashing of teeth to have to bruise my feet against the
clog that Fate has cast between my legs upon their quiet
journey—against that—I can't help it—I am and remain
most excessively sensitive ; and as I'm what I am, and
nothing can alter me in that respect—so long as I'm able
to hold out at all—I now am staking everything, in uttermost
impatience, on clearing my path of this clog once for all *
Luckily I can pretend to myself that it completely suits
my present inner situation, to direct my attention exclusively
outward awhile. I expect you won't allow yourself to be
altogether duped thereby ; and if you were to suppose I might
unhesitatingly prefer to cultivate my inner concentration
in some agreeable retirement, amid congenial surroundings,

---

* Unquestionably the " clog " can bear no other meaning than his
long-standing financial embarrassment ; all kinds of schemes for capital-
ising the labours of his brain are now his uppermost consideration, as
may be seen in the letter of Dec. 12 to Otto, and the next two or
three to Mathilde Wesendonck.—Tr.

as for instance with you two, and—finally indifferent toward
their outer fortunes—devote myself to the continual creation
of new works : if you were to suppose this, let me tell you,
you would be perfectly right (tho' it must not go beyond
ourselves, of course). But I believe, as said, it will now
become possible to delude myself into the other course ;
and that's assisted very much, nay, wellnigh determined,
by my latest relations with my whole world of so-called
friends in Germany. It really is incredible, how things
stand there ; so *incredible* that I gladly withhold it from
you, since you hardly could believe it in the end. Thus
I'm convinced, e.g., that you would tax me with exaggeration
and misconception if I tried to make it plain to you how
truly hostilely, or at least entirely unconscientiously, this
Ed. Devrient has behaved to me ; so I'll merely tell you
that I long had been prepared for it, and wasn't at all
surprised when at last I found it out. I gladly excuse him,
however : everybody has his hobby-horse, and his is a
normal well-regulated theatrical institute, without digressions
into a domain not to be trodden in the daily round. In this
sense he was instinctively against my work from the first,
and only the young Grand Duchess's enthusiastic wish
propelled him on—head-shaking and half sulky all the way.
Well, he has triumphed now ; he openly avers that I've
reached the point of the impossible.—Whether the young
enthusiastic woman's-heart will not retire into itself, cowed
by the experienced, calculating man—the " wise man," if you
will—what do you say ? I'm certain the young Grand Duke
will.—

But look you, child, it is this and its like that stirs my
old pugnacity again, a little : I'm foolish, but—the very
fact that I live is a folly ; you cannot but admit it. The
Impossible itself might tempt me ; and my committing
myself here to Paris, e.g., long seemed to me the last im-

possibility of all. Yet I have a quite peculiar gauge for the Impossible, and that points inwards : whether I carry it through, I shall learn from nothing save my mood, my inclination to pursue ; and I therefore shall deem that impossible for which I lose all zest at last. That may easily occur ; disgust has a terrible sway with me, and once it plainly shews itself, it is invincible ; wherefore I shall not strive against it, and to it belongs the judgment of what may be possible to me. Often do I detect it, and it casts me down for wretched days : then it gets stilled again by this or that surprising advance, sympathy, budding intelligence, where I never had hoped for them. Then Maya weaves its veil opaque once more, a lightning instant of full rayed-out truth confronts me ; hindrances incite, risks enflame—and—we shall see which keeps the field, disgust, or—lust of battle ?— I cannot yet decide. But were I one of those fortunates to whom Fate gave gold and silver also when it gave them pride and talent, my fondest wish would bear me now to you in Rome for 2 fair months ; I know it. Now go you children well alone : I'll see how I can bend my fate, then some day I'll come too. Good luck accompany you ! A thousand heartfelt wishes !—

R. W.

98.

Paris, Dec. 19, 59.

Best Birthday-child,

Do I arrive in good time ? Is to-day the very 23rd ? Maybe the day is right, perhaps, but how about the present ? What could I give the child ? I am so poor now, my well of gifts has run quite dry ; it is as if I hadn't known for ages what it feels like, to come by good ideas, put them on paper, impart them !—The only thing that would consent to occur to me, was just a kind of last conclusion of my own last (?) work ; and truly that has been no bad idea. Listen how it came about :—

You know Hans wanted to conduct the prelude last winter, and begged me to make it a close.* At that time no inspiration could have come to me : it seemed so impossible, that I flatly declined. Since then, however, I have written the third act and found the full close for the whole : so, while drawing up the programme for a Paris concert—the particular temptation to which was my wish to get a hearing of this Tristan-prelude—it occurred to me to outline that close in advance, as glimmering presage of redemption. Well, it has succeeded quite admirably, and to-day I send you this mysteriously tranquillising close as the best gift I can make for your birthday. I have written the piece out for you pretty much as I play it on the piano to myself : there are a few nasty stretches in it, and I expect you'll have to fish up some Roman Baumgartner to play the thing to you, unless you would rather play it with him à quatre mains ; in which case you must adapt the right hand part for both your hands. Now see what you can make of the onerous present !—Better will you understand what I have penned as explanation of the whole prelude for my Paris audience : it stands on the other side of the specimen of caligraphy.

---

* As a matter of fact, Hans von Bülow was the first to give the *Tristan* prelude, and that "with the composer's kind permission" (see programme of Hans' Prague concert, March 12, 1859). According to the *Neue Zeitschrift's* report on the second performance (Leipzig, June '59— see p. 147 *n. sup.*) Hans had provisionally supplied a needful close himself : it would seem that this has misled certain programme-compilers into attributing to *him* the Close always played at concerts when the so-called "*Liebestod*" is not tacked on ; just as foolish and impossible legends were current once, that von Bülow had helped in the general instrumenting. Wagner's own Close is of course the only one published (see full score of the separated Prelude, Breitkopf & Härtel), and it is that reproduced on the lilac facsimile of the enclosure to this letter 98 together with the explanatory programme, a translation whereof the reader will find in *Prose Works* VIII. pp. 386-7.—Tr.

Ivy and vine you will recognise in the music, though, especially when you hear it on the orchestra, where strings and wind alternate with each other; it will come out quite beautifully. I expect to hear it in the middle of January, when I'll hear it for both of us.

And now, many hearty good wishes and greetings from my cold Paris, where we're almost perished with snow, ice and frost! How is it in your part of the world? Does Rome come up to expectations? Let me hear very soon; I do need a word from you!—

Fare you well, be blest and deeply reverenced!—

Your

R. W.

99.

January 1, 1860.

Lady-friend, I'm still alive! The most notable news I can give you for the New Year.

God knows how I came to flatter myself I should receive a greeting from you to-day; for our letters are very slow now, and not to be reckoned on. From the date of your letter I have made out to my sorrow that mine to you can not have arrived on Dec. 23; consequently I can't expect a greeting in return myself to-day.

But I am glad to know that you, and all of you, have reached Rome happily and safely. Your letter shews me that I can very well leave you to fend for yourself now; you have opened your eyes, and—see. Perhaps you had made an oversight of that before. Now see and behold for me as well: I need someone to do it for me, and no one would I rather let see for me, than you. With me there's something queer about it; I have repeatedly found it so, and most definitely at last in Italy: I'm uncommonly acutely affected awhile by any considerable effect on my eye, but —it does not last long. It certainly does not come from my

eye being insatiable ; but it seems that as sense for observing
the world it doesn't suffice me.*   Perhaps it is going with
me as it went with the eye-loving Goethe when he exclaimed
in his Faust: "How grand a spectacle! but ah!—no
more!"—

Perhaps it may come from my being too decidedly an
ear-man ; but I, of all people, pass such long periods entirely
without any sort or kind of sustenance for my hearing, that
neither would that appear to meet the case.   There must
be some indescribable inner sense, which is altogether clear
and active only when the outward-facing senses are as if
a-dream.   When I strictly neither see nor hear distinctly
any longer, this sense is at its keenest, and shews its function
as creative calm : I can call it by no other name.   Whether
this calm is all one with that plastic repose which you
mean, I cannot say ; merely I know that this calm of mine
works from within to without, with it I am at the world's
centre ; whereas so-called plastic repose seems to me rather
the application of outward forms to the allaying of inner
unrest.   If I feel myself in that inner unrest, no picture,
no work of plastic art can take effect on me : it rebounds
like a flimsy ball.   Then nothing but a gaze beyond, will
serve me to see what can calm me.   And this, too, is the
only gaze that affects me sympathetically in others—this

---

* Taken in conjunction with p. 138, this entirely bears out the contention of Dr. Geo. M. Gould (Philadelphia) and myself, that a great
deal of Wagner's malaise proceeded from eye-strain.   As hinted in
a footnote to *Life* iv, 151, though I still reserve details, one of the most
eminent ophthalmologists in London has lately informed me that he
tested Wagner's eyes in 1877, and found the patient to have long been
suffering from astigmatism—a defect of curvature then quite recently
discovered, but far more common than most of us suspect.   In 1860
Wagner would about have arrived at that critical period when the ocular
changes incidental to advancing middle-life are attended with more active
pain etc., such as we know from a letter of Minna's (see p. 254 *inf.*) to
have been the case.—Tr.

gaze over the world and away. It also is the only one that understands the world ; thus Calderon gazed, and who has turned life, and bloom, and beauty, to more wondrous poetry than he ?—

Goethe in Rôme is a very delightful and most important occurrence : what he garnered there, fell to everyone's good ; and thereby he decidedly saved Schiller the need of seeing for himself. The latter could thenceforth make excellent shift, and shape his noblest works ; whereas Goethe pushed his lust of the eye to a hobby, in time, and at last we find him bitten with a mania for collecting coins. He was a whole and utter eye-man.

If we let him lead us where are things to be seen, we are sure to be splendidly led. In Rome you've done quite right to go with him ; at his side may a feeling of gracious repose descend on your eyes of a child ! See for me as well ; and let me ever hear such exquisite reflections, as this first time !—

There isn't much to say about myself, child. A man who is running from pillar to post, to get a fitting concert-hall to open its doors to him, ought to be no concern of yours in Rome : he oughtn't even to tell you how he feels about it.

But give Otto my kindest regards, and tell him that much is soon likely to come to a head ; on the first of May I think of opening my German Opera in the Salle Ventadour. All the best German singers are accepting with enthusiasm ; Frau Ney, [Frau] Mayer-Dustmann (Vienna), Tichatschek, Niemann and others, have sworn themselves under my banner, even with readiness for financial sacrifices. I've a notion I soon shall get everything fixed ; then Tannhäuser and Lohengrin to begin with, and practice of Tristan meanwhile, so that it may be played somewhere about from the 1st to the 16th of June. Thus—I must try to help myself, but it doesn't sound like Rome !—

You knew I had a mind to pass an interval in nothing but some outward occupation like this: now I have been compelled to, particularly through the miscarriage of the Carlsruhe Tristan. My whole present scheme is directed at nothing but the possibility of treating myself to my Tristan: after that, I shall most likely let it drop again. I have nothing further in view; I've quite enough bother with this—and were I Goethe, I'd come to you people in Rome to-day, you may be perfectly sure!—

And now for a beautiful, bright, sunny year! I feel uncommonly glad at your being in Rome, under Italy's sky! A thousand heartfelt greetings to Otto and the children.

With faithful love,

Your

R. W.

100.

Paris, January 28, 1860.

I must make up my mind at last, Child, to give you breathless news about myself. It has been my refreshment in the thick of it all, to think how I would collect my thoughts and give you a nice calm retrospect of all I have gone through: but I am not at the end yet; nor shall I ever be, it seems. Wherefore no more fruitless dallying, and a few lines of certainty instead.

All that I have experienced is as nothing against one observation, one discovery, which I made at the first orchestral rehearsal for my concert; since it has determined the whole remainder of my life, and its consequences will henceforth tyrannise me. For the first time was I getting my prelude to Tristan played; and—scales as if fell from my eyes in regard of the immeasurable distance I have travelled from the world during these last 8 years. This little prelude was so inscrutably *new* to the bandsmen, that I positively had to lead my men from note to note as if exploring for gems in a mine.

Bülow, who was present, confessed that the performances attempted of this piece in Germany had been taken on trust by the audience, but in themselves had stayed entirely unintelligible.* I succeeded indeed in making this prelude understanded both of orchestra and audience—ay, people assure me, it called forth the deepest impression of all; but don't ask me *how* I managed that! Enough that it now stands sharp before me, that I dare think of no further creation until I've filled the fearful gap behind me. I *must* present my works first, and *what does that not mean ?*—

Child, it means my plunging into a slough of suffering and of sacrifices, in which quite likely I shall go to ground. All, all *may* become possible ; but only on condition that I have ample time and leisure for all, that I may take my singers and bandsmen forward step by step, have no reason for hurry, need break off nowhere out of want of time, and always have things well in hand. And what does that mean ? The experiences of this concert, with its skimpy time-allowance, have told me : I need to be *rich ;* I need thousands on thousands [of francs] to sacrifice regardlessly, to buy myself space, time, and willingness. As I am not rich—well, I must endeavour to make myself so; I must let my older operas be given here in French, so as to devote the considerable proceeds to disclosing my new works to the world.—That's what stands before me ; I have no other choice, so—here's to death and extinction! 'Tis my one

---

* See pages 147 and 198. Hans had arrived in Paris Jan. 17 (en garçon), to help in Wagner's concerts, chiefly with training the chorus, also to give pianoforte recitals of his own.—Tr.

remaining task, and for it my dæmon holds me still to life.
Folly, would I think of aught beyond : I can look to nothing
but these awful travails of the world-birth of my latest
works.—

O stay in Rome ; how happy I am, to know you so
out of the world! Behold, regard, consider, all beauteous
things and fair ; you are doing it for me, and my comfort
shall it be to gain those pregnant pictures through your
eyes ! 'Twill be both cooling-draught and cordial for a
man a-quake with fever ; thus, and now—you're my last
consolation !—

Just two words more, anent my outward happenings.
After the most unheard-of torment, stress and toil, I arrived
at my first concert-performance last Wednesday.* The
evening was nothing more nor less than a festival ; I can
but say it. The orchestra was already fired to white
enthusiasm, and hung upon my eye, my finger-tip. I was
received both by it and the audience with endless cheers,
and each of my pieces bore me éclat, amaze, entrancement.
The sensation is quite immense ; strange experiences, con-
versions, feuilletonists (Patrie) rushing to kiss my hand.—I
myself was dead-beat. On that night I took my last
initiation into suffering : I must, I must trudge on,—it was
indeed my last remaining task. The flower [*Tr. u. Is.*] has
to open to the world, and pass away : keep *you* its stainless
buds !—

Many sincere good wishes to Otto ; tell him I love
him ! Farewell, my precious, noble child ! Live softly

---

* January 25, 1860. The main body of the programme was that of
the three Wagner-concerts at Zurich seven years before: it consisted
of the *Holländer* overture, the choral " march," introduction to act iii,
Pilgrims' chorus, and overture of *Tannhäuser;* then a pause, followed
by the prelude to *Tristan und Isolde*, the prelude, Bridal-procession
scene, introduction to act iii and Bridal chorus, from *Lohengrin.*—Tr.

and inwardly on, and strengthen me thereby! With
loyal love

Your R. W.

101.

Paris, March 3, 60.

I mean to make to-day for once a feast-day : I will write
to you, Lady-friend ! Advisedly and with kind consideration
I have often dropped the pen which I repeatedly had taken
up of late to write you. My need is great, and I wish to
earn its fulfilment ; so I'll see what friendly scraps of news
I can scrape together for you.

First I'll describe what now stands on my chimney-piece
—in place of a *pendule.* 'Tis a singular object. On a mount
of red velvet is spread a silver shield, the length of its rim
filled up with emblems from my poems, from Rienzi to
Tristan u. Isolde. Upon this shield, within a silver wreath—
one bough of laurel, the other oak—lies a massive silver
sheet of music, half rolled up : on this roll leading themes
from my operas are carved in musical notation, A beautiful
silver pen rests in the twigs of the wreath, above the sheet
of music ; the boughs are bound together by a golden fillet,
on which stands written :

"Des rechten Mannes Herz muss überströmen in
der Sonnenhöhe grosser Männer,"—and then : "Dem
hohen Meister gewidmet in aufrichtiger Verehrung von
Richard Weiland."*

This Richard Weiland is a simple citizen of Dresden,

---

* "A true man's heart must e'en brim over in the noontide of great
men"—: "Dedicated to the exalted Master, in sincere veneration, by
Richard Weiland." Glasenapp informs us that the sender, son of the
historical painter Wilhelm Weiland, was born in 1829, and had devoted
himself to literature ; for a short time he appeared on the acting stage,
but, in view of his youth, that can scarcely have been until after Wagner
himself had left Dresden.– Tr.

whom I never knew there, but who paid me a visit once
at Zurich—in the Asyl—and furnished me that droll criticism
of the Prague representation of Tannhäuser with his simple
statement that the overture, which merely lasted 12
minutes under myself at Dresden, was 20 minutes long.
—I found his gift, with a most unassuming note, awaiting
me one evening when I came home fagged-out by coaching
my choruses.—So I now have the baton * and this piece of
plate.

Here my concerts † have gained me some very firstrate
devotees.

GASPÉRINI, a kind doctor of great skill and education,
but seemingly about to give up his profession for literary
and poetic work ; a man of fine, refined exterior and great
warmth of heart, only perhaps a shade wanting in energy,
—belonged to me even before my arrival, and is now the
most zealous and persistent champion of my cause. He
has got the " Courier du Dimanche " to open to him for
that.—

In VILLOT I have won an admirable brain, a clear and
delicate mind of unusual culture, emancipated from all
prejudice. This man (who married off a son the other day)
is Conservateur des Musées du Louvre, and as such has
entire custody of the [national] art-treasures. He has
written a history of the Louvre collections, a giant work
that cost him 15 years of unremitting toil.—Now imagine
it : this man had possessed *all* my scores long ere I made
his acquaintance, has studied them closely, and now is quite
happy at my being able to get Härtels to supply him with
a Tristan partitur already.‡ He has quite surprised me

---

* A gift from Frau Wesendonck, after a design by Semper.

† See page 204 ; the second took place Feb. 1, the third Feb. 8.—Tr.

‡ It is to Fr. Villot that Wagner dedicated the famous " Music of the
Future " a few months later—Tr.

by the keenness of his judgment, especially anent the capabilities of his own nation ; to which he belongs completely as regards expression, whereas he far transcends it in his spirit : his is a very handsome and distinguished head. I have not yet taken advantage of his offer of a minute inspection of the treasures of the Louvre, with himself for cicerone, and probably shall be unable to for a long, long time.

Among several others, I may also mention the novelist CHAMPFLEURY, whose brochure, outcome of a first impression, I have already sent you : he has a very pensive, sad, appealing eye. His friend the poet BAUDELAIRE has written me a couple of wonderful letters, but does not wish to be presented to me till he has finished some verses with which he proposes to honour me.—I have told you of FRANCK-MARIE :* he has written a good deal about me, but personally remains a stranger yet.

Then there's a young painter, GUSTAVE DORÉ, who already has a great name here : he has made a drawing, intended for the *Illustration,* representing me as conductor of an orchestra of spirits in an Alpine landscape. Further, there are numerous musicians and composers, who have declared themselves for me enthusiastically ; among them GOUNOD, a suave, good, purely but not deeply gifted man ; LOUIS LACOMBE, LÉON KREUTZER, STEPHAN HELLER. Of importance as a really profound musician is Sensale,† who will play me my scores by and by.

A Mr. PERRIN, of note as painter, past Director of the Opéra comique, and presumably future ditto of the Grand, is most devoted to me, and has written very beautifully about me in the Revue Européenne.

BERLIOZ has fallen victim to envy ; my efforts to keep

---

* Another missing letter ?—Tr.   † Obviously Saint-Saens.

friends with him have been frustrated through the brilliant
reception, to him intolerable, of my music. As a fact, he
finds himself seriously crossed by my appearance in Paris
on the eve of a production of his Trojans ; moreover, his
unlucky star has given him a wicked wife, who lets herself
be bribed to influence her very weak and ailing husband.
His behaviour to me has been a constant hovering between
friendly inclination and repulsion of an object of envy. Very
late,* yet so as not to be obliged to record the impressions
of a repeated hearing of my music, did he publish his report,
which you will probably have read. I could but deem right
to reply to his ambiguous, nay, rancorous allusions to the
" Music of the Future" ; an answer you will find in the
Journal des Débats of February 22.†

ROSSINI has behaved much better. A jest about my
unmelodiousness had been fathered upon him, and greedily
colported even into German papers. Well, he expressly
dictated a disclaimer, declaring that he knew nothing of
mine but the Tannhäuser march, which had given him the
greatest pleasure, and moreover, that, from all he knew of me,
he held me in high esteem. Such seriousness in the old
Epicurean surprised me.—

Finally I have yet another conquest to announce, namely
of a Marshal, MAGNAN, who attended all 3 of my concerts,
and displayed the greatest interest. As I unfortunately am
bound to want such a man well-instructed about me, for
sake of certain circles, I paid him a call, and was really
astonished at his expressions : he had had to hit out left
and right, and couldn't conceive how people could hear
anything else in my music than just such music as Gluck

---

* Journal des Débats, Feb. 9 ; see " A travers Chants."—Tr.

† See *Prose Works* III. ; further, the passage about Rossini is
developed in vol. IV. of the same collection.—Tr.

and Beethoven had written, only with the special stamp of genius "of a Wagner."—

I can't unearth a single copy of my concert-programmes for you to-day; but you shall have one yet. Then you will see that they did not turn out too *intime*. I laid your reflections to heart, and even the words upon Tristan [cf. p. 198] contained nothing but a note about the subject.—

Now I'll tell you a little more about the concerts. The string-instruments were capital, 32 violins, 12 violas, 12 violoncellos, 8 double-basses: an uncommonly sonorous mass, the hearing of which would have caused you great joy, only the rehearsals were still too inadequate, and I couldn't quite extort the proper *piano*. The wind-instruments were merely partly good; none of them had energy. To specify: the oboe remained pastoral all the time, never rising to passion; the horns were miserable, and cost me many a sigh (their wretched blowers excused their repeated false entries by the disconcerting effect of my signal); trombones and trumpets had no brilliance. Everything was atoned in the end, however, by the really great enthusiasm for me that possessed the whole orchestra from first to last desk, and proclaimed itself so openly throughout the performances themselves that Berlioz is said to have been stupefied.

Thus the three nights turned out positive festivals, and as far as demonstrations of enthusiasm go, the Zurich festivals were a mere shadow compared with them; the audience was riveted from first to last. I had made a new close for the overture of the "flying Dutchman," which pleases me much, and also made an impression on my hearers [cf. *Life* iv, 301]. But childlike shouts of joy broke out directly after the natty melody in the Tannhäuser-march, and as often as that melody returned, the same explosion was repeated; a frank child-heartedness which put me in quite a good humour, for never yet had I heard such immediate

14

outbursts of delight. The Pilgrims' chorus was sung very tamely and ineffectively the first time; afterwards it went better. The Tannhäuser - overture, played with great virtuosity, always earned me many a call. The prelude to Tristan wasn't played to my liking before the third concert: on that evening it much rejoiced me. The audience, also, seemed thoroughly stirred by it; for, when an opponent ventured to hiss—after the applause—such a storm broke forth, and so intense, protracted, and continually renewed, that poor I hardly knew what to do on my platform, and had to motion people to leave off, for God's sake, I was satisfied; but that sent the temperature up again, and once more the storm broke loose. In short, I never passed through such a thing before.—

All the pieces from Lohengrin produced an immense effect from the beginning; orchestra and audience almost carried me on their hands after each. I can express it no otherwise—they were festival-nights.—

And now the child will be asking in wonder, why I am not content with such beautiful experiences, and look so dolefully ahead?—Eh, thereby hangs a tale,* but all I can say, is: Festival-keeping is easy—and—I want no feasts; such nights remain something beyond me, they are intoxicants, nothing else, and leave the after-effects of all inebriation;—if I only were differently built, tho', it might pass. As a matter of fact, I have made a long stride; so I might take a good rest now, wait comfortably for what is coming next, and what folk assure me is certain to come— Fame, Honour, and all else? A precious fool I should be! Think of it: I was distracted all the evening of my first concert because a certain Receveur Général had not arrived yet from Marseilles; and what about this individual?—He

---

* The enormous pecuniary losses faintly hinted toward the letter's close.—Tr.

was the wealthy man who, *Gaspérini* had assured me, was keenly interested in my proposal to get my operas performed in France, and might easily be induced to give me his energetic support in it. I had nothing in eye but the possibility of a first production of the *Tristan* in May, in Paris with German singers; that was the solitary goal toward which I was steering, on which I staked everything, and in particular the frantic strain of these 3 concerts. My wealthy man was to run over from Marseilles; the success of my music was to make him declare himself prepared to give the needful guarantee for the said operatic adventure. Finally the man arrives, for the third concert: he has a big dinner on that night, at Mirès'; still—he does come to the concert, for an hour, and—proves a magnificent Frenchman, immensely delighted, but afterwards sceptical of a German operatic enterprise, and so on.—

So I had again been a regular child! Really, I always know it beforehand; and yet one hopes—and dares—because a goal stands out before one, a goal one deems so requisite. And all the use of me, all the sense remaining in my life, is solely to look at that goal and overlook everything that lies between myself and it. Only in sight of that goal, indeed, can I still live; how can I live, if I'm to turn my eye from the goal and plunge it in the gulf that parts me from it?

Maybe others should do that for me, and hold me in the air; but who has a right to ask that of anyone? Does not each of us live with a goal in his eye, only that it just is not the goal of the eccentric? So it happens, child, that once again the stupid master must look deep and long into the gulf alone:—ah, how he feels in his heart then! No scene in Dante's Hell has ghastlier abysses!— Indication enough.—And the goal (?), for all that, remains the only thing that keeps life in me!—But how to reach it?—

Yes, Lady-friend, 'tis the truth: once more all's night around me! Had I no more goals, it were easily otherwise; but now I have simply to climb out with untold toil and trouble from the gulf in which I lately had to plunge again with wellnigh deliberate blindness. Not yet can I so much as see the plateau whence to fix my gaze upon the goal again.—When I last perceived the ineluctable necessity of staking all and everything at present on a first production of my Tristan, I also told myself: With this goal in eye, there can now be no abasement more for thee; all and aught thou doest to attain to means and power, can hold nothing to shame thee, and whoso might not comprehend thee if he saw thee treading unaccustomed paths, thou might'st reply to him: "What know'st thou of my goal?" —For, he alone can comprehend me, who first has comprehended that.—

Well, every day brings forth new plans; now this, now that contingence looms before me. I'm so indissolubly banned to this work, that I would gladly bring my life as sacrifice—in sober earnest—and swear to will to live not one day longer, when once I have produced my work. So perhaps it's not inconsequent, that I should now be possessed with the notion—instead of all the labours and humiliations I should have to undergo to arrive at the required means through "Parisian successes"—just of taking up the simplest cross and going to Dresden, getting myself tried, passed sentence on, and—pardoned, for all I care; to be able, unmolested then, to seek on the spot for the best German theatre, produce my Tristan there, and dissolve the spell which so holds me now that nothing else seems worth an ounce of trouble. Indeed it appears wellnigh the most rational course; methinks it resembles an unpardonable love of self, to refuse any manner of torture or shame that might lead to my work's redemption; for

what am *I*, without my work?—And add to that this
other: I *don't believe* in my operas in *French ;* all I do
toward that end is against the inner voice which I can
deaden but with levity or violence. I believe neither in
a French Tannhäuser, nor in a French Lohengrin ; to say
nothing of a French *Tristan.* My every step towards it,
too, remains unblest: a demon—my dæmon?—is at work
against me in it all. Only at command of a despot could
all the personal obstacles be beaten back, that rear
themselves against my advent to the Paris Opera-house ;
but I've no true zeal to compass that. Before all, what
concern of mine are my old works, grown all but indifferent
to me? Repeatedly I catch myself in the most utter lack
of interest in them. And then the French translations ! I'm
bound to think them clean impossible ; the few verses
translated for my concert cost unspeakable pains, and were
insufferable ; neither is a single whole act from my operas
translated as yet, in spite of endless labours, whilst what
thereof exists is odious to me. Moreover, the tongue itself
is one of the principal reasons why everything here remains
strange to me ; the torment of a conversation in French
fatigues me hugely, and I often break off in the midst of
an argument, like a castaway who tells himself : " Indeed
it isn't possible, and everything's in vain ! " Then I
feel too deplorably homeless, and ask myself : Where dost
thou, then, belong? A question I can answer with
no country's name, no town's, no hamlet's ; all, all are
foreign to me, and wistfully I often look towards the land
Nirvana. Nirvana in its turn, however, soon changes into
Tristan ; you know the Buddhist theory of the world's
creation : A breath perturbs the heaven's translucence :—

; it swells, condenses, and at last the
whole wide world stands forth, in prisoning solidity. 'Tis my

old, old fate, so long as I've such unredeeméd spirits still
about me !—

I have something homelike still about me, tho', which
I'm soon to be deprived of—Bülow. The poor young man
is slaving himself to the bone here, and I get little enough
of him ; he cannot visit me often, yet it's a comfort even to
know that he's here. Dear Heaven, it does me so much
good, to be able to converse naturally ; and that I now can
do with him alone. He is and remains most attached to
me, and it often is touching to get behind the secret pains
he constantly is taking for me ; whereon he turns quite
mournful if I tell him that it all can not avail. But I want
to give him one delight before he goes, and tell him : You
have sent him greetings through me.—

I have now to submit to a little business being done
with me, to try and clear a little of the fearful havoc the
expenses of my concerts have left behind them. One
[Belloni ?] proposes that I should give the identical concert
thrice at Brussels, under conditions which ensure me a small
profit. I suppose I shall have to ; so be prepared to hear
from me next from thence. Of London, too, one speaks to
me. It's sad enough ; but I cannot die as yet, you know.—

And now it will be well, Lady-friend, if I draw to a
close : I clearly see there's no more friendly tidings to
squeeze out, and already I've much overstepped the line.
However, my heart is somewhat lighter since at least I've
been able to write you again : thanks for affording me that !
And many kind messages to Otto and the children ; let me
hear how you all are doing. With faithful love

Your

R. W.

102.

Paris, April 10,.60.
But dearest, precious Child, why so absolutely not a line ?

Must I always ask first ; can't one so much as write to poor me without waiting to have to answer ?—I'm really quite uneasy ; I wrote Otto not so long ago :* no reply from him either ! So nothing is left me save dreaming. I eke things out with that, dream much and often ; but even pleasant dreams have something to alarm me, because one has to bear in mind, according to the rules of dream-divining, that when the object of solicitude appears to us well and serene, the very slightest excess denotes the opposite. But what a sorry aid are dreams ! If one remembers much of what one dreams, itself that points to nothing but the vacancy of our waking existence, and I always think of [Keller's] green Henry, who finished by nothing but dreaming.—

O you bad child ! Even your last letter—and that was ages back—told me so little, all but nothing, of yourself : is *my* silly fate to be ever the sole thing worth talking of ? I almost doubt if these lines will catch you still in Rome : it would be just like the pair of you, to start away without a word of warning when or whither ! You see, I scold : a few days since I might have drawn it milder ; but I'm getting crosser every day.—

Please write me reams on how you are, what you're seeing, how you pass your time, what acquaintances you've made, how it goes with your welfare, and everything of that sort. Indeed you did promise to give me a peep into your camera-obscura now and then ; and all at once totally ex-communicated ? Oh, it's easy to see where you live !

I almost ought not to breathe a word about myself for this once : but what do I know of your own news ? Nothing, except that I don't know : true philosophic consciousness ! And of myself?? Neither head nor tail is to be made of that in my lifetime, dearest child, above all by a

* Not published ; perhaps lost in the post.—Tr.

level-headed person. For instance, I am felicitated now by all common-sense people, and all the world thinks me swimming in bliss and delight since I've attained the quite incredible, and one of my operas is to be produced at last in Paris. "Can he possibly want *more ?*" they say. And just think : I have never been more weary of the whole affair, and to each of my congratulators I snarling shew my teeth.—That's the man I am ! Nobody can satisfy, and nothing suits me. So people let me be; and with that I must put up, in the end.—Toward yourself, tho', I'll not behave so churlishly.—

You know, child, that our sort of folk look neither right nor left, neither before nor behind ; that Time and World are matters of indifference to us, and only one thing sways us—the need to unburden our bosom : accordingly you also know what alone, in reality can lie at my heart. But were it otherwise,—had I already finished with the inner store, and henceforth durst merely look around and keep in view my works' results, the conditions I call forth, the service of which I may be,—then I might find enough of serious and edifying entertainment if I looked around me. I cannot contradict my new French friends when, looking forward to the possibility, nay rather, certainty of a great effect even of my Tannhäuser on the Paris public, they see in it a factor of unprecedented weight, to which they assign an importance to be compared with nothing else conceivable.

A man who can look calmly at the life of so gifted but incredibly wasted a nation as the French, and interest himself in all that makes for its ennobling and develop-ment,—I can't find fault with such a man, if he beholds in the reception of a French Tannhäuser an absolutely vital question for these men's adaptability. Reflect how starved is all French art ; that poesy, more strictly speaking, is altogether foreign to this folk, which knows nothing in its place save rhetoric and eloquence. Owing to the exclusiveness of the French language, and its inability to adopt the poetic element foreign to itself by means of transference from another, there remains but one way open to bring Poesy to bear upon the French—the way of *Music*. But then, you see, neither is the Frenchman constitutionally musical, and all his music he has gotten from abroad. From of old the French musical style has been formed by mere contact with Italian and German music, and strictly is nothing but a cross twixt these two styles. But Gluck, if you look at him closer, taught the French nothing more, than how to bring music into accord with the rhetorical style of French Tragédie—at bottom there was no question here of genuine poesy—wherefore the Italians have been able to keep almost the whole of the field for themselves even since his time. For it has ever been a matter of mere manner in the rhetoric, but apart from that, as little of music as of poesy.

Well, the havoc hence arisen, and increasing to this day, is simply past belief. To find out the capacities of the singers at the Opéra, I was compelled a few nights since to hear the new opus of a Prince Poniatowski; oh, my feelings!! What a longing seized me for the very simplest mountain-vale in Switzerland!! As I came home it was exactly as if I had been murdered, and every possibility had vanished into air. Yet I have learnt how the very ghastliness of an impression may simply add force to the countereffects, and make them of greater scope. "You see *how* it stands," friends said to me, " and *what* we await and demand of you!" Those who tell me this, are men who have not set foot within the opera-house for 20 years, had frequented none but the Conservatoire and Quartet concerts, and finally —before knowing me—had studied my scores; not mere musicians either, but painters, men of letters—even of the State. They tell me, "What you bring, has never been remotely offered us before ; for with music you bring us full poesy ; you bring a whole, and wholly self-supported, independent of every influence that hitherto has been ex- erted by our institutes on the artist who wished to present himself to us. Moreover, you bring it in perfection of form, and with the greatest power of expression : the most ignorant Frenchman himself could wish to alter nothing of it ; he must receive it entire, or reject it in the lump. And there resides the great significance we attach to the coming event : if your work is repulsed, we shall know what's the matter with us, and give up hope ; if it's welcomed, and that at one blow (for a Frenchman can be influenced no other way), we all shall breathe once more ; for it is not literature and science, but only the directest art of the Theatre, the most universal in its operations, that can stamp itself deep on the views of our national spirit. However,—we feel sure of the greatest and most abiding impression."—

In fact the Director himself, now that he knows the subject better, is boasting to everybody that with Tann- häuser he can reckon at last on a real "succès d'argent."

In Brussels, too, I had many a talk with a remarkable old man, a very witty, shrewd and seasoned diplomat ["Papa" Klindworth], yet who recommends me from his heart not to lose sight of the French : let one think and say what one likes, it remains undeniable (according to him) that at present the French are the actual prototype of European civilisation, and to produce a decided effect upon them is to operate upon the whole of Europe.—

It really all sounds most encouraging, and I suppose I cannot get away from the importance I'm to be of to the world. But strange to say, I don't care much for Europe or the world, and at bottom of my heart I tell myself :

What business of thine is it all? As said however, I perceive that I shan't get away from it : oh, my dæmon takes good care of that ; the surest guarantee for my indefeasible effect upon Europe is—my want !

I tell it you quite candidly, so that you may form no false notions about me,—may not believe, for example, that the said vain assumption is driving me to anything which strictly lies beyond me. Those Paris concerts have brought me to an incalculable plight : even Brussels I undertook for nothing but to help myself out of the hole, and that also turned out the opposite ; so that on my departure (much as Rossini once said after the fiasco of a "carefully" wrought opera, "Si jamais on me prend à soigner ma partition") I told myself, "Si jamais on me prend à faire de l'argent !" Germany stays mum to me, and if ever I'm to meet with Tristan and the Nibelungen in my lifetime, I must contrive veritable miracles now, to keep my head above the waters of this blessed life. So I accept the hopes of my Paris friends, in particular of my Opera-director ; and as every grand chance has an unfortunate knack of being a trifle behindhand, for the present I'm not half disinclined to sell myself to a Russian general, who is shortly to arrive here to acquire me for a S. Petersburg Tannhäuser expedition.* I pray you to join in my laughter : indeed there is no other way to help me out of the ridiculous contradictions in which this redemption-craving world leaves its anticipated saviour !

Meanwhile I must gather my wits, to write a—grand ballet. What do you say to that? Have you doubts of me ? You shall beg my pardon for them by-and-by, when

---

* Though the S. Petersburg offer (a bona fide one) would have placed £1,000 in Wagner's pocket on the spot, and an equal amount later on, he honourably declined it for sake of the Paris Grand Opéra—which eventually brought him worse than nothing; see letter of June 5 to Otto.—Tr.

you hear and see it. Thus much to go on with: not a note, not a word of my Tannhäuser will be altered; but a ballet there imperatively had to be, and that ballet was to occur in the second act because of the Opéra's abonnés always reaching the theatre somewhat late, after a heavy dinner, never at the commencement. Well, I have declared I could accept no dictates from the Jockey Club, and should withdraw my work; I mean to help them [the authorities] out of their straits, however: the opera needn't begin before 8 o'clock, and then I'll add a decent culmination to the unhallowed Venusberg.

This Court of Frau Venus was the palpable weak spot in my work: without a good ballet in its day, I had to manage with a few coarse brush-strokes, and thereby ruined much; for I left this Venusberg with an altogether tame and ill-defined impression, consequently depriving myself of the momentous background against which the ensuing tragedy is to upbuild its harrowing tale. All later reminiscences and warnings, whose grave significance should send a shudder through us (the only explanation of the plot), lost wellnigh all effect and meaning: dread and instant trepidation kept aloof from our minds. But I also recognise that, when I wrote my Tannhäuser, I could not have made anything like what is needed here; it required a greater mastery, by far, which only now have I attained: now that I have written Isolde's last transfiguration, at last I could find alike the right close for the Fliegender-Holländer overture, and also— the horrors of this Venusberg. One becomes omnipotent, you see, when the World but exists as one's plaything. Naturally I shall have to invent the whole thing for myself, to be able to prescribe the smallest nuance to the ballet-master; it is certain, however, that nothing save Dance can lend effect and execution here: but what a dance! The good people shall stare in amazement at all I'll have hatched there. I haven't arrived at jotting anything down as yet: I will here make my first attempt with a few indications; don't be surprised at its occurring in a letter to Elisabeth!

VENUS and TANNHÄUSER remain as in the original directions: but—the three GRACES lie couched at their feet, locked picturesquely in each other's arms. A whole tangle of children's limbs surrounds the couch; these are the slumbering Amoretti, who have fallen atop of one another in their childlike romps, and then asleep.

All around pairs of lovers are resting on projections of the grotto. In the middle only Nymphs are dancing, teased by Fauns whom they seek to elude. The movement of this group increases: the Fauns become more boisterous, the Nymphs' coy flight incites the males of the reclining pairs to their protection. Jealousy of the forsaken females: waxing effrontery of the Fauns. Tumult. The Graces rise and intervene, enjoining seemliness and order: they in turn are accosted, but the young men chase the Fauns away: the Graces reconcile the couples.—Voices of Sirens are heard.—Then a tumult from the distance. The Fauns, bent on vengeance, have summoned the Bacchantes to their aid. The Wild Hunt storms on, after the Graces have reclined once more in front of Venus. The yelling retinue brings with it every kind of animal monster: from these a black ram is selected, and diligently examined to see that it has no white spot: amid cheers it is dragged to a waterfall: a priest fells it and offers it up, with dreadful gestures.

Suddenly, amid wild huzzaings of the throng, the northern Strömkarl (known to you *) emerges from the foaming water with his marvellous big fiddle. He plays up for a dance, and you may imagine all I must invent to give this dance

---

* Among Mathilde Wesendonck's poems is a ballad on the Nicker. [Neither this incident, nor that at end of the preceding paragraph, is embodied in the final version.—Tr.]

its fitting character. More and more mythological freaks are brought on, all the beasties sacred to the gods; even centaurs at last, who stamp among the rioters. The Graces are afraid to quell the hubbub; then in utter despair they fling themselves upon the mob : in vain ! Turning to Venus, they look around for help: with a wave of her hand she now awakes the Amoretti, who rain a perfect hail of darts upon the rioters ; more and yet more, their quivers are ever replenished. Then all form more definite pairs; the wounded reel into each other's arms ; a general frenzy of desire. The arrows, whirring wild of aim, have hit the very Graces ; no longer are they mistress of themselves.

Fauns paired with Bacchantes rush forth ; the Graces are borne off on the Centaurs' backs ; all stagger toward the background : the [young] couples lie down : the Amoretti, shooting still, have gone in pursuit of their quarry. Approaching lassitude. A mist descends. From greater and still greater distance sounds the Sirens' cry. All becomes hid. Deep quiet.—

Finally — — Tannhäuser awakes from his dream.*—

Something of that sort. What do you say to it ?—It tickles me, to have been able to bring in the eleventh variation of my Strömkarl, for that explains why Venus and her court have moved off north : only there could one find the fiddler meet for these old gods to dance to. The black ram also pleases me, tho' it I could replace : shouting Mænads would merely have to carry in the murdered ORPHEUS ; his head they would cast in the waterfall,—whereon my Strömkarl would spring up. Only, without words that's less intelligible ; what is your opinion ?—I wish I had Genelli aquarelles to go

---

* It will be observed that the two cloud-tableaux of the ultimate version are not even suggested here. Some seven weeks hence, however, they are introduced into a more detailed draft, together with a third tableau—Diana and Endymion; see the "Wagner number" of *Die Musik*, Feb. 1905.—Tr.

by : he used to make these mythologic orgies very plausible. I suppose, however, I shall have to help myself again, tho' I still have several details to devise.—

So I've been and written you another Kapellmeister letter, don't you think ? And a ballet-master's letter into the bargain this time. Won't it put you in a good humour ?

And yet you do not write to me ? Nor Otto either ? O you bad, bad people ! Wherever am I to get letters from, to give me joy, then ? And you know perfectly well that nothing else can give me proper joy ! Yes, one thing—when I give myself something to do with you.

Only yesterday the Brussels people sent my photographic portrait after me, which to me appears highly successful ; so of course I thought at once of you. If you will write me very nicely soon, and tell me about when you're returning to Zurich, I'll send to Herr Stünzig, or whomever you name, this picture that will tell you how I look now ; and let it be hung above the piano in the picture-gallery. As you've taken all your house to Rome with you, there won't be a single friend to welcome you on your return if I don't put in an appearance, at least in the picture-room.

Only imagine my having clean forgotten Otto's birthday this time ! I knew quite well what March brings round, but the day, the day I couldn't think of [16th]. Moreover, I had absolutely nothing fit to give him, so you must ask him to wait till next March : evidently I shall be a rich man by then, throwing millions all round me.—Apart from that, remember, my dear child, that I still have nothing upon earth but you ; that for you, through you, with you, do I live, and all my pastime has for me this only charm—that I can make it voice to you my lack, and you give ear to it so fondly. Adieu, my child ! A thousand heartfelt wishes : if they're too many for yourself, then give of them to your good man and children. R. W.

103.

Paris, May 2, 60.

I really can't let May come in, best Child, without sending you another sign-of-life to Rome, as I presume you will not stay there much longer. Could anything withhold my hand from writing you to-day, 'twere only that I have so absolutely nothing right to tell you; however, you already know that it isn't what I write *about* to you, that possibly can count, but the mood in which I write it. According to that the topic would be a matter of indifference, were it not that my mood itself, to be exact, is my only topic that can interest you; and just about that there isn't much to say. How *could* I be in brilliant mood now?—Let that pass.—Is my mood quite worthy of your sympathy? Neither about that can I clear my mind; but the voice deep down within me says: It should be otherwise!

God knows for what I still exist! So far as it's a matter of my will, I have no reason to congratulate myself on my endurance: the lucid intervals are far too rare. Perhaps even they will vanish altogether some day; and yet—I still await them—hold out, wait—and drag my life on in the night!—

Your recollections moved me very much. It is incredible, what devastations of one's being one can bear; the overplus would prove a lamentable fraction, might it not also be a thing sublimely great. In good moments I venture to flatter myself with the latter: what is greater than complete abandonment of happiness for the whole breadth of existence, and restriction to unique instants? Of a surety, the vulgar alone is broad of life and insistent, the noble but strength of resistance; affirmation nothing, negation all.—And the artist?—Poor fool, he's dupe enough of his own consciousness; but he's very cunningly contrived to weather the eternal conflict. Yes, to be in perpetual conflict, never to arrive at full inner repose, ever to be hunted, lured, and hurled aside,—indeed that is the life of seething whence his inspiration blossoms like a flower of despair.—Oh, I know it, and you can but feel it with me: who would fain be other than he is?

Well, my mind has grown clear as to the choice which now faces me, but not yet as to how I ought to choose,— nor will that choice, apparently, depend at all on me; but *It* will choose, the *Brahm*, the neuter. And the choice is this:—either to *reproduce* my works, or *produce* new ones.*

The first is tantamount to shouldering all the consequences of the affirmation of life, until they crush one. If I mean to disclose my finished works to the world for virtually the first time, and make it feel all that it owns in them through wholly adequate performances, in that alone I have an undertaking which must utterly consume the very strongest dose of vital force. Then all else is a by-road, every plunge within an act of treason,—then, ho for without, everything outward, subjecting of the world to me, belonging of myself to it alone, letting myself be betrayed, humiliated, racked, destroyed by it, to pass into its conscience. Then will I say to it, as Jesus to His disciples at the Last Supper: " Ye know but the milk of my doctrine; now shall ye taste of its blood ; come and drink, that I may be within you!"—†

---

* "Entweder meine Werke *aufführen*, oder neue *ausführen*." As a rule I prefer to restrict the term " produce," in this connection, to the first *performance* of a work, but an exception is demanded here by Wagner's deliberate play on words.—Tr.

† There is no text in the Bible exactly corresponding to this allusion (the nearest being Cor. I. iii, 2, and Heb. v, 12-14); but in the working-out section of Wagner's own *Jesus of Nazareth* (1849) we find the following assigned to act iv, which includes the Last Supper: " Jesus, ' Ye have tasted but

Or the second:—I renounce all possibility of ever hearing my works, and consequently of disclosing them completely to the world. 'Tis a sacrifice, and yet—so far as my own pleasure is concerned—perhaps a mere alluring dream ; for the voice distinctly tells me, I shall never reach enjoyment or satisfaction through performance of my works, and there will always be left a secret pang that tortures me the more as I must conceal and deny it, no doubt, not to rank as utter madman. And if I renounced that :—oh, the vision of bliss that dawns on me then ! In the first place, total personal poverty ; not another care for the least possession. A family that adopts me, stills my very modest needs, to which in exchange I transfer all that ever may be mine ; there to do and follow naught beyond the writing of my final works, everything I still have in my head. Then I also leave it calmly to my saving dæmon, to summon him who shall disclose my works to the world some day—it being left to my good pleasure to have him presented to me, or to let things pass without a murmur if I thought the man impossible. That—that were my wish, my settled choice—had *I* a voice in it!—

The choice's settlement will indicate *which* was more needful. If none but *I* can reproduce my works, it will happen ; I'm certain of that!—If none but *I* can write the works I have still in my head,—then *that* will happen. Now, which would be the harder task ? Or—which would be of greater *moment ?* I rather incline to the former. Probably it is more indifferent to the World-spirit, whether a few extra new works of this kind shall be bestowed on the world, than that the essence of this kind of work should be disclosed to the world wholly intelligibly. Oh, it is

the milk; not the gall of my doctrine. My death shall give to you the gall, that ye may be steadfast in doing the work that is needful ' (See Eph. iv, 13 and 14)."—*Prose Works* VIII, 308.—Tr.

obvious : with the essence of a thing one never reckons quantity ; that's inessential, but the main affair is the inner capacity of the entire kind. If I completely disclose this, I thereby fire the consciousness of other units, who will then be able to multiply the spark. Thus may we also account for the uncommon individuality and multiplicity of the Italian school of painting, the Spanish school of poetry, and so on. Consequently (I believe I am safe in assuming) it is of the greater moment to the World-spirit that I should disclose my finished works to the world through perfect performances ; and on the widest possible terrain, since the few on whom the spark can fall to use are very rare, very dispersed alike in time and space. With new works, on the other hand, in a certain very deep sense—intelligible to the World-spirit alone—I now can but repeat myself, no other essentiality can I reveal any more.

So a choice would come off very badly, and it will be impossible to consult my wish thereon. Yet a middle course may be found even here, and a mocking mirage floats before me : namely, that I might perhaps combine the two by turns, or find sweet rest again the battle over, and finish my works in the end. Oh, It is never at a loss for snares ! But I *know* my dæmon ; and there are serious hours when I know everything, no snare can trap me, and yet—I resolve to bear all. To-day I'm writing you in such a mood ; be good to me, respect and love me ! I deserve it—for my sorrows' sake !—

Many thousand greetings. Let me hear soon, when I am to begin addressing to Venice. I shall answer Otto presently in Latin, since that has become his pet tongue. And he's right ; what was sung to him yonder in Latin is glorious [Sixtine chapel—Palestrina ?]: I know it well !

104.

May 23, 60, Paris.

I broke open your last Roman letter this morning in bed, and viewed what it contained [her portrait and Otto's as birthday gift, see p. 232. Maurice came back to tell me my bath was ready; he found me bathed in tears, and silently withdrew.

My child, the gods honoured me yesterday with the finest day of this year. It had never been entirely bright and fair before: on my early-morning walk of yesterday for the first time I was greeted by an absolute clear sky, with an invigorating easterly wind to boot; everything green and gleaming. Without the faintest cause for gladness at my individual lot, living from one day to the next in the most tottering uncertainty, daily compelled to defend myself, as if besieged, against continual attacks upon my quiet—yet it was well and bright with me; the gods loved me, and that made me smile. Nothing approached me, nothing met me with a greeting, except the heavens and the lovely breeze, which had shunned me so long; but that sufficed, and fairest visions filed before my soul. For sure, I pondered, everywhere 'tis fine to-day, and what tho' I receive no greetings, full many a someone will be thinking of me and saying: See, the gods do love him!—How childish I still am, how easy to be coaxed! The sky and zephyrs, sunshine and green of May, relieved you of the trouble, this time, of scaring dull care from my brow. Please thank them a little!—

What I else have only known in bouts of exaltation, turned this time to a quiet calm resolve—to delight myself by some good deed addressed to others. At home I found the latest number of the Journal des Débats; in it an article by Berlioz on Fidelio. I had not seen Berlioz since my concerts: thereafter he had let himself be enticed into

greater and greater animosities and ill-concealed attacks;
I had been the more obliged to give the unhappy man up,
as any contrary attempt would inevitably have appeared to
him an insult. However, I was much delighted by this
article on Fidelio, and braving every possibility, nay, probability of his totally misunderstanding me, I wrote him
somewhat as follows: " I have this moment read your
article on Fidelio. Accept a thousand thanks for it! It
is quite a special joy to me, to hear these pure and noble
accents of expression of a soul, an intellect, which so
completely understands and makes its own the inner secrets
of a creation by another hero of art. There are moments
when the witnessing of such an act of estimation transports
me almost to a higher pitch than the appreciated work
itself; because that testifies so plainly that an endless chain
connects great spirits, which through this solitary link are
saved from ever falling to incomprehension." *

How rejoiced I shall be, if he takes that in good part.
To be sure, upon reading the article through a second time
I remarked how infinitely remote from mine is Berlioz'
standpoint, even in this valuation of Beethoven; he still
pays far too much regard to the artwork's outward features,
and consequently an attention beyond my comprehension
to the manifestations of applause wherewith it is received.
Nevertheless I could see how solitary is Berlioz' station
even on that step, and how foolish he is to deprive himself

---

* The passage in quotation-marks is an almost literal translation of
the "pigeon-French" note to Berlioz which Wagner had transcribed
for Liszt the day before, save that the address " Cher Maître" and the
concluding sentence, " Si je m'exprime mal, j'espère pourtant, que vous
me ne comprendrez pas mal," are omitted above.—N.B. The letter to
Liszt of May 22, 60, does not appear in the English edition of the
Wagner-Liszt Correspondence, as the original, evidently buried among
the papers of Princess Wittgenstein, was not published until 1900
(*Bayreuther Blätter*, pages 3-4 for that year).—Tr.

of the sole refreshment possible in such a situation, un-grudging welcome of his next-of-kin. But envy—: good God ! !

—So my thoughts roamed tranquilly ahead, and lit on Liszt. Of him I know truly nothing that has not shewn him to me in a strictly amiable light; his shadows do not lie in his character, but solely in his intellect here and there : on that side he is easily influenced, and gets lost in weaknesses. It was long since I had written him ; * even my great grief at the loss of his son [Dec. 15, 59] was expressed to him merely through others [Bülows ?]. Business there is none between us, and to so dear a friend I can't write otherwise than intimately ; but, to be certain that one's confidences are always being made to *two* [i.e. Liszt *and* Pss Wittgenstein] is really past abiding,—it turns the whole thing into pose and jugglery. And that's the fact : Liszt has become a man without a single secret to himself ; neither is it a union of hearts, but his plainly abused weakness, that has reduced him to an unlovely dependence. At last I

---

* As a matter of fact, Wagner had written him from Brussels on the 29th of March, but apparently without receiving any answer either to that letter or to its predecessor of Nov. 23, 1859. Similarly, when Wagner reproaches himself in his letter of May 22, 60 (see last footnote), " On the 22nd of October I thought of you, of course, but did not write you. Why ? I can no longer remember," his memory really *is* at fault; for letter 298 in the *W.-L. Corr.*, dated " Paris, Oct. 20, 59," begins thus : " I hope, dear Franz, these lines will reach you punctually on the 22nd. Accept my hearty congratulations on your birthday," etc., etc., fully half a page being devoted to the warmest utterances of affection, by side of which Liszt's meagre " Herzensgruss zum heutigen Geburtstag von Deinem Franz Liszt "—the telegram referred to at end of this paragraph as " the most ardent felicitation "—quite pales to insignificance, making one realise how very thankful Wagner was for such small mercies. Similarly, the metaphorical " hand-squeezes " would seem to have been strangely one-sided at this epoch, for Wagner's gift of the *Tristan* full score itself (through Härtels) roused no Weimar echo until many weeks after.—Tr.

regretfully, but definitely declared to him—or rather to the pair, alas!—that I could write to him (or them!) no more. So the poor fellow sacrifices all in silence, and suffers all as if he could see nothing else for it; yet he goes on loving me as heretofore, just as he remains a noble, precious creature in my sight. Imagine then, how touchingly a greeting steals to us from time to time; from time to time we find the means of giving each other's hand a hidden squeeze, like a pair of lovers severed by the world. Thus only yesterday the most ardent felicitation on my birthday arrived for me by telegraph; * how I smile and rejoice then!—

And so the day passed: I remained in unruffled good spirits, mentally enjoying, almost for the first time, that sense of ease and happiness of the bodily robust who is conscious of no reason for his well-being just because it proceeds from a harmonious balance of his vital forces. To you I've little need to name the source whence this feeling wells for me; 'tis that itself which gives this health, and so exquisite it is, that still I feel how very seldom can a fine day bring me such untroubled harmony again. At evening, Jupiter shone wondrous bright on me— he's standing at full brilliance now—according to our Schopenhauer's conceit he is the star of the fifty years old, and I still lack three of that; but I shall live to see them : will Jupiter stay true to me, and shine upon me then? Oh, there still are starless nights to come, I know them all, the dread and dreary through the which I have to steer :—Shall I then espy the star again; will Jupiter shine for me when

---

* As may be seen in the letter already twice referred-to in these notes, the telegram arrived just as Wagner was *concluding* that. letter itself.— N.B. The princess had set out for Rome just four days previously; nevertheless the "lettre pleine d'effusion de Wagner" is despatched to her three days before its writer himself is answered : " Je vais lui recrire et m'imbiber aussi de son *Tristan*," writes Liszt to Carolyne May 28.—Tr.

my need of a lodestar is direst ?—I asked. The wondrous
evening answered me with balmy breath, and cooled my
eye.—

A couple of young Germans, whom I chose entirely at
random, came round at night. Before leaving, they gave
me no peace till I played them the prelude to Tristan again,
over which all the young-folks have gone completely mad,
particularly when it comes to the new close. That close,
in fact, I had to play them a couple of times more : then
I bundled them off, and laid me down. To-day I awake,
and your letter is brought to my bedside. But there, child,
there, I can depict no more—wherefore not a word about
the portraits of you both !—You shall have mine as soon
as ever I know *when* I'm to address it to Zurich. It's the
best of my portraits, quite remarkable to myself for having
succeeded so well in very unpropitious circumstances, and
especially for having caught so calm and unconstrained a
facial expression. I was very much out of sorts, yet plagued
by the Brussels bandsmen to leave them my photograph
as souvenir ; it rained (Otto knows how it *can* rain at
Brussels), and I didn't want to go to the studio. Finally,
late in the day, behold me called for once more : I had
no umbrella, was to conduct again that evening, had to
mount five flights of stairs, and expressed to the artist my
utter indignation at being expected to bring off anything
endurable under such conditions. The aplomb with which
the artist (an extremely good one) treated me, put me in
a really good humour, and with the remark : " Well, all
things are possible if you can do anything with me," I
took my stand in complete amazement, thinking to myself :
" I daresay it will turn out quite good enough for the
Brusselers." I now remember realising, also, how incredibly
rapidly the functions of the brain obey the passing mood
and can link the nearest with the most remote. I had

been photographed before in Paris, and, without my being aware of it, the brute of an artist had thought fit to pose me in a most affected attitude, my eyes cocked sideways: the resulting portrait is an abomination to me, making me look, as I've protested, just like a sentimental Marat.* That wretched effigy has been used for the *Illustration*, and—still more hideously distorted—since gone the round of like illustrated journals (even in England now).—Well, my abhorrence of it instinctively led me at the Brussels operation to try for a more seemly expression, to give myself without a grain of affectation a tranquil, reasonable look. And the very irony of this whole process brought me to the right frame of mind in a twinkling: all my surroundings vanished, and quietly I gazed across the world as if it weren't the least concern of mine. Merely a wish remained, mayhap, to see my Jupiter: perchance it may strike you that he really did ray down a glimmer on me.

Now I've told you all about my birthday, and everything connected with it. Yesterday you dipped your goblet in the fountain [of Trevi], and drained a cup for me as well: O my child, how fair a thing you wished me then! Believe me, no fonder aspiration could the gods fulfil me, than to let you drink me welcome to that fount; through you to learn Rome's fairest mysteries, the which I have to thank already for so great a happiness, since they have been so dear and salutary to yourself. So let us set our hopes on Jupiter!—

---

* Plainly this is the portrait facsimiled on page 73 of Mr. Chamberlain's *Richard Wagner*, notwithstanding that at first sight there the signature appears to be " Paris. 6 Mai 1861 "; the last cypher, however, is so imperfectly inked that it might equally be an " o." Even supposing that date to be really " 186*1*," there would be nothing to prevent Wagner from bestowing the Paris likeness on an importunate acquaintance over a twelvemonth after it had been taken ; whereas the above description fits it to a tee.—Tr.

105.

Paris, July 22, 60.

Am I really to write at last on this dark page I so repeatedly have squared to hand? Am I to despatch you another account of myself? Or shall I wait until at least a day of sunshine gives pure sky to animate me with a breath of cheerfulness that I might gratefully devote to you?—Not even that boon will shew itself! West and South keep on prevailing, to tune my poor nerves to their lowest pitch. Which shall it be, then? Maybe you'll fret yourself more than you need, if I keep silence!

Even yourself, can you actually form a clear conception of my life? I scarce can credit it, for perhaps it is not possible. I have lived to make the strange experience that I must end by withdrawing from almost every sign of sympathy extended to me, because I'm pulled up everywhere at last against a point where my odd position toward the world, and everything I do therein, falls victim to misunderstandings so manifest that I can but feel how people really take me—strictly speaking—for a sort of hypocrite. It is becoming very difficult, however, even to explain what I mean by that; so that this perception in turn remains my secret, and the only consolation left me in face of the world is a curious one: that what it fancies it beholds in me is a thing it treats as common to us all, quite natural, and therefore not particularly blamable.*—

---

* These and the ensuing dark sayings rather suggest that the gobemouches had lately been busying themselves with that generous assistance in recognition of which Mme Kalergis became owner of the "orchestral sketches" of *Tristan*—an act of generosity thus reported by Liszt in a letter of July 11 to Pss Wittgenstein—"La ligne sur Mme Kalergis dans la lettre de X se rapporte au service qu'elle vient de rendre à Wagner, en comblant généreusement le déficit de ses concerts de Paris, par l'avance de plusieurs milliers de francs. C'est un beau trait qui m'a causé une très agréable surpris, et dont j'ai été directement informé par une courte lettre de Wagner, que j'ai communiquée à X." To Frau

No one, I am sure, could have less gladness, pleasure, or merely recreation, fleeting stimulus of any sort or kind, than I. Whatever I do or try to, never for a moment does it enter my head to prepare *myself* a pleasure, an enjoyment, by it; were it only since I've learnt to see more and more distinctly that what I sought has never thriven, but always turned into the opposite. To me this is so evident, that after a trip to Fontainebleau the other day—whither I had been attracted by the promise of fine trees—I took a firm resolve to think of no further distraction of any kind this summer, because so much, regarding which I've grown extremely sensitive, made me finish by recognising even in that trip an experience more replete with pain than pleasure. Not a soul invades my solitude whom I'm not more pleased to see depart; at any stirring of the inextinguishable desire for intimacy, or were it but some trifling change, I have come to impress on myself that all conceivable fulfilment could only give me pain, and quietly bide at home, aware that I should never find the very tiniest refreshment tho' I sought it. I expect there's hardly anybody who can figure this entire and utter resignation, and least of all if one has children!—

And with all this unheard joylessness of existence to be moving in a world still, amid requirements and regards that almost always cast on me the light, in others' eyes, of one who shews himself inordinately grasping,—at last that leads me to the strangest sentiments in respect of this world. I tell you openly, the bitterness I have often confessed to you is disappearing more and more from me, and contempt is usurping its place. This feeling is not passionate:

Wesendonck the transaction can scarcely have been a mystery, for the reference in letter 114 (*vid. inf.*) points to a prior communication thereof either to her husband or herself.—Mme Kalergis is the lady whose name by a second marriage (de Moukhanoff) adorns the dedication of the reprint of Wagner's *Judaism in Music* some nine years hence.—Tr.

no, it gives me more and more tranquillity; but no longer
is there a relation of mine to anyone whatever, in which this
feeling doesn't take the upper hand completely. And that
spares my heart much: it's far less vulnerable now;—I can
despise where formerly I was enraged!—

So I pour my heart out much less freely, also, reflecting
that I'm not the man for understanding through my actions,
and hoping that something at least of my works will meet
with understanding some fine day. Yet I may tell you
thus much: my sense of purity alone confers on me this
power. I feel myself pure of heart: in my inmost depth
I know that I have ever wrought for others only, never
for myself; and my perpetual sorrows are my witness.—

But joy? Ah, nothing more can give me joy! And
that's my solace: any joy, in which I caught myself, were
my arraigner, and it were over with my right of proud
disdain.—

Thus to-day I am able to inform you with a curious sense
of satisfaction that the notification of repeal of my banish-
ment from Germany, delivered me a few days since, left
me utterly cold and indifferent. Telegraphic congratulations have been raining cheers upon me: not a single one
of them have I answered. Who would comprehend it, if
I told him this is nothing to me but the opening of a new
field of suffering, of suffering that certainly outweighs all
chance of any kind of gratification, in measure as I see
nothing in front of me but sacrifices on my own part?
Whoever draws by accident a step too near me, appears
to understand this of a sudden; but 'tis nothing save a
whiff of understanding; he turns his back, and ere long
he thinks I'm shamming after all. And those, too, are
the middling best; as for the remainder—Disgusting's
the word

I have a friend, however, of whom I grow fonder and

fonder afresh : my old surly-faced and yet so deeply love-filled Schopenhauer. When I've been fumbling the farthest and deepest, what a quite unique refreshment all at once, to dip into the pages of that book ; to see my sentiments so wholly understood and scheduled, but in that other tongue withal which soon turns sorrow to an object of cognition, transposing everything from Feeling to the cool, consoling marble of the Reason, and while it shews me to myself, at like time shewing me the whole wide world ! What a marvellous exchange is that, and of the most beatifying order ! And ever new is this effect, because it constantly is stronger. Thus calm is given, and contempt itself ascends to love : for all self-flattery has gone ; clear knowledge cools the brow of pain ; the creases smooth, and sleep regains its soothing power. And how beautiful [? *], that the aged man knows nothing of all he is to me, of what I'm through him to myself !

And now please let me call to mind a very different sort of friend. Laugh as you list, but I speak of a perfect angel I've always about me, a being of unswerving kindness, that cannot so much as look at me without lavishing a whole heap of glad caresses on me : 'tis the little dog you destined for me once upon your bed of sickness ! Words fail to express the affection of this matchless beasty. Each afternoon we lose ourselves together in the Bois de Boulogne ; then I often think of my old peaceful Sihlthal ! Fare you well, dear kindly soul, and have my thanks !—

---

* I cannot help thinking that Wagner meant to say "wie Schade "— " what a pity ! "—instead of this puzzling " wie schön."—Two months after the above was written, the Frankfort philosopher died (Sept. 21). He and Wagner had never met, nor even exchanged an epistle ; for the complimentary copy of the *Ring* poem was sent to Schopenhauer unattended, Dec. 1854, and the *Tristan* poem direct by Härtels Dec. 1858 *without* the draft letter quoted p. 76 *sup.*—Tr.

106a.

[Paris, beginning of August 1860.]

Heaven help us, what a poet I must be! I am growing quite presumptuous—this never-ending translation of the Tannhäuser has made me so conceited. Just through being compelled to follow word by word, I've discovered at last how concise and unalterable even this my poem is; one word, one shade of meaning dropped, and my translators and self have had to admit that an essential point was sacrificed.* At first I did believe in the possibility of minor alterations, but we've had to give up all and sundry. I was quite astounded; and then, comparing this with other poems, I found I really knew but few to which I could ascribe a similar quality. In brief, I've been driven to acknowledge to myself that just the poem could absolutely not have been done better,—what will you say to that? It is rather in the music, that I can make improvements; here and there, to particularise, I shall give the orchestra richer and more expressive passages. The only scene I mean to recast entirely, is that with Venus: I found Frau Venus stiff; a few good features, but no true life. Here I have added a fair number of verses; the Goddess of Delight herself becomes affecting, and Tannhäuser's agony real, so that his invocation of the Virgin Mary bursts as a cry of anguish from his deepest soul: at that period I could never have made a thing like this. For its musical execution, though, I still need very good humour, and haven't the remotest notion whence to get it!—

There will soon come out a prose translation of the four pieces, Holländer, Tannhäuser, Lohengrin and Tristan, for

---

* Edmond Roche and Rudolf Lindau, assisted afterwards by Charles Nuitter.—The whole subject is exhaustively dealt with in an interesting article by Dr. Golther in the special "Wagner-number" of *Die Musik* 1903 (No. 16).—Tr.

which I shall write a preface meant to give my friends here some enlightenment on the formal side of my artistic tendencies.* I have just been going through these translations, and that compelled me to take stock of every detail of my poems once again. Yesterday the Lohengrin moved me very much, and I cannot help considering it the most tragic tale of all, since the *Versöhnung* really is only to be found if one casts a quite terribly far glance on the world.†

Only the profound hypothesis of Reincarnation (*Seelenwanderung*) has been able to shew me the consoling point where all converge in the end to an equal height of redemption, after their divers life-careers, running severed but side by side in Time, have met in full intelligence Beyond it. On that beautiful Buddhist hypothesis the spotless purity of Lohengrin becomes easy to explain, in that he is the continuation of Parzival—who first had to wrest to himself his purity ; in the same sense would Elsa reach up to Lohengrin in her rebirth. Thus the plan for my " Sieger " would appear to me the sequel and conclusion of the Lohengrin : here " Sawitri " (Elsa) fully overtakes " Ananda." Thus were all the awful tragedy of life solely to seek in sunderance by time and space ; but as Time and Space are nothing save *our* modes of viewing, have no reality apart from that, so to the man of perfect sight even the utmost tragic grief should be explainable as nothing but the

---

* "Zukunftsmusik," *i.e.* "Music of the Future"; see *Prose Works* III.—Tr.

† To prevent this sentence being twisted to an arbitrary significance, I have retained the German word *Versöhnung*, which may literally mean either reconciliation, atonement, or expiation. Here, in light of the next paragraph, the idea is that of an ideally ' happy ' ending, but of such effected by extension of the conflicting factors to *one* point of rest, beyond the bounds of personality, just as with the chief characters of the three other dramas named above.—Tr.

individual's defect of vision.* So it is, I believe; and in full truth the solitary point at stake is a matter of the Pure and Noble, which in itself is griefless.—

I can write you nothing but such babble—the only worth the pains; and with you alone have I a care to babble of such things! Then Time and Space, their contents naught save want and agony, take wing! But ah, how rarely am I in heart for such babbling!—

The Tristan is as great a wonder to myself as ever. It is becoming more and more inscrutable to me, how I was able to create a thing like that; upon reading it through again, alike my eye and ear went wide agape! How terribly I shall have to pay for this work some day, if I mean to place it whole before me! I distinctly foresee the most unheard-of sufferings; for there, I can't conceal it from myself, I've overstepped whatever lies within the range of our executive achievement: supremely talented performers, the only ones equal to the task, are very rare arrivals in the world. Yet I cannot withstand the temptation, were it merely to hear the orchestra!!—

Parzival has been much awake in me again; I'm seeing more, and clearer, in it every day. Once the whole is finally mature within me, the carrying this poem out ought to be an unexampled joy for me; but many a year may run ere then; also I should like to let it rest, for once, with poetry alone. I'm staving it off as long as I can, and only busy myself with it when it takes me by main

---

* "So müsste dem vollkommen Hellsehenden auch der höchste tragische Schmerz nur aus dem Irrthum des Individuums erklärt werden können." At risk of appearing to play into the hands of my friend Dr. Gould, I have been obliged to give this clause half a diopter clearer definition than that of the original. Greater difficulty is presented by the next sentence: "und in voller Wahrheit handelt es sich durchaus nur um das Reine und Edle, das an sich schmerzlos ist"—for one cannot be quite certain, to *what* the "handelt es sich" refers.—Tr.

force ; but this curious generative process makes me forget my whole misery then.—

Would you like me to babble of that? Didn't I tell you once, that the fabulous wild errand-woman of the Grail is to be one and the same with the temptress of the second act? Ever since that dawned on me, almost the whole of this subject has grown clear. This strange uncanny creature that slavelike serves the Grail-knights with unwearying zeal, fulfils the most untold commissions, and lies cowering in a corner till she's told to execute some office of uncommon hardship,—at times she vanishes entirely, no one knows whither or how. Then suddenly we meet her once again, worn, gruesome, wan and haggard ; yet tireless anew, serving the Holy Grail like a hound. Of its knights, tho', she betrays a secret scorn : her eye seems ever seeking for the right one,—already has she fancied to, but never found him ; nor what she's seeking, does she really know : it is sheer instinct.—When Parzival, the dullard, comes into the land, she cannot turn her gaze away from him : some strange thing must be passing in her ; she knows it not, but fixes on him. He shudders—but it fascinates him also: nothing does he understand. (Here—Poet, set to work!) The working-out alone can speak here ; yet listen to a hint or two, just as Brynhild lent her ear to Wotan :—

This woman is in an inexpressible state of disquiet ; the old esquire has remarked it of her oft before, as the time drew near for her to vanish, but her condition this time is at utmost strain : what is taking place in her? Does she dread another disappearance, fain would be dispensed therefrom? Does she hope to be allowed to—end at last? What is she hoping of Parzival? Plainly, she looks to him for something never-heard,—but all is vague and shadowy, no knowledge, only craving, gloaming.*—Huddled in a

---

* "Kein Wissen, nur Drang, Dämmern." Here we may certainly

corner, she is present at Anfortas' scene of agony : sphinx-like, with curious scrutiny she stares at Parzival; he, too, is stupid, comprehending nothing, open-mouthed—stays dumb. He is cast forth : the errand-woman of the Grail sinks shrieking of a heap, then vanishes (she must roam again).

Now can you guess who is the wondrous witching woman found by Parzival in the magic castle whither his knightly temper leads him ? Then guess what goes on there, and how it all turns out, for I tell you no more to-day.—

106b.

August 10.

I am writing you this second sheet many days later,—how many, I do not know : " Schon zähl' ich nicht die Tage mehr ! " Everything here is one murky monotony : cares and disagreeables in ever novel shape,* but ever the same. Completely joyless ; but not stormy : rather, slinking. On the contrary, calm, full resignation ; naught to—expect ; nothing—to hope ; scarce aught—to wish. Quite used to the caprices of my fate ; bending my back to my mission ; patient, even as regards the weather. And this weather has its lesson for me : it is, that one can alter nothing, must get accustomed to it. The same with all the moral constellations that surround us : there raging is of no avail,—only enduring !—But now and then a light springs up, within. When all has withdrawn there from without,

---

detect the germ of "Durch Mitleid wissend" (such an enigma to the average German of the 'eighties).—It is unnecessary to indicate the differences between this concept and the final story.—Tr.

* See the letter of June 5, in which Otto had been told of the approaching demolition of Wagner's little Paris house for street improvements. About this date he must have been engaged in his attempt to recover the remaining two years' rent, which he had been obliged to pay down in advance (perhaps because of his having no legal standing, as refugee).—Tr.

unsatisfied, the inner life grows light and warm. Surely that is the Tristanesque Night: "Barg im Busen uns sich die Sonne, leuchten lachend Sterne der Wonne!"

All that I could tell you of my existence, appears to me so futile; yet maybe that's the hardest thing of all to understand. Such a career as mine must ever cheat the onlooker: he sees me in acts and undertakings he deems to be my own, whereas at bottom they are quite alien to me: who marks the repugnance that often is filling my soul? All that will be understood one day, but only when the sum is finished and the balance struck. Then folk must find that this Unusual was really but to be accomplished *thus*, and they'll learn—though without being able to apply the lesson to the next case. It has arrived at this: to others I seek to explain but little now; as I have none save a sense of unmitigated suffering, I may as well suffer this too—for I know that it must be. Still: the day of clearing up will come—things are shaping that way—and the world will clap its eyes on many a thing it had not allowed itself to dream of. I say this without for a moment concealing from myself the impossibilities on which I'm marching: Germany lies open to me at last, and I'm feeling my first true shudder; for I haven't an idea as yet, where Tristan's to be born. Ah yes, now the trouble's about to begin!

So the Paris Tannhäuser distracts me, gives time to meditate on Germany, precipitate nothing, and—what is of vast importance!—perhaps the means to adopt the only attitude toward German reproductions of my newer works to enable me, with patience and tranquillity, to prepare there for the best. Should this succeed—how strangely would that sum have then worked out whose figures puzzle everybody now, since nobody can square them.* And yet—I

---

* Apparently alluding to some remark of Otto's re the writer's finances.—Tr.

admit it most modestly—there has been as good as no true calculation of my own in it.—But let us quit this Jack-o'-lantern dance of worldly will and weening: we rank for little else therein but sorrow !—

I can tell you nothing more of Parzival to-day, however, for it's all in a very embryonic stage as yet and indescribable. I'll narrate you an old story instead, which made a great impression upon me the other day through its individuality and profound characteristique. In a volume of Ct. de la Villemarqué's " Les contes des anciens Bretons," where I found the oldest versions, from the Mabinogion, of the legends handled later by French poets—e.g. of Artus, Parcival, Tristan, and so on—I also lit on the tale of Erec and Enide, whereof I still "possess" a medieval German adaptation * in my whilom Dresden library—without having read it. The tale runs pretty much as follows :—

Erec, after long warfare, has brought Enide home to wife ; his land he has secured against assaults of foes on every side ; such miracles of bravery has he wrought, that in his own and all men's eyes he can but rank as most un-vanquishable hero ; so he finds no further cause for fighting, and lives in peaceful bliss for nothing but the love of his fair wife. This dismays his people and his friends ; they fear he will unman himself and lose his power, and blame the too great influence of the gentle dame. She herself begins to grow alarmed, and chides herself for being cause of what all deem this serious change in Erec's nature. Careworn she wakes one morning, looks sadly on her slumbering spouse, and down upon his naked breast, from which all bravery seems flown, fall two hot tears. Waking, he overhears her words, " Oh, must the blame be mine, that hero-strength has

---

* By Hartmann von Aue, who followed Chrêtien de Troyes [the paradoxical "possession" is to be explained by a brother-in-law's guardianship.—Tr.].

hied from him?" Marvelling—with the instant sensibility of noble natures—he fancies he must read her plaint to mean that she is longing now to be, or haply to become, a worthier hero's wife. This strangely subtle film of jealousy determines him forthwith : "God forbid that I should stay thy hand from joining with a worthier knight's above thy husband's corpse!"—he cries. At once he bids saddle for himself and Enide, takes hurried leave of all, fares with her alone into the world, and orders her continually to ride before him, and whatever she may hear or see, never to turn round her face to him, and never breathe one word to him except he ask her. Far in the forest, three robbers come riding towards them : she cannot help but warn Erec. "Did I not command thee silence?" he upbraids her, defeats the robbers, slays them, gives their horses bound together into Enid's charge, and bids her ride still farther in advance of him, driving the horses before her. So they fare on in silence. The same adventure is repeated, only with progressive increase of the danger, of Enide's alarm, Erec's wrath and victorious exploits. Enide hardly dares own to herself her fearful weariness from the long journey without rest or refreshment, for how much more terrible must Erec's exhaustion not be,—Erec, who has ceaselessly to undergo the most stupendous combats? At last he calls a halt ; he bids her repose on a flower-strewn mead, a countryman brings food, wine, and so on. Erec goes aside while she revives herself, and merely wets his parched lips at a spring. He lets her fall asleep, and watches by her. Then they set forth once more, farther and still farther, to the most unheard, most perilous adventures, and ever passed through as before.

Finally, after doing battle with a fearsome giant, Erec returns to Enid's resting-place exhausted unto death, and swoons to the ground. O her lamentations ! Then comes a

knight with lordly retinue—an enemy of Erec's ; the latter
girds himself to yet another fight : he crashes down, as dead.
Seized with burning love for Enid, the Graf bears her off to his
castle, together with her husband's body.   Enid is forced to
appear in the banquet-hall ; the Graf wooes her hand ; beside herself for woe, she cries aloud : " O Erec, liv'dst thou
yet, what man had dared to woo me ! "   The door flies open :
that piercing cry has woken Erec out of death.   One glance
reveals him all ; he slays the foe, clasps Enid to his bosom,
begs her ne'er to doubt him in the days to come, e'en tho' he
be not ever fighting, and with the overjoyed fares home !—
    What do you think of it ?   Are not these whole men ?
So ineffably tender that nowadays we can't conceive of them
at all ; the frightfulest expenditure of strength, from an
excess of refinement of feeling !—
    So sheet 2 is full, as well,—goodbye !   Kind regards to
Wesendonck ; I shall write him soon.   A thousand thanks
and constant love !

R. W.

107.
Paris, Sept. 30, 60
My dear precious Child.
    Hitherto it had only been unwellness that seemed to
seem to allow a pause in my affairs ; to-day, however, I
must wrest me a free hour for once—if free I mean to be.—
    Ah, how the child is revelling in Raphael and paintings ;
how beautiful it is, how sweet and reassuring !   Only myself
does that manner of thing refuse to so much as touch : I still
am the vandal who, after a whole year of residence in Paris,
hasn't got the length yet of a visit to the Louvre !   Does
that not tell you everything ?—
    And how goes it with me otherwise ?—Imagine that
I'm trying now with all my might to pump up music, as
Venus has got to take singing-lessons !   How do I feel

with it ?—You know I'm always writing dumb (or rather,
invisible) letters to you. In one of them I wrote a deal
about two tiny Indian birds that had come into my home
here, and I would not let be given away because they sang
quite exquisitely in the summer, and always cheered me
up at breakfast ; the little cock and little hen had each
its own peculiar stave of melody, most delicate, most
melancholy. At last, on my return from the Rhine expedition about mid-August,* I hear the hen not at all, and her
mate doing nothing but twittering, striving with more and
more distress to find his stave of melody again :—in vain,
he could not take it ; he was *unable* to sing any more ! I
had not noticed it myself, but merely heard, that birds grow
dumb at summer's end and don't begin their song again
till Spring draws nigh ; so I judged that their affairs were
finished thereabouts, and they forgot their singing just
because they no longer felt a need of it. But this taught
me something different : my little male seemed quite astonished at himself, that he had lost his tune and no attempt
could bring it back to him. It took strong hold upon my
mind, this alienation of the inmost nature, this failure of
the power of melody. To whom does that belong, then,—
to the bird, or to someone who simply lends it him ? Certain
it is, that nothing save a state of ecstasy renders him capable
of melody ; at the proper time this state becomes so much a
habit to him, that when the other season comes, he's quite
aghast at seeing the magic suddenly reft him. I suppose
he gets used to it at last ; something inside must tell him,
in Spring he'll have the power to sing again !

Much did I write you on that theme ; for his twittering

---

* To Otto Aug. 23 (a Thursday): "Last week I made a few days'
trip to the Rhine, to wait on the Princess of Prussia at instigation of
the embassy;" it was with Minna, whom he fetched from Soden baths
Aug. 13.—Tr.

and painful chirping lasted for some time.—But now, imagine
it—another letter!—one morn his little wife starts twittering
—and gets her whole tune correct! Fully ten times in
succession did she pipe it!—I was beside myself,—what
could it mean? Was it an anomaly? Are there exceptions
in Nature too? Be that as it may, the little hen had
managed it, though I have not heard her since.—

Ah, if the sky would but clear for once! How am I
to put up even with that for over a year? It's no use
grumbling, though; in spite of sky and autumn days,
compose I must. And I've been literating also; I shall
send you the book very soon [cf. p. 239]. The verses for
my Tannhäuser are not in German trim yet: I'm giving
you the draft after which they've been carried out in French.
And those French verses I have had to compose! What
do you say to that? God knows! everything comes right
n the end; but how?—Yet all this occupation comes in
pat; it masks the world-estrangedness in which I shall always
remain. Hold out I must; it is the will of that same power
which bids my dickybirds to sing and cease. But as for
any actual thinking of myself, I dare not often do it; for
nothing's there but dreary waste. That I have to try and
people with affairs; and if the latter go against my grain,
why! cares merely make one live longer; and Care is aye
a faithful dame.—

But don't entertain any false notions! I'd bind myself
by violence to nothing, and least of all engage in this Paris
Tannhäuser, for instance, were I obliged to importune for
aught here, to say nothing of making a sacrifice. On the
contrary, I put a good face on this foolish game since people
bring so good a face to meet me. As far as reproductions of
my works go, never in my life have I been so well-treated,
nor am I ever likely to be again: no matter what I ask, is
done; nowhere the smallest withstanding. The pianoforte

rehearsals have now commenced, and time is devoted in the very best sense. Every detail is submitted to my approval : thrice have I rejected the plans for the scenery, before they drew them to my mind ; but all will be perfect now, and—even if it doesn't attain the ideal—at any rate the representation will be the best that has taken place yet, or can take place again for ever so long. My pillar of strength is my giant Niemann ; the man has inexhaustible capabilities. He's almost raw at present, and owes everything to instinct until now ; but he has nothing else to do, for months, than let himself be led by me : we study it all to the very last dot.— For Elisabeth I have likewise a half-novice, Sax : her voice is wonderful and not yet spoilt, her talent promising ; she's completely under my thumb.—Venus—Mad. Tedesco, expressly engaged for me—has a superb head for her rôle, only the figure is just a shade too ample ; talent very considerable and well-suited.—Wolfram gave us the greatest trouble of all ; finally I got a Sig. Morelli engaged, a man of magnificent presence and splendid voice : I must try how to coach him. Luckily the opera isn't to be given till I'm perfectly satisfied with the rehearsals ; and that's of weight— I couldn't let so momentous an offer go begging !—The Opéra people already have taken a liking to me ; there is no constraint in any of my relations with them now ; they have begun to understand me, gainsay me in nothing, and are delighted at all the fine doings ahead.

So everything would be well, if it were only a little better with the rest of my existence. There nothing helps : I wake up sad, and sadly go to bed. The bad weather may have something to say in it ; but the moments of wellbeing are growing all too rare, and disquiet, ay, dread, stretch ever broader.—

But don't pay too much heed to these complaints : after all I still am open to the greatest sense of wellbeing, so soon

as any really fine impression comes. On my last birthday,
you know, it was the east-wind did it ; to-day we've had the
first autumnal fog, which forcibly reminded me of Zurich.
Perhaps it means fair weather, and that will help me
much.—

Already I've been working a bit at the music of my new
scene. Remarkable : all the inward-empassionate, what I
might almost term the feminine-ecstatic, I could do absolutely
nothing with at the time I wrote my Tannhäuser ; there I've
been compelled to throw down everything and build anew,—
in fact, I'm horrified at my erst property-Venus ! Well, that,
I'm sure, will go much better this time (especially if the fog
brings good weather) ; but the brisk, the joy-of-lifed, all this
is good in the Tannhäuser, and I cannot make the smallest
alteration there. Further, whatever bears the legend's scent
about it, already has the atmosphere : Tannhäuser's lament
and penance thoroughly successful, the [instrumental] group-
ings not to be improved, except that I have had to touch
up passionate features now and then elsewhere ; for instance,
at Tannhäuser's outburst in the finale of the second act I
have replaced a very tame passage for the violins by a new
one, which is very difficult, but the only one to satisfy me.
I can ask anything of my orchestra here, however ; it's the
first in all the world.

Enough of Tannhäuser.—From time to time I've also
gossiped much with you on people I had met : for the
moment I know of nothing to single out, without giving
it an air of more importance than it has. On the whole,
I continue to lead a thoroughly lonely life ; nothing suits
me better. Yet my loneliness itself is often one of dis-
content : what helps me then ?—Sweet memories, and—
sleep.—

Having taken a great dislike to plans, I have projected
absolutely none as yet, even for a production of the Tristan ;

I keep thinking the right thing is bound to turn up of itself some day. Meanwhile Queen Victoria has taken it into her head to want to hear my Lohengrin this winter; the director of Covent Garden Theatre has looked me up, and the Queen wants Lohengrin in English. It would have to be in February, but I know nothing more precise about it, nor even if I shall be able to entertain it. It would be droll, though, were I to hear this work in English for my own first time !—

And now I shall soon be moving out; from the 15th of October on, my address is 3 Rue d'Aumale. It is a smaller dwelling, and I hope not to have to write either poetry or music in it, as all it's fit for is a counting-house. I half lost my law-suit; not a sou of compensation do I get. Ah, when have I ever arrived at anything? This has been a bad, a most unlucky business; the house itself, which I chose just for sake of its quiet, had become noisy beyond all bearing through the demolition of this quarter. They declare that my propriétaire was unaware of it: quite possible !—

Well, child, with you it has fared better; my only consolation! Heaven bless your lovely pictures, and the portrait above all !* I quite expect to see all that, myself, ere long.—A thousand kind regards to Otto; I'll write him the very next time.

Just one thing more. On the Rhine, not far from Rolandseck, blonde slips of children got on board, then off again,—quite in the children's way: one of them looked, in fact, like Myrrha! How well I knew that you were once at home there !—

A thousand greetings, and the whole of my heart !—

R. W.

---

* Clearly that which now figures as our frontispiece.—Tr.

And now for the draft of the new Tannhäuser verses.

Get out your book! Turn to "Venus (breaking into wrath)"—after Tannhäuser's third stanza—down to the words :

"Zieh hin, Bethörter, suche dein Heil!
"Suche dein Heil, und find' es nie!"—

Then something like this is to follow :—

"Die du bekämpft, die du besiegt,
"Die du verhöhnt mit jubelndem Stolz,
"Flehe sie an, die du verlacht ; " [*etc.**]

108.

Oct. 24, 60.

A hurried word, my dearest Child!

Your last lines made me profoundly and heartily glad, —as one always feels after alarm.†

The [missing] letter must have got here on a most unlucky day, just as I was packing off my servant, whom I had previously had the greatest difficulty in tolerating. He had frequently committed the offence of forgetting my letters and carrying them about with him for days, if they

---

* The whole of the new draft dialogue is given in the German edition of these letters, but a reproduction is quite needless here, as the only variants from the modern textbooks (down to 1901) are the following : "*Sclaven nie*," for "Sklave, weich!" "*gespart*"—for "erspart"—and a tiny point or two in punctuation.   On the other hand, though the form given in modern textbooks prior to the very latest edition (1901) is that of Wagner's *Ges. Schr.* ii (1871), the wording differs considerably in the revised German score : a riddle solved at once by that article in *Die Musik* (cf. p. 238), where Dr. Golther shews that the music for this new scene was *set* to the French translation, and therefore Wagner had subsequently to re-adapt his German draft to fit it.—Tr.

† See letter of Oct. 20 to Otto : "On the 1st of October"—meaning Sept. 30, unless the letter spread over two days—"I wrote your wife ; I'm much disturbed at having had no news since then, as I hoped to find at least a word of welcome on my entry into my new abode."—Tr.

had been handed to him by the postman ; for which I had often blown him up severely. Now—it was precisely in that week that I sent him about his business ; he had to quit my house in half an hour (for good reasons). Another letter, also, has never reached me : now everything is clear,— whether from knavery or fright, he didn't give the letters up, on leaving.—I shall try to hunt him up ; if that doesn't succeed—ah ! you must write me all over again. I give everyone exactly as much trouble as I give myself : we must bear it between us.

I am very fatigued : people here are too unremittingly industrious for me. Not the least irritation—but very great strain !

A thousand fine greetings !

I must be off again !

Just one more greeting, tho' !

R. W.

109.

Paris, Nov. 13, 60.

Dear precious Child, fair kindly soul, have thanks for all your messages !

You shall have a brief bulletin from me as often as possible.

I am picking up—very slowly—but still picking up. —I have scarcely any recollection of the first week of my illness, but now my mind is gradually clearing.* For

---

* Two or three days after letter 108, Wagner had been compelled to give up his attendance at the opera-house, owing to what is vaguely described by contemporaries as "a typhoid fever, the crisis of which was marked by all the symptoms of inflammation of the brain." The term "typhoid," however, must not be read in its specific modern sense, as in those days it was indiscriminately applied to almost every kind of so-called 'low' or 'nervous' fever. More probably it was an actual case of subacute 'brain-fever,' brought on by worry and nervous strain (including that of the eyes—see this letter's next sentence).—It really is

several days I was almost totally blind ; now I'm uncommonly weak, amazingly emaciated, with eyes deep-sunk. You know that I am never wholly free from pain, which nothing save nervous excitement could numb : now that I have to avoid all excitement, you may guess what is left of me !—

Yet, too much is dangled in front of me still, and Life, I suppose, will soon have back the whole of me !

Yesterday I was taken for a drive to the Champs Elysées, with a little walk in the sun, which did me good.   I'm coming round ; moreover, I've recovered patience.—

In my humble new abode the three Roman prints hang framed above and round my couch !—

Adieu for to-day ;   I can write no longer !—Thanks, a thousand thanks, and deep fidelity of heart !—

R. W.

---

instructive to compare the above with Minna's report to the Berlin friend next day (Nov. 14, 60) : " Richard has certainly been ill, but thank God ! is now so far recovered as to have been able to take a walk with me again, and consequently he thinks of attending the rehearsals of his Tannhäuser after another few days. His illness lasted quite a fortnight in all, and he brought it on himself through some over-exertion in teaching their parts to the two lady-singers who are employed in the Tannhäuser [also, be it said, through " a removal at which I was the only person, on my side, who could speak French "—R. W. to Otto, Oct. 20.—Tr.]. In addition he may have caught a slight cold, and as his nerves are always quite excitable enough, that made them worse ; he was also very feverish. But Richard was not actually confined to bed, as I have already heard that the newspapers somewhat strongly exaggerated ; which is disproved by the fact that Wagner is shewing himself to the Germans here, receiving them, etc.—Unfortunately Richard is a very impatient invalid, and at such times always vents his spleen on me. He will not obey, when one kindly entreats him to anything ; for instance, he wouldn't keep warm, and so brought on an inflammation of the eyes through another chill. But that also is happily got over, with the help of our excellent doctor [Gasperini], so that he is able to write and read again now " (Die Gegenwart, Oct. 1899). One could have wished for a word of sympathy with his present feebleness.—Tr.

110.

Paris, Nov. 17, 60.

Here comes another bulletin, my Child.

I'm mending—tho' the pace is very slow : the weather will not favour me a bit, but keeps throwing me back! Still I've attended to a first affair,—I have been to the bookbinder. The pianoforte [Bülow's ' vocal '] score of Tristan has at last appeared ; I had given Härtels orders to send a few copies to Zurich direct, among them one for Frau Wille ; but naturally I was not going to polish Freundin off like that: I bade a copy come to Paris, to be bound here after my own heart and despatched to you by my own hand. Well, it came at the very worst stage of my illness : imagine my distress ! I had to see it lying there, without the power to attend to it.

But I have been to the bookbinder now. That it will turn out after my wish, alas ! I'm bound to doubt ; these people are all so horribly devoid of ideas ! Probably I shall have to content myself with something quite ordinary, and you will have to make the best of good intentions. In any case it will take long enough before it's finished, and you'll have to reckon it as birthday-gift and Christmas-box in one !—

For the rest, I feel so—dead : I can describe it no otherwise. A becalming without a puff of interest in existence ; the future productions of my latest works all dream and haze ; not a trace of wish or zeal within me ; my wretched nerves always aching and much below par ; nothing but the moment's excitement to give my state a better look !— And still—it goes, and go it will—but how ? God knows !— Why on earth are there spots on the sun ? Bright weather is still the best aid.—Monday [19th] I mean to attend a rehearsal again : I must learn to be duly composed.—

But, what a charming idea, your little dog ; do tell me

its name! Was that a master-stroke of friend Otto's?—
Believe me, you'll get plenty of joy from the beasty; there
is something wonderfully composing in association with
dumb animals. I congratulate!

And now sincerest thanks for the kind messages that
came into my sick-room : I'm worried at their having ceased
for several days. Surely you are not ill yourself? Do
reassure me !—

And a thousand hearty greetings to Wesendonck ; he
shall hear from me soon.

Good-bye and health be with you!

Your

R. W.

111.

[Latter part of November.*]

Merely a few lines, Lady-friend, but they will tell you
enough !—

I'm doing my utmost to be able—by taking the greatest
possible care of myself—to attend rehearsals regularly every
day ; and this is how I manage it :—

At 10 o'clock I go to bed, remain sleepless as a rule
for 3, 4, to 5 hours ; then arise—very weak—about 10
in the morning ; after breakfast I lie down again, undertake
nothing, don't write a line, read a very little ; then dress
myself, go to the Opéra—for 1 o'clock—attend a rehearsal ;
come home dead-beat between 4 and 5, lie down again
and try to doze ; dine at $5\frac{1}{2}$, then recline once more, receive
nobody except the doctor—not to have to speak ; read a
little, and commence afresh as above.—

---

* I have reversed the German volume's order of letters 111-112, and
consequently altered the date there conjectured for this one ("Dez."). I
have done so, not only because of ample internal evidence, but as we
have documentary proof that Wagner resumed his superintendence of
the Opéra rehearsals on the 20th November.—Tr.

You will see from this, how profoundly ill my wretched
nerves are. Never must I sing again ; the way I used to
render whole acts from my operas, however seldom, can
never be re-attempted : it is just those, always superhuman
exertions, I have to pay for now. Neither of my old
conducting of an orchestra can there be any further talk :—
accordingly, I don't know how I am ever to get to the
end of my life-task !—Still, much is to be expected of
rest, great care and graduation, and at any rate I shall
improve in time.—

It is like you, to have thought of approaching my poor
self on the spot : yet I also think, Dame Reason's right.
Wait for Tannhäuser, and perhaps not even the first
performances, but until I shall already have recuperated
somewhat : in a condition like my present, I can't be said
to exist at all. Please seek Otto's kind opinion !—

I was delighted with what you told me of Frau Wille :
I had thought as much, and am cross with her for nothing
more. I really do know what she's worth, albeit she is
not made for action ; often we do not need this energy,
tho', but simply comprehension and good-feeling : and of
what value it is, to have found that !—Greet her for me
from my heart !—

And sincerest love to all your family, together with the
good Papa ! Weak and full of woe, but faithful aye and
thankful, I remain Yours

R. W.

112.

Paris, 3 Rue d'Aumale.

Dec. 4, 60.

In haste a heartfelt greeting to the precious Child, an
some relief !—

During the past week my recovery has made good

17

progress. Strength is returning; I'm looking better ; people are pleased with my appearance.—

So it has been a serious warning. It made a great impression on me: I am carefully mapping my future, to be able to fulfil my life-task ; yet I have hopes, again, that I can fulfil it !—

Are you better satisfied, dear Liege ?

As for Tannhäuser, we'll bide our time ; I don't conduct the band myself, and the rehearsals over—all is over !—

Soon more from the

LIVING.

113.

For the 23rd December, 1860.

I find I have still a sheet left of my colour,* Lady-friend ; so it shall bear you my felicitation on your birthday.

What shall I wish, what offer you ? An utmost toilsome, unresting existence makes—*Rest* appear to me the wishful thing ; I long for it myself so yearningly, that I needs must wish it others too, especially my Dearest, as sole and highest good. It is so difficult to win to : in whom it was not born, he hardly ever will acquire it, and nothing but a total crushing of his native character can bring him this victor's-prize. Who remains in life like this, staking his nature again and again on this life, may have grown very tranquil—almost completely so, in fact—as regards much in its broader issues ; but the little everyday affairs of life will ever sting him, make him lose all patience and repose.

How curiously it fares with me ! All that sets the world in motion, almost without an exception, leaves me cold and unmoved. Fame has no sway at all, with me ; Profit only in so far as I may need it to keep me independent :

---

* Pale lilac, like most of these letters' originals ; see the *Tristan* facsimile.

of taking any *serious* step for either, I never could dream. To prove my point is also quite indifferent to me since I've learnt how unutterably few men are capable of so much as understanding their fellows. Further, my very natural and pardonable craving, to witness a fully adequate representation of each of my works, has very much cooled down of late, and particularly in this last year; renewed contact with bandsmen, singers, and so on, has again wrung many a sigh from me, and fed my resignation with strong food on this side too. More and more have I to mark how measurelessly far I've strayed from this—in our modern life the quite invariable—basis of even my own art-fashionings, and willingly do I admit that if I suddenly cast a glance now on my Nibelungen or the Tristan, I startle as if from a dream, and ask myself: " Where wast thou ?—Thou wast dreaming! Set wide thine eyes and see: lo! *this* is the reality."—

Yes, I will not deny it, I strictly hold my later works for downright inexecutable. And if the inner prompting ne'ertheless revives, to realise a possibility e'en here, in turn that's only possible through letting my poor brain roam off again into the dream-world ; where untold, never-precedented aids arise, and I trust myself with the enormous power to draw them to me. Faced with an unbroken series of experiences, however, of incredible weakness and superficiality in all the persons and relations whereon the possibility of my assumptions had reposed, here also Resignation gains more and more predominance, and lends me that passivity which turns with terror from a useless strife. I have come to thinking very little of it now.—

So, if aught invigorates me for the present Tannhäuser affair, it is strictly nothing but my nature's inextirpable propensity to rouse itself beneath the influence of artistic aims. With difficulty can I force myself the whole day

long, to take an interest in the thing; but once I'm at
rehearsal, the immediateness of art resumes its hold on me:
I squander myself and my forces—and literally for a thing
that leaves me quite indifferent.—

In truth that is my case!—

Yet see!—how the whole breadth of heaven parts this
from the view which not alone the world, but all my own
acquaintances, nay, e'en my most devoted friend, still take
of me. I can truthfully say that it is almost solely this
mad but ineradicable opinion of everybody who draws near
me, that gives me pain: I may preach, waste anger, argument, or indignation,—I'm ever answered by the smile of
pity for a momentary loss of temper! If people then could
only plumb my silence, when, pale and outwardly indifferent,
I suddenly break off, withdraw into my shell!

O my child; where am I then to find my only, only
solace?—Once I did find the heart and soul that wholly
understood me in such moments, and held me dear because it
understood, and knew it understood me *so!* See, to this soul
do I flee, then, let sink my limbs as one fatigued to death,
and dip my head in the soft æther of its kindly thought.
All that I lived through once, the untold emotions, cares
and sorrows of that past, dissolve as from a storm-cloud
to a quickening dew, which laves my burning temples;
there do I feel refreshment and at last repose, sweet rest:
I am beloved—am known!—

And that repose, I lay it at your feet! In gracious consciousness of all you are to me—the angel of my calm, the
guardian of my life—may you also find the noble fount
to steep the arid paths of your existence! Share you my
calm, accept it from me whole to-day, as I enjoy it at this
instant when I sink my soul entire in yours! My wish
this, this my offering!

R. W.

114.

Mardi Gras [February 12, 1861].

Fat Tuesday shall grant me a quiet morning at last, Lady-friend, to tell you just a little of myself.

When I've a headful of nothing but the hundred details of my present task, there seems to me no sense in speaking of myself to you ; for this was ever the distinction of our intercourse, that instinctively a sublimation of the truer core of thought and action alone appeared to us worth heeding, and, so to say, we felt ourselves emancipated from material life forthwith, so soon as we but met. So, if I hunt all the lumber out of my head, to get it clean-swept for you, of course there's nothing but the marrow left there, and no more need to talk about my plague. In return, a gloaming melancholy then girdles-in the soul, and shews us all the things without in their true empty light ; for nothing really is of solid worth to him who feels how much he has to sacrifice if he would yield an import to the semblance of reality.—

What comforts me amid the many plagues that Art imposes on me, is that it can appear to you in cheerful light. You have and dote on paintings, reading, studying, hearing ; and of it all you hold alone to what seems nobly worth to you, untouched by what you suitably may leave unheeded. All your accounts, even the latest of this winter, agree herein—that on you the blessing is bestowed of placid calm enjoyment. The deeper sense of that enjoyment will have been revealed to you by now ; haply for you it is the same as my activity, perchance my want, for me.—Yet I often entertain the thought that I myself were capable of such enjoyment, and nothing but my mission held me back. Of course, when I reflect on what I'm able to endure, I can but wonder at myself, and deem that oft so ardent wish for quiet and secluded rest entirely unjustified ; and yet a certain inner peace is my constant companion,—the peace of deepest and completest resignation. An altogether uninvidious, but all the surer incredulity has won possession of me : I hope for absolutely nothing more, and in particular —despite occasional airings of my sometimes most communicative temperament—the whole of my relations to such as come in contact with me are so extremely flimsily based that it would be impossible for any shock to damage them ; if an individual has approached me somewhat close to-day, and I lose sight of him for months—or quarters, or half-years—that doesn't make a grain of difference in our mutual relations.   I am never unsociable, but unspeakably indifferent ; habituation nowhere gets a hold of me.

You ask about my female company ?   I have made a few acquaintances, but not so much as made myself at home with one.

Mad. Ollivier [Liszt's elder daughter] is highly gifted, even dazzling of nature, . . .   I'm thinking, how it is that we so seldom see each other. . . .   It is much the same with all the rest of my acquaintances : the odds are so against my profiting by any better-cultivated intercourse, that I willingly resign on every hand, and just accept whatever whim or hazard brings into the house.   Among others . . . there is a Frln von Meysenbug,* who is staying here as governess to Russian children. . . .   When brought to see me, she had this in her favour, that once in London, years ago . . . I had treated her very badly in a fit of ill-humour ; the recollection touched me, and now . . . she finds herself more at her ease in my company . . .

---

* See Wagner's letters to her, included in the volume of *Letters to Otto Wesendonck et al.*, where will also be found her interesting account, as eye-witness, of the *Tannhäuser* disaster.—It should be remarked that the dots in the above are faithfully reproduced from the German edition, notwithstanding the difficulty of fitting some of them in without affecting the sense ; obviously they represent allusions to third parties, with whom (apart from Minna) we are in no way concerned.—Tr.

As for the so-called higher world, a lady whom I knew quite superficially in earlier days [1853] has drawn greater attention from me this time, than before ; it is Countess Kalergis, niece of the Russian chancellor Nesselrode. Surely I have told you of her once already, . . . She was in Paris some time last summer, hunted me up, and induced me to get Klindworth over from London to make music with her. Entirely among ourselves, except for Berlioz, I sang the second act of Tristan with Mme Garcia-Viardot ; we also did some music from the Nibelungen : it was the very first time since I left you.—What made me more attentive to this lady, was the observation of a singular weariness, a disdain and loathing of the world, that might have seemed indifferent, had I not quite plainly noticed with it all her profound longing for music and poesy, which appeared to me of moment in such circumstances ; and as her talent was considerable in that direction, at last she did not leave me without interest. Moreover, she was the first person I have met who surprised me—quite spontaneously—by a truly magnificent grasp of my situation . . . [cf. p. 234].

Frau v. Pourtalès, wife of the Prussian ambassador, seems to be not without depth, and at least to have distinguished taste.—

Quite a racy nature is that I have detected in the wife of the Saxon ambassador, Frau v. Seebach . . . I was surprised by a certain gentle glow that gleams beneath the lava here : she could not understand how anyone could overlook the intense warmth of my conceptions, and thought it questionable to take her own young daughter with her to the Tannhäuser. Such curious acquaintances one makes, you see, but they're nothing more—than acquaintances ! . . .

Ah ! child—let us drop all that ! And believe me, one drags along one's way just so, with toil, with toil,—scarcely caring to render account to oneself of how one does it. All wishing is in vain : toiling and moiling is the only method to forget one's misery.

Your decision not to come to the Tannhäuser, my child, had much depressed me—as you surely will be able to conceive—simply because it robbed me of the pleasure of seeing you so soon again. I was bound to endorse all the reasons combining to influence you, as valid for your inner self, since I have always done wisest when I took the pains to understand you, and enriched, ay, often-times corrected, my own feeling by adopting yours. I was sad—and said nothing.—But Otto lately wrote me that, after all, you meant to come with him for the event. Look you ! that gave me such a grievous inner joy ; for I knew you had done yourself injustice, and that made me so [un]happy that I hardly dared to hope for a fulfilment of the promise.—And now Otto has just written me again, that—you would *not* accompany him. Once more it troubles me unspeakably, as you may well imagine !—

Now listen to a quiet word from a friend who again has just battled through much : —

This first Tannhäuser-time will hang a load about my neck ; I do not think it a propitious season for the silent need of our two souls. Much that is needless will not be avoidable,* whilst everything will take an outward and unedifying turn. Accordingly I needs must hold it better to accept your meaning, and await a more equable season to present you for the first time with an entire work of mine so carefully prepared in execution as here is the case with this Tannhäuser : then, and in calmer mood, the performance itself both must and will have much to offer you, and we shall taste it tranquilly.—

---

* Undoubtedly, a very painful encounter with Minna.—In the upper paragraph an "un" must surely have been dropped by the German printer.—Tr.

Yet if I admit you all that, ought I to conceal from you
that every point in it vanishes before the bare thought of
seeing you again—were it only for an hour?—No, my child,
it shall not be concealed from you; and were you still to
come at risk of having little sight of me and my true self,
I still—the egoist I!—should count the hour thrice-blest in
which I once again could gaze into your eyes!—But, enough!
You know it all better than I!—

For the nonce I have a little rest, to wit, not those daily
rehearsals; but the last second of my working-time is always
claimed by countless extras. The rehearsals go ahead with
unexampled application, at times beyond my comprehension,
and at any rate we are in for a performance quite out of the
common. Niemann is right-down sublime; he's an artist
of the very rarest water. The succeeding of the other parts
will be rather an outcome of artifice; yet I hope that by extreme attention we shall succeed in covering up the strings.—

And now, a thousand greetings from my heart! Thank
Otto most sincerely for his firm allegiance: whatever he
may meet with here, I know he'll bear it, and surely carry
back a strong impression with him.

Adieu, Lady-friend!

The first performance still stands fixed for Friday 22;
yet Otto should be prepared to wait for it till Monday 25.

[*The three notorious nights at the Grand Opera, when
Tannhäuser fell victim to the Jockey Club's deliberate plot,
occurred between this letter and the next. As the first performance did not take place till March* 13 *(second* 18, *third* 24), *it
is to be presumed that Otto arrived too early for anything but
the dress rehearsals, and had to leave before the actual débâcle.
—Tr.*]

115.

Paris, April 6, 61.

Best Child, I think you did me an injustice when you
shewed yourself a little sensitive at my having merely
forwarded for you to read, the other day, a not insignificant
letter that had reached me, without accompanying it by
a single word of my own. Has silence lost its meaning to
you, and could you possibly imagine that in such a case
I really had nothing to say? Nay, that would *not* be right
interpretation.—

To tell the truth, I'm tired of eternally giving my friends
concern; from the whole objectionable Paris adventure I
have no other residue than this bitter feeling. The disaster
itself left me fairly indifferent, at bottom. Had I made for
mere outward success, I should naturally have had to tackle
many things another way; but that's—just what I can't.
In my mind that success could only count as a result of
the thing's inner succeeding: the chance of a truly fine
performance of no matter which of my works had tempted
me; so soon as I was forced to abandon that, I was already
done for and defeated. What actually occurred to me, was
the appropriate punishment for my giving way to another
illusion; it affected me no deeper. The representation of
my work was so foreign to me, that its reception didn't
really matter, and I could look on at it all as a spectacle.
Whether the incident may have consequences or not, is a
point that still leaves me cold: all that I feel in its regard
is—lassitude, disgust.—

Indeed the only thing that stung me, was the quick
recovery of consciousness that from such incalculably mad
odds, as those of a Parisian success of one of my most
intimate works, my whole lot in life must so onerously
depend withal. This is so cruel and insane [a fate] that
for a while it really seemed to me the most sensible course,

to renounce, and radically, an existence so utterly awry and undisposable !

I am wearying my friends past all conscience, and dragging loads along with me that I really cannot bear much longer.—Good Bülow, who felt my pain most deeply, has been probing German soil to find a somewhat reassuring outlook for me. I have—little trust, and suppose that in the search for rest I must gradually wear myself down till I find the last rest. Yet I have duties that keep me still erect ; Care lends me life anew.—

Nothing further can I tell the child about myself; but I reserve a broad smile for the very next time, that—deceived by falsely judged appearances—one thinks one may congratulate me prematurely,—as happened to me not so long ago.—

Whither, my child, has flown the comfort of those Calderon evenings ? What evil star was it, that robbed me of my only worthy haven ?—Believe me, whatever you may hear that sounds unlike it,—when I left that Asyl my star was doomed to its descent; I can but fall and fall !—

Never—never let a contrary belief arise in you ! Hold fast to that alone ! I do not murmur, I complain of nothing :—it had to be ; but, if you would remain just to me,—never forget it yourself !—This I still have wished to say to you : oh, stamp it deep upon your mind !—

And now give Otto my best greetings. His presence in that evil time afflicted, rather than rejoiced me, albeit I protest from my whole heart that his care and sympathy, his entire being, profoundly moved me. Personally, however, I could be so absolutely nothing to him ; it was one perpetual racket, and the real miscarriage of my undertaking so exactly coincided with the period he was here. I suffered most at those rehearsals, during which my work grew more and more unrecognisable and alien to me. The performances, on the contrary, had the mere effect of purely physical blows, that simply woke me from my soul's distress to consciousness of—my outward misery; the blows themselves I felt but superficially.—

Tell Otto also that there will shortly be a report by myself to read, presumably in the Leipzig Illustrirte, on the whole Paris Tannhäuser affair ; * I had promised a relative something of the kind.—

Fare you well, Lady-friend !

In a few days I must go to Carlsruhe for quite a brief stay, then speedily return, as I still have far too many things to settle here.—

With a thousand greetings !

R. W.

[*Bülow's diplomacy had been at work, sounding the Grand Duke of Baden as to Wagner's "outlook"—see p. 267. Wagner goes to Carlsruhe, obtains a promise that* Tristan *shall be given in September, and returns to Paris by April 24 ; whence he starts for Vienna May 7 or 8—in search of special singers, and in response to an announcement of " Lohengrin,"—arriving there May 9.—Tr.*]

116.

Vienna, May 11, 61.

I have just attended the rehearsal of my Lohengrin ! I cannot lock away the incredibly moving effect of this first hearing, amid the fairest and most affectionate circumstances, artistic and human, without imparting it at once to you. Twelve years of my life—what years !—have I passed through !! You were right, when you so often wished me

---

* Dated " Paris, 27th March 1861," it appeared in Brockhaus' *Deutsche Allgemeine Zeitung* the day after this letter was written ; see *Prose Works* III. 347-360.—Tr.

this delight; but nowhere could it have been offered me
so completely as here! Ah, were *you* two here to-morrow!!
A thousand sincerest wishes!

R. W.

117.

Paris, May 27, 61.

Just arrived back here [26th] I find the Child's dear letter
forwarded after me from Vienna, which was to have delighted
me there on my birthday. The effect of these lines has
been indescribably beautiful, now that Wiedersehen lay
between:* a dream had become reality, to melt once more
to dreamlike memory!

So there still are means of heartiest invigoration and
encouragement! They are ours, and ever do we win them
afresh, because our consciences are pure and free. For sure,
we shall hail each other oft again, and every Wiedersehen will
weave a lovelier, nobler bloom into the garland of our life!

A thousand faithful greetings from the lately sped!—

At Carlsruhe I had a very pleasant time with the
Grand Duke; his delight was great when I informed him
of my firm resolve to give preference to a settlement there,
over any other in Germany. Whatever he can do towards
assisting me to a suitable abode, he will with alacrity.—

I find Liszt still here,† and shall have a longer sight

---

* Having left Vienna on the 20th or 21st, he clearly paid the Green
Hill a flying visit for one night en route for Carlsruhe; the nearness
of the latter city to Zurich perhaps had much to do, not only with
the "resolve" recorded a few lines lower, but also with the domestic
'catastrophe' vaguely suggested in the next two letters.—Tr

† Liszt writes a friend in the second half of May, "Wagner will be
back in 4 or 5 days.—He left a few lines for me ere starting—the same
day as I arrived here" (i.e. the 7th or 8th). The "bösen, schwierigen
Periode" of the next sentence in the above must chiefly refer to the
serious financial embarrassment in which Wagner had been plunged by
deprivation of *any* returns from the Paris *Tannhäuser.*—Tr.

of him this evening at my rooms . . .—For the rest, my child, I now am face to face with a bad, a difficult period; by the beginning of July, when I should re-cross the Rhine in that event, may I have everything well behind me: that's what you must wish me! Meanwhile little Tausig who started from Vienna after me, and punctually caught me up at Carlsruhe—helps me now and then to a playful smile. I look upon him as partly a gift from yourself!—

And many thanks for the pretty presents which I found on retiring to rest and egoistically packed up at once.* The wreath I left for you; I know you will make fine use of it!

My heartiest greetings to Otto and the children! Thanks and love to yourself!

Your

R. W.

118.

Paris, June 15,

1861.

What a time it is since I wrote the most excellent Child,—and yet there were a lot of thanks to be said for the dear last letter!—

I'm living dreary, soul-less days away, have zest for nothing in the world, neither for work of any kind, nor for anything else; scarcely can I drive myself to write the most in-cumbent letter! Perhaps I might describe my state as a preservation of patience: complete uncertainty—is all that I can distantly convey!—

I go out little now: disgust with everything is great.— I am simply trying to kill time, and read Göthe just as it

---

* Presumably at the villa on the Green Hill, with a departure early next morning before his hosts had risen. The wreath would be an operatic trophy from Vienna.—Tr.

comes; of late, the campaign of 1792. 'Tis a total lethargy, and the fish on dry sand is quite an apt emblem of me.

Liszt and Tausig left a week ago; I was glad to be rid of them—in my present state! No matter who, is not the right one, and naught avails me. How strange must Liszt's occurrence in my life appear to me! I met him first just 20 years ago in Paris, at a time when—in the most precarious outward plight—I had already conceived a great loathing of the world in which he dangled glitteringly and dazzlingly before me; and now, when I have to repent my driving by my fate for once towards that world again, when I am renewing the experience of my youth so thoroughly, and nothing, no pretence, no mirage, can move me any more to lift a finger up to it,—now Liszt must once again be basking in the sun there, under my very eyes! . . .* No one knows better than himself what it is, that is to be attained there; wherefore it will be judging him more correctly if I assume that, as his object stays denied him too, he likes to intoxicate himself now and then with a semblance . . . I couldn't accompany him any-whither, and so saw little of him; but I've promised to visit him for a week or two at Weimar, where he intends bringing out some big symphonic works.—

Ah! my child, if I had not you, my look-out would be bad! Hold firm to that belief, and faithfully!—And let that cover all that I could say!—

But a life I have no longer. Perhaps I shall somewhat pluck up heart again—particularly for work—when I have got away from here; if only that can be effected soon!—

The solitary thing to rouse me is the Tristan scheme. Do think it over, how you can get Papa to pass the autumn and a portion of the winter in Vienna this time; I'm sure it would do you good as well! I would let you both look after me, as long as I remained there; for I

---

* Again the dots are reproduced from the German edition.—Tr.

am going away alone,* and shall put up meantime at
Kolatschek's. Then you could listen quietly for once to
all I shall have brought to a hearing, Tristan, Lohengrin,
Holländer and Tannhäuser—: it really ought to make your
winter quite a homelike one again.—

Well, we'll have another debate about that.—And now
my best and heartiest wishes! And all that's good and
kind to Otto, the children, and the whole Green Hill,

from Your

Grey

R. W.

119.

Paris

78 Rue de Lille. Légation de Prusse.

July 12, 61.

My Child, I am writing you from the hôtel of the Prussian
embassy, where I have found sanctuary for the few weeks
I still must keep to Paris. In front of me I have a garden
with fine tall trees and a basin with two black swans,†
over the garden the Seine, and over the Seine the garden
of the Tuileries ; so that I can breathe again a little, and at
least am in ordinary Paris no longer.

---

* The virtual separation from Minna (it never became a formal one)
was evidently a settled thing by now, and two days before the next
in this series of letters, "After we had lived through four more ghastly
days in the [dismantled] rooms, she set off comfortably [for Soden baths]
together with the parrot" (to Malwida von Meysenbug, July '61).—The
Kolatschek of the sentence's end perhaps was Dr. Adolf, who also had
been a refugee in Switzerland, and in whose short-lived *Deutsche
Monatschrift* portions of *Opera and Drama* had appeared in 1851 before
the book itself was issued ; but we hear no more of him.—Tr.

† See the beautiful Albumblatt "Ankunft bei den schwarzen Schwänen,"
dedicated to his present hostess, and instinct with all the touching
melancholy of the moment. What detained him in Paris till nearly the
end of the month, was the supervision of a translation (Nuitter) for the
French vocal score of his *Holländer*.—Tr.

My household goods have been packed again, and sent to the depôt here : where they will get unpacked, some day, God knows ; in all probability I shall never see them more. I am wanting my wife to settle down in Dresden, and take them to herself there ; for my part, I can think of no more settling down. This the upshot of a last, hard, infinitely miserable experience ! 'Tis not appointed me, to cultivate my muse in the lap of a cosy home ; each attempt to defy all the frowns of my fate, and indulge a longing so innate in me, is more emphatically frustrated every time, from within and from without ; the dæmon of my life throws every cunning semblance to the dust. 'Tis not appointed me, and every sought-for rest becomes the source of most acute disquietudes.

So I shall vow the remnant of my life to roving. Perhaps it will be granted me to rest my limbs from time to time beside some shady well, and here or there refresh myself : the only benefaction still to grant me !—

To Carlsruhe I *am not* going ! !

From this indication of results you may infer the latest happenings in my life, both inner and outer.—

At the last there even died the little dog that you once sent me from your sickbed ; mysteriously suddenly ! It is presumed that a cart-wheel had struck him in the street, injuring one of the little pet's internal organs. After 5 hours passed without a moan, quite gently and affectionately, but with progressive weakness, he silently expired [June 23]. Not a foot of ground was at my disposal, to bury the tiny friend in ; so I sneaked and forced my way into Stürmer's little back-garden, where I buried him myself by stealth beneath a bush.—With that little dog I buried *much* !—So I intend to wander now, and on my wanderings I shall have companion no more.—

That tells you everything !—

18

I shall be able to send you a carte-de-visite presently : Liszt, who sat to every photographer in the place, compelled me to a sitting also.* I have not been to fetch the cards yet, but will do so by and by.—

Keep well and cheerful ! Many hearty wishes to Otto and the children ! All my love to yourself!—

R. W.

120.

Paris, July 25, 61.

I meant to come to you for two days, before my journey to Vienna ; now Liszt has knocked that on the head. On the 5th and 6th of August he is giving big music of his own at Weimar (Faust etc.), and had arranged for me to pay him a brief visit ; then I learnt that he was expecting friends from far and wide, a crowd I did not want to mix in, and sent him word I shouldn't come ; but as that appears to touch him to the quick, I shall have to go, unless I wish to wound him seriously.

That frets me, since it makes my Zurich plan impracticable, but I've been thinking whether you perhaps could come instead to Weimar for the 5th and 6th of August ; which really would be very interesting to you both, were it only as pretext for staying away from St Gallen. Do you think that Otto could be brought to see it ?—If not, I shall rely all the firmer on you both for Vienna ; where you would

---

* See the request in her letter of June 24 (p. 345 *inf.*).—Hereafter I shall have a word to say on the ominous coincidence, that not one of Mathilde's letters of earlier date than poor Fips's death has descended to us, though Wagner had had a portfolio "expressly made to lock away thy keepsakes and letters " (p. 34). Here I merely refer the reader to p. 278, l. 18, my note on p. 283, and Wagner's letter to Otto of June 25, where that death had been already termed " almost inexplicable," and "the manner of it, everything—has much afflicted me . . . particularly in present circumstances."—Tr.

have to arrive by the end of September at latest, and stay as long as you possibly can.—

I do not write you, for fear of distressing you ; but I think, if anything, too much of you !—The sense of strangeness in this world is growing on me ever stronger. In truth, I know not why I should endure this parody of life.

God knows whether the Tristan will revive me ; if I dip into the score by accident, sometimes I stand aghast at the thought that I may have to hear it soon.—I am astonished afresh, how little of one people strictly can know, how utterly different I am when alone, and when I mix with others ; often I've to laugh at the phantom which steps before them then !—

But why continue ?—

How goes it with the health ? Are the baths acting well ?—Strength ! we still need it !—

I shall start on Monday [29th] ; a quick reply will catch me here still. Then Weimar till the 6th of August. Then— Vienna, K.K. Hofoperntheater.—However, I'm sure to write if I don't see you.—

Be saluted from my deepest heart !

R. W.

121.

Vienna, Aug. 19, 61.

Letter-writing is a funny thing, Lady-friend One sets apart an hour at last, and vows it to communication ; but what is such an hour, when plucked from out the midst of this eternal churn of life, impressions, moods ? For sure, a letter of the sort tells little, and we couldn't correspond at all with those we love, were that churning not to be assumed as known to them through sympathy.

I had to agree with your Weimar letter at once, when I saw that your visit might have interfered with Vienna.

Grant Heaven the sacrifice's recompense be not withheld us!
Amen!

At Weimar there naturally was no question of peace
and enjoyment. From far and near they trooped around,
to see me once again—or see me; literally, I had to relate
my whole life's history to some fresh person each half-hour.
Despair at last inspired me with my old mad pranks, and
everybody was delighted with my jocularity; but I *dared*
not turn serious, since I can no longer be so without almost
dissolving into tears. 'Tis a long-standing fault of my
temperament, and now is taking more and more the upper
hand: I fight against it, tho', as much as I can, for fear
of some day weeping myself all away.

A feeling is growing upon me, that I have pretty well
got to the end of life's journey: there has long been no
question of goal, but the pretext also, maybe even the excuse,
will fail me soon. Don't misunderstand me, if I confess
with mildest candour that it is ever growing harder to me,
to hold anything worth serious consideration: nothing grips
me any more, and all belief is lacking; there's only one
way left to bring me round,—to weep together with me!—
That is precisely what good Hans did, and Liszt as well:
the good old Frommann also came and helped! And really
it did help me, in a sort, to bear the other people's praises
of my courage, their talk of fame and glory.—So I departed
from Weimar in quite an amicable mood, and above all,
I took away a very charming memory of Liszt; who is
also leaving Weimar—where he has been able to plant just
nothing—to fare at first into the vague. His Faust really
gave me great joy, and its second part (Gretchen) made an
unforgetably deep impression on me. What filled me with
great melancholy, was that all this could only be performed
with quite unusual mediocrity: everything had to be seen
to in *one* rehearsal, and Hans, who conducted, did wonders

to make the execution even tolerable. So, this has been the goal of all the sacrifices of our lucky Liszt, too—that he could not wring from this wretched world so much as the bare material for a good performance of his work! How profoundly that reflection confirmed me in my resignation! And I had to learn much besides, on this occasion, that shed a final light upon my own position in the world. I learnt exactly how it stands with all the princes from whom I have felt driven to expect a little, more or less, for some time past; now I know that even the best of them, with the best of will, is impotent to do anything for me. That honestly was good for me, and not a grimace could I pull at it; but I have a feeling that it must soon be over now, and—in sober truth!—I'm glad of it!

Well, I've been in Vienna several days [since the 14th]. A good-natured enthusiast, Dr. Standthardtner, has lent me his home for a few weeks, while the family is away; after that I shall have to fend for myself, or perhaps find someone else who'll put me up! Unfortunately my tenor, Ander, is still out of voice, and the study of Tristan is delayed thereby; but as I have nothing else in view, and should harm the undertaking if I left Vienna, I am awaiting whatever the stars shall decide about this final scheme of mine, which, like the last flutter of the veil of Maya, still chains me to this life. The people here are good to me; but none of them actually knows the danger into which I am dragging them with my Tristan, and perhaps it all will still become impossible as soon as they find out. Isolde alone [Frau Mayer-Dustmann]—a little of whose part I lately went through with her—has an inkling of what is at stake. How horrified they will be, one fine day, when I blurt out that they all must go to ground with me!—

Down to now I can testify that I have never duped anyone wilfully. When the management inquired my terms, it was impossible for me to ask or stipulate for money; the only thing I bargained for, was that my singers and the orchestra should be most studiously saved for me a whole month before the projected first performance. That gives me the requisite composure; for I am drawing near my last goal now, and know that I can do something toward reaching it only by waiving every kind of obligation.—

So come, my child, and the sooner the better! I'm a dreadful egoist to urge you to it, and unless Otto is very fond of me, he has cause enough not to fall in with my petition.* But this is a last word: the course and meaning of the world are dead against me; I can stamp my last clear imprint on it only if I do not give the smallest thought to sparing of myself. For your comfort I may say, however, that I am in surprisingly good health; my appearance is capital, so everybody tells me, and my patience has steeled itself quite cheeringly. Merely, I'm excessively soft; for instance, human beings' treatment of dumb animals makes me grieve more than ever. Also I am clearer-sighted than of yore, and getting to make less and less use of Illusion. So venture it, my child!

I'll write you another time about my journey with Olliviers [from Weimar] viâ Munich and Reichenhall (near Salzburg). A thousand good wishes! Every kind thing to Otto and the children! Adieu, dear Child!

                                                        R. W.

        (Seilerstätte 806,
            3rd floor, Vienna.)

---

* Last June 25 Wagner had written Otto, "I know the great cares to which you are exposed at present," and three weeks previously, to another person, "I am entirely bereft of means . . a best-proved friend, upon whom in such circumstances I might have counted for certain, is completely paralysed just now by the American crisis—owing to the character of his business" (see Glasenapp's *Das Leben R. W.'s* II. ii, 328).—Tr.

122.

Vienna, Sept. 13, 61.

I have really had three lovely hours ; so Lady-friend shall hear about them :—

The other day I was driven to the country-seat of a Hungarian family, Graf Náho [Nako], which boasts of having been the first and red-hottest devotee of my music in Vienna. An amiable young man—Prince Rudolph Liechtenstein, who picked up his equally estimable and very gentle wife en route—conducted me to the foot of the chain of hills where Schwarzau lies. A wonderful site : were the plain filled up with water, it might easily pass for a Swiss lake. The equipment of the castle, of extraordinary taste, betrayed the rarest sense of fantasy in choice, arrangement and invention. The countess, a lady verging on the end of her thirties, with large, surprisingly intellectual black eyes, is celebrated for her singular natural talent in music ; she maintains a private orchestra of Gipsies, in whose midst she sits down to the piano and they improvise the most marvellous stuff for hours together. I feared I might find her stuck-up, perhaps affected : her mien soon reassured me. The seriousness of her sense of beauty was still better taught me by some astonishingly well-executed copies of the finest Vandyck portraits, as to which she remarked that they had cost her much trouble since she unfortunately had had no regular instruction in painting either ; anything like her studio I have never seen. At lunch we touched on books ; she was reading Tschudi's " Fauna of the Alps " at present. Then in came a magnificent light buckhound, followed by a spendid raven-black Newfoundland of gigantic size ; both were indescribably delighted by their mistress's caresses. We fell discussing the bearings of the animal world to man ; I propounded my pet theme, and found a most sympathetic audience, even to the full height of my

articles of faith. The Gipsy band was in Hungary at the
moment, so the countess tried to give us an idea of the
way she improvised with them, alone at the piano, and
very original and fascinating it was. Soon she dropped in
motives from Lohengrin, and that ended in its being *my*
turn to go to the piano. I was gratified by the beautiful
hush with which it was all received. Only the Graf, a
fine tall thoroughbred Hungarian, thought needful to keep
telling me about my works' impression ; I bore it with much
patience, however, as the scraps of conversation he had
heard about me were related with an inexpressible good-
nature. Young Liechtenstein I found a prey to touching
melancholy : he had entered the diplomatic (*politischen*) career
after having chosen naval service in first youth, but was
growing more and more aware how little he was made for
politics.—The day passed in just enough walking and driving
to induce an agreeable fatigue. Next morning I had to
be called very early, as I had a rendezvous with my singer
Ander at Mödling, which lies on the road from Schwarzau
to Vienna. Everybody assembled again for breakfast on
the terrace in the freshest morning air, and with two other
Hungarian magnates—Zichy and Almasy, who incessantly
spoke of their horse-breeding—I began my journey back,
as far as Mödling ; where I was set down at 8 o'clock, in
glorious weather. It was still too early to make a call on
Ander ; moreover I was tired of so much talking, and finally
of hearing others talk ; so I determined to belong all to
myself for a while first. I took a chaise and drove into
the lovely ravine of the Brühl [the Liechtensteins' property].
There stands a place of entertainment, deserted at that
hour of day. Behind the house lies a garden with an outlook on lush fields and hanging woods, magnificently
lighted by the early sun. There I sat down, and passed
—alone, in silence—that first fair hour whereof I wished

to tell you. I left the spot profoundly comforted, beatified, at peace !

The second fair hour was that when Lady-friend expressed to me the very thoughts which I had felt in that first hour. That Ulrich v. Hutten was guiding her pen, but made her prophecy the more significant. The whole full soul of my existence stepped to me, interpreted that hour's silence, and the angel breathed its kiss of blessing on my brow.—That was the second fair hour.

And what of the third ?—

It was an unawaitedly fine success. The Flying Dutchman (the only opera of mine that can be given during Ander's continued indisposition) was set down for yesterday. I had heard this opera again a little while ago, when it left me very discontented, annoying me in particular by some very grave misunderstandings in the interpretation and the musical tempo, as also by a good many crudities in the rendering of the female chorus. So I had the two principal singers, the chorus, and the Kapellmeister called together yesterday morning for a little talk. It chiefly concerned the big scene between the Hollander and Senta, to whom I briefly but definitely explained the needful ; they seemed to be struck at having missed such obvious points. Chorus and Kapellmeister were similarly instructed.—As the representation had become a matter of routine already, and it was impossible to call the band together too, it would have been easy for these renovations to throw the whole thing out : the greater was my joy at the performance. A new spirit had entered into all. The Kapellmeister himself was astonished at the precision with which the amendments were executed ; my two singers were positively *sublime* in those particular places, but from beginning to end it all was seizing, ay, overwhelming to myself ! I can't help saying it : 1 have experienced many a beauteous thing, and yet must call last night my third fair hour !—

Let that be enough for to-day! The happiness of those three hours ought not to be alloyed ; and therefore—nothing more from me to-day! Out of mist and grey I stretch my hand to thee and cry : This has been possible.—Courage, then, courage! The fairest hour is still to come!—

R. W.

123.

Vienna, Sept. 28, 61.
Kaiserin Elisabeth
Weihburg Gasse.

O my noble glorious child !—

Almost I ought to write down nothing else to-day, than that ejaculation, for all that I could add thereto is immaterial! Music is turning the whole of me into an exclamatory being, and the sign thereof, at bottom, is the only punctuation to suffice me, when once I leave my tones! 'Tis the old enthusiasm, too, apart from which I can't subsist; and sufferings, troubles, ay, peevishness, ill-temper, all take on this fanatical tinge with me,—which surely also is the reason why I give so much distress to others!—

See! What can they not bring to pass in Zurich? One might ransack Vienna, Paris and London, to find aught in photography to touch what your Herr Keller has achieved!* Ah, child, how beautiful you are! No words can breathe it!! By God! this heart is fit to be a dwelling-place for kings : the poorest beggar who resides therein must feel his head upsoaring to the clouds!—And the birth-pangs of the highest birth are written also on these cheeks that

---

* In all probability this is the carte-de-visite facsimiled in Herr Steiner's "Neujahrsblatt" for the Zurich Allg. Musik-Gesellschaft 1903. The portrait—a good deal handsomer and more "queenly" than that of the oil-painting—has been deemed too small for reproduction in the present book, but perhaps may eventually be used elsewhere.—Tr.

once had smiled so child-like!—Eh! God, too, dwells within
the child!— Ye there, obeisance deep!!———

Do you think to-day a little late, to bring my thanks?
—But it is only to-day, that I can get at last to anything.   I'm
just resurging from all sorts of worries, of which the queenly
dame must hear the leastest little.   Moreover, I have moved
again!   An acquaintance who had placed his home at my
disposal hitherto—since he was away with all his family—
is coming back immediately; and as the luck never falls
to unlucky me, to light on decent hospitality (I must except
the kind Prussian ambassador in Paris), nothing remained
but to tuck myself into an inn again.   So I am quartering
here for some months, and here have I at last unpacked
my little flying—Dutchman's—chattels; among which the
big green portfolio has also come to light once more.   I
had kept it locked up since Lucerne; so I hunted out the
key, to take a good look at my treasure again.   Heavens,
my feelings!   Two photographs, the birthplaces of Tristan:
the Green Hill with the Asyl, and the Venetian palace.
And then the birth-leaves with first sketches, curious embryos;
the dedicatory verses, too, wherewith I sent the finished
pencil-sketches of the first act to the child: how I rejoiced
in these verses, they're so pure and true!   The pencilling
of the song—I found that too—whence sprang the Night-
scene: God knows, this song [*Träume*] has pleased me better
than the whole proud scene!   Heavens, it's finer than all
I have made!   It thrills me to my deepest nerve, to hear
it!—And to carry such an omnipresent after-feeling in one's
heart, without one's being overjoyed!!   How were that
possible?—I locked the portfolio nice and fast again; * but

* In pursuance of my note to page 274, it should be remarked that
not a word is said here of Mathilde's early letters, diary, etc.; whereas there
is apparent purpose in that "kept locked up since Lucerne," seeing that
the photograph of the Green Hill did not arrive till the præ-Minna

the latest letter with the likeness, I opened that once more :— and out came my ejaculation !! Forgive, forgive me !— I'll exclaim no more !—

And least of all should I do it now, when I'm addressing my lines to you at Düsseldorf, whither you have gone to tend a poor sick mother !—How deeply the thought distresses me, that I can be of no comfort whatever to her ! I have to thank her for something so ineffable—and perhaps my very name must not be spoken in the patient's presence ! This I fear in all modesty, as you may well believe !! But on the day when you see her just after my letter, do tell her that you wish her patience, convalescence and recovery, from a *doubled* heart !—

Now I'm to look forward to the 20th of October, am I not ?—I am thinking of all the fine things which I mean to prepare for the pair of you here : the Holländer and Lohengrin you shall hear at once and frequently, and even of the Tristan there is hope now. My singer's in possession of his voice again, full of hope and zeal ; so the study is at last to commence in real earnest.

Now, my blessing on you, dear ones !

Many kind wishes to Otto and the children—who are with you, I presume. All that is noble and eternal to the Queen !

R. W.

[Here a letter is obviously missing ; see Frau Mathilde's of October 23. About a fortnight after receipt of the last-named Wagner paid the Wesendoncks the brief Venice visit recorded

---

Paris period—cf. pp. 177 and 184. This " big green portfolio," which " she sent me once to Venice " (p. 307), must not be confounded with that other locked portfolio he bought for himself at Geneva (p. 34), the fate whereof is so dark a riddle.—For the references to the *Tristan* sketches etc., see pages 16-17, 58, 80, 307, and 311.—Tr.

below, then returned to Vienna Nov. 13, only to find it useless to wait any longer for the "return of a tenor voice into the throat" of his sole available Tristan.—Tr.]

124.

Paris, 19 Quai Voltaire,
Dec. 21, 1861.

Were you by any chance thinking I should not congratulate you on your birthday? But there, you knew my Christmas-eve is antedated by a day!—

Prosperity and happiness, with all my heart!—

I have cast myself into the arms of my old beloved :— Work has me once more, and to her I cry : " gieb Vergessen, dass ich lebe! " [*Tr. u. Is.* ii.]

I left Vienna three weeks since, direct for Paris. Nobody wanted me; I can't produce the Tristan ere a twelvemonth —a twelvemonth how and where? I have had no happy time of it. Metternich's invitation alone kept faith, but in consequence of the mother-in-law's sudden death an unexpected relative had come to Paris and seized the apartment meant for me; I can't move in before the beginning of January. I couldn't stop in Vienna ; nowhere else was I welcome ; so I started for Paris right at the beginning of December, and am making shift till January with a small room on the Quai Voltaire. I have got so far, however, as to look forward to the imminent blessing of reception into a well-regulated household with good attendance, and without any outlay needed for nice sustenance. I'm sure you will be glad of that!—

Here I am taking the greatest of pains to deny myself; if it doesn't succeed altogether, I make the pretence, to myself at least, as if people weren't aware of my presence : for three days in succession, now, I've contrived to be obliged to speak to no one (that horrible speaking!). At the

restaurant I saw Royer, director of the Grand Opéra, but
pretended not to notice him ; very soon afterwards I saw
him again, and meantime had read the announcement-of-issue
of a translation by him of some lost stage-pieces by Cervantes : of a sudden the man interested me. It was droll
to find myself accosting him, talking with him for fully
half an hour, and so completely ignoring the opera-director
that our only topic was Cervantes. He sent me his book
next day. The poet's preface moved me beyond words :
what profound resignation !—

I have often to laugh out loud when I raise my eyes
from my work-bench to the Tuileries and Louvre straight
opposite, for you must know that in reality I am in Nürnberg
now, and mixing with somewhat blunt, three-cornered folk :
there was nothing else for it, but to get among such company. The journey back from Venice to Vienna was most
lingering ; two whole long nights and a day I sat helplessly
wedged between Erst and Now, driving home into the grey :
a new labour it must be, or—an ending ! Unfortunately
my visual functions are growing ever duller ; nothing rivets
my gaze, and each locality, with all that appertains thereto—
were it the greatest masterpieces in the world—distracts
me not, remains indifferent to me ; my eye I have for
nothing but distinguishing of day from night, now, light from
gloom [cf. p. 200]. It really is a palsying against and toward
the Outer ; I see no pictures more, save inner ones, and
they clamour for nothing but sound. But no empassioned
vision would consent to lighten me on that grey journey ;
the world itself appeared a toyshop ; and that took me
back to Nürnberg, where I had passed a day last summer
and there are plenty of pretty things to see. At once it
resounded to me as an overture to the Mastersingers of
Nuremberg.

Arrived back at my Vienna inn, I worked the ground-plan out in curious haste ; it made me feel quite well, to find how clear my memory had remained, how fluent was my fancy in invention ! 'Twas a rescue, nothing less ; just as the advent of insanity may even save one's life ! So I wound up left and right, thrust the twelvemonth's bolt on Tristan, politely thanked for invitations to triumphs in various cities of my exquisite German fatherland, and—finally arrived just where I am, " zu vergessen, dass ich lebe ! "—

Your own home-coming, across the sainted Gotthardt, cannot have been precisely pleasant ; yet I was glad that you were not beside me on the journey to Vienna ! For once I was so narrow-hearted as to congratulate myself on having to accuse myself of no complicity in a discomfort for yourself and husband ; neither did Iphigenie [his own revised version of Gluck's] come off punctually on the day supposed [Nov. 16]. On the contrary, it calmed me to think of your reaching the green hill sooner, where you could gladden yourself with the children once more.

Your husband's condition grieves me much ; he is a palpable hypochondriac. It really is to be doubted whether the seclusion of Zurich is beneficial to him ; for it will have been remarked that amid the distraction of great cities, much company and so forth, he thinks far less about himself, and then is perfectly well. Probably he is not made for fruitful self-absorption : reading can help him but little, since he lacks too much of what one must gain in comparative youth and cannot make up for later ; so he falls into unprofitable brooding. I believe, dear Lady-friend, that you ought seriously to contemplate some change in this direction ; for it is evident, especially to one who has been away from you some time, that it is a question here of maladies which have their root far oftener in little, than in deep complaints.—

Perhaps you'll smile at my solicitude and my advice ?—

Ah! I know it's not my rightful business. But when one
has arrived at helping oneself the way I now am doing,
one becomes quite presumptuous, and tries to take too
much upon oneself, maybe, in seeking to help others also.
At least this presumption, however, is kindly meant; so
don't be angry with me for it!—

And now forgive me for my Nürnberg mastersingers!
They'll come by quite a pithy meaning, and quickly make
their tour of all the German theatres, perhaps by the
beginning of next winter, when I shan't trouble my head
much more about them.

The production of the Tristan still remains my eye's
chief mark. That once successfully effected, I have not
much more to do upon this earth, and would gladly lay
myself to sleep beside Master Cervantes. For my having
written the Tristan I thank you from my deepest soul to
all eternity!—

Now fare you well! Reign calmly on, both learn and
teach! Patience already is yours: and that I now have
learnt myself! A thousand fine wishes for the birthday!

Your

R. W.

125.

[Paris, end of December 1861.]

My best and heartiest thanks, my Child!—*

I reply to you with a confession. It will be needless
to speak it plainly out: everything in and about you tells
me that already you know all. And yet I feel impelled
to give you certainty on my side also :—

At last I am fully resigned! †

---

* For her letter of Dec. 25 and the scenario mentioned later.—Tr.

† The most delicate of all possible allusions (confirmed by the letter's
close) to an event impending, in the Wesendonck household, for the
middle of next June.—Tr.

One hope I never yet had given up, and believed that I had earned it hardly : to find my Asyl once again, be able again to live near you.—One hour of Wiedersehen in Venice was enough, to shatter that last fond dream !

I had at once to recognise that the freedom which is needful to you, and to which you must hold fast for your continuance, you can never maintain so long as I am near you. Only my remoteness can confer on you the power to move free after your own will ; only when you have nothing to purchase, have you no price to concede.

I cannot bear, for price of my proximity, to see you cramped and put upon, dependent, ruled. For I cannot requite to you that sacrifice, because my presence then can offer you no more ; and the thought that the poor mite I can be to you in such conditions is bought with all your liberty, with human dignity itself, would make me feel that nearness in itself a torture.

Here soothe avails no longer.—I see, you feel and know it yourself ; and how should you not, the first of all ? You have known it long, and earlier than I, who have long remained within my secret heart the incorrigible optimist.—

It was that, that alone, which weighed like lead upon my soul in Venice, not my plight, nor my other mischances. Those are indifferent to me in themselves, and have been ever since I knew you. You would scarce believe the utter callousness wherewith I cast the die in all these things : in truth they do not touch my feeling anywhere, or but in passing ; and that with mere relation to the lot which really might be due me, wherein there would be no such thing for me as failure or success.—

I adhere to it : to me it is a comfort to know you endowed with tastes, and in a social position, that can confer upon your pain a soft, idyllic character. For my part, I shall

19

merely strive to square my outward life in such a way, that
unmolested I may obey my creative inner impulse, retained
in all its freshness. I need a settled home for that, above all
else : I shall accept it under whatsoever conditions ; for I
can bear everything, everything now, since nothing weights
me, and Life with all that it involves has no more sense
for me at all. Where and how?—is boundlessly indifferent
to me ; I want to work : naught further ! Then for yourself
as well can I be something quite apart : I know it, and you
know it too ! The grisly Last is over : Venice, the journey
back and three ensuing weeks—O horrible !—now lie behind
me !—So, courage ! go it must !—

I shall send you oft a morsel from my work. How you
will open your eyes at my Mastersingers ! Keep your heart
secure against *Sachs*, or you'll fall in love with him ! It's
an extraordinary work. The old draft afforded little,*
next to nothing. Eh, one must have been in Paradise, to
discover what may lurk in such a thing !—

Of my life you shall hear the merest necessary—the
outermost : inwardly—rest assured of that !—*nothing whatever*
will occur again, nothing but artistic creation. Consequently
you will be losing just nothing at all, but will gain the only
thing I have of worth—my works. We shall see each other
now and then, though, shall we not ? Void of all wish then :
wherefore also, wholly free !—

So ! A remarkable letter is this ! You can hardly

---

* Sent to Paris by Mathilde Dec. 25 ; see her letter of that date.
This scenario had been lent or presented to her long before, and must
thereafter have been returned to her ; for it is mentioned in her list,
page 366, and was also in her possession till her death. The main body,
all of it that had previously been made public in Germany, will be found
in *Life* ii, 383-5 ; its entirety in the " Bayreuth number " of *Die Musik*
1902.—The allusion to " Paradise," of course, is taken from the " Cobbler-
song " (act ii), which accompanied the present letter ; see facsimile.—Tr.

(Eva ist auch der Name des jungen Mädchens;
das soeben mit ihrem Geliebten auf einem
Fluchtversuche begriffen ist.)

Sachs.

Jerum! Jerum!
Hallohallohe!
Oho! trallalei! O he! —
Als Eva aus dem Paradies
von Gott dem Herrn verstossen,
gar schuf ihr Schmerz der harte Kies
an ihrem Fuss dem blossen;
Das jammerte den Herrn,
ihr Füsschen hatt' er gern;
und seinem Engel rief er zu:
„da mach' der armen Sünd'rin Schuh';
und da der Adam, wie ich seh',
an Steinen dort sich stösst die Zeh',
Dass recht fortan
er wandeln kann,
so miss' dem auch Stiefel an!" —
Jerum! Jerum!
u. s. w. —

O Eva! Eva! schlimmes Weib!
Das hast du am Gewissen;
dass ob der Füss' am Menschenleib
jetzt Engel schustern müssen!
Bliebst du im Paradies,
da gab es keinen Kies:
ob deiner jungen Missethat,
hantier' ich jetzt mit Ahl und Draht;

und ob Herrn Adam's übler Schwäch'
versohl' ich Schuh' und streiche Pech'!
    Wär' ich nicht fein,
    ein Engel sein,
Teufel möchte Schuster sein!"
    Jerum! Jerum!
        u. s. w.

O Eva! hör' mein Klageruf,
    mein' Noth und schwer Verdrussen'!
Die Kunstwaar' die ein Schuster schuf,
    sie tritt die Welt mit Füssen!
    Gäb' nicht ein Engel Trost,
    Der gleiches Werk erloos't,
und rief mich oft in's Paradies,
wie dann ich Schuh' und Stiefel liess'!
Doch küsst der Engel und die Stern,
Dann schaff' ich Werke für das Herr,
    und bin im Ruh'!
    Hans Sachs ein Schuh—
    macher und Poët dazu..
        Jerum! Jerum!
            u. s. w.

Ein andermal der
Probegesang! und den
der junge Ritter versucht'!

believe what ease it gives me now, to know that you know
that I know what you long have known!

And now for a Cobbler's song!—

Adé, my Child!

The
MASTER!

126.

Viel Glück, und dass es blüh' und wachs'
Das wünscht von Herzen euch Hans Sachs.
Something new in the old year!*—

Good-Year.
R. W.

127.

Paris, 19 Quai Voltaire.
January 7, 62.

My Child, I am still here! End of the month I think
of transferring myself to Wiesbaden.—I confess to feeling
weak enough to need a friendly word.

I am not pleased with myself thereat!

Yet the Mastersingers help: for their sake I'll hold out!
Adieu!

R. W.

128.

[February 3, 1862.]
POGNER.
"Und du, mein Kind, du sagst mir nichts?"
EVA.
"Ein gutes Kind, gefragt nur sprichts." †

---

* Enclosing Walther's verses "Am stillen Herd . . . da lernt' ich auch
das Singen." [The words in the text, modelled on Sachs' favourite rhyme,
convey to *both* the Wesendoncks "every good wish for its thriving,"
and one's thoughts fly at once to the Master-cobbler's speech that ushers
in the quintet of act iii.—Tr.]

† "And thou, my child, say'st nothing to me?"—"A good child only

So, some children do not understand being asked in the third person.

The old enthusiasm tried to stir.   I had a mind to beg you people for an evening's rendezvous at Basle, to read my Meistersinger to you.   It came hard to me, to renounce the old custom ; yet be it must, and I daresay you will thank me for it!—

I have packed my manuscript up for you, however, and it's just going off to you instead.*   Mind how you find your way about : it looks dreadful in places, with blots of ink too. It would be amusing to me, to see if you made it all out.

At times I had to stop work for laughing, at times for crying.   I commend to your notice Herr Sixtus Beckmesser. David, too, will win your favour.

For the rest, don't get misled : all that there is in it, has been made expressly by myself.   Merely the eight lines with which Sachs is saluted by the people, in the last scene,

---

speaks when asked "—*Die Meistersinger* act ii, save that "folgsam" ("obedient") now takes the place of "gutes."—Probably a letter, or telegram, is missing between 127 and 128, as Mathilde *had* answered on the 16th Jan.—*vid. inf.*—In the German edition this letter 128 is conjectured as of the end of January, and inferentially, from Paris; but it now appears to have been written from Carlsruhe on the date assigned above.   As its contents, however, round off the composition of the *Meistersinger* poem, no object would be served by detaching it from the group of "Paris letters."—Tr.

* Dr. Golther informs us that this manuscript, the "much corrected" original poem, was also found among Frau Wesendonck's papers :—its first act is dated "Paris, 5. Jan. 62," its second "Paris, 16. Jan. 62," its third "Paris, 25. Jan. 1862 "—the date in each case being terminal.   The remarkably caligraphic facsimile-edition now obtainable at Schott's is not taken from *this*, but from the fair copy made by Wagner for his own use, clearly just before the present letter, and from which he read aloud at Mainz two days later (see p. 300).   From the books of that firm we further learn, through Dr. W. Altmann, that Wagner had despatched a copy of the whole new scenario from Vienna the 19th of November 1861 on approbation, i.e. fully six weeks ere renewing acquaintance with his sketch of sixteen years ago (p. 290).—Tr.

are from SACHS' own hymn to Luther; the names of the
master-tunes and 'tones' (with exception of a few invented
by myself) are also genuine. Taken all round, I am surprised
at what I've been able to make of the meagre notes.

To-morrow I go to Mainz, and thence to Biebrich or
Wiesbaden, to seek a nest in which to hatch into music the
master-egg I've laid.

Should you want to write to me, before you hear from
me again, please address aux soins de *J. B. Schott's Söhne in
Mainz.*

God keep you, my Child !

Best greeting from the

MASTER.

❃

AFTERMATH

LETTERS OF FEBRUARY 1862
to
JUNE 1871

❧

129.

Biebrich, Feb. 13, 62

Does the wicked Child intend, perhaps, to let the Master know absolutely nothing more about her? I should have been so glad to hear how the Meistersinger pleased her; I'm getting half afraid she may be ill!—For my part, I remain here till late autumn (and let us hope, the finish of my composition), Biebrich c/o Architect Frickhöffer; where I have taken a year's tenancy of a couple of nice rooms, magnificently situated on the brink of the Rhine, close to the palace [Duke of Nassau's], and am fitting them with odds and ends of hired furniture. My only property, among it, is the famous tea-machine with mug; but I expect to shake down very soon. If the Child would only write from the Green Hill!

R. W.

130.

Biebrich
Feb. 16, 62.*

Freundin!

You do wrong to pay any heed to me; this time it positively shames me. I was unaware, and accordingly uneasy. One word sufficed, one mournful, hopeless word! O how much happier to be dead oneself, than see a loved one die!—So it is moving over you, and you are receiving one initiation after another! To the serious mind it *is*

---

* In answer to a brief note unpreserved; see Wagner's pathetic letter to Cornelius of March 4, '62 (*Fortnightly Review*, July 1905).—Tr.

initiation : thought and feeling blend in it to one; it feels the deepest-thought, and knows how direly true that is !

For your mother I have shed a tear-drop big with meaning ; for yourself, be welcomed to this solemn realm where I am now a denizen, and whence alone I still can look upon the world,—can even see it bright of semblance, since I look no longer *into*, but *from out* the night !

Leave the Meistersinger quite aside ; the manuscript belongs to you ; I had no other purpose than to render you your property !

Heartfelt greetings to Otto and the children !

R. W.

Biebrich
(bei Architect Frickhöffer).

131.

Biebrich,
March 12, 1862.

I wrote you once from Paris lately that you should hear little of my life thenceforward, but solely of my handiwork, because the first could never have a meaning more. But how when I cannot get to work, when life takes all my energy ? Must the solution then be such a dubious gap as this, when I have kept you so long waiting for a thankful sign of life in answer to your letters, to your gift ?—Even to-day I can tell you nothing further, than, I hope to start work at last to-morrow ; there has been an interruption of six weeks, during which I have done nothing but "live"— if so one may call it.*

---

* March 6 he writes Roeckel : "My wife surprised me by coming over from Dresden to help me ; she was 10 days here." Minna had arrived about the 20th of February, as Wagner writes Frau Betty Schott on the 22nd that he is at Darmstadt with his wife for a performance of *Rienzi*, and to Cornelius on the 4th of March that he said good-bye to her "the day before yesterday." By a strange fatality Mathilde's "little box

I am thoroughly settled here now, have two chambers hired for a year, the pianoforte, book-case, renowned divan, the three Roman engravings and the old Nibelungen print; facing my desk hangs the photograph of the Green Hill also, in a window-recess the Palazzo Giustiniani. The site is extraordinarily beautiful, hard by the Rhine, the [ducal] palace close beside it. The house itself stands quite alone, and may God preserve it from further inmates! It is very handsomely built, on speculation, and contains one lovely big suite, which I would gladly see occupied by some decent body.* A beautiful, quite spacious garden; the birds in the [duke's] park keep up a contest of song with those on the island opposite; the nightingales are numberless, they say, and positively deafening in their season. So here will I await my Mastersinger destiny!

Best thanks for the letter with which you really shamed me! You read too soon, and wrote to me too early; you should still have left me in the corner for a while. For the rest, I couldn't help remarking that this was in fact the first time you had made acquaintance with a poem of mine on paper, and not through my reading it out; also, the difficult manuscript must have given you much ado,—eh! it all is so different, when one has to struggle on alone. I've read it several times aloud, though, lastly at the Grand

---

and *Meistersinger* letter (p. 350) arrived also in those same ten days, and Minna's blind resentment dashed her husband's last fond hope : " There's no more doubt of it ; it is impossible for me to live with my wife any more " —he writes Cornelius, and to Roeckel April 5 : " My wife has now obtained the full Dresden amnesty for me [Saxony had been *excepted* in 1860], but I shall not budge from here ; where I have housed myself quite endurably, and—down to the present—have splendid calm for work."—Tr.

* " Eine ganz wunderhübsche grosse Wohnung, in welche ich gern etwas anständiges wünschte." Presumably the said "big suite" was temporarily inhabited by the landlord, with whom Wagner soon fell out over that person's neglect of his (F.'s) mastiff.—Tr.

Duke's in Carlsruhe [March 7], when they listened very well, if nothing like so well as great big Micky,* and the rules of the Tabulatur were the very things that made them laugh most. Why, child! *that's* just the point of all the strange pedantic stuff; one has got to laugh. With Walther's songs you lack the melody, by all means there the indispensable affair ; I set these verses to the melody all ready in my head, and that of course you can't conceive. Just hear how easily it runs tho' ; e.g.

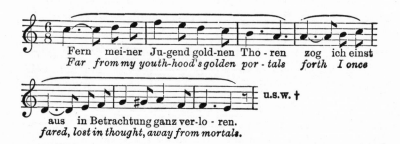

Fern   mei-ner Ju-gend gold-nen Tho - ren   zog   ich einst
Far   from my youth-hood's golden por - tals   forth   I once

aus   in Betrachtung ganz ver-lo - ren.
fared, lost in thought, away from mortals.

Of the whole affair the Folk hears nothing but the melody : guess my riddle who can !—

The first time I read it, was at Schott's in Mainz, the 5th of February. I had had to abandon the idea of reading it first to yourself, but was determined to have some compensation for you ; so before my departure from Paris I wrote to Vienna, telling Cornelius (of whom you'll hear more in due time) that he must be at Schott's in Mainz on the

---

* See pages 14 and 134, *Micke* or *Miekchen* being a pet abbreviation, generally of Marie, in this case of Myrrha, to whom Frau Wesendonck had evidently read the poem. From the remainder of the paragraph it is clear that the lady's "no. 5" originally contained a much more detailed criticism ; unfortunately it seems to have been the identical letter which "fell into Minna's hands at once" (see previous notes and p. 350).—Tr.

† Of course one must supply a flat *b* for key-signature, but the above, so Dr. Golther tells me, is a faithful copy of Wagner's MS. sketch. Alike words and music entirely differ from the finished work.—Tr.

evening of the 5th or I should call him "Sie" again. It was just like [Schiller's] Bürgschaft: all the rivers had flowed over, as you know, many trains stopped running, great danger everywhere: no matter, on the tick of 7 my good Cornelius enters, and travels back to Vienna next day! Now I would have you know what a poor devil he is, how he plagues his soul with lesson-giving to earn 40 fl. a month; but—he loves me dearly, and you have seen what store I set by him.* Do write him, child; he loves you too.— He lives at "Weissgärber-Pfefferhofgasse 30 Wien," his full name is "Peter Cornelius," and he's also a nephew of the celebrated painter.

Now fare you well, and accept my very best greetings. I could not write before to-day; I had to wait for good humour. Adieu, my Child!

R. W.

P. S.

Ah, the lovely pillow! Look at me, now; to pocket such a thing as that without a word! Nicely spoilt!!

132.

Biebrich a/ Rh.
May 22, 1862.

Dear Lady-friend,

To-day is my birthday: someone has sent me flowers into the house [cf. *Meistersinger* iii]. I have been ill, and only yesterday could I get into the park again. Of yourself I durst think little now, as I can help you in nothing more and simply cherish silent wishes for your welfare;

so I sat all lone.

Suddenly there came an inspiration for the orchestral introduction to the third act of the Meistersinger. The most

---

* In his invitation, as a fact, Wagner himself had undertaken to pay the travelling-expenses.—Tr.

engrossing climax of this act will be the moment when
Sachs stands up before the whole assemblage, and is greeted
by the people with a mighty outburst of enthusiasm, whereon
they chant with clarion tongue the first eight lines of Sachs's
ode to Luther (the music for which is ready). For the
introduction of this 3rd act—the curtain rising upon Sachs
seated in deep thought—I now shall give the bass strings
a soft and mellow, deeply melancholy strain to play, that
bears the character of utmost resignation ; then the solemn-
joyous melody of the " Wacht auf! Es rufet * gen den Tag ;
ich hör' singen im grünen Hag ein' wonnigliche Nachtigall,"
sounded by horns and sonorous wind-instruments, will be
added thereto as bright evangel, and developed more and
more by all the band.

It has become clear to me that this work will be my
most consummate masterpiece, and also—that I shall [live
to] consummate it.

But I wanted to give myself a birthday present ; I'm
doing so, by sending you these tidings.

Take care of yourself, attend to your health, and—if
think of me you must—picture me always in the frame
of this birthday-morning mood ! It will be a comfort to
you, and you will flourish too, for sure !—

Best wishes from

Your

Richard Wagner.

133.

Biebrich

June 9, 1862.

Dear Lady-friend,

For days and days have I been intending to write dear
Myrrha and thank her for the share I'm sure I must ascribe

---

* The word stands thus in the MS., instead of "nahet." [N.B.—
The brief explanatory programme contained in *Prose Works* VIII., p. 388,.
was not written till seven years later.—Tr.]

her in the lovely cushion ; but she also must get used to my
ingratitude, which doesn't consist in actual want of thanks,.
but in so frequent omission to attest them. Such attesta-
tions are agreeable, flattering effusions, wherewith one flatters
and delights oneself the most : I seldom come to execution
even of such pleasant projects now ; all trends with me
towards a last and serious close, so it is but with sadness
I can look at e'en the flowers strewn upon this final road.

The poem you sent me to-day is very beautiful—quite
masterly, I think ; only, the point of the legend now appears
to me otherwise. There flattering hope is given the nixy,*
but I for my part understand no hope now, have become
impervious to nothing so much as its suasion ; in its place
I understand that happiness we have not first to hope for,
but truly in ourselves are masters of. Perhaps you will
remember how I told you once in days gone by, that as
life went on I had ever grown more vividly aware that Art
would never furnish me a happiness beyond conception till
every good of life were reft me, all, all were lost, and any
possibility of hoping cut away. I remember also in my
thirtieth year, or thereabouts,† having asked myself in inward
doubt if I really did possess the grit for an artistic individuality of highest rank ; in my works I could still trace
influence and imitation, and only with misgivings did I
dare look forward to my further evolution as a thoroughly
original producer. Well, at the time when I told you the
above—that period of strange passion—on a lonely walk one
day the possibility suddenly occurred to me of losing one
boon whose possible possession must from of old have
seemed to me unthinkable ; and then I felt the time would
come for Art to acquire a quite new meaning in my eyes

---

* See "Religion and Art," *Prose Works* VI. p. 249, and cf. p. 221*n*
sup.—Tr.

† Therefore between the *Holländer* and *Tannhäuser.*—Tr.

a meaning altogether wondrous,—the time when not a hope would ever have the power to snare my heart again.

Thus has the full meaning of the old Messiah-legend also dawned on me at last. They were waiting for a liberator and redeemer, of the seed of David, a king of Israel : everything came true; palms were strewn before him ;—only, the unexpected occurred, for he said to them, " My kingdom is not of this world." * So do all the nations yearn and strive for their Messiah, who shall fulfil their wishes of this life : he comes, and says to them, Give wishing up itself !—'Tis the ultimate solution of the great Wish-riddle,—which you must admit that your friend Hutten and the others did not understand.

Myself, I have no wish left, save to be able to work. Even to the representation of my works my wishes extend no longer, and compulsion thereto I accept as an unavoidable calamity. To Vienna I have been definitively invited for the autumn, to produce the Tristan : that disturbs me now. Yet it irks me also to be driven in my work [by Schott ?], for, the way I'm working now, I cannot do it quickly. Assured leisure were what I most could wish : if I cannot attain it, I suppose I still must feel the pain of life; but its anticipation would enhance the pleasure of creating. I should like a haven in the most complete and utter solitude, and that is very hard to gain.—

Accept my felicitations yourself ; give my kind regards and thanks to Myrrha, as also to your husband, to whom I still owe hearty thanks for his last letter !

From my heart Yours

Richard Wagner.

---

* Slightly expanded, the same parable is narrated to Malwida within a week (see *Letters to Otto etc.*), whilst an immature variant is to be found thirteen years earlier in the working-out section of *Jesus of Nazareth* (*Prose Works* VIII. 297-9).—May the "Wunsch-Räthsel" toward the paragraph's close be a lapsus calami for *Welt-Räthsel, i.e* "Riddle of the World" ?—Tr.

[Between this and the next came three letters to Otto, whilst a fourth bears the same date as our no. 134—see Letters to Otto. The master had meanwhile left Biebrich for Vienna, arriving mid-November, to prepare for the eternally deferred production of Tristan und Isolde. On the day before no. 134 he telegraphs to a disciple that he is " half dead" from the rehearsals for his concerts of the 26th and New Year's day.—Tr.]

134.

[Kaiserin Elisabeth,]
Vienna, Dec. 21, 62.

I had a beautiful sweet dream of you last night, directly after falling asleep. May it betoken you good—all the good I wish you, cherished Friend, with all my heart!

It affected me much, midst all the stress and misery of the present, that a dream should still remind me of your birthday in good time. That was fine, and I observe that Dream at least still cares for me.

Fervent greeting!

Richard Wagner.

[For Frau Wesendonck's three-line reply vid. inf.—Wagner's outward history between nos. 134 and 135 is sufficiently indicated in no. 136. He had returned to Vienna the end of April, only to find his Tristan still postponed, and writes from his new ' home' in what then was an outlying suburb.—Tr.]

135.

[To Frau Eliza Wille, Mariafeld.]

221. Penzing bei Wien
June 5, 1863.

Dear honoured Lady,

In a day or two I mean to write to Wesendonck's again at last ; only—it can only be to *him*. I am too fond of

20

the wife, my heart is so melting and full when I think of her, that it is impossible for me to address her with that formality which would be more incumbent on me now, in her regard, than ever; neither can I write her from my heart without an act of treason to her husband, whom I sincerely prize and honour. What, then, is to be done? for I also cannot keep it wholly buried in my heart; *some* human soul, at least, must learn how it stands with me. So I tell it you: She is and stays my first and only love; I feel it plainer every day. That was the summit of my life; the trembling years of beautiful distress I lived beneath the waxing spell of her proximity hold all the sweetness of my life. It needs but the remotest ground, and I am back amidst them, all saturated with that magic atmosphere which takes my breath still, just as then, and leaves me nothing but a sigh. And were there no stimulant else, yet dreams would do it; dreams that refresh me every time they shew her to me.—Now tell me, friend, how *can* I converse with this lady as now it should and must be?— Impossible!—Ah, even do I feel I dare not see her any more; in Venice once already such a wiedersehen made me right unhappy: only after I had entirely lost that memory, did she become to me again quite what she was before. This do I feel: fair will she ever remain in my eyes, and never will my love of her turn cold, but I dare not see her face to face; not under this awful constraint, which— imperative as I acknowledge it—must be the death-knell of our love. What am I to do, then? Should I leave my dearest in the fallacy that she has grown indifferent to me? But oh, that falls so hard!—Should *you* relieve her of that fallacy, would that be doing good? I know not!—And life will slip away at last; O misery!—

Since my departure from Zurich I have been strictly living as in exile; what I sacrificed then, no tongue can tell!—'Tis my solitary craving now, to arrive at |least at household peace again, be left to live for work alone. By dint of untold exertions I have bought myself at least the possibility of founding a hearth once more, which I henceforth have to tend entirely alone. Repeated attempts have convinced myself and friends that a continued dwelling with my wife is clean impossible, and thoroughly injurious to us both ; so she is living in Dresden, where I provide for her abundantly beyond my means. She cannot quite compose herself as yet, and I am forced—with strenuous subdual of recurrent accesses of pity—to adopt an attitude of sternness, without which I should only prolong her sufferings and rob myself of all prospect of peace. I can truly say, this trial is the hardest I have ever borne ; but there!—I am renouncing all, and wish for nothing but a working rest ; the sole relief to clear my conscience and make me really free!—

And now, my dear, do be beseeched and tell me often of our lady-friend,—you love her still, I hope, and she is likewise true to you ? Indeed it is too hard to know so infinitely loved a being's life so utterly remote and alien, without the power to cast a glance upon it anywhere. What I may learn through her husband, you will comprehend, cannot shew me the Lady-friend to whom I dare protest undying love e'en tho' I never mean to see her more. Never?—'Tis hard,—but so it must be!—

I have just been opening that green case, again, she sent me once to Venice. How many an agony of life has been passed through since then, and yet to be encompassed at a touch with all the old, unspeakably beautiful charm! Sketches for Tristan there, for the music of her poems!— Ah, dearest friend, 'tis true one loves but once, whatever of intoxicant or flattering this life may bring our way! Yes, I know it now, now first completely, that I shall never cease to love but her. You will respect the innocence of this avowal, and forgive me that I make confession to yourself?

Good-bye, and be a friend to
Your
Richard Wagner.

136.

[*To Otto.*]

221. Penzing
bei Wien.
June 6, 1863.

Best Friend,

I really must have news of your two selves at last! Of mine you will learn something worth hearing only when I can tell you I'm at work again ; for happenings, however manifold, have no more actual sense for me. My Russian travel, St Petersburg, Moscow, with all the episodes attached thereto, only influenced me in so far as it was to contribute to freeing me from all such things and conducting to a haven of work. Under terms and conditions like those, my bitterness regarding the heap of people who have more surety and ease than they know what to do with is often very great, and gives me an ironic undertone to almost every act of kindness shewn me. When I reflect on the states of unrest into which I have fallen since quitting Zurich, I cannot but accuse my fate of hardness ; for it is solely the chance of finding rest again to write my projected works at last, that lends this foolish hunt for it a meaning.

Well, I have traversed my fiftieth birthday, and had wellnigh to felicitate myself on keeping it in total solitude! My rural dwelling was thereafter treated to a torchlight procession [June 3] which I attended rather absent-mindedly. Just as the line of lights was drawing

near across a bridge, the most splendid full-moon rose above
the tree-tops of the Schönbrunn garden, and gazed in
mystical sublimity upon the mummery beneath. Even
during the singing, a couple of young people who were
with me up above heard naught from me but exclamations
at the glory of the moon. It was the old familiar, unique
friend, that drew to me above this childish stranger world—
exactly as it used to cross the distant wreath of Alps and
move athwart your garden to my—Asyl!

—Asyl!—How often have I thought, ere this, that I
had found a haven!!—This last time I was so in need
of an abode of rest, that, with eyes for nothing save a quiet
dwelling with a garden, I took the very first that came;
a week later, and apparently I should have settled at
Bingen. While that hung fire, I heard of this; indifferent
as to where, I closed with here; and now I've but one wish,
that at least it may be granted me to stop here till my
end!— As things stand in Germany and with myself, the
only chance I see of bringing that about is by dint of
periodical excessive strains, journeys to Russia and suchlike; though I cannot conceive how I'm to sustain them
for long. Some day folk will read it perhaps in my
biography, and many a one will wonder; for I naturally
shall come to grief on one of those occasions. If you want
a notion how such undertakings tax me, compare for a
joke the three Petersburg photographs,* which were taken
at the commencement, with the Moscow one for which I
sat a fortnight later!—However, it has got to be!—

For all that, I haven't lost my old mania for fitting up
the dwelling of my final choice as tastily as possible; should
your household care to make a trifling contribution,† from

---

* See Mr. H. S. Chamberlain's *Richard Wagner* p. 70.—Tr.

† See postscript to this letter, and openings of the next two.—Tr.

no one would it be more welcome—as you must be aware. For you really are the only ones to whom I belong on this earth, in a measure ; to that pass has it come, and I can make no fresh beginning. That I belong to you, you both have earned with griefs and sacrifices of all kinds.

—What did you think of the Swiss villa the Grossfürstin Helene of Russia presented me with? Weren't you a little afraid of getting me slung about your neck again ? Luckily the villa stands in the same place as the 50,000 fr. which I'm supposed to have netted in Russia. How welcome it must be to all my German patrons, to know that I'm ∗so sumptuously provided for and it hasn't cost them a penny !—Well, well, it's just my usual fate, to figure as the enviable !

Ah, dearest friend, enough about myself ! Once I am back at my Meistersinger, you two shall hear again ; I'm so distracted at present, that I can collect my wits for nothing. Still better, if you gave me prompt occasion by heartily-begged news of yourselves ; for which I'm longing much !

With a thousand good greetings,
Your
Richard Wagner.

I would gladly have a pretty good-sized portrait (photographic) of your wife, please ; the Green Hill already hangs framed in my room.

[To Mathilde henceforward.]

137.

221. Penzing bei Wien.
June 28, 1863.

Freundin,

A beautiful, beautiful portfolio arrived to-day ; it is destined for the Meistersinger. I have managed down to now quite capitally with the green one, which I unpacked again the other day (—I have settled once more!—) and behold! all kinds of sketches and strange leaves therein, all tucked into a corner. Dear Heaven, it looked like Tristan still, inside there! Never mind; the mastersingers had to creep in too. Now, don't be cross with me for once, I'm not a proper Master yet; even with my music I haven't got much beyond the 'prentices (so God knows how it all will turn!): wherefore the perfectly finished shall always go into the new portfolio, and look so grand that I'll tell myself each time I peep at it, "Come, you're already a bit of a master,—tho' nothing like so much as she who sent you the Master-portfolio"; but the unfinished (alas! and how much about me is unfinished!) shall jog along in the big green one meanwhile, with all the gleanings from old wondrous days. I really am more faithful than you may believe, and perhaps than you are sometimes made believe about me; so the mastersingers, if ever they're to come to anything, must come into the world *partout* in the same old green portfolio: God only knows what luck 'twill bring them! But whatever gets quite straight at last shall move, as said, to the new brown one; already there are 40 pages of full score inside,—tho' I've no idea at all what luck 'twill bring.

How am I to make that intelligible to you?—Admit, it's hard for so unfinished a mastersinger to write you; e.g., if I were to tell you, A master ought to have repose, I must confess at once that *I* have none, and—what's worse!—am never like to have any. That's the hideous truth which has now become quite plain to me: I've no repose! I cut myself entirely loose from men, relations, every sort of intercourse at last, because at bottom all torment me— that's how I am!—and furnish me a nice still dwelling; every nook in it has to fit to my mind, I'm a-fever to make

it all immensely snug and comfortable, for I tell myself,
There shall you stick, pass all your time there (fortune
favouring) and stay entirely alone.—To be alone: ah! the
bliss that thrills through me anon, when I tell myself that
—before I actually am alone. Good: I get alone—foolish
man, as if my heart weren't yoked to me!—and then at
last my full unrest explodes, now in the likeness of care,
new of craving. I yearn for a presence, since *nothing* save
presence can soothe—believe me, the god of peace and
happiness, his name is " Presence "—and—have to do without
it. So I take up at first with my serving-folk,* who soon
grow fond of me ; then a dog is added. Not that I have
procured myself a new one,—I've a horror of everything
now now, all new associations, even with a dog; but thieves
broke in, the other day, and stole a gold snuffbox which
the Moscow orchestra had given me as souvenir ; that
grieved my old Baron who lives below, and he placed his
old retriever at my service. So the dog now sleeps in my
rooms at night, and will not quit me even in the day ; he
clings to my heels wherever I go. His name is Pohl ; he's
brown and strong, but aged already, as I said: ere long
he'll die,† like Fipps and Peps,—the pity of it !——To
resume : I fancy I shall reach no true repose. Even as
regards the Meistersinger I'm still mistrustful, earnestly and
calmly as the brown portfolio stares at me.—

Can Otto be cross with me for not having written to
him so long? Well, I did write him as soon as my
birthday was over—the so momentously awaited 50th [cf.
p. 231]—lest he might think I only wrote him when I wished
to bother him for something ; but if it were not for yourself
I really shouldn't have known if he received my lines or

---

* A most excellent couple, man and wife, named Mrazek.—Tr.
† Pohl survived the whole Munich period, and died in January 1866
at Geneva.

no. How goes it with his health; does his throat still
trouble him? I hope for good news of him.

How stands it with beautiful Switzerland? Is the lake
as vivid green and blue as ever; and the mountains with
their fields of snow?—Children, indeed you chose yourselves
a lovely land, and oft-times does a longing for it seize me;
once I hoped to die there some fine day! Methinks I was
often more restful there, upon the whole, than I am now;
Swiss scenery like that has something tranquillising! A
sunset I no longer know; just a couple on the Rhine of
late. But no residence would come to hand there, so I'm
seated here for the sake of some fine tall trees which I have
in the garden; and the abode is restful,—not myself! However, I told you that before.—

And how do things fare with yourself? To you Hans
Sachs came easy; to me he still comes hard. Art also
can be serious—not life alone! Adieu, Lady-friend!

Stay kind to
Your
R. W.

138.

Penzing, August 3, 1863.

Dearest Meisterin,

According to your last dear lines * I might strictly have
looked for "further particulars" from Schwalbach. Meantime
I ran over to Pesth, whither I had been invited by the
Hungarians, to give two "concerts." † I got back a few

---

* An unpreserved letter of July 15, which would fall between nos. 7
and 8 of Frau Wesendonck's own group, evidently announcing her departure for a 'cure' (see end of the present one).—Is it necessary to
explain that the only possible English equivalent for *Meisterin* in this
connection would be "Lady-master," with allusion to her verses of
"7a"?—Tr.

† July 23 and 28; including the *Meistersinger* overture, which he had
given first at Leipzig to an empty house the year before (Nov. 1, 62).—Tr.

days since, and found at least the promised lamp; which I find most beautiful and masterly, and would have you freely thanked for.—

With my haven it's so-so, really curious! The need of a more permanent foothold, with a suitable pleasant abode, had become overpowering; I felt that only from a similar base could I look out on the world once more—for a final time—to discover how things stand twixt it and me. Well, I find they don't stand for the best, and heartily repent having laid out my poor hard earnings on securing the expensive basis for that step in knowledge. As nobody seems inclined to take me in, I should have put my few thousand Russian roubles to better use by buying myself into the first Italian hospice and leaving the world to go its way; for I really don't see any need of me in it. It is the honest truth I'm telling you, and calmly from the bottom of my soul! Were I to count up all the queer mischances that have dogged me since my departure from Switzerland, you yourself could only see therein a wellnigh systematic reckoning of Fate's, to turn me from my purpose. I have no luck; and it takes a little luck to keep a man like myself under the delusion that he belongs to the world.—

Meisterin, it is not well with me, and I'm aweary of life, —as I plainly ascertained the other day, when at instant peril of death. It happened near Pesth on the Danube, in the same boat two young Hungarian cavaliers had sailed from Rotterdam to Pesth. A spirited lady, Gräfin Bethlen, mother of six children, had undertaken to steer; at a sudden squall she grew alarmed, and brought the boat too near the wind; the waves dashed it against a raft, and it cracked in two. Well, compassion for the mother seized me, but so singular a sense of comfort for my private self, so buoyant and so bracing that our young-folks could hardly contain their wonder at my conduct, as they would rather have expected great excitement from such a nervous man as me. When they began praising me—for I did a little toward the rescue—I had almost to burst out laughing!

What *is* the use? Dying is no such easy job, especially if one's time hasn't come yet; and that must be the case with me, except that I cannot see at all what I am spared for. To be something, perhaps, to my dear ones!? Could I be less to them when they know that I am dead, than now when I'm cut off on every side and merely suffer? Personally I can be nothing more to anybody,—and my spirit? That remains with them, whilst it quickens *my* heart no more. I have no zest any longer,—for nothing. All devoutness fails me, all concentration; a deep, restless distraction sways my inner man; I have no present, quite palpably no future, of belief not a speck. To be sure, the right artistic function, the representing of my own new works, might have made a great difference; but my return to Germany has dealt the death-blow to that. It is an abominable country, and a certain [Arnold] Ruge is right in saying, "The German is low."* Not a trace of hope exists there, and you may judge how it stands with my erst-presumed high patrons, when I tell you that I have been ·invited to repeat my Vienna concerts by the Czechs of Prague, the Russians, the Hungarians, whereas I am certain that my precious Germans would decline me if I made an offer of myself. In Berlin the Intendant refused to accept my call, and so on; since my return from Russia I haven't found it possible to look up a soul belonging to this theatre as yet: my loathing of these people is so strong, that I am incapable of undertaking anything else for which I should require them. Everybody who knows anything, finds that perfectly natural; only, it also means

---

* Or "abject"—*niederträchtig*—see "German Art and German Policy," *Prose Works* IV, 92.—Tr.

the close of my career. Believe me, it is a strange feeling, to know that even you are really not acquainted with my works ; I have simply to conduct a morsel of them properly, and even the most gifted and experienced of my disciples at once admit that they had as good as no conception of the piece before. What, then, is my spirit, what my works? —without me, they exist for no one! Yes, that makes my humble person of great weight to me ; only—this personality itself exists for none but me, and that's a bad business. Something, no doubt, may be said on the other side, including words of comfort, of emphatic flattery ; but it avails with me no longer : I hear they are words, even see it when they're written—as for that matter, nearly all my intercourse with men is carried on by letter now.

What am I to do with my haven, then, despite portfolio and lamp? A knotty point, especially with my great distraction. I turn and twist it in my mind : If I set myself a term again, a fixed number of years—say five,— how am I to start gaining them? That is growing very difficult, and to tell the truth, I *don't* know how. My needs are increasing, I've a double household to keep up— two altogether wretched ones !—so my *person* has occurred to me. Nobody asks for my works, the world pays heed to nothing save the virtuoso ; now want has shewn me that I also am a virtuoso. At the head of an orchestra I appear to produce that effect on these people ; the Hungarians, who hadn't a notion of my music, and live on nothing but Verdi etc. at their National-theatre, took in each single number from my Nibelungen, Tristan, Meistersinger, with quite incredible alacrity,—manifestly because it was *I* who presented and performed them. So, now that I am pondering how to gain my "time," I tell myself that I must make a concert-tour ; and that's what it most probably will come to. The worst of it is, I cannot stand it long

or often, my over-exertion at such performances and
rehearsals passes all measure ; yet I mean to try.   Perhaps,.
if I were to ask you, you could arrange me such a " concert "
of new scraps at Zurich itself; only it might be hard to
contrive there, as my poor " person " needs very many
other persons, to make a personal effect.   Be that as it
may, you will shortly hear of my giving concerts again
here or there ; some will exclaim, " Didn't we tell you, he
wants to make money ? "—perchance a few others, " They
say, he wants to die ! "—

Perhaps it will end all right, tho', and my Asyl (the
how-many-eth ?) stand me in good stead for once ; the
lamp will shine, portfolio fill, and—a tea-set (my old one is
not get-at-able !) agreeably refresh me.*   God ! everything
is possible, and although my nerve-racked body's always
feeling aches and pains, my doctor [Standhartner] laughs.
each time I ask him if it must not turn into a fatal illness
soon.   That ought to brisk one's spirits up ; and in truth,.
however wretched is one's health, it's health of a sort.
Only, I can bear with solitude no longer ; the old retriever,.
given me by my landlord, is really not enough.   With my
50th year I came by a positive yearning for a daughterly
element ; at Berlin a little while ago [end of April] when
Bülow presented his baby girl to me with the regret that
it was only a daughter, something flashed upon me and I
told him, Be glad of it, for thou shalt have great joy of
this daughter.   Recently a maiden of 17 years and unim-
peachable birth was recommended to me as gentle, willing
to serve, and uncorrupted ; so I took her into my home,.
to dish me tea, look after my things, and be present at
table and of an evening.   God bless me, the trouble I had

---

* See pages 118 and 356 ; it is clear that Wagner uses the present
tense here in a future sense, though Frau Wesendonck's answer mistakes.
it.—Tr.

to get the poor child out of the house again without
wounding her feelings! She was bored to death, longing
for town again, but took every pains to conceal it; so that
my only way to create myself a relative happiness at last,
by getting rid of her, had to be on the pretext of my
journey [Pesth concerts, end of July]. Dear Lord! and yet 'twere
so simple to please me; how well I can get on even with
my servants, I know by experience. I thought of Vreneli,
who waited on me at Lucerne; she couldn't leave. Now the
elder sister of the girl sent home has applied to me; she
is more experienced, staid, seems well-disposed, and isn't
unagreeable; so I almost think of making one more trial
with her.* You see how it is; I have to try for everything
with money now—presumably because I have so much of
it!—I'll let you know how it turns out.

And now I perceive that I must put a little stopper
on my writing, or Otto will have a right to tax me with
exciting you! To tell the truth, best friend, I find it hard
to write a letter to you; all the sweet that comforts me at
times now, is nothing but a memory, lies back among the
past. Of that I cannot, must not write; and what remains?
How gladly would I tell you of a real pure joy, an agreeable
experience from the present; but whence derive, without
inventing? I have already told you I was nearly drowned,
and that is all!—Should I write you how I have been
fêted and applauded by the public here or there? Indeed
I count it to those gentry's credit, and pride myself no

---

* Eccentric as the episode may seem in itself, it disposes of the
ridiculous legends—founded on a Viennese dressmaker's bills—that the
writer used to dress himself in female garments. Long ago I had been
struck by the "we" in one of the crumbs of that correspondence
flaunted by addle-brained purveyors of gossip, and felt more inclined to
credit Hanslick's story of "a pretty ballet-dancer"; but the amazing
innocence of the whole arrangement is proved alike by its narration
to "Elisabeth" and her unrebuking answer.—Tr.

little on my stirring people with my music to wellnigh
the same enthusiasm as is wont to be evoked by ballet-
dancers and that class of artists ; but God forgive me, I'm
glad each time it's over, and do not think of it again if
I can help it. Perhaps it's sheer ingratitude—one of my
proved chief vices, you know.

Here and there an agreeably-cheating apparition of
more charm does flit across my gloom. For example : at
Pesth I had a lovely bud-young singer, with the most soulful
naive voice, for the rendering of cantlets of my Elsa ; she was
Hungarian, pronounced German with delightful correctness,
and probably had never heard anything right about music
before in her life. I was quite touched, that my music
should alight on something so pure and unsullied ; and the
good child in her turn seemed so touched by myself and
my music, that for the first time in her life she really felt.
The outbreak of these feelings was inexpressibly pretty
and moving, and many a one might have thought the
damsel had conceived a sudden love for me : so that is
someone else to have to " write " to.—

See, I'm telling you all the good I can ; but I really
know of nothing more, and am not even sure if you will
count the last tale to my " good."—Still, it gives the letter
a turn, and will enable you to tell your husband something
of me after all. The poor fellow seems to have been having
his full share of trouble ; I won't mention America (I have
enough for myself with my Germany !) but to be continually
plagued with a horrid pain in the throat, that often prevents
him even contradicting (as he very amiably confessed
to me), is misfortune enough and to spare. He thinks he
will have to get into a situation, for once, where he wouldn't
be tempted to speak at all ; I'll propose to him to exchange
with myself for a couple of months—when I'm at Penzing,
be it understood : *not* when I'm giving concerts, as he'd be

done for in a fortnight then.—Really Otto must be heartily
sick of me! How he has tried to help me all along;
how often has he thought things *must* go right with me
at last,—and ever I am stranded on the same old spot,
nothing will fructify,—all's thrown away! Yes, and I
believe it myself, all's squandered on me : sportsmen have
a catchword about having "ein Waidmann gesteckt," i.e.
one is under a spell that balks one's shot,—maybe that's
the case with me!—

Now I don't know where to send this letter; July 15
you wrote me from Zurich that you would be back there
in 3 weeks at the outside; wherefore I think it safest to
assume the 3 weeks are run out, and put the old address on it.

Farewell and be thanked a thousand times for your
existence; you still exist,—so I suppose I, too, must co-exist
a little, in a fashion! Best greetings to husband and
children; they're to go on thinking decently of me. The
long sheet of gossip is ended; may it not make you too
dismal! Remember that at least I have been still able to
write it!—Adieu, best Meisterin!

Your
R. W.

139.

Dear Child,

A mighty big letter—to which I have nothing of account
to add for the moment—went off to your address at *Zurich*
a few days since. As you are stopping away so much longer,*
please let it be sent on to you (not that it's very amusing).

A thousand greetings!

Your
R. W.

Aug. 7, Penzing.

---

* Then there must be a *second* letter ot Ǝrau Wesendonck's missing
between nos. "7 and 8," for hers dated August 9 (no. "8") replies to the
said "gross mächtiger Brief" itself.—Tr.

140.

Sept. 10, Penzing.

Maybe I ought to have written you before, Best friend—
perhaps you were expecting it?—but I'm living in such
pressure now,* that I can find no sense at all to write
you. Once I had a fanatical idea of begging you to do
something enormous for me ; but I had to dismiss it again
with a mournful smile,—I'm a man of ill-luck! Also I
expected to be called to the Rhine by the end of August
for concerts (Darmstadt, Carlsruhe), which would have enabled
me to visit you all, and moreover to take a mountain-trip
in my old land of cure to patch up my terribly ailing lower
man ; but nothing came at all of Darmstadt, and I am
asked not to go to Carlsruhe ere the end of October. Now
that's just about the time I ought to have some engagements
in the east again, so that everything will crowd together ;
and yet I must put up with it,—in fact my present chief
trouble is due to this all having dawdled so long.—

Good Lord, how I repent my settling here, already ; and
yet I staked my all on first securing fixity of tenure,—so great
was my need to plant my foot again, no matter where or
how. It has fared with my hard-earned Russian spoils as
with the man in the play who curses his luck for having
won a prize in the lottery, since he can prove it has cost
him much more than he gained. What congratulations on

---

* " Nun leb' ich aber so im Drucke, dass ich gar keinen Sinn finde,
an Sie zu schrieben." I am not sure that the " so im Drucke " may not
mean " so in the press," as a serial essay on " The Vienna Opera-house "
appeared in a local newspaper about this epoch ; see *Prose Works* III.,
also the end of this letter and the postscript to no. 143. As to the
" etwas Enormes," of the next sentence, upon reference to Frau Wesendonck's of August 9 it would seem that the idea Wagner had momentarily
entertained was that of asking to be allowed to return for a while to his
old " Asyl" of five years ago ; in which case the " Unglücksmensch "
would mean " a man who *brings* ill-luck," cf. " Einen Unseligen labtest
du " etc., *Die Walküre* act i.—Tr.

my Russian fortune have I not received!—and from whom?
From creditors of whose very existence I didn't know. Ah,
how pleased everybody was, that I had been so well supplied
and no one need bother about me again!—

I am going to Carlsruhe, to make a last trial whether
anything is to be expected for me from a prince's protection.
—Do not say that I'm a "helpless" man [cf. p. 355]: rather,
where no one else, at any rate, can help me, I can now
help myself and alone; but where my contemporaries might
have helped me, posterity will apprehend—presumably very
soon. Then it will be patent how easy it would have been
to help me, and *what* the world would have gained if my
last good years of creation had not been so wretchedly lamed.
—Yet if *I*—to forestall that future wonderment—now do
for myself what people then will do for my monuments, what
rubbing of hands all around! And the nation would like
to be still more " united."

Well,—I still hope to make it possible to visit you in
Switzerland, perhaps *before* Carlsruhe; but *perhaps*—I shall
have vanished beforehand, without leaving a trace. Oh, to
cease sounding; for the last echo of one's chord to die away
in space!!—

There we are; fine stuff I'm writing you! Of course
I oughtn't to send it off, but you did the same thing once
yourself, and insisted that written was written,—and really,
to have to speak to one's best friends in studied periphrasis,
revokes all impulsion to speak. I admit that I am foaming
now, and presume beyond all bounds; but it's the last
paroxysm, I feel, the last paroxysm: then I shall drop
my hands and give the horses their heads—whithersoever
they will! Never will I trouble for my life again, save
this one time!—Child, that's what I am passing through—
and so, enough!—

I cannot advise you to come to Vienna yourselves

[cf. p. 357]. Art?—not a rap; Opera completely wretched and disgraceful. I have *nothing* more to do with the theatre; God knows whether you even would find me here, for I'm on the bounce at any instant. Such a bounce may bring me to yourselves, however, for a couple of days; if things go fairly with me, I shall come before Carlsruhe—as said—end of October.

What a letter!—Forgive me, I cannot do better with it!—Perhaps another time! A feeble remnant is still left *within* me, whereout—perhaps—something still may be made!

The very best of greetings!

R. W.

141.

It is a load on my mind, that I fell upon you so ungovernably with my laments the other day. If you can forgive me, it will be harder for Otto to, and that agitates my heart!—

Something would appear to have "got into my bones"—as people say; I fell ill, and was so for a week.—That did me good, and I have come to order *in* myself; so it only remains to get so *with* myself as well. Toward that I have an extremely arduous time next ahead of me, toils and hardships of all kinds; but they will be the *last*.—

In October I shall visit you *in any case*. Entreat me kindly, precious friends; I hope I shall be welcome to you!

From my heart,

R. W.

Penzing. Sept. 20, 63.*

---

* See Frau Wesendonck's answer of the 23rd. The "announcement" mentioned in the first sentence of Wagner's next letter is not preserved; in fact, from hers of Oct. 20 it appears to have never reached her.—Tr.

142.

Penzing, Oct. 17.

I must correct my announcement of yesterday, and acquaint you that my Carlsruhe concert cannot take place till the 14th of November. Therefore, if you should have any kind reassurance to send me, particularly as to Otto's condition, I would beg you to address it for the present to Penzing still.

With heart's devotion

R. W.

143.

No doub. you will guess, Lady-friend, of what weight your letter has been to me! I told you a while ago that my resolve could not be talked about, but only gradually disclosed by execution; and now you answer me quite rightly, La vie est une science,—it must be learnt and practised [cf. p. 360]. I believe I am ripe for it, and know but one desire now : Repose and work!—

Of my enterprises for this winter much still remains vague ; all I know for certain, is that I have to make one final effort, not to achieve, but to close behind me. The day after to-morrow (Oct. 31) I go to Prague (Black Horse) for 2 concerts; Nov. 10 I reach Carlsruhe; the 14th is the concert there, and should Otto have so far recovered as to be able to bring you thither, I fancy I may promise both of you a fine impression. Thence on, uncertainty pervades my plans : roughly, between then and Christmas I have concerts in prospect at Breslau, Löwenberg in Silesia (Prince of Hechingen), Dresden, perhaps Hanover, and probably Prague once more. Possibly St Petersburg will then take March and April, conceivably Kieff and Odessa the previous January also; perhaps, too, Pesth again. You may imagine the state of my poor nerves in view of such

geography ! It seems almost criminal to myself, but nothing
else is left me.

Now, I should like in the interval, if you will put me
up, to find brief rest with you ; perhaps about Christmastide ; possibly even from Carlsruhe. Don't be astonished—
tho' it be only for a few days—if I drag out the portfolio
and try to work a little. Moreover, I have a petition as
regards my board : please send me lunch and dinner to
my room ; meals in common to be reserved for special
festivals, and at your special invitation.—Otto's recovery
is to me a veritable gift from Heaven ; we here (I and
the doctor) quite share your opinion that this illness has
been a crisis of most beneficial consequences. All this
is very beautiful and profoundly gladdening to me.—

Now accept my earnest heartfelt thanks again for your kind
letters.—Salute Otto and the children from a loyal heart ;
they are all to be good to me ; Yourself as well !

Your

R. W.

Penzing, Oct. 29, 63.

I am sending Otto a brochure [cf. p. 321*n*]. You will
judge by it how placably I think of issuing from the world,
but will also infer the said issue's necessity from the certainty
of my knowledge that even such practical, simple proposals
will find no hearing.

[*As Frau Wesendonck's reply speaks of a chance of Otto's
deing well enough to take her to Carlsruhe, it is possible
that they heard the* Meistersinger *overture and Sachs' Cobbler-
song there, either Nov.* 14 *or at the concert's repetition on the*
19*th. In any case the next we hear of Wagner is from the
Green Hill, where he arrives between the* 20*th and* 22*nd, and
sends Herwegh an invitation in the name of his hosts the*

23rd, for that evening. Presumably he spent the best part of a week on the Green Hill, for he does not reach Mainz till the 27th, en route for the concerts mentioned below.—Tr.]

144.

Penzing, Dec. 15, 63.

A mere brief note !

I have been back since the evening of the 9th inst. Arrival in the dwelling which Fate has assigned me as home had a tristely comforting effect on me. Everything was warm and snug, Franz and Anna [Mrazek] pleased to see me, no ill befallen ; only Pohl had so fretted at my absence that he really was much aged. It was 'an odd feeling, to be surrounded with familiar beings and objects not one whereof I knew a year ago.

The dismalest is my great exhaustion. This the upshot of my " art-tour "—that I cannot dream of either continuing or repeating it. *Impossible* to go to Russia ; but whatever's to become of me without that aid, I vacantly inquire.

At Löwenberg I found a very good-natured man in the Prince, but unfortunately he is too old, and has been too much imposed on, to be able to be of use to me. At Breslau I found myself thoroughly shamed, and cut a very sorry figure in my own eyes,*—but an old acquaintance turned into a famous new ; Frau Wille's sister, Fr. v. Bissing, came to Löwenberg and Breslau for the concert. My great fatigue and agitation, for which she made most kind allowance, permitted no true freedom in our intercourse ; nevertheless, the few hours were of deep value for us both.

Cornelius will come out every day to me, I hope, in spite of wind and weather. I am trying with singularly bitter pains to keep myself this Asyl.

---

* A snub administered by a wealthy resident whose assistance had been half promised ; see Glasenapp II. ii., 440-41.—Tr.

Let me hear good of you soon, and greet husband and children from the heart of

Your

R. Wagner.

145.

A thousand fervent heartfelt greetings for the birthday! I can offer you no gifts but of the heart now; my fancy still refuses me its old-accustomed services; 'tis musing on repose and paths that lead thereto.   In spirit I shall be among you, tho', and taste full lovely visions of the family-feast!

A thousand good wishes with the greetings!

R. W.

Penzing, Dec. 21, 63.

[*Thus the last unconstrained exchange of letters is prompted on the selfsame day* (vid. inf. p. 363), *and the prime cause of the ensuing twelvemonth's silence must be sought in some third factor, perhaps some unrecorded appeal to the husband for renewed assistance in the serious financial straits above-foreshadowed.   Next March it is Frau Wille who is asked whether the Wesendoncks can accommodate the composer with* "a work-room either in the principal building, or in the little neighbouring house I occupied before," *to enable him to complete his* Meistersinger—*the entire first act whereof had just been sent to Schott—by that summer's end.   Who conveyed the refusal, we do not know precisely; but within a fortnight we find Wagner escaping from Vienna creditors and taking, literally, taking shelter at Mariafeld, where he reaps the Willes' hospitality for barely a month (see* Letters to Otto etc.).   *Then comes that miraculous transformation-scene, rescue by Ludwig II. of Bavaria at the beginning of May; followed by the master's establishment in Munich and the removal*

thither of the faithfulest of his disciples, Cornelius, Hans von
Bülow, and the latter's wife.—This in explanation of the next
letter, which itself is a reply to Frau Wesendonck's of Jan. 13,
1865.—*Tr.*]

146.

[Munich, mid-January 1865.]

Best Child, I think it would be best to send the whole
portfolio ; I pledge myself, with all that's dear to me, that
it shall return to its lady-owner unimpaired, and rather
enriched than diminished. It would fall hard to point out
everything that might need copying and despatching to
us ; so it's better that I should search among the things
themselves.

It required a strong inducement, to get me to take any
part in this, but my young King is just the man to set it
all in order ; he has the right pertinacity, and all his
instigation springs from his own self. Now Semper has to
build me a splendid new theatre (there's nothing else for
it already), the best singers are to be fetched from all ends
to represent my works, and—all my writings, of no matter
when, must be culled from all hidden portfolios. Knowing
that he must not give me much to do with it, he [the King]
tactfully turns to my friends ; and that's what he has done
in this case also [cf. p. 363]. At his often-repeated request,
you see, I had had to state what I had written, and whither
it had disappeared ; so I had to denounce the big portfolio on
the Green Hill too,—I couldn't help myself. But no harm
is meant ; simply, he wants everything collected, to take it
in his charge and know that he possesses me entire.

Ay, child, *he* loves me ; there's no gainsaying it !—

If things don't go quite right with me despite all that,
no doubt there may be reasons. The lighter grows my
freight of faith, the higher my insurance,—already I believe

in next to nothing, and to fill that void it needs a quite prodigious ballast of royal favour! Once I was to be had cheaper; now my clairvoyance is terrible, and the illusion anent that fearful weakness everywhere, which shrunk back from me as from a madman, is becoming hardly possible to me again.* Yet I do all I can, and still gladly await something better from men; in which my young King just assists me. He knows all, and—wills!—so I myself am bound to will too, tho' it often strikes my soul as strange.—

Best greeting to the Green Hill!—They told me lately, it had been offered for sale this summer; is that so?— Whither away then?—Am I quite too inquisitive?—Ought I to renew my kind thanks for the Christmas present? Did the big Micky expect it? Scarcely! There's another old letter to read,†—shall I find that in the portfolio?—

Adieu! I recollect with love!

R. W.

147.

[Munich, Spring 1865.]

Freundin,

The Tristan will be wonderful.

Will you come??

Your

1st performance 15th May.

R. W.

---

* Cf. Sept. 9, 64, to Frau Wille: "I had *really been abandoned* by all my *old friends*,—literally *you* alone still believed in me"; and exactly a month later, "Your silence alarms me. Surely you received a letter of mine a short while back?" (*Letters to Otto etc.*).—Tr.

† Dr. Golther tells us "the letter does not exist," evidently considering that the reference is to the enigmatic "Brief an * * * " in Frau Wesendonck's list (*vid. inf.*); but I am inclined to think that this "noch einen alten Brief" is figurative (probably also the "Christmas present") —an indirect appeal for renewal of old friendship.—Tr.

[*No one from Zurich came to hear* Tristan (*see the letter of next September to Frau Wille*), *the first public performance of which had eventually to be postponed to the* 10th *of June owing to* "*Isolde's*" *indisposition. A few weeks afterwards, however, Wagner extends an olive-bough to Otto, in the shape of a beautiful epistle, one passage wherein has so often been misinterpreted that it will be as well to give a somewhat closer rendering than heretofore :—*" The disturbance that drove me from you six years back should have been avoided : it so estranged my life from me, that you yourself, as I, did not really know me again when I last approached you once more. This [latter] pain should also have been spared me : to myself it seemed as if it might have been possible, and beautiful, very beautiful would it have been, ay, sublime, if it had been spared me,—but one must not ask for the sublime,—and I was wrong.—Now much has altered with me. Everything around me has become fairly new" *etc.* (Letters to Otto). *Here the* " ich hatte Unrecht " ("*I was wrong*") *most clearly refers, not to the* " Störung, die mich vor sechs Jahren von Ihnen trieb "—*which, by the way, should be* " seven " *if it does not actually refer to the unlucky Paris expedition—but to the estrangement which commenced in the winter* 1863-64.

From the time of the said letter and its reply, July-August 1865, *friendly relations with Herr Wesendonck were re-established, and we find letters sent to him at not unfrequent intervals down to the end of* 1870. *The only one to Frau Mathilde still extant is the next and last of our series, though the sweet lady's own simple words of* 1896 *should be recalled here :* " *After his second marriage** Wagner's first visit with his wife was paid to ' Mariafeld ' near Zurich and to the ' Green Hill ' at Enge. The Festivals at Bayreuth we never*

---

* August 1870; Minna had died in January 1866.— Tr.

*missed.   Down to the master's death we remained in friendly
commune with him.*"—Tr.]

148.

Honoured Freundin,
Would you perhaps mind searching among the manuscripts of olden time, kindly preserved by you, for a sheet
of music——
At Weber's last Resting-place,
chant for 4 male voices, and let me have a copy of it in
case you find it?   You would be heartily obliging Your
RICHARD WAGNER,
who with his wife sends you very best greetings.
Tribschen.

June 28, 1871.

---

*To supplement these later letters, we find the following
private dedications :—*
Written in the pfte (vocal) score of Die Meistersinger :
" To his valued friends on the Green Hill, in grateful
remembrance,

Richard Wagner.
May 1868 "—

In that of Siegfried :
" For the cherishing of ancient memories, as also in
continuation of the Green Hill library, with grateful
greeting,

Richard Wagner.
Tribschen, August 14, 1871 "—

In that of Götterdämmerung :

" To his honoured friends of the Green Hill, with old fidelity and gratitude,

                                        Richard Wagner.
Bayreuth, May 13, 1875.

And it dämmered after all !   R. W."

Mathilde Wesendonck

1864

After a Basrelief by Joseph Kopf.

FROM HER TO HIM

TALES AND LETTERS,

1859 *to* 1865.

❧

As the succeeding 14 *letters, and the few poems included therewith, are published in the German edition as the "only existing replies to the master's," and as they do not commence till so late, I preface them with a couple of tales from an earlier period—tales that bear their personal allusion on their face. These I borrow from Frau Mathilde's little book of "Märchen und Märchenspiele," reprinted in* 1900 *from its original issue of March* 1864 *and dedicated on the one occasion to her children, on the other to her grand-children. As to the first tale,* "The Stranger Bird," *it certainly was written* circa *Christmas* 1858-9,—*see Wagner's " thanks for the lovely fable" pp.* 95 *and* 98 *sup. ; the date of the second cannot be assigned so positively, since the reference at foot of p.* 159 *is puzzling—no " Föhrenmärchen" being included in the said collection,—yet Wagner's reference on p.* 158 *to the Erard, which he had christened* " the Swan" (*p.* 57), *makes July* 1859 *a presumable birth-time for this.—W. A. E.*

The Stranger Bird *

❧

IT was a wonderfully mild Spring day ; the earth looked like a freshly opening rose in the fragrance of the morning dew. The rays of the noonday sun enticed and coaxed the blossoms forth, without scorching them ; for they still were shy and doubtful, all ignorant of their power, like a lover with his child-sweetheart ere the dear secret has slipped from his lips. So the sun made itself as handsome as it could, and smiled, and never seemed tired of gazing. And every glance became a flower. Forget-me-nots sprang from its childlike honest eyes ; its earnest sacred trust was shewn in violets, its love in the rose, and its innocence in snow-drops. The wounds, however, that its thorns made, were changed into purple-red strawberries ; its tears fell into the flower-cups like nourishing dew ; the deep sighs from its bosom fluttered through the air and gave a good shake to the fresh-clad trees and shrubs to see that every leaf was quite secure and not merely pretending. But the strange thoughts which flitted through its head became little birds, who made field and forest, hill and vale, brim over with lovely music. If a human soul but heard that sweet carol, it filled him with such joy and pain that he knew not whether to laugh or cry ; but his heart remained devoted to the pretty songsters all his life. When the music stopped he would

---

* In the Englishing of these tales and letters of Frau Wesendonck's I have had the valuable assistance of a friend, "Evelyn Pyne," who also has kindly translated the accompanying verses.—W. A. E.

grow sad, for it left deep longing in his breast; he felt as tho' cast out of Paradise a second time, and remained solemn and grave all the rest of his days. Yet peace was within him, and no more idle wish for passing empty pleasures.

Now, one of these little birds was hopping gaily on before a tiny lassie, who was trying in vain to catch the pretty warbler in her small white apron. Playfully teasing her, the bird would now come close, and then skip far away, drawing its tiny pursuer to and fro through field and thicket. Out of breath and tired at last by such a chase, she sat her down upon a stone beneath an old gnarled beech-tree. As it threw its shade across her burning face, she wiped the perspiration from her forehead, while her little heart went pit-a-pat as if it needs must burst. Before her, perched upon a branch, the bird sat silent.

It was late in the afternoon by now; the setting sun was gilding the topmost crests of the distant hills as tho' seeking to save himself by this warm embrace from the death he seemed hastening to. But their faces soon grew pale, and down he sank into a sea of dreams, while long crape-like shadows moved across the darkening earth. The little one wished to go home, that her mother might not grow frightened about her; but each time she stood up, the bird on the bough began to sing, and it sounded as if he were weeping and crying, until it drew her by force to her seat again. So she picked up her little basket, took out her supper, and listening all the while, began to eat it. The crumbs she strewed around, for the dear little creature's sake; but it did not seem hungry, and paid no heed to them. The shadows grew longer on the ground; the patches of light in the wood became smaller and smaller; whilst aloft in the sky, here and there, a pale star peeped out dim and misty. At last she got up, filled her little basket with sweet-smelling wildflowers to take to her mother, and made

ready to go. Then suddenly the bird sang out quite loud
and clear:

> Baby mine
> sweet of eyne,
> do not pine.
> Fairies fine
> shall be thine
> where stars aye shine:
> follow, follow me!

The flowers dropped from the child's hands, and she
ran after the songster, who no longer seemed so anxious
to escape her, but kept quite close, and carolled as he
hopped on before her. How pleased she felt to understand
his language! It almost seemed to her that he would
perch tamely on her shoulder ere long, and let himself
be taken home, and never fly away again. In her mind
she already saw her mother's joy at welcoming so rare a
guest; the narrow cabin widened out into a palace, and
her quick little heart leapt high at the thought that it
would never feel lonely any more. How often had she
sat at the slit of a window in the poky little room, and
looked out longing for a playmate. Hard work and poverty
had held her captive with iron hands; not for her had
been the heedless games of childhood; and so she had
been ripening before her time towards the serious things
of life. How briskly now her busy hands would move, if
she might listen to the bird's bright singing all the while.

So sweetly befooled, she followed the teasing little
creature as it flew lightly on ahead through the spicy
evening air, never guessing how all this wandering to and
fro must hurt the poor lassie's little wounded feet. Often
did its feathers seem to her of clearest azure, then again
dark red like glowing carbuncles, or shining green like
emeralds that one may see through; at times even, he

22

looked quite black, and only on his breast there gleamed the loveliest tints! But soon she lost all sense and feeling, and fell exhausted on the wood's soft moss. Deep silence reigned around; only the rivulet sang in the distance, and the wind lightly toyed with the ruddy gold crowns of the fresh-leafed oak-trees. The bird himself had withdrawn to the thicket, and snugly tucked his head away beneath his wing.

Then a splendid dream arose in our poor little maiden's soul. She saw the pretty golden stars come down from heaven, as if to play with her; and as she looked, lo! they were children like herself and others. Only they had tiny golden wings, and such beautiful big eyes, much more beautiful than even the loveliest children have; and whoever looked into them became quite well, no matter *what* had ailed him! Some of these children had dazzling deep-blue eyes, like Joy herself when she comes down to men; others were darker, and seemed both grave and pitiful, like Mercy when she looks on the woe of the miserable. But all of them embraced and danced in wondrous rings, and figures past her understanding, while unseen harmonies made music for it all. Our little girl knew the sounds, had heard them once before, and they made her more happy than tongue can tell!

These large-eyed children of the sky had lovely playthings, all made of purest silver, that never broke however carelessly they handled them. Soon one of them came close to her, offered her its toy, and held out its little hand to lead her away. She tried to rise, but all in vain: her limbs felt as heavy as if they had been bound to the earth with chains; she could stir neither hand nor foot. "Give me thy little wing," begged she softly, and the child-angel loosed one from its shoulder there and then, to give her. Already her two little hands were stretched out to take it,

her eyes were turned toward Heaven : it stood wide open—
glory and splendour streamed down from a thousand
sparkling suns, while hymns of God resounded to eternal
blessedness and everlasting peace. " Ah ! " she sighed, " Up
there ! how happy I should be up there, with all the saints !
But mother would grieve if I did not come home ; and
who would there be to take care of her, and keep her
when she grows old ? " A tear fell from her eyes, hot
and heavy ; then—she gave the little wing back. Heaven,
angels, singing, all had gone, and sobbing she awoke.

On the ground lay the little basket, its withered flowers
overturned. In haste she picked it up, and ran off as
fast as her feet would carry her. Without thinking, she
struck the pathway to the cottage. A sudden rustling
among the bushes in front made her heart beat high ;—alas !
it was only a grey sparrow, whose simple twitter chirped
its morning-hymn to the Creator !

The Swan

THE apple-trees were white. With snow ? Well, with
flower-snow ! God looked down at His work, as on the
seventh day of Creation, and found it good. The azure-
blue Heaven gazed on the sweet-smelling flower-decked
Earth, and a happy smile came over his face as he saw
his faithful likeness far below in the depths of the sea.
He felt mightily drawn toward the cool water, like Narcissus
to his never-to-be-won Beloved, and he could not leave
off looking at his image, hanging over it with endless longing
and pain. Often does he weep from deep emotion, and
his tear-drops trouble the beloved picture in the depths.
Then furious anger seizes him, the sapphire pillars of the
vault of heaven tremble, terrible furrows gash his glorious

face, his eyes flash fire, and the firmament rumbles with the thunder of his voice. Then he casts his nets of gold toward the desired one, and in a thousand gleaming hues a golden bridge arises o'er the waters.

At even, when the golden stars and silver moon adorn the sky's dim garment, the watchful sun shuts close his eye, that he may not behold himself in all his majesty; for were that possible, 'twould be the end of the poor earth; no power could hold him back from her, and his fierce ardour must destroy her. So, never have they met; they have but looked at one another, and each has borne the other's secret in their breast. And that is why so many a gift of Heaven lies hidden in the deep, deep sea. Seldom is a mortal told about them, because he is a chatterbox; only the swans are in the nixies' confidence as well as man's, and what they know thereof they trust it to a song. But the song only tells it to such as ought to know it; to all the rest it says just nothing. But I once knew a swan, and from him I've gotten all I know.

The Lord of the Worlds once sent the swan to guard that likeness in the deep, to say and sing of His longing and love. His lordly plumage He formed from the incense of the divine spirit, from morning-fragrance and sea-foam. Proudly arching his dazzling neck, the swan glides up the silver stream, and many a lovely song flows from his breast. His hurrying foot ploughs furrows in the crystal surface, and friendly little ripples gaily dance around him, skipping and foaming in their teasing play. When their pranks become too rough for him, he broadens out his mighty wings above the waters, the wavelets quake back in their terror, and the god's Beloved trembles in the depth.

One day he saw a child upon the shore. It was building little huts of sand, as busily as if its play were very serious work. First he looked at the child, then at her game. The little one would not let that disturb her in the slightest, nor even seemed to notice him. Once their eyes did meet— but then she went on playing as if quite alone. That look had sunk in both their hearts, though, and clove so firm that never could they pluck it out.

From that time forth the swan came often to the spot where the little one played on the shore ; he found more and more pleasure in the child's innocent ways and simple charm. Ere long he could hardly tear himself away, and only with a sigh would he return at evening to his lonely watch upon the darksome waters, then hasten back at earliest dawn to that dear spot to which his soul seemed chained. The maiden scarcely wondered at his presence ; she fancied, so it must be and never could be else. Had she not seen the golden sun ascend each day, that sank from sight on yester-eve ? Did not the sky, whose features lowering clouds had almost turned into a stranger, yet always clear again to friendly gaze upon the earth ? Unsullied joy beamed from her deep-blue eyes, and her unfearing little heart would rock itself in sweet content.

The swan oft brought her sea-shells filled with ivory foam, or purple corals, glistening roses of the deep ; at parting he would often leave a snow-white plume behind ; and she would deck herself with them and clap her little hands for joy to see how fine she looked. But when he told her of the marvels he had seen on distant journeys— the ways and customs of strange peoples,—proud cities rising from the sea,—the colours of all countries rippling from swift masts,—the heaven's beauty and that glorious image of it in the deep, whose guardian he himself had been elect—then, then she would forget her play, her eyes would hang upon his lips, and to her it seemed that all these wonders were arising from her own child-soul, and she were roaming with him on the billows' glassy paths.

He shewed her next the pure and noble pearl, transfigured symbol of dumb griefs, and taught her all the difference twixt true and false. And then she grew more trustful toward him, stole her arm round his white neck, stroked down its glossy feathers, and nestled her wee head beneath his wing's soft down. All at once he felt as if he thus must carry her away, and never let her leave him any more. How wearisome the cold far-off Beloved of the Sky appeared to him; how foolish now, for aye to guard her! "O," in his impious arrogance he cried to the All-ruler, "Come down from Thy golden throne, come down to men, and learn from them of love and happiness! Thy bride is cold and feelingless as Thou; guard her Thyself, since none will rob Thee of her!"

Hurrying breezes sped his words aloft to the great Father of all worlds. In burning wrath He hurled His thunderbolt against the dauntless heart of His best-loved singer. Whereon the air grew full of wailing, earth shuddered, and the sun hid his weeping face beneath the sea.

The swan let fall his dying head on the maiden's lap, and singing he passed away. Dyed red with his blood were her bosom and cheek, as she tenderly bent over him, and their souls became one in the ebb of life's last breath.

When the Lord of Creation beheld what He had done, grief seized Him for his favourite. He sent His messengers —an angel-host—to gather up the swan's white feathers to trim His garment's starry hem. The child was never seen again.

❧

Her Letters

1.

I have pitied you so often in this hot weather, for it must indeed be stifling in Paris. Perhaps you are taking refuge again in the Bois de Boulogne, only one has to pay for even that by some exertion. It is really beautiful now on this green hill, and the moonlight nights are lovely past compare. It is long since we had such a summer; it really makes one feel quite superstitious, and almost afraid to go to bed lest everything should have changed before the morning.

Last week we made a little excursion with the children to Baden-Weiler, the ancestral home of the Princes of Zehringen. It is an hour by rail from Basle, and already bears quite the physiognomy of the little Baden land below; fine nut-trees, woodlands, hills, pastures, and in the distance the silver ribbon of the Rhine. I suppose that will be something like your future home; pleasant, quiet and lonesome, I almost fear too lonesome, as far as concerns the society of refined, intellectual, artistic people; there Paris spoils one. Lessing is a taciturn, almost over-modest creature, whose strongest passion is hunting; Schirmer is simply primitive; the Grand Duke?—but you must know him better than I. Our German princesses are mostly brought up in very homely fashion; they learn to keep house, that is to say, to eke out their pocket-money, and touch us by their simple unassuming manners. The Grand Duchess, however, has attractive features. Her portrait hangs on the wall of the Roman Bath at Baden-Weiler, together with the Duke's, in a gold frame; whilst the former reigning couple have to content themselves with a plain black one, hung in a corner. Perhaps in fifty years or so the young people may be advanced in their turn to the black frame, while a new star shines in the gold one, and the grandparents have utterly vanished. It was quite a picture of the age.

Last Saturday there was a concert in the Frau Münster-Kirche ; Papa Heim conducted, but was unequal to his task. Schmidt of Vienna sang an air from the Creation ; a grand voice, that stays clear and distinct even in the softest passages ; he must make a splendid König Heinrich [*Lohengrin*]. His powerful physique also pleased me, and it seems at least made for endurance, for he is eternally singing, now here, now there ; but his programme is terrible, calculated for none but the most commonplace audience. A portion of Gluck's Orpheus and Euridice was given, and greatly moved me. Most lovely is that passage where Orpheus goes down into Hades, and the spirits of the nether world thunder out at him their cries of No ! No ! while the harp-strains glide so sweetly and softly between them, teaching us to trust in the ultimate triumph of the beautiful. I should very much like to hear the whole opera some day.

Frau Dr. Wille came into town for the concert, and spent the night with us. She gave me many kind messages for you, and I presented her with the Rhein-Gold. Sunday morning we breakfasted on the north terrace and chatted a great deal about you. Keller, Dr. Wille, Köchly and his wife came to lunch, also old Fräulein Ulrich, whom you may perhaps remember ; we are very fond of the old lady, with her original ways.—How I chatter ! But perhaps it may cheer my friend up, or even recall old times to him. He knows a great deal, but thank God he does not know what grey hairs mean yet ; ebb and flow, light and shade, that is youth. A greybeard has no moods such as you describe in your last letter,* and do not we know that they come and

---

* See the signature of no. 118, page 272.

go? That is my comfort. As I sit here on the balcony
and write, the mountains are glowing rose-red in the
sunset; would I could fix a reflection of their tender gleam
on this little page, and waft it into your soul!

I am so glad you are going to Weimar; for all that,
Liszt is the one man nearest to you; do not let him fall
from his place in your heart. I always remember a lovely
remark of his: "I value people by what they are to
Wagner." As for Vienna, we will see if fortune favours us :
at least it is pleasant to think of. I have just heard for
the first time from the Princess [C. Wittgenstein] from
Rome. She frequents none but the Nazzarenes there,
the Christian, churchy painters. That serves her purpose,
which she is carrying through with iron resolution, altho'
she must be frightfully ennuyé with it all. Apart from
Cornelius and Overbeck there is not much pleasure to be
found amongst them; of course I am referring to living
artists.

And now to beg a favour, which you shall grant me when
occasion allows. I have had a little photographic album
given to me, and have already several likenesses of friends in
it, carte-de-visite size like my own; in a few seconds one
can get a dozen taken. Now of course I possess your large
photograph, but the little book would so like to have one
too, and the place for it remains vacant; you will not deny
the little book its whim? It will be very patient, and the
Child will be patient too, and not worry the Master with
writing for it; he must only do it when he wants to, for if
he always consulted the Child I fear he would have enough
to do. Meanwhile she is trying to harden herself by
strengthening baths, but they are somewhat exhausting, and
seem to steal away the little strength remaining to her.
Nevertheless a good result is promised.

Now it has grown dusk, the mountains stand pale and

lifeless over there, and all is very still. Peace, Peace, may
the blessedest peace descend on your heart also !

Your

Mathilde Wesendonck.

June 24. 61.

Next morning. Last week the Pasha of Egypt came
up here, and afterwards went on to the Bürkli terrace, where
they played the Pilgrims' chorus and Evening-star a few
minutes later. The sounds came across to me quite plainly.
—Sulzer is back at Winterthur, making a pause in his cure.
While he was looking at the pictures I was doubtful about
his eyesight ; but later on, in the garden, when he wanted
to distinguish some very large flowers on an evergreen,
he was obliged to use double glasses. I was very sorry,
for the flowers are light blue, and stand out most distinctly
from the glossy green of the leaves.—Now one more good
wish ! Is this not a real gossipy letter !

2.

Your last lines made me feel very sad ; * for a long time
I could not answer them. The thought of our meeting in
Vienna had grown so familiar, that at last I felt perfectly
sure of it. To tell you the truth, for ever so long I did
not believe in it ; and now when faith had come at last,
I have to give it up again ! What we leave in the hands of
the future, is taken from us for the moment, perhaps for
ever ; the moment is our very own, but who can tell what
the dim Mother hides in her dark bosom ?—Foreseeing the
difficulties that might confront the birth of a Tristan,
it was chiefly our meeting that lay in my mind ; and

---

* A letter, now missing, that must have come between nos. 123 and
124. [Moreover, Frau Wesendonck herself clearly sent two letters between this and the one last-printed ; see pp. 275 and 281.—Tr.]

had we known that you would only stay such a short time in Vienna, we should certainly have come sooner. It was not to be!

But now I cannot rest. We will go and waylay the Mother where she still is awake; Otto and I intend starting for Venice on Monday. We shall not stay there long, however; in a fortnight, or three weeks at most, we shall be back again. It will strengthen, refresh, and stimulate us, before the winter sets in, as I hoped Vienna would have done. For, even if life does appear an idyl here and there, a proper gaze would soon find out the material for tragedy; * reciprocal short-sightedness protects mankind from this discovery. Then "seeing" is painless in itself, but "being" always painful; you worshipper of Schopenhauer, you really should know that! It follows that the people who see *much* and are *nothing*, are certainly the happiest! And "to be happy" is the main thing, is it not? To be great, to be good, to be lovely, does not satisfy man; he wants also to be happy,— strange caprice! It seems to me that if one were either of those three, he would never need the hollow, toilsome apparatus of the other! Yet, what do I know of it?

There have been great changes among the notables of this place. Gottfried Keller has been made Town Clerk and taken possession of Reg.-R. Sulzer's old quarters in the Chancellery. Thus the poor mother of the "grünen Heinrich" has lived to taste the joy of seeing her son a recipient of outward honours and dignities as well!

Moleschott, moreover, has been called to the University of Turin as Professor of his faculty. His life here had been entirely forlorn of late, and almost friendless.

---

* This clause is of great significance in connection with the close of Wagner's letter of two months hence, page 288; whilst the next few sentences are obviously ironical, and meant to convey the fact that the writer herself is not happy.—Tr.

And last but not least [in English] your Herwegh has received a summons to Naples, as Professor of " Comparative Literature." It was high time, for his affairs were perilously near to utter ruin. Perhaps he may retrieve himself through an honourable occupation so suited to his favourite pursuits.

The worthies here are shaking their heads over the levity of de Sanctis ; but for my part I am glad that a few well-sounding names should get noised abroad for once : it is such a very rare thing in Germany. What is sounded there, rings mostly false, and only those whom people do not talk about are worth the trouble.

What will be the next tidings from my friend ? I share with him the chagrin of his latest disappointment. Whither will the Fates lead him next? Will a time ever come, when *he* can take a rest on our green hill ? Let us hope on, altho' it seems so hopeless ! Thanks for the photograph, and sincere affection !

                                        Mathilde Wesendonck.
Octob. 23. 61.

3.

I have just been reading the sketch of the Meistersinger.* I think it excellent, and hope you will make great use of it ; it is full of subtle touches which may save you much extra labour. My blessing on the resumption of this work ! I rejoice at it as at a festival, for in Venice I hardly dared to cherish such a hope.

You have brought to naught one silent Christmas treat I had promised myself. You were to have received a letter on my birthday—now it lies in Vienna ! A little box, containing sundry trifles we had happened to speak about, was to have taken you by surprise on Christmas day : I had

---

* That of 1845 ; see pages 290 and 364. Since letter "2" Wagner had paid his visit to Venice.—Tr.

prepared all this with so much pleasure, working at it with such haste and eagerness, in the secret fear lest it should not be ready until too late ; and now I shall probably receive it back from Vienna ere long !—

The translation of Cervantes is a most valuable find. I conclude that the manuscript is beyond suspicion ? It would certainly be difficult to imitate Cervantes plausibly [cf. p. 286].

Thank you so much for your kind letter [no. 124], which at least brought your handwriting back to me, altho' I could not quite recognise my friend's usual exalted mood.

And now receive sincerest wishes and regards

From your

Mathilde Wesendonck.

Decbr. 25. 61.

4.

I have been dipping into the biography of Schopenhauer,* and felt indescribably attracted by his personality, which has so much that is akin to your own. An old longing came back to me, to look into that inspiredly beauteous eye for once—that deep mirror of Nature which is the common heritage of genius. I recalled to mind our personal commune ; before me I saw the whole rich world you yourself had unlocked to the childlike mind ; my gaze clung with rapture to the magic edifice ; higher and higher throbbed my heart with fervent gratitude ; and I felt that nothing of all this could ever-more be lost to me ! As long as breath is in me, I shall aspire and strive on ; and that is your doing. Schopenhauer himself you were not to know, and your tone-creations were never unlocked to him : What does that matter ?—he would smilingly exclaim to-day—

* W. Gwinner, "Schopenhauer aus persönlichem Umgang dargestellt," Leipzig 1862.

We two belong to the Whole; an eye that looks on loneliness is our [joint earthly] lot!

The book contains an excellent portrait, in which the crass assertion of photography is beautified and transfigured by the spiritual might of the man himself.

Some day when you leave Paris to come nearer to me, I shall enjoy sharing a book with you, at least now and then, without having to trouble you to go to the embassy for it.* My poor little box has come back to me, and I have set it dolefully aside. When once you settle down somewhere, I shall certainly smuggle things into your house again, as surely as the goblins pursued the poor peasant.†—How fares it with the health—and with the work?

> Yours in her heart!
> Mathilde Wesendonck.

Jan. 16. 62.

5.

The winged lion on your desk has woken up; ‡ spirit and strength are his symbol. He shakes the troubled dream from his limbs, and tosses his mane; that gladdens me, and I will think of nothing else. Let what comes from without be left to Fate; within dwells the foe, in one's own breast.—

Scarcely ever, so it seems to me, has the fountain of your poetry gushed forth with greater copiousness and originality, than this time. Also, it is but a kind of justice to yourself, to give that indestructible deep Humour, so

---

* " Ohne Sie auf das Ministerium zu bemühen "—clearly the Austrian embassy in Paris, official residence of the Metternichs (cf. p. 285), to which there is reason to believe that Zurich packets had been addressed during the past twelvemonth or so.—Tr.

† See pages 20, 74, 80 and 118.

‡ A Venetian letter-weight with the Lion of San Marco, a present from Frau Wesendonck.

considerable an ingredient in your character, its due pre-
ponderance for once. Together with his brother Amor,
the little boy-god has come down from the heights of
Olympus to the human heart ; and only where the one
was glad to stay, would the other enter in.

I feel as though I had climbed a high hill, and were gazing
at a wondrous evening-glow, the Hymn of all Creation !

Greeting and farewell !

Your

Mathilde Wesendonck.

[Feb.*] 19. 62.

6.

I knew it well : dreams do come true [p. 305]. The more
reality withdraws from us, the more do dreams keep watch.
May Heaven still send you many such a dream !

Your

Mathilde Wesendonck.

Decbr. 23. 62.

7.

Lay these leaves among the others in the green portfolio !
I will write shortly ; in the meantime I let myself be nursed
and cared for, like a sick child. My kind regards to the
doctor [Standhartner ?].

Your

Mathilde Wesendonck.

July 3. 63.

---

* The German edition gives the month as " Jan.," but that cannot well
be, as the letter most plainly refers to the completed *Meistersinger* poem.
On the other hand, if Feb. 19 be the correct date, only a fragment of the
original can have been preserved ; see page 300.—Tr.

7a.*

Mir erkoren—	[*Chosen for me—*
Mir verloren—	*Riven from me—*
Ewig geliebtes Herz.	*Ever belovëd heart.*

Cf. Tristan u. Isolde.]

Hast heard the nightingales' enraptured singing,
while o'er the trees her garlands May was flinging ;
but when sad Autumn doubtful days is bringing,
no little bird dare set its song a-ringing.
The mountain-peaks that high as heaven are winging,
their chill renunciant silence them enringing,
flush red, thou seest, in mute despair close-clinging,
when nears the goddess in sun-chariot swinging.
O question not, reluctant answer wringing!
Much have I borne of fortune's bitter slinging,
but This my lips' close lock shall ne'er be springing—
'tis why my songs so sorrowfully I'm stringing.

What chalice holds the radiant shine
of all the great gold sun?
And thou so small, O heart of mine,
yet wouldst confine
earth's joy of all, in one?
Sweet love's infinity
shut in a cell,—
and heaven's eternity
by life's dream tell?

---

* It is to be assumed, of course, that these verses were written at
various dates within the past eighteen months or so (e.g. the one
un-sent for his birthday), though all despatched together. Their printed
arrangement, also, may not entirely correspond with their order of origin ;
yet the " nightingale " poem would seem, from its contents, to be really
among the earliest of the series.—W. A. E.

In the heart that is sad and weary
there sobs a depth of woe,
as bitter and black and dreary
as the sea, in its deep, deep flow.

And sighs like the winds are moaning
now here, and now there, o'er the floods,
where memory's light, atoning,
as tender as evening broods.

While hope like a boat is sailing,
by longing drawn back to shore,
amid the wild breakers quailing,
she fareth home never more.

When dark grief with overshadowing pinion
fearsome on thy trembling spirit sinks,
and a-weary of the ever-changing,
thy strest soul its every chain unlinks ;
from thine eye Illusion's veil has fallen,
and thine Eden flies from thee like foam ;
while from graves the pallid ghosts are stalking,
and things real seem but dreams a-roam ;
all existence fades to empty show,
Being figures but as Not-being's foe —
real alone thy heart-throbs then remain,
with their e'er-affirming sobs of pain.

On the 22nd May 63.
Dwells a soul both strong and fair
prisoned in the blossom there,
that with all her being's care
lives and weaves in sunlit air ;

23

that with ever tireless strife
one thing seeks—a fair flower-life ;
that, altho' the golden sun
thousand sister heads hath kissed,
envies not each happy one,
flowers toward the light she missed :
him alone her fair face turns to,
him alone her sweet breath yearns to ;
and—if he forget her quite—
shuts her gentle eyes and light,
lays her little flower-head low,
breathes one sigh—grows silent so.

———

Heart, what woe couldst thou endure,
wert but as a flower pure ?

———

A deep deep grave I fashioned
and laid my love therein,
with all my hope and yearning,
tears that mine eyes were burning,
joy, grief, and all akin.
And when they each slept soundly,
I laid myself therein.

———

8.

You can well believe, Friend, how heavily your momentous
letter [no. 138] has weighed upon my heart to-day ! But I do
not grudge the cares you thus prepare me, for I most gladly
suffer with you ; my whole nature feels ennobled by permission to share your griefs. However mournfully these
written symbols gaze at me when I ask them for their
meaning, yet how dear and friendly is their glance when
I remind myself, they come from him, and were written

just for thee! Friend, I am afraid you might say much
harm to me, and I should still be fond of you!—

You "joy-unholpen man" ("*freudehelfeloser Mann*")—
an expression I noticed once in Walther v. d. Vogelweide,*
and promptly in my secret heart applied to you ; whoever
could help you, would indeed be fortunate! My head swims
when I think of all the misery which haunts you ; with the
exception of a few fine moments like that perilous "good
one" you describe to me so charmingly [p. 319], and which
fall to your lot more than to anyone else's, Fate still remains
your debtor. I know this, and grieve for it with all my
soul, yet can find no empty word of consolation, because
I have no hope it ever can be otherwise. I need not tell
you how terrible it is to me, to see you thus hunted round
the world for the sake of giving *concerts ;* were the sky
itself to re-echo the crowd's acclamations, it could never
make up for your sacrifice. I follow your so-called "*triumphs*"
with bleeding heart, and turn almost *bitter* when people
hold them up to me as something to be thankful for. All
I feel then, is how little people really know, that is to say
understand you ; and—then I also feel—that I do know—
and love you!—But how little can one person do, against
the thousand-headed monster that calls itself the world ;
one might shed one's heart's blood to its last drop, and yet
not win one tiny morsel of affection from it. So it is, and
so no doubt it was before us.

The portfolio and lamp are not to cumber your Asyl ;
they shall become "Wanderers" like yourself, when once
you leave it. But, supposing you wished to get rid of this
Asyl later on, would it be so very difficult to do so?
Have you bought, or merely rented it? And do you
not think that a residence so close to Vienna, even if only

---

* Lachmann's edition, p. 54; l. 37.

for sound of the thing, is useful and desirable for you in artistic respects? My heart, indeed, is ever calling you back to Switzerland; but then this heart of mine is egoistic, and ought not to be listened to. Putting that *first* one aside, would an Asyl in Switzerland be out of the question? Until now my tears have guarded that against other inmates; only I despair of being able to do *more*, for the immediate future.

With regard to musical conditions at Zurich, you would find a nucleus in the Orchestral Union there, i.e. a permanent band of 30 strong which furnishes the service of the theatre, the highly respectable Musik-Gesellschaft, and Garden-concerts without number, under a conductor named Fichtelberger, who perspiring manages to beat a Beethovenian Symphony to pieces. Papa Heim, who formerly belonged to the malcontents (be it said en parenthèse), has since been elected to the Committee, and is so proud of his new dignity that he plays the paternal monarch, i.e. is pleased with everything. Besides this society, the Heisterhagen and Eschmann Quartet still flourishes, in which a young man named Hilpert, apparently quite musical, has taken the place of Schleich. Should you seriously propose to favour us with a musical performance conducted by yourself, I would suggest that you have a nice long rest on the green hill, allow yourself to be taken care of by the Child, and then and there discuss the future.

You tell me nothing about your work, except that the portfolio is filling up. And I am to let you drink your tea out of strange teacups? Cruel man, to grudge me the pleasure of sending you a new tea-set! Do you not know that my only consolation for such gloomy letters is the power of satisfying your little wants? You might leave me this one satisfaction!

When I am back in Zurich I will get a little dog and train it; and then, when it has grown very fond of me, you shall have it—nicht wahr?

I leave early on Sunday, perhaps for a few days yet at Homburg, where Otto is taking a "Silence-cure," and we hope to be home again toward the end of next week. If Switzerland should prove beyond your reach in course of the next two or three months, we will come to Vienna or wherever you like. I will not write about your accident, except to say Thank God your life was spared!

It has grown late, and I am writing in haste—but I could not stay silent, it made me too miserable. May you be feeling brighter when you receive this! And now my sincerest remembrances; I am and shall remain your friend. We will loyally stand fast.

Your

Mathilde Wesendonck.

[Schwalbach] August 9.* 63.

To share each other's joys and sorrows, is still a blessing left us!

9.

Septbr. 23. 63.

Otto has been laid up for three weeks with rheumatic fever and inflammation of the muscles, and I am nursing him day and night, without, however, having gained much ground as yet. His condition is most painful, and complicated by many ups and downs—also, I am afraid, very lingering. Griesinger will be called in consultation tomorrow, and I am hoping great things from his skill. Under these

---

* Probably this is meant for "19," as the 9th of August, 1863, was itself a Sunday (see line 4 above).—Tr.

circumstances you will understand, Friend, why I was silent. The misery of your state of mind chilled my blood itself; I felt that I was helpless there. I was to tell myself forsooth, that all the gifts of Nature, even the most glorious, are squandered if uncrowned by empty external success ; that they are nugatory in and for themselves, and he who owns them above others, possesses but the right to greater wretchedness! It made me almost bitter, to think you would have me believe that; my religion and my belief (which really are one and the same) are vowed to nothing save the Thing in itself. I cannot understand at all, how anybody can at once scorn and seek what people call success, i.e. applause. Only the sage, methinks, who asks nothing from the world, should venture to despise it ; the man who uses it, becomes its accomplice by mere contact with it, and can no longer be its judge. You are at once a knower and accomplice in the last degree : you rush at every new illusion, apparently to sweep from your breast the disappointment of its pre-decessors ; and yet no one knows better than yourself, that it never can or will be. Friend, how is this to end? Are not fifty years experience enough, and should the moment not arrive at last, when you will come to full agreement with yourself?—

To-day I have received your welcome message,* which has done me infinite good, and I now can pluck up heart again to believe in your coming. What sincere joy it will give me, to prepare you a nice quiet rest ! In Switzerland the autumn days are often very beautiful, and even in winter it is most pleasant in this home of ours. Should Otto's illness drag on longer than expected—which

---

* Between this sentence and the last, she clearly had received his letter of the 20th.—Tr.

Heaven forbid!—would it perhaps be possible for you to keep the Christmas holidays with us?   Meanwhile I hope with all my heart, both for your sake and our own, that it [i.e. your coming] may be earlier.

Greeting and love
from Your
Mathilde Wesendonck.

10.

Your "yesterday's," to which you refer, unfortunately has not reached me, but I thank you for yours of to-day. [See p. 324.]

I am hoping to see you soon in Zurich, whether before or after the Carlsruhe performances.   Our patient is getting better day by day; still, we are entering the 8th week now, and his strength returns but slowly.   Nevertheless we are hoping that this crisis may have paved the way for a beneficial change in Otto's general health, which long had left much to be desired; and in that we are supported by the verdict of the doctors.

Now, *auf Wiedersehen* in good earnest, and greetings from all the heart of

Your
Mathilde Wesendonck.

Octob. 20. 63.

11.

Octob. 27. 63.

Dear Friend,

I am more and more possessed by the thought that we soon shall see you in our midst, and it will be a real sabbath of the heart to me, to make your stay as pleasant as possible.   I believe our home contains the elements of a familiar fellowship, without gêne or other sacrifice for individuals : la vie est une science, says a clever Frenchman, a science that has to be studied. At times a calm comes o'er the sea, the heavens shew no cloud ; and so in human life are intervals when Fate seems to be holding its breath. May such an interval be ours !

What I so sincerely wish and try for, is such a very little thing that perhaps it will only draw a smile from you. It is at least to see you with us once a-year, and so at home that every nook and cranny in the house is quite familiar, and the children don't grow strangers to you. I have constantly striven to keep fresh in their memory your former living with us, and to this day the children only know the Asyl by the name of Uncle Wagner's garden. The idea of seeing it fall into strange hands had long distressed me, but I am at last beginning to feel safe about that ; for the little house has now been included with the rest, and is treated as belonging to the larger plot by way of kitchen-gardens and the like ; and again, because part of the lower storey has been converted into Carl's schoolroom and his tutor's room. In this way the châlet comes under my special care, and I have been given the duty of guarding it from decay or dilapidation. I need hardly tell you that even this affords me a sort of melancholy pleasure ; you yourself know only too well what a solace the heart seeks in such things,—things which in themselves are nothing, and the crowd so readily calls "useless," yet where all is of weight to the heart. That ever retains its ideal, in which the world has neither part nor lot ; it opens to a golden key, and has vanished when the world imagines it has locked it fast.

I do hope I shall soon hear about you and your plans ! The lovely iridescent autumn days are over now, and frosty friend Winter stands without the door ; within, however, all grows warm and bright. Otto's recovery goes on as fast as we could wish, and I hope the last traces of his illness will soon have disappeared entirely. Keep up your courage also, and hold in affectionate heart

Your

Mathilde Wesendonck.

12.

To the Black Horse at Prague I send you a kind greeting : I read your brochure yesterday, and could not help laughing, it seemed to me such utter irony [cf. p. 325]. Be sure you send me from there the programme of your performances ; the last thing which reached me from Prague bore the motto of the Faust-symphony.* Much in human life is doomed to oblivion, very little is unforgetable, but according to that little is determined the whole worth of existence itself. " To be, or not to be," is the question here also, and the cross is ever laid on the " to be."

I would very gladly come to Carlsruhe, but Otto's strength is not quite re-established ; he can bear so little yet, that we avoid all excitement. Nevertheless, perhaps it may be possible between this and the 14th ; he displays a wish for it himself.

And now my sincerest regards to you, and prepare yourself for the green portfolio ; I hope we shall succeed in providing you with quiet. If you should care to bring one of your flock with you, such as Bülow or Cornelius, he will be equally welcome. I trust the green hill will grow dear to you once more !

Your

Mathilde Wesendonck.

Sunday Evening
[November 1 (?) 1863].

---

* Meaning " overture," which had been played there last February ; in 1855 he had rejected the idea of dedicating it to herself, on account of this same depressing " motto."—Tr.

13.

Every scrap of your news, beloved Friend, is a thought from you to me, and as such, the dearest greeting my heart could desire; so, many thanks for each communication, however short [cf. p. 326]. Between us, indeed, it needs but a token now, as it were a visible bond to lead us through life, in presence of the infinity of that world-of-feeling to which we both belong. The weft of the mysterious weaver who intertwined the threads of our mutual fate is not to be unravelled, but only to be torn asunder; "Wisst Ihr, wie das ward!—" *

I understand the gloom, the exhaustion you are feeling, and know what it must cost you to go to Russia. Nowhere can I find rescue or counsel, alas! for, altho' I wildly rack my brains, no light will come; so I would rather be silent, than try to comfort you with empty words of hope in which I have no belief myself. It is humanity's most mournful lot, to recognise an ill without the power to root it up; 'tis born with us, and like a leprous malady we pass it on against our will.

It was a pleasure to me to hear that you had met Frau v. Bissing [Frau Wille's sister] at Löwenberg and Breslau; blessed are those who do good upon earth! They are in truth the only blessed!—Our friend [Frau Wille?] has just left me; she stayed the night here, and we chatted of ne'er-to-be-forgotten happy hours.

Father Christmas has also been here; he said he was going to Vienna, to deck a friend's snug dwelling. I thought that very nice of him, and should dearly like to have kept him company. However, Father Christmas has a special privilege over all the world; so I only bade him

---

* From the Norns-scene *Götterdämmerung*, a motto long since used by Wagner, in another tense, for the "Album Sonata" dedicated to Frau Wesendonck (see *Life* iv, 131).—Tr.

be *sure* he went to the right man's house, and gave him his address. Now he begs a kindly welcome.

The children are brimful of anticipation. The tree is to be lit in the dining-room, surrounded by a glory of Raphaels ; the effect will be quite fine.

Remember me to Cornelius, and do not forget

Your

Mathilde Wesendonck.

Decbr. 21. 63.

14.

My Friend,

In a letter received to-day, Frau v. Bülow asks for some of your literary manuscripts which are in my possession. I have looked through the portfolio, but of course I cannot think of sending anything away, unless at your personal wish. As it is hardly possible that you will remember which strayed leaves and leaflets are gathered in my portfolio, I am sending you a list of the whole contents ; will you please tell me *whether* and *what* I am to forward.

I conclude, of course, that you are aware of the projected publication of your works by his Majesty [cf. p. 328]. I was so very glad to see from the amiable lady's lines that you are well, and have gathered your dear ones round you.

And now with greetings from my heart, and hoping to be affectionately remembered,

Yours

Mathilde Wesendonck.

January 13. 65.

PARIS PERIOD

Der Freischütz. [*Prose Works* VII.]
On German Music. [*Ibidem.*]

Caprices esthétiques ; from the diary of a dead musician
    [Probably " The Virtuoso and the Artist," which originally
    appeared in the *Gazette Musicale* as " Fantaisie esthétique d'un
    musicien" ; see *P.W.* VII.—Tr.]

A Pilgrimage to Beethoven, weighty recollections from
    the life of a German Musician ;

A Pilgrimage to Beethoven (Conclusion).   [*Ibidem.*]

How a poor Musician came to grief in Paris : tale
    [" An End in Paris," *ibid.*]

A Happy Evening.   [*Ibid.*]

Queen of Cyprus (Abendzeitung) ;

Queen of Cyprus (continuation).   [*Ibid.*]

Rossini's Stabat Mater (Zeitschrift f. Musik).   [*Ibid.*]

Revue critique, Gazette musicale.   [" Pergolesi's Stabat Mater ";
    ibid.]

Die Feen.   Grand romantic opera in 3 acts.—*

Der Venusberg, romantic opera in 3 acts ; draft
    [*Tannhäuser.*]

Draft for Wieland the Smith [*Prose Works* I.]

---

* It should be observed that from this point forward Frau Wesendonck's classification into "periods" is wholly inadequate, and for the
greater part incorrect.   Most of the contents, excepting the "drafts," have
been incorporated in Wagner's *Gesammelte Schriften ;* of the remainder
only the "letters" remain unclear, especially the enigmatic "Siegfried's
Brief," which I can but imagine to be a lapsus calami for that concept
of a letter to Schopenhauer reproduced p. 76 *sup.*   At Frau Wesendonck's
death the only item still preserved among her papers was the *Meistersinger* draft of 1845 ; the rest had merely been "taken care of" by her,
as we may gather from Wagner's letter of June 1871 (at which date
he was publishing vol. ii of the *Ges. Schr.*), and undoubtedly were
restored in course of time to Wahnfried—after being returned to her
in the interval between his last two printed letters.   The *Tristan*
sketches etc., and those for the first three members of the *Ring des
Nibelungen*, together with the 1861–2 manuscript of the *Meistersinger*
poem, were former presents to Frau Wesendonck, and therefore not
included in her list.   Of special interest in the above are the drafts etc.
for the *Ring* poem, which it is to be hoped may soon be given to the
world.—Tr.

Draft for the Young Siegfried.

The Young Siegfried (poem).

Draft for Siegfried's Tod.

Siegfried's Tod I. (poem). [*Prose Works* VIII.]

Preface to Siegfried's Tod.

Siegfried's Tod II. (poem). [*Götterdämmerung?*]

The Saga of the Nibelungs. ["Nibelungen Myth," *P.W.* VII.]

Das Rheingold (draft).

Das Rheingold (poem).

Die Walküre (draft).

Die Walküre (poem).

Letter on the Goethestiftung, to Liszt.—[*Prose Works* III.]

Siegfried's letter.—[? !]

To Herr von Ziegesar. [A letter-concept ?]

On a Zeitschrift f. Musik. ["On Musical Criticism," *P.W.* III.]

DRESDEN PERIOD

Draft for Lohengrin.

Art and the Revolution. [*Prose Works* I.]

The arts of Poetry, Sculpture etc.

Artistry of the future. [For the last two headings see "Art-work of the Future," *Prose Works* I.—Tr.]

The Genius of Community. [See "Communication," *ibid.*

Judaism in Music. [*Prose Works* III.]

Letter to * * *

To the Dresden Kapelle.—["Toast" etc., *ibid.* VII.]

To a State-functionary (poem). [1848-9.]

Dame Want (poem). [Ditto.]

Theatre-reform (Dresdener Anzeiger Jan. 16, 49). [*Prose Works* VIII.]

What relation bear Republican endeavours to the Kingship ? (Dresdener Anzeiger). ["Vaterlandsverein" address, *ibid.* IV.]

Artist and Critic, with reference to a particular case
(Dresdener Anzeiger). [*Ibid.* VIII.]

Programme to Beethoven's Ninth Symphony.—[*Ibid.* VII.]

Beethoven's overture to Coriolanus. [*Ibid.* III.]

Beethoven's Heroic symphony. [*Ibid.*]

Gluck's overture to Iphigenia in Aulis.—[*Ibid.*]

A close for Gluck's overture to Iphigenia in Aulis.
[Full score?]

Remarks for the performance of the opera " Der fliegende
Holländer." [*Prose Works* III.]

Draft of Die Meistersinger, comic opera in 3 acts.—[1845.]

Speech at Weber's last resting-place in the cemetery
at Dresden. [*Prose Works* VII.]

Cantata sung at Weber's grave-side [,composed] Novbr.
10, 44, Dresden.—[*Ibid.* ; cf. p. 331 *sup.*]

VALEDICTORY

(W. A. E.)

❖

VALEDICTORY

Upon closing this unique correspondence, instinctively one asks oneself: Would Wagner and Frau Wesendonck have been happier in the long run, had they adopted the alternative suggested on page 25 and left their respective homes together? As with all conjectures regarding things which might have been, one cannot answer positively; yet I believe, such happiness might have been possible in 1852-3 indeed, but *not* in 1858 and onward. Otto would certainly have been riper for that separation in the later year; but —leaving aside all danger from the physical and mental condition into which Minna had gradually fallen—the love of Richard and Mathilde had sublimated into something too ethereal by the time of its declaration, not to run risk of dispersion by the inevitable shocks of daily intercourse. Besides a gifted brain and inbred tact, it needed an unusually strong character, really to be a prop and moderator to a genius whose ideas of practical life had become so largely tinged with that transcendency which stamps his artworks. In 1868 he asks his sister Clara: "Whence could it come, that I fashion something different from others, were I not also different myself?" Absolute poverty, complete retirement from the world, might have charmed him with its grand simplicity; for that, however, I doubt if Mathilde's bringing up, and more especially her sumptuous surroundings, had well prepared her. Affluence was unattainable by Wagner, to the end of his days: in its absence the delicate hothouse plant might uncomplainingly have drooped and pined away.—And later, three years later? The spiritual enactment of Sawitri was very beautiful, most holy; but it could not fit for ever with existing claims upon a matron. When Mathilde gave it up at last against her will (p. 347) involuntarily she took the wiser path—for her husband and herself at least.

Terrible were the perils to which she thus exposed her hero, robbed at almost the same moment of all home in this world—for

a second time—and all hope for the next. Awhile he might drown
his sorrows in a masterwork of comedy that owes its lovable chief
character, and even some traits in its heroine, to his chastened
"resignation"; just as he had told Frau Ritter close on three
years back, he was living "only since the deepest self-experienced
woe again and again presented itself as but another artwork to
be shaped." But sooner or later a reaction from this objectiveness
was bound to set in: for a spell he "hardly knew himself," and
the blackest of palls might have shut him in at any instant. Thrice
happy he, that then at last he found the chosen vessel of companion
gold, after an act of sacrifice that raises "good Hans" of flesh
and blood to a higher plane than ever reached by Ludwig, Liszt
or Otto: "She knew that help could be extended me, and
helped she has."

Perhaps the highest evidence of that companion vessel's true
nobility is furnished by the bare existence of the present book.
"It had been Richard Wagner's wish"—a preamble to the German
edition informs us—"that the accompanying leaves should be
destroyed.—Frau Wesendonck did not regard herself as exclusive
owner of the letters addressed to her; she silently preserved them
for posterity, and willed their publication.—The Wagner family
renounced all author's rights, in this exceptional case, and ceded
them to the departed lady's son and grandson, who have arranged
that the Stipendiary Fund [for enabling needy artists etc. to visit]
Bayreuth shall benefit thereby." This step's impersonality is an
honour in itself to all concerned, yet it might have been easy to
devise a mode whereby the identity of the whilom owner should
have been hidden from all but an intimate few: in that such a
mode was not adopted, we have not alone another proof of the
devotion of Richard Wagner's widow to his memory, but also of
her splendid sense of justice. Only by publication *in full* could
vulgar slanderers, who had dared to fret Frau Wesendonck's last
span of life, be put to shame; only thus could the good name
of that sweet friend and her descendants be cleared triumphantly.
Ah yes, ye glib resuscitators of forgotten hearsay,—ye who recked
naught that your silver-haired prey was neither blind nor deaf as
yet,—when ye killed her your doom was sealed!

When death so suddenly descended on her in the month of

August 1902, Mathilde Wesendonck was making ready for presentation of these letters to posterity.* Their accomplished German editor, Prof. Dr. Wolfgang Golther, tells us that in autumn 1903 her heirs entrusted him with the precious legacy : " Frau Wesendonk herself had partly prepared the edition.† *Everything* was to be published unabridged and unaltered, and direct from the originals that lay before me. A few letters, which I have specially noted, only existed in Frau Wesendonk's transcription; their originals appear to have been lost. Merely a handful of quite immaterial and minor omissions have been effected, out of regard for living persons ; omissions indicated every time by '. . .' The letters and leaves were to be arranged, explained and introduced [see later]. . . . Among them lay a few to Frau Wille and Otto Wesendonk, which have been included as directly bearing on the rest. . . . The 14 letters by Mathilde Wesendonk are the only answers preserved."

---

* It is most touching, to learn from Dr. Golther's preface that the pencilled ' composition-drafts' of *Tristan und Isolde* had been carefully gone over by Frau Wesendonck with pen and ink, to ensure their permanence ; how we should like to know *when !* They are dated by the master himself: act. i, Oct. 1 to Dec. 31, 1857 ; act ii, May 4 to July 1, 1858 ; act iii, Lucerne, April 9 to July 16, 1859. For the first act he wrote the verses reproduced page 17 *sup.;* above the second act, the words " *Noch im Asyl*"—" Still in my haven." Only in a very few passages of the second act did the voice-part differ from its final form, whilst the introduction of that act began with what is now its ninth bar.—The ' orchestral sketches,' i.e. the phase immediately before fair copy of the final score were never among Frau Wesendonck's belongings (see p. 234), but their dates are also given us : act i, Nov. 5, 1857, to Jan. 13, 1858; act ii, July 5, 1858, Zurich, to March 9, 1859, Venice ; act iii, May 1 to July 19, 1859, Lucerne. The last pages of the fair copy were completed Aug. 6, '59 (p. 161), and despatched to Härtel's next day.—On her printed copy of the poem, a birthday present 1858 (p. 94), Mathilde inscribed Isolde's words : " Mir erkoren—Mir verloren—Heil und hehr, kühn und feig—Todgeweihtes Haupt! Todgeweihtes Herz ! "—The pencilled ' composition-drafts ' of *Rheingold, Walküre* and the first two acts of *Siegfried*, with many a brief personal jotting or hieroglyph on their margins, were also preserved by the lady, in dainty cases of red leather ; their dates will be found elsewhere.

† Her preparation, Dr. Golther privately informs me, consisted in the said transcription (about ⅓ of the whole) and a few marginal notes.—N.B. Here I have respected Dr. G.'s omission of the " c " from the surname for the same reason that I *retain* it in the letters themselves,—*vid. inf.*

What a pity it seems, that there should be no more than those fourteen ; and how mysterious ! Had they all been destroyed, one could have understood it so much better, for that was the case with Frau Charlotte von Stein's to Goethe ; she asked for them back, and burnt them. Perhaps Frau Wesendonck did ask for hers ; but why preserve *none* of earlier date than June 1861 ? Her diary of 1858, with sad infrequent letters down to the Wiedersehen of April 1859,—a begging of these back, though Wagner had once decreed that they " shall not be given out again " (p. 34), we could easily understand on the eve of his departure to rejoin his wife next autumn ; their prompt destruction also. But her letters from Rome of winter 1859-60 : surely there can have been as little reason for depriving us of these, as for withholding those now published. Looked at from whichever side, I am forced to the conclusion that *Minna destroyed the whole bundle* just before laudanuming Mathilde's living present, Fips,—a doing to death so plainly hinted page 273.* It is too long an argument to set forth here, but Minna's final letter to her Berlin friend, of the next December, most distinctly connects the Paris ' catastrophe ' of summer 1861 with sudden discovery that " the pair *remain* in love " (see *Die Gegenwart* already-cited). That terrible shadow ; are we never to emerge from it ?—Let us return to pleasanter parting thoughts.

Had Frau Wesendonck lived long enough to finish her labour of love, I think an introduction to this correspondence would have been written by herself. Knowing her fondness for the letters of Wilhelm von Humboldt to *his* Freundin (p. 79)—most incorporeal of all platonics—I fancy she would have taken as text the following passage from that Freundin's preface :—" For a length of years this correspondence was my highest boon. What I required of sympathy and solace, of counsel and encouragement, of cheer and elevation, and finally of knowledge and enlightenment on higher truths, I drew from this exhaustless store that ever lay nigh to my hand. Such

---

* As to the " It is presumed " on that page—which would scarcely harmonise with the directly-preceding *räthselhaft* (" mysteriously," or " unintelligibly," " inexplicably ") if Wagner meant to convey his own surmise—it is quite possible that the original MS. had " *Vermeintlich*," i.e. " Allegedly," where the German now reads " *Vermuthlich*." He had used this " *Vermeintlich* " before, to Liszt (p. xxxiv *sup.*), concerning Minna's opium-habit.

a correspondence is society which leads to closer insight into character. It cannot be a secret, the whole world might know its contents ; but it was written to myself, and thus the *ark* of my life's covenant ; so I kept in silence and concealment what was penned for me alone, what indemnified me for serious deprivations, rewarded me for many griefs. . . . I viewed it as a never-stanching fount of higher life, whence for long years I drew strength and courage, and won whatever ripeness I might gain. In truth I needed for my mind no further sustenance, for my meditation no more copious matter, for my instruction no other book, for my soul no clearer light. Most kindly would the noble friend subdue his powers to my apprehension ; and thus, whatever He might talk to me about, to me He ever was intelligible, lucid, and convincing. If we differed at times in opinion, that difference arose from the externals of our lives [they never met but once, a quarter of a century before]. But my soul's-friend remained the guiding principle of all my spiritual life ; from one letter to the next I lived in thought with him, and, broken as my health was, that formed for me a thriving inner life. . . .

"For years since his death have I lived on these letters. Plunged in my friend's ideas, and pondering withal on this unique relation and what had thereby ripened in me for all time and all eternity, it often seemed to me not right that so much truth, such greatness and such goodness, should perish wholly with myself. True, for me alone had it been written, adapted to my individual sense ; but the truths were expressed so lucidly, the sure paths to inner calm and happiness so gently and so clearly pointed out, that a knowledge of them must be salutary for every seeking mind. —And all this to descend into the grave with me, with me be turned to dust?—"

So Mathilde's legacy has been fulfilled ; the wish of Richard Wagner also,—for the originals exist *no* longer.

And now for the needful final word on my own humble share in this production.

First as to the spelling of the lady's name. In face not only of the letter facsimiled herewith and several others addressed to myself (of no interest whatever to the public), but also of all her published works and the volume of Wagner's letters to her husband—I cannot bring myself to follow the example of her heirs and deprive her marriage-surname of its "c." * To my mind, such a step is an interference with literary documents, for there can be no possible doubt that Wagner never wrote about, or to Mathilde or her husband, with elision of that "c"; notwithstanding that family pedigrees now may prove the simple "k" to be the true orthography. As Mathilde Wesendonck, then, shall she still be known at least in England—with due apologies to her descendants.

Then as to punctuation—by which I do not mean the commas, but full stops and suchlike. It is always a moot point when letters come before an editor for publication, and there is no fixed rule for its settlement, since private correspondence is hardly ever over-careful with these aids to sense. In the present case I find Wagner's sentences often divided up in a manner unfamiliar to me ; wherefore I have exercised a faithful translator's liberty, and punctuated as I myself deemed most in keeping with the context. Here and there it has been a choice between two evils, I admit; but the German edition stands always open to the more exacting inquirer, and he may be left to strike the balance on these minor matters, as also on an occasional (a very occasional) redistribution of paragraphs.

Chronology.—Except with letters "58a" and "111-112," I have made no alteration in the order of any subsequent to no. 55 ; *before* that number I have radically rearranged the Zurich group in the light of internal evidence. Naturally my rearrangement can claim no other authority than that of a working hypothesis ; I believe, how-ever, it will be found an assistance to the reader, and Dr. Golther himself has courteously given prominence in the eleventh and following German editions to a table of comparison which I sub-mitted to him some six months since. Broadly speaking, the said table (unnecessary to reproduce here) will be found a sufficient guide to any student who may desire to check my work ; unfortunately, however, I have revised my own arrangement since in three or four particulars. My best apologies to Dr. Golther.—N.B. The

---

* As the German edition of these letters appeared on the very eve of my going to press with vol. iv of the *Life of Richard Wagner*, I hastily struck out the "c" from every mention of this surname that was not an actual quotation there ; but I have since repented of my haste, and now the "c"s are all restored in readiness for a possible (?) reprint.

letters of *Wagner* constituting my first and last groups will be found subdivided into smaller grouplets in the German edition.

To conclude, I have grateful thanks to tender to my publishers; to Dr. Golther and my friend Herr C. F. Glasenapp, for various elucidations; and above all to an English friend, "Evelyn Pyne," for her assistance in giving the due feminine flavour to our joint translation of *Frau Wesendonck's* tales and letters, also for her sole and beautiful translation of that lady's poems. Just seventeen years ago I had the honour to publish in the now defunct *Meister* an Anniversary Ode by "Evelyn Pyne"; four lines therefrom shall now form my apostrophe:—

> "Sing of strong Love the redeemer,
>   Self-less who comes but to save:—
> Deathless he lives in thy music—
>   Tearless we stand by thy grave."—

WM. ASHTON ELLIS

Easter 1905.

HORSTED KEYNES.

INDEX

Following a plan which I have found work satisfactorily in similar cases before, I do not *repeat* in this index the figures denoting tens and hundreds for one and the same reference, excepting where the numerals run into a fresh line of type : thus

Calderon, 14, 6, 23, 65, 201, 67, will stand for
Calderon, pages 14, 16, 23, 65, 201, 267.

Numerals followed by "*n*" are references to footnotes, whilst those enclosed within brackets indicate that the subject is only indirectly mentioned in the text.—W. A. E.

A.

A., Madame, 175.
d'Agoult, Countess, 53 (?).
Ahasuerus, xli, 147.
Aldridge, Ira, 9.
All Souls' day, 69, 72, 182.
Allg. Musikzeitung, xxxvii, ix, lii, 194*n*.
Almasy, Count, 280.
Alps, lix, 32, 5, 58, 100, 1, 7, 11, 2, 113, 62, 207, 309, 13, 21, 45, 52.
Altenburg, Weimar, 164.
Altmann, Dr Wilhelm, xxxii, 179*n*, 292*n*.
America, xxii, xxxviii, 105, 10*n*, (126), 128, 278*n*, 319 ; see New York.
Ananda and Sawitri, (xxxvii, xl), lv, lxii, 8, (25, 42), 54-6, (82), 97, (117), 239, (288, 306, 20).
Ander, tenor, 277, 80, 1, 4, 5.
Anfortas, 140-3, 242.
Apollo, birth of, 150 ; Delphi, 165.
Arthur, King, xxxvi, 244.
"Asyl" (Zurich), viii-xi, xvii, xxx, xlv, lvi-lxi, 12-5, 26-8, 31-2, 57, 61, 64, 88, 99, 147, 52, 9, 92, 6, 206, 67, 283, 9, 309, 13, 21*n*, 7, 30, 56, 60, 371*n*.
Austria, 87, 90, 129 ; see Vienna.

B.

Bach, J. S., 155.
Baden, Gd Duke and Duchess, 64, 101, 79, 96, 268, 9, (277), 300, 22, 343 ; see also Carlsruhe.
Badenweiler, 343.
Basle, 4, 292, 343.
Baudelaire, 207.
Baumgartner, W., xix, 11, 160, 98.
Baur, 10 ; see Hotel.
Bayreuth, xl., (179-80), 330, 2, 70.
Bayreuther Blätter, xiii, 76*n*, 229*n*.
Beckmesser, 292.
Beethoven, xlviii, 209 ; *Egmont*, 133 ; *Fidelio*, 228-9 ; last sonatas etc., 193 ; symphonies, 7*n*, 8, 20*n*, 356.
Belloni, (214).
Berlin, lx, 175, 89, 317 ; opera-house, 186, 315.
Berlin friend, Minna's, xxii, v-vi, xxxiv, lix, 254*n*, 372.
Berlioz, 182, (184?), 193, 207-9, 28-30, 263 ; *Romeo*, 121 ; *Troyens*, 208 ; wife, xxxv, 208.
Berne, 11, 12*n*.
Bethlen, Countess, 314.
Bible, 8, 79, 145, 225, 304.
Biebrich on Rhine, 293-305.
Bingen on Rhine, 309.

Bissing, Frau von, 326, 62 ; Myrrha, 108*n*.
Bodmers, the, 10.
Bonapartism, 129, 81.
Bordeaux " episode," xl, i, viii-ix.
Bourgeois et Dennery, 19*n*.
Brahm, the, 225.
Breitkopf and Härtel, see H.
Brendel, 175*n*.
Breslau concerts, 324, 6, 62.
Brühl ravine, 280.
Brunnen, 168.
Brünnhilde, 13 (81), 100, 44, 56, 68, 177, 241.
Brussels, 218, 30*n* ; concerts, 214, 9, 232 ; photo., 223, 32-3.
Buddha, 53-5, 103, 56, 7, ; and Art, 56, cf. 69.
Buddhism, lv, 8, 53, 156-7, (197), 213, 225, 39 ; mendicancy, 73-4, 103-4.
Bülow, Cosima von, lx-i, 328, 63, 9, 370.
   ,,   Hans von, lx-ii, 175, 8, 84*n*, 198, 203, 14, 30, 55, 67, 8, 76, 328, 61, 70 ; daughter (Blandine), 317.

C.

Çakya-Muni, 53-5.
Calderon, 14, 6, 23, 65, 201, 67.
Carlsruhe, 101, 30, (163?), 177, 83, 202, 68, 9, 70, 3, 92*n*, 300 ; concerts, 321-5, 59, 61. See Devrient.
Carvalho, 176, 9.
Cervantes, 19, 22, 286, 8, 349.
Challemel-Lacour, xxxv, 174.
Chamberlain, H. S., *Richard Wagner*, 45*n*, 233*n*, 309*n*.
Champfleury, 207.
Charnacé, Countess, 175, 93.
Chemnitz, xxi, xxvi.
Chillon, l.
Chrétien de Troyes, 143, 244*n*.
Clara, Wagner's sister, see Wolfram.
Cleobis and Biton, 159.
Como, 110.
Constitutionelle Zeitung, Dresden, 191*n*.
Cornelius, painter, 301, 45 ; *Nibelungen*, 192, 299.
   ,,   Peter, composer, 297*n*, 8*n*, 300-1, 26, 8, 61, 3.
Courrier du Dimanche, Paris, 206.
Crespi, painter, 112.
Czechs, 315.

D.

Dante, xl, 8, 165, 211.

Danube, accident on, 314.
Darmstadt theatre, 298*n*, 321.
David, King, 304.
   ,,   *Meistersinger*, 292.
Delos, island of, 150.
Delphi, oracle at, 165.
Deutsche Allg. Ztg., 136, 268*n*.
Devrient, Eduard, 14, 164, 79, 83, 196 ; see Carlsruhe.
Dolgorucki, Prince, 77, 92.
Donner, *Rheingold*, 133.
Doré, Gustave, 207.
Dräseke, Felix, 160, 6, 8.
Dresden, xiii-iv, xxi, iv, xxx, 100-1, 153, 89*n*, 91, 205-6, 12, 44, 73, 98-299*n*, 307, 24.
Dunkirk, xxxviii.
Düsseldorf, xxxviii, 284.

E.

Eddas, the, xxxix, 181*n*.
Egmont, see Beethoven, Goethe.
Egypt, Pasha of, 346.
Elberfeld, xxxviii.
Elisabeth (*Tannh.*), 186, 221, 49, 318*n*.
Elsa (*Loh.*), 239, 319.
" *Engel, Der*," 16.
English, 7, 10, 28, 156, 251, 348 ; journals, 233 ; " God save the King," 137. See London.
Erard, Mme, 57.
   ,,   pianoforte, 35, 41, 56-8, 69, 71, 2, 80, 7, 8, 95, 113, 7, 23, 58, 64, 7, 92, 299.
Erda-scene, *Siegfried*, 168*n*.
Erec and Enide, 244-6.
Eschenburg, Prof., 7.
Eschmann, Zurich musician, 356.
Ettmüller, Prof., 181.
European culture, 8, 157, 9, 218.
Eva (*Meistersinger*), 291, 370.
" Evelyn Pyne," 335*n*, 75.

F.

Fafner, 13, 4.
FAUST-OVERTURE, li-ii, 7*n*, 361.
Fazy, Maison, Geneva, 33*n*.
FEEN, DIE, MS. (score ?), 364.
Fichtelberger, Zurich conductor, 356.
Fiddle-note, long-drawn, 42.
Fips, dog, 175, 237 ; death, 273, 4*n*, (278), 312, 72.
Fischer, Dr Georg, xxxi.
   ,,   W., Dresden, xxx, iii ; death, 191.
FLYING DUTCHMAN, see HOLLÄNDER.
Fontainebleau, 235.

Franck-Marie, 207.
Franz, Robert, 14.
Frederick the Great, xxxix, 142.
French : art, 37-8, 184, 206-7, 16-8;
language, xxiii-iv, 174, 9, 213, 4, 7,
238, 360 ; nation, 178-9, 207, 11, 6,
218 ; poetry, medieval, 143, 244.
Fricka (*Walküre*), 8.
Frickhöffer, Biebrich, 297, 8, 9*n*.
Frommann, Alwine, xxvi, 276.
Fugues, 8.
Fünf Gedichte, xxxix, 16-7, 58, 307 ;
see *Träume*.

G.

Ganges, the, 157.
Garcia-Viardot, Mme, 263.
Garibaldi, 137, 45.
Garrigues, Malvina, 179*n*, (330).
Gasperini, Dr, 178, 206, 11, 54*n*.
Gegenwart, Die, xxii, v, viii, xxxiv,
254*n*, 372.
Geibel, dramatic poet, 144.
Genelli, 222-3.
Geneva, vii, xii, 31-4, 284*n*, 312*n*.
Genius, xlii, iv, lx, i, 75-6, 95-6, 120,
148, 82, 216, 24-5, 9-30, 347, 58, 69.
German art, 37-8, 147, 51, 5.
Germany, xxxviii, xlii, iii, 27, 64, 87,
100, 4, 28-9, 79, 96, 208, 12, 9, 32,
236, 43, 67, 87, 8, 309, 10, 5, 9, 22,
348.
Geyer, Ludwig, 45*n*.
Gipsy music, 193, 279, 80.
Giulay, Count, 153.
Glarus, Alps, (lix), 6*n*.
Glasenapp, C. F., 189*n*, 205*n*, 78*n*,
326*n*, 75.
Gluck, 6, 208, 17 ; *Orpheus*, 344 ; see
Iphig.
Goethe, vi, lxi-ii, 19*n*, 79, 93, 112, 30,
200-2, 70, 372 ; *Egmont*, 122-3, 33-
135, 7 ; *Faust*, li, 72,174, 200 ; *Tasso*,
120-3, 5, 35, 57 ; *Werther*, 18*n*.
Golther, Dr Wolfgang, xxxix, lii, 18*n*,
22, 94*n*, 238*n*, 52*n*, 92*n*, 300*n*, 29*n*,
371, 4-5.
Gondola, 36, 42, 4-5, 77, 88-92, 100.
GÖTTERDÄMMERUNG, lv, 362; pfte.
score, 332 ; poem, MS., 365.
Gottfried von Strassburg, 142.
Gould, Dr. G. M., 200*n*, 40*n*.
Gounod, 193, 207.
Graces, Three (*Tannh*.), 221-2.
Grail, Holy, 23, 94, 140-4, 241.
Greek art etc., xxix, xxxix, 150, 9, 65.
Green Hill, the, viii, xi, xix, xxxviii,

lvi, viii, ix, 13, 7, 8, 20, 5, 32, 3, 4,
38, 44, 51, 7, 81-2, 8, 99, 101, 9, 11,
113, 8, 22, 44, 6, 9, 59-63, 9, 73*n*, 86-
187, 223, 69-70, 2, 4, 87, 97, 313, 20-
332, 43-6, 8, 56-63 ; photo., 177, 84,
283, 99, 310.
Gries, 126.
Griesbach, Frau, Jena, 130*n*.
Griesinger, Dr, 357.
Grimm, Bros., 20, 74*n*, 106.
Gurnemanz (*Parsifal*), 241.
Gwinner, W., 349*n*.

H.

Hagenbuch, F., Zurich, xix.
Hamburg, xlvi ; Exchange, 137.
Hanover theatre. xxxi, 324.
Hanslick, E., 318*n*.
Härtels, xxxii, lviii, 18*n*, 21*n*, 135, 46,
151, 5, 7, 67*n*, 98*n*, 206, 30*n*, 55,
371*n*.
Hartenfels, Dr, 128*n*.
Hartmann von Aue. 181*n*, 244*n*.
Haydn, *Creation*, 344.
Hechingen, Prince Hohenzollern-, 324,
326.
Heim, Emilie, xxvi, xlix, l, 7.
  ,, Ignaz, xxvi, l, 20*n*, 72, 126, 75,
344, 56.
Heine, Heinrich, xliii, 137.
Heinrich, Hôtel Baur, 10.
Heinse's *Ardinghello*, xliii.
Heisterhagen, Zurich musician, 356.
Helene, Gd Duchess, Russia, 310.
Heller, Stephen, 207.
Herold, Mme, 176.
Herwegh, Georg, 4, 14-5, 148-50, 61,
325, 48.
Hewitz, Frau, 179*n*, (183).
Hilpert, Zurich musician, 356.
Hohenlohe-Schillingsfürst, Prince, 164.
HOLLÄNDER, DER FLIEGENDE, xliii:—
French translations : prose, 238 ;
verse, for score, 272*n*.
Hero, xli, vi, 28, 96, 283.
Overture : new close, 209, 20.
Vienna perf., 272, 81, 4.
Holtzmann, Adolf, 8.
Homburg, 357.
Homer, 6.
Hornstein, Robert von, xxv, xliii, v-vi,
l, iii-v, viii.
Hôtel Baur au Lac, Zurich, xxxviii,
liii, vii, ix, 10.
Hotels : Geneva, 33*n*, Prague, 324, 61 ;
Vienna, 282, 305.
Hugo, Victor, 184.

Humboldt, W. von, 78-9, 90, 2, 4, 9, 372-3.
Hungarians, 279-80, 313-6, 9.
Hutten, Ulrich von, 281, 304.

.I.

Idea, Platonic, 75, 96-7.
Idealism, xlii, 37-8, 48-9, 52-3, 65, 82, 85, 95-8, 112, 21, 52, 94, 200, 24, 233, 9-40, 61, 81-2, 360, 9.
Illustration, Paris, 207, 33*n*.
Illustrirte, Leipziger, 268.
Indian legends, lxi, 8 ; cf. 81, 152, 93.
Intelligenzblatt, Zurich, 148.
Iphigenia in Aulis, Wagner's revision of Gluck's, xxxii, 19, 287, 366.
Isola bella, 35.
Italian : art, 37-8, 87, 9, 112, 99, 217, 227 ; language, 88, 92.
Italy, xii, 33, 99, 122, 9, 94, 202, 314 ; see Rome, Venice.

J.

Jesus Christ, 8, 79, 140, 3, 225, 304.
Joseph of Arimathea, 140, 2.
Journal des Débats, 208, 28.

K.

Kalergis, Countess, 234-5*n*, 63.
Kant, 79, 93, 4, (95, 239-40).
Kaulbach, 192.
Keller, Gottfried, vi, lv, 11*n*, 344, 7 ; *Der grüne Heinrich*, 215, 347.
Keller, Zurich photographer, 282.
Kieff, 324.
Kilchberg, near Zurich, lviii, 100.
Kirchner, Theodor, 13, 129.
Klindworth, Karl, li, 128*n*, 263.
„   " Papa," 218.
" Kobold," (20), 74, 80, 105, 6, 18, (350).
Köchly, Prof., 127*n*, 344.
Kolatschek, 272.
Königsberg, xxii.
Köppen's *Hist. of Buddhism*, 53, 156, 157.
Kreutzer, Léon, 207.
Kundry (*Parsifal*), 94, 241-2.
Kurwenal (*Tr. u. Is.*), 77, 119, 58.
Kutter, New York, 14.

L.

Lacombe, Louis, 207.
Latin, 227.
Latona, 150.
Laussot, Mme, xl, cf. xlviii.

" Lazarus," 15.
Leipzig, xlix, 147, 51, 3, 7, 313*n*.
Lessing (?), 343.
Liechtenstein, Prince R., 279, 80.
Lindau, R., 238*n*.
Liszt, Franz, xxxiv, xlvi, l, iii, vii, 12; 65-6, 87, 106*n*, 29, 33, 4, 55, 64, 80*n*, (229*n*), 230-1, 4*n*, (260), 269, 71, 4, 276-7, 345, 70 ; *Bohémiens*, 193 ; music, 144, 7, (184 ?)—*Faust*, 271, 4, 6.
LITERARY WORKS, Wagner's :—
  Art-work of the Future, 365.
  Beethoven, 37*n*, 78*n*.
  Communication, xli-iii, (xlvi), 365.
  German Art and Policy, 315*n*.
  Homage to Fischer, 191.
  Jesus of Nazareth, 225*n*, 304*n*.
  Judaism in Music, 235*n*, 365 ; cf. lii.
  Liszt's Symphonic poems, 13*n*, 121.
  Manuscripts of, 328, 31, 63-6.
  " *Music of the Future*," 206*n*, 38-9, 248.
  Opera and Drama, xliii, (xlvi), 272*n*.
  Vienna Opera-house, 321*n*, 5, 61.
LOHENGRIN, xliii, 5, 131, 280 :—
  Hero, 57, 97, 239.
  Performances : Dresden, 153 ; Leipzig, xlix ; Vienna, 105, 268-9, 72, 284, 344 :—contemplated : London, 251 ; Paris, 201, 3, 13.
  Poem, 239 ; draft of, 365 ; French prose-transl., 238.
  Selections : concert, xlvii, 204*n*, 10; 319 ; milit., 90.
  Wagner hears for first time, 268-9; cf. 251.
London, li, ii, 7-9, 128, 200*n*, 14, 62, 263, 82 ; Covent Garden, 251.
Lope de Vega, 18*n*, 9*n*, 20.
Löwenberg concerts, 324, 6, 62.
Lucerne, xix. 20, (26), 81, 105, 12-69, 174, 7, 91, 2, 283, 318.
Luckemeyer (Mathilde's parents), xxxviii, 38 ; mother, 284,—death; 297-8; brother, 14*n*, 126, 8, 80*n* ; sister Marie, 9.
Ludwig II. of Bavaria, 327-9, 63, 70.
Lugano, 110.
Luther, Sachs' ode to, 293, 302.
Lüttichau, von, xxviii, 189.

M.

Mabinogion, 244.
Magdalene, Mary, 8.
Magdeburg theatre, xxi-ii.
Magenta, battle, 153.
Magnan, Maréchal, 208.

Mainz, 17, 292*n*, 3, 300, 26.
Mannheim theatre, xxxii, 103.
Marat, "sentimental," 233.
Maria Stuart, see Schiller.
Mariafeld, (87), 150, 327, 30.
Marriage, youthful etc., xli-ii, 45-6, 73, 79, 85, (93), 134.
Marseilles, 194*n*; magnate, 210-1.
Maurice, Paris servant, 228, 52-3.
Maya, veil of, 197, 277.
Mayer, Elisa, *Humboldt*, 78.
Mayer-Dustmann, Frau, 201, 77.
Max, Archduke, Austria, 104.
Mecca, 142.
Medea, 37.
Meister, *The*, 375.
MEISTERSINGER, DIE :—
  Concert excerpts, 313*n*, 6, 25.
  Music, 297, 9, 302 : act i, comp., 298, 304,—scoring, 308, 10, 1, 3, 317, 24, 7, 56 ; act iii, chorus and introduction, 301-2; unused theme, 300.
  Overture, 286 : performed, Carlsruhe, 325 ; Leipzig and Pesth, 313*n*, 6.
  Pfte score, 331.
  Poem, 285-300, 50-1, 64*n*, 70 ; "Tabulatur," 300.
  Scenario **1845**, 290, 348, 64*n*, 6 ; **1861**, 292*n*.
Melot (*Tr. u. Is.*), 77, 158.
Messiahs, 219, 304.
Metternich, Princess, 285, 350*n*.
Meyer, Johanna C. (Planer), xxi.
Meysenbug, Malwida von, xlii, vi, 262, 272*n*, 304*n*.
Milan, 35, 110-2.
Minna, see Wagner.
Mirès, 211.
Mitleid (compassion), xii, v, xx, xxxii-xxxiii, liii, v, vii, 27, 47-51, 63, 73, 85, 120, 67, 242*n*, 75, 8, 9, 84, 98, 307, 14, 38, 54, 7.
Mödling, near Vienna, 280.
Moleschott, Prof., 347.
Moon, the, 36, 42, 4-5, 309, 43.
Morelli, barytone, 249.
Mornex, 11, 2*n*.
Moscow, 308, 9 ; snuffbox, 312.
Mozart, *Zauberflöte* ov., 7*n*.
Mrazeks, Wagner's servants, 312, 26.
Müller, Alex., xvi, xix.
  ,,   Franz, 12.
Munich, xxxv, 19*n*, 108*n*, 54*n*, 79*n*, 278, 312*n*, 27-9.
Muotta-Thal, 6*n*.
Murillo, engravings after, 192.
Music, 44-5, 208, 47, 82, 319 ; of the

Future, 147, 208, 39 ; and Poetry, 36-7, 93, 121, 65, 78, 84, 217-8, 38, 240, 300.
Musik, Die, 104*n*, 222*n*, 38*n*, 52*n*, 90*n*.
Myth, xxxix, 142, 50, 7, 9, 65-6, 351.

N.

Nako, Ct & Ctss, 279-80.
Naples, 348.
Napoleon III., 129, 81, 208, 13.
Nassau, Duke of, 297, 9.
Nature, egoism of, xliii, 46, 52-4, 8-9.
Nesselrode, 263.
Neue freie Presse, xlv.
Neue Zeitschrift für Musik, xxii, 13, 147, 75*n*, 91*n*, 8*n*.
Ney, Frau, soprano, 201.
New York, xxxvi, viii, 14*n*, 128*n* ; see America.
NIBELUNGEN, RING DES, xliv, (8), 219, (226-7), 259, 63, (308) ; compos. sketches, 364*n*, 71*n*; concert excerpts, 316 ; poem, l, v, 12*n*, 97, 168, 94,—sent to Schopenhauer, 237*n* ; sale of, lviii, lx, 157, 67*n*, 8. See also RHEINGOLD etc.
Nicker, 221*n*, 303.
Niemann, Albert, 201, 49, 65.
Night, 31-2, 6, 45, 69, 81, 107, 212, 224, 31, 43, 83, 6, 98.
Nirvana, xl, 213, 353.
Nuitter, Chas., 238*n*, (248), 72*n*.
Nuremberg, 286.

O.

Odessa, 324.
Oederan register, xxi.
Olliviers, xxxiv, 262, 78.
Oratorio, 8.
Orpheus, 222, 344.
Otto, Kaiser, 19.
Overbeck, 345.

P.

Palazzo Giustiniani, Venice, xv, viii, xxx, 35, 44, 77-8, 87-9, 99 ; photo., 177, 283, 99.
Palestina, 227.
Palleske's *Schiller*, 102-3, 63, 8.
Paris, xxiii-iv, xxx, iv, xli, ii, lv, vii, 6, 18, 57, 68, 105, 28, 54, 9-62, 173-275, 82, 3, 5-92, 8, 300, 30, 43, 50 ; Bois de Boulogne, 237, 43 ; catastrophe, 269-75, 369, 72 ; Champs Elysées, 181, 254 ; Concerts, W.'s, 198-211, 3, 9, 28 ; Conservatoire,

217 ; German Opera plan, 201, 11 ; Grand Opéra, 207, 13, 7—see *Tannh.* ; House, W.'s, xxxiv, 180-3, 189, 92-3, 242*n*, 51, 4, 72*n*, 3, 85, 91 ; Jockey Club, 220, 65 ; Louvre, 206-207, 46, 86 ; Salle Ventadour, 201 ; Seine and Tuileries, 272, 86 ; Théâtre lyrique, 176, 9.

PARSIFAL, see next reference.

Parzival, lx, 239, 41 : ideas for drama, 50, 93-4, 7, 136, 40-4, (226), 240-2, 244 ; mus. theme, 22-3.

Patrie, Paris, 204.

Patti, Adelina, 128*n*.

Penelope, xli.

Penzing, Vienna, 305-27.

Peps' death (dog), 9, 312.

Perrin, Paris dir., 207.

Pesth : boat-accident, 314 ; concerts, 313, 5-8, 24.

Philharmonic concerts, London, 7-9.

PIANOFORTE WORKS, Wagner's, 4*n*, 5, 198, 272*n*, 362*n*.

Pilatus, Lucerne, 113, 59, 60, 4, 7.

Planers, the, xxi-v, xxx, xliii ; mother's death, xiv.

Plato, 136 ; see Idea.

Plutarch, 177, 81.

Pogner (*Meistersinger*), 291.

Pohl, dog, 312, 7, 26.

„ Richard, lx.

Politics, xxiv, xxxvi, 79, 87, 129, 31, 136, 48-9, 53, 91, 280.

Pollert, Frau, soprano, 13.

Poniatowski, Prince, 217.

Posa (*Don Carlos*), 175, 89.

Pourtalès, Countess, 263, 72, 83.

Praeger, Ferd., xlviii-ix, lix-lx.

Prague : concerts, 315, 24, 61—H.v. B.'s, 198*n* ; theatre, 206.

Prakitri, 193 ; see Sawitri.

Professors, 7, 18, 21, 56, 144, 60, 347-8.

" Providence," xxviii, 79, 135.

Prussia, 146, 263, 72, 83 ; Princess, xxxv, 247*n*.

Pusinelli, Dr Anton, xiii, xxvi, ix, xxx, xxxiv, 102.

Pythia, 165.

Q.

Quai Voltaire, Paris, 285, 91.

Queen Victoria, England, 251.

R.

Raphael, 112 ; Mad. d. Sedia, 192 ; Green Hill copies, 246, 346, 63.

Reichenhall, 278.

Reincarnation, lvii, lxi-ii, 51, 4-5, 239, 370.

Revolution, xxiv, xlii, vi, 185.

Revue Européenne, Paris, 207.

RHEINGOLD, DAS, 11*n*, 133 ; compos. mus., xlvii-viii,—MS., 371*n* ; pfte score, 344 ; poem and draft, xliv, 365.

Rhine, the, xxxviii, 247, 51, 70, 97, 9, 313, 21, 43.

Rich, the, xlv, 47-50, 73, 9, 197, 203, 211, 23, 308, 69.

Richard, C., 19.

RIENZI, lvii, 11*n*, 2 ; Darmstadt, 298*n* ; Dresden, xxiv ; Hanover, xxxi.

Riga, xxii-iii, 37*n*.

Rigi, 113, 27-8, 32-3, 7, 45 ; Kaltbad, 162, 4.

RING, see NIBELUNGEN.

Ristori, 37-8.

Ritter, Frau, xxxi, xl, vii, lx, 72, 91, 131, 4, 370 ; daughters, xl, vi.

Ritter, Karl, xxxi-ii, l, iii, iv, 32, 45*n*, 72, 4, 6, 88, 9, 91, 101, 6, 10, 28, 134, 8.

Roche, Edmond, 177-8, 238*n*.

Roeckel, August, xxxv, xli, vii-ix, lii, lv, 298-9*n*.

Rolandseck, 251.

Rome, 39, 110, 38, 94*n*, 7, 9, 201, 2, 204, 15, 23, 4, 8, 31*n*, 345, 72 ; Sixtine chapel, 227 ; fountain of Trevi, 233.

Roses, 18, 26, 81, 103, 52.

Rossini, 28, 19.

Rotterdam to Pesth, 314.

Royer, op. dir., 218, 9, 86.

Rue d'Aumale, 251.

„ de Lille, 272.

„ Newton, 181.

Ruge, Arnold, 315.

Russia, 77, 219, 62, 308-10, 4, 5, 21, 326, 62.

Rütli, 163.

S.

Sachs, Hans, 290-3, 302, 13, 70.

S. Anthony, 112, 3.

S. Gallen, (lvii), 274.

S. Gothard, 20, 110, 2, 7, 287.

S. Petersburg, 219, 308, 9, 24.

Saint-Saens, 207.

Saints, lv-vi, 54, 82, 112-3, 7, 48, 51, 314, 39.

Salzburg, 278.

San Marte, 136*n*, 42.

de Sanctis, 21, 126, 37, 348.

Sawitri, 8, 193, 369 ; and Elsa, 239.
See Ananda.
Sax, Marie (Sasse), 249, 54*n.*
Saxony, King, xxxv, 13, 100, 89*n.*
Schack, Count A. F., 19.
Schandau, xx.
Schiller, 78, 9, 93, 5, 102-3, 63, 8, 90,
  201, 301 ; Committee's invit. 189 ;
  Don Carlos, 175, 89 ; Letters to
  Lotte, xxix, lii, 129, 30-1, 81 ; *Maid
  of Orleans*, 189 ; *Maria Stuart*, 37-8.
Schirmer (?), 343.
Schleich, Zurich musician, 356.
"*Schmerzen*," 16.
Schmid, A., *Gluck*, 6.
Schmidt, basso, Vienna, 344.
Schnorr, Ludwig and Malvida, 179*n*,
  (330).
Schopenhauer, xlv, li-v, (42, 6-9), 52,
  59, 75-6, 8, 93, (97-8,.112, 48, 52,
  165), 181, 2, (224-7), 231, 7, (261),
  347, 9, (353), 64*n.*
Schott, 17, 292*n*, 3, 300, 4, 27.
  ,,   Frau Betty, 298*n.*
Schulthess, Zurich bookseller, 19.
Schwalbach, 313, 57.
Schwarzau, near Vienna, 279, 80.
Schweizerhof, xxi, 132, 50, 3, 4, 6, 63,
  164, 7 ; see Lucerne.
Seebach, Frau von, (247*n*), 263.
Seefeld, Zurich, 10.
Seegessern (Schweizerhof), 153, 4.
Seelisberg, liii-iv, 9, 113.
Semper, Gottfried, 15, 140, 86-7, 206*n*,
  328.
Senta (*Holl.*), xli, 28, 281.
Sex-problem, xlii-iii, viii, 46, 8, 53-5,
  75-6 ; see Woman.
Shakespeare,, 148, 50 ; *Hamlet*, 361 ;
  Othello, 9.
Sicily, 181, 3.
Sieger, Die, lv, vi, lxi-ii, (28, 41), 54-
  55, 239.
SIEGFRIED, 100, 18, (336) : music, lviii-
  lx, 13, 21*n*, 56, 68*n*, 77, (270, 1),—
  box missing, 122, 8, 36 ; pfte score,
  331 ; poem and draft, xliv, 365 ;
  ' sketches,' 371*n.*
Siegfried's Tod, poems, draft and pre-
  face, xliv, 365.
Sihl-Thal, lviii, 100, 237.
Silence, 22, 43, 5, 86, 9, 98, 163, 81,
  260, 4, 6, 75, 80-1, 352, 8, 62 ;
  "sounding," 64, 189, 286.
Simplon, 35.
Sina (Baron?), Venice, 87.
Soden baths, 247*n*, 72*n.*
  ,,   Count J., 18*n.*

Solferino, 158.
Spanish literature, 18-23, 142, 227 ; see
  Calderon.
Stachelberg, 6*n.*
Standhartner, Dr, 277, 83, 317, 25, 51.
Stars, 36, 44, 88, 90, 277 ; comet, 44;
  Jupiter, 231, 3.
"*Stehe still*," 17, 58, 60*n.*
Stein, Charlotte von, vi, lxi-ii, 19*n*,
  372.
Steiner, A., *Neujahrsblatt*, xiii, xxvi,
  282*n.*
Strakosch, 128*n.*
Strassburg, 19.
Strömkarl, 221, 2.
Stünzig (?), Zurich, 223.
Stürmer, (?), Paris, 273.
Sulzer, Jakob, xvi, xxxvii, 14, 346, 7.
"Swan" (pfte), 57, 71, 2, 113, 334 ;
  see Erard.
Swans, The black, 272*n.*
Switzerland, lii, 28, 72, 101, 5, 60, 77,
  217, 79, 310, 3, 21, 56, 8.

T.

Tägliche Rundschau, Berlin, xiii.
TANNHÄUSER, xliii, 238, 50, 303*n* :—
  Ballet, 219-23.
  Cut in act ii, 186.
  French translations, 174-5, 8*n*, 213,
    238, 48 ; prose, 238.
  Hero, 97, 186, 221, 2, 38.
  March, 208, 9.
  Overture : perf., Paris, 210 ; Strass-
    burg, 19*n* ; Zurich, xliv ;—time-
    length, 206.
  Paris : hopes of, 179, 82, 201, 3, 13 ;
    Grand Opéra production, 216-20,
    243, 8-9, 53-68, (286).
  Paris version, 220-3, 38, 46, 8,
    250, 2.
  Performances (other) : Prague, 206 ;
    Vienna, 272.
  Poem, 238 ; draft, 364.
  Selections, concert : Paris, 204, 9-10;
    Zurich, xlvii—milit., Venice, 90.
Tappert, Wilhelm, xxi, xxxv.
Tasso, Jerus. Delivered, 123, 6, 8.
Tasso, see Goethe.
Tausig, Carl, 24, 136, 270, 1.
Tedesco, Mme, 249, (254*n*).
Tichatschek, Joseph, xiv, xxx, 189*n*,
  201 ; wife, xxvii.
"Transitions," artistic etc., 184-8.
"*Träume*," 16, 7, 80; 283.
Traunblick, Salzkammergut, xxxviii.
"*Treibhaus, Im*," 17, 23.

Treviso, 107.

Tribschen, lake of Lucerne, 154n, 331.

TRISTAN UND ISOLDE, 64, 82, 105, 288 :—

Composition-draft, mus. : act i, 15-7, 283 ; act ii, 22n, 4, 57, 118, 52, 185 ; act iii, xii, xix, xx, 105, 17-139, 46-55, 8, 9 (completed), 220, —themes, 123, 7 :—M.S., 158, 204, 364n, 71n.

Hero and heroine, xxvii, xl, lxi, 17, 36, 77n, 96-7, 140, 53-5, 220.

Mabinogion, 244.

Music, Wagner on, 79, 105, 24, 65, 168, 77, 85, 90-1, 240, 75, 88 ; sings, 263.

Orchestral draft : act i, 18, 21 ; act ii, xviii, 24n, 36, 41, 64, 7, 71, 5, 79, 80, 7, 92-111 ; act iii, 130, 2, 9, 144, 5, 56, 8—fair copy, 132, 46, 151, 5, 60, 1n :—MS. 234n, 371n.

Pfte (vocal) score, 255.

Poem, viii, lx-lxi, 14, 42, 65, (81), 121-2, 42, 52, 243, 85, 352, 71n ; first idea, li, lv ; prose-draft, lx ; publication, xxxii, 91n, 4, 121-2, 237n, 371n ; translation, French prose, 238.

Prelude, 130, 213 : concert-close, 198-9, 209, 32 ; perf. :—Leipzig, 147n, 98n ; Paris, 198-9, 202-4, 210 ; Pesth, 316 ; Prague, 198n, 203, (315—also at W.'s other concerts of that year).

Production contemplated, xxvii, 86, 119, 204, 19, 40, 3, 50, 5, 9, 88 : Carlsruhe, 64, 101, 30, 77, 9, 81, 183, 96, 202, 68, 73, 92n ; Dresden, 189n ; Munich (effected), 179n, 329-30 ; Paris, 201-2, 11-3 ; Vienna, 271, 2, 5, 7-8, 284, 5, 7, 304-5, 15, 46.

Score, proofs, 166, 90 ; pubd, 206, 230n, 1n.

Sketches, prelim., 283, 307, 11.

Trümplers, the, 10.

Tschandalas, 54, 193.

Tschudi, *Fauna of the Alps*, 279.

Turin University, 347.

Tyrol, 100.

U.

Uhlig, Th., xxiv-v, xl-vii, 167n.

Ullmann, B., manager, 128.

Ulrich, see Hutten.

„ Frln, 344.

Usinar, 8.

V.

Vandyck, 112, 279.

Venice, xii, iii, viii, xxvii, xxx-ii, 34-5, 41-2, 86-7, 9, 100, 1, 4-5, 11-2, 8, 128, 36, 227, 84, 6, 9, 90, 306, 7, 47, 348 : Café d.l. Rot., 89 ; Giard. publ., 35, 88, 100 ; Grand Canal, xviii, 35, 36, 44, 69, 77, 87, 8, 9, 107 ; Lido, 42, 4, 88 ; Piazza S. Marco, 35, 77, 88, 90 ; Piazzetta, 35, 44, 87, 8, 100, —lion, 350 ; Rialto, Foscari, Grassi, 87 ; Riva, 100. See Pal. Giust.

Venus, 112 : *Tannh.*, 220-2, 38, 46, 9, 250.

Venusberg, (186), 220-3, 364.

Verdi, 316.

Verona, 100, 10.

Vicenza, 107.

Victoria, Queen, 251.

Vienna, xxxv, 87, 105, 201, 68-70, 4-286, 92n, 301, 4-27, 44, 5-9, 55, 7, 362 ; concerts, 305, 16 ; Schönbrunn, 309 ; Theatre, 268, 81, 315, 23,—see *Tristan*.

Villemarqué, Ct de la, 244.

Villot, F., 206-7.

Violin, 42, 209, 21, 2, 50.

Vischer, Prof. F. T., 18.

Vreneli, (126), 154, 61, 7, 9, 76, 318.

W.

Wagner, Cosima, 330-1, 69, 70.

Wagner, Minna, vii, ix-xxxvi, xliii, vii, xlix, lii-lxi, 3, 4, 9-14, 22n, 5-6, 32, 37n, 51, (63), 70-1, 85, 101, 2, 175-176, 89n, 90n, 1, 2n, (214, 24, 8), 247n, (249, 58, 62, 3, 4, 5, 7, 70-2), 273, 4n, (278), 283-4n, 98-9n, 307, 316, 69, 72 :—birth and marriage, xxi-ii; brother-in-law, xiv, xxiii, v, vii, 70 ; death, xxxv, 330n ; laudanum, xv, xxxiii-iv, 372 ; letters, xviii, ix-xx, ii, iii, v-xxxiv, lix, lx, (160, 2, 4), 200n, 54n, 372.

WAGNER, RICHARD :—

Abode, viii, xi, ii, vi-viii, xx, iii-v, xxxiv, liii, vi-ix, 3, 4, 10-3, 26-8, 33, 5, 6, 8, 44, 56, 61, 87-8, 99, 105, 13, 8, 24, 6-7, 35, 50, 3-6, 63, 164, 7, 75-8, 80-3, 9, 92-3, 247, 51, 254, 69, 71-3, 7, 9, 83, 5, 9, 90, 293, 7-9, 305, 7-17, 21n, 5, 6, 50, 355-6, 62.

Animals, xxv, lv, 19, 47-50, 169, 278, 279 :—birds, 12, 3, 26, 98, 117, 43, 167, 247-8, 99 (cf. 302, 52) ; dogs, 9, 86, 255-6, 79, 99n, 357,—see Fips ; horses, 107, 46-7, 280.

WAGNER, RICHARD (*continued*) :—
Box lost, 122, 8, 36.
Christianity, 32, 79, 141, 3, 5, 51, 166, 238, 304.
Colour, 18, 64, 88, 126, 32, 92, 258.
Conducting, xxi-iv, xliv, 8, 16*n*, 20, 62, 4, 128, 79-80, 2, 93, 5, 202-10, 257-60, 305, 13-27, 55, 6, 62.
Creations, xi, xx, xlvii-ix, lv-vi, 24, 37-8, 42, 8, 54-6, 75, 8, 93-7, 106, 121, 4-5, 44, 5, 7, 50, 2, 6, 65, 73, 184-6, 8, 91, 7, 200, 2, 16-8, 26-7, 238-41, 50, 86-7, 90, 8, 303, 22, 7, 370 ; their performance, xiii, xxiv, xxxi, xliii, 60, 2, 86, 101, 5, 10, 125, 8*n*, 74, 8-80, 95-6, 202-4, 11-3, 219, 20, 5-7, 43, 8, 55, 9, 66, 72, 277-8, 81, 304, 15-6, 9, 28, 55, 8.
"Dæmon," xii, 22, 31, 43, 58, 85, 173, 4, 97, 204, 13, 9, 24-7, 73.
Death, xli, li, 23-4, 6, 8, 31, 4, 42, 46, 7, 50, 7, 8, 61, 4, 6-71, 9, 81, 82, 94, 109, 18, 40-1, 4, 53, 4, 82-3, 185, 90, 1, 2, 203, 12, 4, 24, 41, 267, 73, 5-8, 86, 8, 97-8, 313, 4-8, 322, 7, 70.
Diary, 31, 4, 9, 40, 3, 64, 5, 7, 70, 91*n*.
Disputing, xli, 3-4, (20), 47, (89), 97, 126, 35-6, 66, 85-8, 91, 259, 319.
Dreams, 31, 3-4, 64, 81-2, 90, 111-2, 152, 66, 83, 200, 15, 26, 8, 59, 69, 305, 6, 51.
Dress, 105, 31, 54, 318*n*.
Engravings (presents), 192, 254, 99.
Exile and amnesty, xii, ix, xxiv, xxxv, 13, 27, 64, 87, 90, 100-1, 3-4, 151, 8-60, 77, 80, 8-9, 212, 3, 26, 36, 299*n*, 315.
Eye-strain, xliv, 138, 54, 99-200, 40*n*, 253-4, 86 ; cf. 232-3.
Fame, 11, 73, 87, 90, 103, 5, 11, 39, 174, 8, 93, 5, 204-10, 58, 76, 9, 80, 287, 308-9, 18-9, 22, 55, 8.
Flowers, lix, 17, 21, 6, 80-1, 108, 12, 118, 52, 61, 301, 3.
Friendship, male, xiii-vi, ix, xxxvi, xli, iv, vi, lvii, lx-i, 52, 60, 2-3, 65-6, 85-7, 9, 144, 5, 7, 55, 61, 4, 175, 87-9, 91, 4, 6, 206-8, 17, 30-2, 236, 59, 62, 71, 4, 6, 7, 300-1, 10, 329.
Ghosts, 32, 63, 81, 2.
Gratitude, xv, xxi, xxxvi, lvi-viii, 5, 15, 43, 65, 73, 7, 104, 18, 35, 55, 162, 93, 223, 30*n*, 7, 54, 7, 65, 88, 301, 3, 8, 14, 9, 20, 9, 31-2.

WAGNER, RICHARD (*continued*) :—
"Grey," 28, 32, 272, 82, 6, 92, 9, 344.
Handwriting, l, liv, 103, 8, 9, 34, 198, 304, 72*n*.
Health, xviii, xx, vii, xxxii, iii, xliv, lv, 5, 9, 12*n*, 20-2, 4, 36, 9, 45, 6, 64, 8, 74-7, 92, 3, 8-9, 107, 10, 2, 122, 4, 32-3, 5, 8, 45, 6, 56, 8, 60, 162, 6-9, 75, 6, 80, 2-3, 90, 231, 4, 246, 53-8, 78, 301, 9, 17, 21, 3, 4, 326, 50, 62.
Lamp, xxv, 36, 44, 77, 89, 107, 314, 316, 7, 55 ; shade, 18.
Laughter and smiles, l, iv, 6, 13, 78, 92, 102, 9, 30, 7, 45, 8-9, 56, 8, 65, 175, 93, 219, 28, 31, 7, 67, 70, 5, 276, 86, 92, 300, 15, 7, 9, 21, 35, 350-1, 61.
Letters missing, 18, 24, 34, 9-40, 59*n*, 68, 91*n*, 4*n*, 103, 90, 207*n*, 284, 92*n*, 323-4, 7, 46*n*, 59, 73.
Loneliness and retirement, xi, ii, v, xviii, xx, v, xlvi, vii, liii-iv, vii, 3, 4, 32-3, 5, 6, 44-5, 60-1, 4, 71, 7, 85, 6, 9, 90-2, 117, 29, 31, 7, 44, 145, 7, 50, 5, 9, 63, 4, 74-5, 80, 2, 187-8, 93, 213-4, 23, 8, 35, 48, 50, 271-5, 80-1, 5-6, 8, 99, 301, 4, 7, 8, 311-2, 5-9, 22, 43, 50.
"Marquise," 127, 53, 4.
Misunderstood, vii, xi-iii, vi, xlii-iii, 38-41, 51-3, 6, 62, 6, 79, 85, 97, 106, 20, 75, 85-8, 91, 4, 212, 29, 234-5, 43, 57, 9, 60, 75, 6, 355, 8.
Money-matters, vii-viii, xx, i, iii, iv, xxvi, vii, xxx-ii, v, vii-viii, xlv, lvi, lviii, 5, 15, 43, 52, 60, 73-4, 104, 5, 126, 54, 6, 7, 61, 7*n*, 76, 95-7, 201, 203, 10*n*, 1, 4, 9, 23, 6, 34*n*, 5, 42*n*, 243*n*, 51, 8, 66-7, 9*n*, 78, 85, 301*n*, 307, 10, 2, 4, 7, 8, 20-2, 6, 7, 62, 9.
"Muse," lix, 13, 22, 80, 189, 273.
Paintings etc., on, 87, 9, 112, 99-200, 204, 7, 22-3, 7, 35, 46, 61, 79, 86.
"Palm," 103, 6.
Passport, 90, 160, 1, 4, 7.
Patience, vii, xi, vii, 27, 32, 85, 92, 98, 137, 51, 64, 89, 95, 232, 42, 54, 258, 70, 8, 8.
Pen, l, liv, 95, 152.
Pessimism, lii, 46, 52-3, 8-9, 125-6, 149, 50, 263, 76-8, 86, 9-90, 8, 314-322, 8-9, 46, 55-8, 62 ; see Schop.
Pfte-playing, xlvii, l-i, iii, lx, 7, 16, 57-8, 65, 72, 80, 118, 23-4, 30, 2, 137, 45, 55, 60, 79, 98, 232 80 ; see Erard.

WAGNER, RICHARD (*continued*) :—
Pillow, 23, 135, 64, 301, 3.
Portfolios, 34, 274*n*, 325, 8-9, 63, 372 :—brown, 310-2, 6, 7, 55, 6 ; green, 283-4, 307, 11, 51, 51 ; red, 149, 51, cf. 371*n*.
Portraits of self, 207, 23, 32-3, 74, 309, 45, 8.
Presentation plate, &c., 205-6, 312.
Reading, xliii, liv, 6, 8, 14, 8-23, 36, 44, 53, 78-9, 92-3, 102, 20, 2-3, 6, 129-31, 6, 41-3, 8-50, 6, 63, 8, 77, 181, 9, 207, 27, 56, 70, 9, 87, (331), 350 :—aloud xlvii, 14-5, 9, (182), 267, 92, 9-300.
Rest, quiet and repose : inner, xx, lviii, 8, 24-5, 7-8, 35, 41-3, 56, 60-64, 6-7, 70, 6, 106, 9, 18, 45, 6, 152-3, 63, 73, 81, 3, 6, 9, 200-1, 225, 8, 31-3, 6, 7, 42, 58, 60, 1, 281, 99*n*, 302, 11-2, 23, 7, 46, 58 ; outer, xi, iii, viii, xxxiii, xlv, liv, lvi-vii, ix, 11-3, 33, 5, 43, 52, 62, 64, 89, 139, 50, 4, 80, 8, 9, 92, 5, 226, 7, 51, 7, 8, 67, 73, 304, 7, 8, 309, 11-3, 24, 7, 56, 61.
Riding, 113, 46-7, 54, 80.
Servants, 32, 77, 8, 92, 126, 54, 61, 169, 76, 7, 228, 52-3, 312, 8, 26.
Singing, l, 13, 133, 68, 74, 9, 82, 257, 263.
Sleep, 16-9, 31-4, 6, 46, 64, 9, 107, 135, 237, 50, 6.
Spring, xliv, 69, 123, 9, 66, 77, 228, 247.
Tea-set etc., 43, 88, 118, 297, 317, 356.
Travel and trips, xii, xlvi, l, ii, iii, 6, 9, 11, 8, 20, 7-8, 31-5, 57, 68, 9, 72, 4, 101, 7, 11-3, 22, 7-8, 32, 3, 137, 45, 7, 57, 9, 60, 2-4, 73*n*, 7, 94, 197, 202, 33, 5, 47, 68-79, 84-7, 90-293, 8*n*, 305, 8, 9, 13-27, 55, 62.
Walking, xviii, xlvii, liii, iv, vii, ix, 6, 35, 88, 100, 7, 17, 38-9, 44, 52, 75, 228, 37, 54, 80, 301, 3, 12.
Weather, lix, 3, 6-7, 35, 57, 65, 80, 100, 7, 12, 7, 20-39, 45, 6, 51-60, 4, 166, 99, 202, 28, 31-4, 42, 8-50, 4, 255, 80, 326, 43.
Weeping, l, 9, 32, 67, 8, 109, 19, 91, 228, 76, 92, 306.
Working-hours, xvlii, liii, lx, 14, 124, 135, 8-9, 46, 52-4, 8, 60, 74, 256.
Zwieback, 129-31, 5, 44, 8, 64, 76.
" Wahlheim," 18.
Wahnfried, 364*n*.
WALKÜRE, DIE, 11*n*, 321*n* :—Music, li,

lii, iv, v, 8,—privately sung, l, 12-3,—theme from act i, 7,—' sketches,' 371*n*, pencilled dedic., li ; Scenario and Poem, MS., xliv, 365.
Wallis, 35.
Walther (*Meistersgr*), 291*n*, 300.
Walther v. d. Vogelweide, 355.
War, 126, 8*n*, 34-7, 46, 8-9, 57, 8, 85.
Weber : *Freischütz*, 137 ; Chant at grave, 331, 66.
Weiland, Richard, 205-6.
Weimar, xlvi, 62, 6, (131 ?), 271, 4-7, 345 ; Gd Duke, lvi, 26, 277.
Wesendonck, Guido, xxxviii, liii, 14 ; death, xxvii-viii, xxxvii, 66-7, 71, 108-109.
Wesendonck, Hans, xxxviii, 288*n*, 91*n*, 347*n*.
WESENDONCK, MATHILDE, vii-xi, xvi-xvii, xx, v-viii, xxxiii, viii-xl, iv-v, xlvii, l-lxii, 369-74 :—
Death, xiii, xxxix, 370, 2.
Diary, 32-3, 50, 6, 67, 372.
Health, 4, 7, 13, 39, 82, 139, 75, 81, 183, 90, 237, 56, 75, 97, 302, 45, 51, 369.
Letters missing, 24, 34, 40-1, 5, 50, 9, 64, 7, 8, 86, 91, 109, 10, 7, 24, 34, 136, 8, 44, 6, 9, 51, 3, 64, 5, 8, 75, 81, 190, 1, 4, 9, 201, 9, 14-5, 23, 4, 8, 232, 46, 52-3, 6, 7, 64, 6, 9, 70, 5, 281, 3-4*n*, 97*n*, 300*n*, 13*n*, 20*n*, 2, 7, 334, 46*n*, 8, 50*n*, 1*n*, 71-2.
Poems, xxxix, 16-7, 58, 80, 133, 7, 221*n*, 303, 7, 13*n*, 34, 5*n*, 51-4, 75.
Portraits, 45, 228, 32, 51, 82-4, 310, 345.
Tales, xxxix, 95, 8, 106, 11, 58, 9, 334-42, 75.
Wiedersehen, xxxvii, 25, 7-8, 36, 9, 69, 72, 81-2, 101, 11-3, 8, 22, 3, 6, 128-31, 44, 6, 9-51, 5, 7, 9, 60-3, 6, 7, 173*n*, 86-7, 97, 233, 51, 7, 64-5, 7, 269, 74-5, 8, 82, 4-7, 90, 2, 300, 6, 321-7, 30-1, 45-8, 56-61, 72.
Wesendonck, Myrrha, 9, 14, 103, 13, 8, 135, 51, 60-1, 3, 251, 300, 4, 29 ; letters to, 108-10, 34, 302.
Wesendonck, Otto, vii-x, ix, xxvi, xxxvi-xxxviii, xlv, lvi-ix, 3-15, 9, 25, 39, 63-65, 9, 103, 5, 6, 9, 11, 3, 8, 22-8, 31, 5-6, 139, 45, 6, 53, 7, 60, 7, 75, 83, 204, 23, 227, 32, 43*n*, 64-8, 71, 4, 8, 91-2, 305-7, 312-3, 8-20, 3, 7, 30-2, 47, 56, 69, 70 :—
—Carriage and horses, 3, 6, 100, 22, 146 ; Children, viii, xxxviii, lviii, 24, 38, 63, 8, 9, 82, 5, 6, 113, 59, 74, 7, 191, 202, 14, 23, 35, 51, 70, 2, 4, 8, 84,

25

287, 98, 320, 5, 7, 34, 60, 3 ; Health, 287, 313, 9, 24, 5, 57-61 ; Letters to, 5, 15, 20, 308-10,—pubd vol., xxxvi, 190*n*, 215*n*, *et passim* ; Surname, spelling of, 371*n*, 3-4.—Also, simple 'kind regards,' 151, 9, 61, 77, 81, 2, 201, 2, 14, 46, 51, 6, 7, 70, 2, 84, 98, 304, 20.

Wesendonk, Karl, xxxviii, 13*n*, 4, 108-110, 52, 77, 360, 70, 1, 3 ; christening, lviii, 118-9.

Wiesbaden, 291, 3.

Wille, Eliza, xlv, 38-41, 51, 65, 8, 108*n*, 131, 61, 77, 255, 7, 326, 7, 9*n*, 30, 44, 262 ; letters to, 22, 34, 85-91, 144, 305-308, 71,—pubd collection, 85*n*, 327.

Wille, Dr François, 74*n*, 86-7, 131, 44, 150, 61, 3*n*, 327, 44.

Winkelried, 181.

Winterberger, Alex., 106, 10, 38.

Winterthur, Switzerland, 346.

"Wish," ix, xlviii, 24, 7, 8, 36, 42, 60-3, 78, 81, 98, 112, 35, 49, 83, 225-7, 33, 242, 55, 8, 65, 90, 304, 12, 7.

Wittgenstein, Pss Carolyne Sayn-, xxxiv, liii, vii, 13, 147*n*, 93*n*, 229*n*, 230-1, 4*n*, 345 ; daughter Marie, liii, lvii, 13*n*, 164.

Wolfram, Clara, xxvi, 11, 2*n* ; letters to, vii, xix, xxxiii, v, 33, 369.

Wolfram von Eschenbach, 136, 41-144.

Woman, xl-lvi, 28, 42, 6, 8, 53-5, 60, 75, 9, 103, 12, 40, 55, 73, 6, 96, 240, 242, 8, 50, 62-3, 77, 9, 306-8, 11, 4, 317-9, 26, 55, 72-3.

Wotan, 8, 13, 97, 168, 241.

Z.

Zehringen, Princes of, 343.

Zeller, Dr, 175*n*.

Zeltweg, Zurich, xxvi, xlvii, (4), 13.

Zichy, Count, 280.

Ziegesar, Weimar, 365.

Zurich, xxiv, xxxviii, liii, 3-28, 63, 122, 6, 52, 60, 7, 79-80, 250, 5, 82, 287, 330, 46 :—
'Catastrophe,' vii-xix, xxv-viii, xxx, xxxvii, xlviii-ix, lx, 22, 4-8, 31-3, 41, 43, 4, 51, 7, 60, 1, 9, 125, 47, 52, (189, 92, 4), 260, 7, 73, (284, 9), 303, 6, 8, 13, 4, 30, 69.
Concerts, xliv, vii, 1, 6, 7*n*, 8, 204*n*, 209, 317, 44, 56.
Lake, lix, 74, 85*n*, 313.
Rathhaus, 144.
Villa, Enge, see Green Hill.

Zwickau, xxi, v, vi, (70).